# BUSINESS ETHICS 92/93

**Fourth Edition**

**Editor**

**John E. Richardson**
**Pepperdine University**

Dr. John E. Richardson is Associate Professor of Management in the School of Business and Management at Pepperdine University. He is president of his own consulting firm and has consulted with organizations such as Bell and Howell, Dayton-Hudson, Epson, and the U.S. Navy, as well as with various service, nonprofit, and franchise organizations. Dr. Richardson is a member of the American Management Association, the American Marketing Association, the Society for Business Ethics, and Beta Gamma Sigma honorary business fraternity.

Cover illustration by Mike Eagle

Annual Editions
*A Library of Information from the Public Press*

The Dushkin Publishing Group, Inc.
Sluice Dock, Guilford, Connecticut 06437

# The Annual Editions Series

Annual Editions is a series of over 55 volumes designed to provide the reader with convenient, low-cost access to a wide range of current, carefully selected articles from some of the most important magazines, newspapers, and journals published today. Annual Editions are updated on an annual basis through a continuous monitoring of over 300 periodical sources. All Annual Editions have a number of features designed to make them particularly useful, including topic guides, annotated tables of contents, unit overviews, and indexes. For the teacher using Annual Editions in the classroom, an Instructor's Resource Guide with test questions is available for each volume.

## VOLUMES AVAILABLE

Africa
Aging
American Government
American History, Pre-Civil War
American History, Post-Civil War
Anthropology
Biology
Business and Management
Business Ethics
Canadian Politics
China
Commonwealth of Independent
    States and Central/Eastern
    Europe (Soviet Union)
Comparative Politics
Computers in Education
Computers in Business
Computers in Society
Criminal Justice
Drugs, Society, and Behavior
Early Childhood Education
Economics
Educating Exceptional Children
Education
Educational Psychology
Environment
Geography
Global Issues
Health
Human Development
Human Resources
Human Sexuality

International Business
Japan
Latin America
Life Management
Macroeconomics
Management
Marketing
Marriage and Family
Microeconomics
Middle East and the Islamic World
Money and Banking
Nutrition
Personal Growth and Behavior
Physical Anthropology
Psychology
Public Administration
Race and Ethnic Relations
Social Problems
Sociology
State and Local Government
Third World
Urban Society
Violence and Terrorism
Western Civilization,
    Pre-Reformation
Western Civilization,
    Post-Reformation
Western Europe
World History, Pre-Modern
World History, Modern
World Politics

Library of Congress Cataloging in Publication Data
Main entry under title: Annual Editions: Business ethics. 1992/93.
    1. Business ethics—Periodicals. I. Richardson, John E., comp. II. Title: Business ethics.
ISBN 1–56134–080–4          658.408

Fourth Edition

Manufactured by The Banta Company, Harrisonburg, Virginia 22801

# To the Reader

In publishing ANNUAL EDITIONS we recognize the enormous role played by the magazines, newspapers, and journals of the *public press* in providing current, first-rate educational information in a broad spectrum of interest areas. Within the articles, the best scientists, practitioners, researchers, and commentators draw issues into new perspective as accepted theories and viewpoints are called into account by new events, recent discoveries change old facts, and fresh debate breaks out over important controversies.

Many of the articles resulting from this enormous editorial effort are appropriate for students, researchers, and professionals seeking accurate, current material to help bridge the gap between principles and theories and the real world. These articles, however, become more useful for study when those of lasting value are carefully *collected, organized, indexed,* and *reproduced* in a *low-cost format,* which provides easy and permanent access when the material is needed. That is the role played by *Annual Editions.* Under the direction of each volume's *Editor,* who is an expert in the subject area, and with the guidance of an *Advisory Board,* we seek each year to provide in each *ANNUAL EDITION* a current, well-balanced, carefully selected collection of the best of the public press for your study and enjoyment. We think you'll find this volume useful, and we hope you'll take a moment to let us know what you think.

Recent events have brought ethics to the forefront as a topic of discussion throughout our nation. And, undoubtedly, the area of society that is getting the closest scrutiny regarding its ethical practices is the business sector. Both the print and broadcast media have offered a constant stream of facts and opinions concerning recent unethical goings-on in the business world. Insider trading scandals on Wall Street, the marketing of unsafe products, money laundering, and questionable contracting practices are just a few examples of events that have recently tarnished the image of business.

As corporate America struggles to find its ethical identity in a business environment that grows increasingly complex, managers are confronted with some poignant questions that have definite ethical ramifications. Does a company have any obligation to help solve social problems such as poverty, pollution, and urban decay? What ethical responsibilities should a multinational corporation assume in foreign countries? What obligation does a manufacturer have to the consumer with respect to product defects and safety?

These are just a few of the issues that make the study of business ethics important and challenging. A significant goal of *Annual Editions: Business Ethics 92/93* is to present some different perspectives on understanding basic concepts and concerns of business ethics, and to provide ideas on how to incorporate these concepts into the policies and decision-making processes of businesses. The articles reprinted in this publication have been carefully chosen from a variety of public press sources to furnish current information on business ethics.

This volume contains a number of features designed to make it useful for students, researchers, and professionals. These include a *topic guide* for locating articles on specific subjects related to business ethics; the *table of contents abstracts* with summaries of each article and key concepts in bold italics; and a comprehensive *index.*

The articles are organized into five units. Selections that focus on similar issues are concentrated into subsections within the broader units. Each unit is preceded by an *overview* that provides background for informed reading of the articles, emphasizes critical issues, and presents *challenge questions* focusing on major themes running through the selections.

Your comments, opinions, and recommendations about *Annual Editions: Business Ethics 92/93* will be greatly appreciated and will help shape future editions. Please take a moment to complete and return the article rating form on the last page of this book. Any book can be improved, and with your help this one will continue to be.

John E. Richardson
*Editor*

# Contents

# Unit 1

## Ethics, Values, and Social Responsibility in Business

Eleven selections provide an introduction to business ethics and social responsibility.

The concepts in bold italics are developed in the article. For further expansion please refer to the Topic Guide and the Index.

# Unit 2

## Ethical Issues and Dilemmas Involving Employees and the Workplace

Sixteen selections organized within seven subsections examine crucial employee-related issues and their ethical implications for management's decision-making practices and policies.

The concepts in bold italics are developed in the article. For further expansion please refer to the Topic Guide and the Index.

**Unit 3**

## Business and Society: Contemporary Ethical, Social, and Environmental Issues

Ten articles organized within three subsections provide an analysis of important ethical, social, and environmental issues affecting both domestic and multinational business operations.

The concepts in bold italics are developed in the article. For further expansion please refer to the Topic Guide and the Index.

The concepts in bold italics are developed in the article. For further expansion please refer to the Topic Guide and the Index.

# Unit 4

# Ethics and Social Responsibility in the Marketplace

Seven selections organized within two subsections describe the practice of incorporating ethics into the marketplace.

The concepts in bold italics are developed in the article. For further expansion please refer to the Topic Guide and the Index.

# Unit 5

## Developing the Future Ethos and Social Responsibility of Business

Five selections consider guidelines and principles for developing the future ethos and social responsibility of business.

The concepts in bold italics are developed in the article. For further expansion please refer to the Topic Guide and the Index.

# Topic Guide

This topic guide suggests how the selections in this book relate to topics of traditional concern to students and professionals in the field of business ethics. It is useful for locating articles that relate to each other for reading and research. The guide is arranged alphabetically according to topic. Articles may, of course, treat topics that do not appear in the topic guide. In turn, entries in the topic guide do not necessarily constitute a comprehensive listing of all the contents of each selection.

| TOPIC AREA | TREATED IN: | TOPIC AREA | TREATED IN: |
|---|---|---|---|
| **Affirmative Action** | 19. Many Minorities Feel Torn | **Employee Conduct & Responsibility (cont'd)** | 14. Why Corporations Can't Lock the Rascals Out<br>15. Silent Saboteurs<br>21. Hazing<br>22. After the Downsizing<br>25. Implementing Business Ethics<br>28. Industry Ethics Edge Upward<br>33. Combating Drugs In the Workplace |
| **AIDS** | 12. Employee's Right to Privacy?<br>34. AIDS in the Workplace<br>42. Magic of Herman Miller<br>43. Sex and Decency Issues in Advertising | | |
| **Apartheid** | 4. A CEO Looks at Ethics<br>5. Corporate Responsibility<br>35. Untouchables<br>39. Ethics of Virtue | **Employee Health and Safety** | 15. Silent Saboteurs<br>21. Hazing<br>34. AIDS in the Workplace |
| **Codes of Ethics (Codes of Conduct)** | 1. Business Ethics: A Manager's Primer<br>2. Ethical Climate for Excellence<br>3. Ethics in Practice<br>7. Understanding Pressures That Cause Unethical Behavior<br>8. Ethics and Profits<br>11. Corporate Ethics Test<br>25. Implementing Business Ethics<br>28. Industry Ethics Edge Upward<br>35. Untouchables<br>38. Social Responsibility, Ethics, and Marketing Strategy<br>39. Ethics of Virtue<br>41. Marketing By Professionals<br>46. Creating Ethical Corporate Structures | **Employee Rights** | 12. Employee's Right to Privacy?<br>13. Balanced Protection Policies<br>16. Stopping Sexual Harassment<br>20. Older Workers Face Age-Old Problem<br>21. Hazing<br>26. Take the Pap Out of Ethics<br>33. Combating Drugs In the Workplace<br>34. AIDS in the Workplace<br>36. Emerging Ethical Issues in International Business<br>42. Magic of Herman Miller<br>45. Pyramid of Corporate Social Responsibility<br>46. Creating Ethical Corporate Structures |
| **Conflicts of Interest** | 22. After the Downsizing<br>26. Take the Pap Out of Ethics<br>29. Parable of the Sadhu<br>36. Emerging Ethical Issues in International Business<br>45. Pyramid of Corporate Social Responsibility<br>46. Creating Ethical Corporate Structures | **Environmental Disregard and Pollution** | 2. Ethical Climate for Excellence<br>5. Corporate Responsibility<br>9. Ethics and Common Sense<br>10. Farewell to Arms<br>30. Shades of Green<br>36. Emerging Ethical Issues in International Business<br>47. Managing As If the Earth Mattered<br>48. Environmentalism: The New Crusade<br>49. Herman Miller: How Green Is My Factory |
| **Consumer Protection** | 10. Farewell to Arms<br>37. Torrent of Dirty Dollars<br>38. Social Responsibility, Ethics, and Marketing Strategy<br>39. Ethics of Virtue<br>41. Marketing By Professionals<br>43. Sex and Decency Issues in Advertising<br>48. Environmentalism: The New Crusade | **Equal Employment Opportunities** | 18. Approaches to Halt Sexual Harassment<br>19. Many Minorities Feel Torn<br>20. Older Workers Face Age-Old Problem<br>21. Hazing<br>32. New Look at Women Executives<br>33. Combating Drugs In the Workplace<br>35. Untouchables<br>42. Magic of Herman Miller |
| **Discrimination** | 19. Many Minorities Feel Torn<br>20. Older Workers Face Age-Old Problem<br>21. Hazing<br>24. Changing Unethical Organizational Behavior<br>32. New Look at Women Executives<br>35. Untouchables | **Ethical Dilemmas** | 1. Business Ethics: A Manager's Primer<br>2. Ethical Climate for Excellence<br>3. Ethics in Practice<br>15. Silent Saboteurs<br>26. Take the Pap Out of Ethics<br>29. Parable of the Sadhu<br>34. AIDS in the Workplace<br>41. Marketing By Professionals<br>47. Managing As If the Earth Mattered |
| **Downsizing** | 11. Corporate Ethics Test<br>13. Balanced Protection Policies<br>20. Older Workers Face Age-Old Problem<br>22. After the Downsizing<br>23. Ethical Values Underlying the Termination Process<br>31. New Trends in Relocation | | |
| **Employee Conduct & Responsibility** | 12. Employee's Right to Privacy?<br>13. Balanced Protection Policies | **Ethics Training** | 6. Examine Workplace Ethics<br>9. Ethics and Common Sense<br>17. Dealing With Sexual Harassment<br>18. Approaches to Halt Sexual Harassment |

# Ethics, Values, and Social Responsibility in Business

Ethical decision-making in an organization does not occur in a vacuum. As individuals and as managers, we formulate our ethics (that is, the standards of "right" and "wrong" behavior that we set for ourselves) based upon family, peer, and religious influences, our past experiences, and our own unique value systems. When we make ethical decisions within the organizational context, many times there are situational factors and potential conflicts of interest that further complicate the process.

Decisions do not only have personal ramifications— they also have social consequences. Social responsibility is really ethics at the organizational level, since it refers to the obligation that an organization has to make choices and to take actions that will contribute to the good of society, as well as the good of the organization. Authentic social responsibility is not initiated because of forced compliance to specific laws and regulations. In contrast to legal responsibility, social responsibility involves an voluntary response from an organization that is above and beyond what is specified by the law.

The eleven selections in this unit provide an overview of the interrelationships of ethics, values, and social responsibility in business. The lead article in this section, "Business Ethics: A Manager's Primer," offers practical and insightful suggestions to managers, enabling them to approach the subject of business ethics with more confidence. The next two articles discuss the significance of the ethical component in management's strategic decision-making. In "A CEO Looks at Ethics," the author maintains that ethics should be built on a foundation of mutual trust among individuals and organizations. The next two articles describe the importance of examining potentially ethical problems in the workplace and creating a positive corporate culture.

The seventh article delineates how a code of ethics, personal values, and ethical instruction are some of the critical ingredients necessary to take into the competitive environment as management endeavors to deal with employees, stockholders, and consumers in an ethical manner. Articles 8 and 9 wrestle with the important question: "Do good ethics and good profits always go hand in hand?" Article 10 predicts that environmental issues will likely be a major area of focus of the government and various consumer groups during the '90s. "The Corporate Ethics Test," the final article, allows the reader to compare his or her ethical choices in 4 hypothetical cases to those of top CEOs.

**Looking Ahead: Challenge Questions**

Do you believe that corporations are more socially responsible today than they were 10 years ago? Why or why not?

In what specific ways do you see companies practicing social responsibility? Do you think most companies are overt or covert in their social responsibility activities?

React to Vernon Loucks' statement in "A CEO Looks at Ethics": "Ethics is simply and ultimately a matter of trust. People act in their economic self-interest. But a system based on that fact must be grounded on mutual trust among individuals and among organizations. A buyer needs to trust a manufacturer, a lender needs to trust a borrower, and so on."

Dr. David Vogel believes that the relationship between ethics and profits is a rather tenuous one. Do you think ethics and profits always go hand in hand? Why?

What are the economic and social implications of "management accountability" as part of the decision-making process? Does a company have any obligation to help remedy social problems, such as poverty, urban decay, and pollution? Explain your response.

From an organizational perspective, what do you think are the major arguments for and against social responsibility?

# Unit 1

# Business Ethics: A Manager's Primer

The application of different ethical maxims to a given situation may produce divergent ethical judgments. The 14 propositions given here should enable management to deal with the subject of business ethics with confidence.

## Gene Laczniak

**Dr. Laczniak** *is Associate Professor of Business and Chairman of the Department of Marketing at Marquette University, Milwaukee, Wisconsin. The author would like to acknowledge the helpful comments of Professors T.R. Martin and Patrick E. Murphy of Marquette University in the development of this article.*

Too many business managers have been shortchanged in their business education. They have been cheated because during their college years their business professors failed to integrate ethical issues into management education. While some practicing managers have taken courses in "business ethics" or "social responsibility," they typically have not learned to appreciate fully the crucial role that ethics plays in business decision making. To a large degree this has happened because many business educators shy away from integrating ethics into mainstream business classes such as marketing, finance, and production.

Why do educators find it so difficult to teach business ethics or, for that matter, to address ethical issues when dealing with other topics of business strategy? Largely for the following three reasons. First, many business educators pride themselves on their analytical approach; in contrast, addressing ethics is associated with a softer type of analysis, and occasionally with a preachy mentality. This might be deemed the *soapbox* factor. A second closely related cause is that the foundation for meaningful remedies in the area of business ethics is perceived as subjective and unscientific. In other words, many business professors feel that ethics is too elusive a subject for extended lecture treatment. This constitutes the *soft* factor. Third, some business educators believe that dealing with business ethics in the classroom will have little or no lasting effect upon the morality of their students; this might be labeled the *superfluous* factor. Consequently, a great many business educators have not given business ethics its proper due in the classroom because of their perceptions that the subject is soapboxish, soft, and superfluous.

This article compiles and analyzes some propositions that are useful for understanding business ethics. These propositions are grouped into three categories: (1) propositions that serve as useful foundations; (2) descriptive propositions; and (3) proscriptive propositions.

## Propositions That Serve as Useful Foundations

*Proposition 1: Ethical conflicts and choices are inherent in business decison making.* This proposition is a logical springboard for appreciating the importance of business ethics because it legitimates the inseparability of business decisions and moral consequences. Substantial support for this postulation is available. One classic study of business ethics reported that at some point in their careers 75% of the responding managers felt a conflict between profit considerations and being ethical.[1] Later studies noted that the majority of managers questioned also felt this pressure to be unethical.[2] Similarly, another widely publicized study indicated that 65% of the managers surveyed sometimes felt pressure to compromise their personal ethical standards.[3]

More importantly, this proposition can provide the business manager with the motivation to discover and analyze the numerous ethical implications of current business practices. For example:

• Is it ethical for pharmaceutical companies to market infant formula in developing countries as an alternative to breast feeding when it is common knowledge that sanitary containers and unpolluted water are frequently not available and that babies will be deprived of the immunological benefits inherent in breast milk?
• Is it proper for a public relations firm to attempt to bolster the worldwide image of a country accused of numerous human rights violations?
• Is it moral for a firm to ship a product designated unsafe

in one market, such as the United States, to another market where the regulations do not apply?

Every business manager can add examples to the ones just noted. The point is that this proposition emphasizes that the ethical implications of business practices are legion.

---

# "...a high organizational ethic could induce a manager with low integrity to behave more properly."

---

*Proposition 2: Proper ethical behavior exists on a plane above the law. The law merely specifies the lowest common denominator of acceptable behavior.* This proposition undercuts the argument that legality is the only criterion for judging acceptable behavior. If this proposition does *not* hold, the study of ethics is extraneous. While some members of the legal profession may challege this postulate, the entire field of moral philosophy rests on its inherent truth. This proposition provides a rationale for examining the compelling argument that ethical propriety and legality do not necessarily coincide. For example, it is not *illegal* to exhort children to ask their parents to buy a product promoted *via* a commercial on a children's television show. Whether such a practice is *unethical*, because it exploits the gullibility of children, can be vigorously debated.

In addition, this proposition provides an opportunity to explore some fundamental differences between legal and ethical perspectives. For instance, the law is a *reactive* institution that applies to situations only after they have occurred. Ethics is usually more *proactive*, attempting to provide guidance prior to a situation's occurrence. Similarly, within the law, a transgression must be proven beyond a reasonable doubt, whereas from an ethical perspective, an action is morally wrong independent of conclusive proof that it in fact took place. For example, suppose the quality control manager of an electrical supply house knowingly sends out Christmas tree lights that could potentially short out because of a design defect and thereby cause a fire. The lights, however, do not malfunction. Legally, the manager is not culpable because no harm occurred; ethically, a violation of trust has clearly occurred. Thus this proposition embodies the concept that the realm of ethics provides guidance for managerial actions and supplements the requirements provided by law.

*Proposition 3: There is no single satisfactory standard of ethical action agreeable to everyone that a manager can use to make specific operational decisions.* Few business executives would question this generalization. This proposition establishes that advocating a particular moral doctrine is not the point of examining the issue of ethics. Rather, while there are many ethical perspectives of great worth, the issue of morality *in general* is at question. In other words, the power and impact implicit in managerial decisions demands an examination of the responsibility for those actions. Thus, ethical considerations are properly examined in reference to the managerial process.

*Proposition 4: Managers should be familiar with a wide variety of ethical standards.* Several ethical maxims are used as the theoretical foundation for a variety of industry statements on ethics. Typical of the more simplistic maxims are:

*The utilitarian principle*—Act in a way that results in the greatest good for the greatest number.

*The professional ethic*—Take only actions that would be viewed as proper by a disinterested panel of professional colleagues.

*The golden rule*—Act in the way you would expect others to act toward you.

*Kant's categorical imperative*—Act in such a way that the action taken under the circumstances could be a universal law or rule of behavior.

*The TV test*—A manager should always ask, "Would I feel comfortable explaining to a national TV audience why I took this action?"

Obviously, these maxims are difficult to apply to specific situations and can sometimes lead to conflicting resolutions, particularly if analyzed in the context of a *case situation*. For example, consider the case of a sales representative who, against stated company policy, routinely pads his expense account vouchers 10% to 15%. However, he does this with the knowledge that his fellow sales representatives and his supervisor do the same thing and tacitly approve of this action. In this circumstance, does the golden rule justify the behavior? Wouldn't the professional ethic imply that the practice should cease? This is a rudimentary illustration, but it underscores the fact that various modes of moral reasoning exist and that the application of different ethical maxims to a given situation may produce divergent ethical judgments.

*Proposition 5: The discussion of business cases or of situations having ethical implications can make managers more ethically sensitive.* Perhaps this is the most debatable of the five propositions ventured thus far because a certain substantial segment of business educators and managers would question its truth. The position of this group is that academic course work cannot instill integrity in a future manager. They believe that students come into the classroom with a relatively intransigent morality. Therefore, classroom efforts directed at personal values are an exercise in futility.[4]

Notice, however, that the proposition as stated promises only the *potential* for increased sensitivity to ethical concerns, not wholesale changes in morality. One expert provides some limited support for this proposition when he reports that a sample of MBA graduates who took a course in business ethics seemed to develop ethical sensitivity over a period of time.[5] Furthermore, other researchers have contended that the academic community has the reponsibility to provide courses in business ethics regardless of their effect.[6] In the view of these experts, such offerings will not transform personalities overnight but will stimulate thinking about ethical issues. In short, sufficient justification exists for encouraging discussion among managers about business ethics, and for the expectation that the effort will have some moral payoff in the business world.

In summary, the five foundation propositions provide a rationale for business ethics as (1) an area of significant managerial concern, (2) distinct from the realm of law, (3) an area, like many areas of management, that has few pat answers but (4) worth exploring because of its relevance to effective and responsible management decision making.

## Descriptive Propositions

With these five foundation propositions, the business manager is now ready to address the specific process of ethical behavior as it occurs in the organization. Unfortunately, little can be definitively stated about how ethical or unethical behavior evolves in a business firm. In part, this is why business ethics are considered subjective or soft—a dimension that was referred to earlier. Nevertheless, a few useful, general propositions can be established for ethics in the organization.

*Proposition 6: There are diverse and sometimes conflicting determinants of ethical action. These stem primarily from the individual, from the organization, from professional norms, and from the values of society.* This proposition underscores the multiple influences that characterize the business environment and shape ethical actions; it also highlights the complexity of pressures that can be part of resolving an ethical question. Consider, for example, the following sample situation:

*Smith University holds as part of its endowment portfolio a large block of stock in the multinational Jones Company. The stock was donated to Smith University by the founder of the Jones Company. The Jones Company is heavily involved in apartheid-ruled South Africa. Members of the university community, especially students and faculty, are pressuring the university to immediately sell all its Jones Company stock. Some members of the community where Smith University is located have even threatened to picket Smith classes. Mr. Courtney, vice president of Finance at Smith and a former diplomat, knows Jones Company to be a model corporate citizen in South Africa, treating black and white employees alike. However, the management of Jones Company supports the existing South African government. Furthermore, Courtney believes the Jones Company stock is extremely depressed at this time and that its sale would not be in the best interest of the endowment fund, the major source of student scholarships. Should Courtney and Smith University sell the stock immediately?*

Notice the multiple pressures that may be present in a situation such as this: *Societal* pressures dictate selling the securities. Moreover, Courtney's *personal* beliefs, stemming from his religion and philosophy, make him shudder at the inflexibility of the South African government. On the other hand, *organizational* pressures dictate restraint, since Courtney and other officers of the university feel the Jones securities will soon appreciate in value. Similarly, from a *professional* viewpoint, Courtney knows that the sale of the Jones stock would be a symbolic act at best and at worst a slap in the face to a company that has been a Good Samaritan in South Africa and a close friend to the university. How does Courtney resolve these conflicting pressures? No precise answer exists. Somehow he takes the various viewpoints into consideration and recommends an action with which he is comfortable. It is even possible that his recommendation, whatever it is, will be overruled at a higher level of the organization.

The foregoing examination of Proposition 6 suggests another proposition. In the last analysis, Courtney must make a decision that will have ethical consequences. Ultimately, the factors and subfactors to which ethics are attributable—influences such as religion, professional norms, societal expectations, and organizational pressures—somehow combine to shape an *individual* decision that is associated with Courtney and according to which Courtney could be morally judged. This leads to the next proposition.

*Proposition 7: Individual values are the final standard, although not necessarily the determining reason for ethical behavior.* The upshot of Proposition 7 is that multifaceted influences affecting the likelihood of ethical action by the decision maker will ultimately be reflected in an individual decision. The action taken will be perceived by others as embodying the ethical values of the decision maker. Introduction of this proposition helps businesspeople realize the individual responsibility inherent in managerial decision making. In other words, no matter what factors lead a manager to make a particular decision, there is a measure of individual responsibility that cannot be denied because in the last analysis the decision was made by a given manager. For example, the product manager who knowingly sends a shipment of unsafe products to retail stores cannot avoid individual culpability by claiming that economic pressures in the organization necessitated the action.

One major organizational implication of Proposition 7 is that management should strive to maintain a laudatory *organizational* ethic because this dimension is somewhat controllable by the organization. This lessens the likelihood that organizational considerations will pressure the individual manager to compromise his or her personal beliefs and behave unethically. Conversely, a high organizational ethic could induce a manager with low integrity to behave more properly. For example, the American Telephone and Telegraph Corporation (AT & T) provides all employees with a copy of a booklet that states that if employees report to outside sources the improper behavior of AT & T management or employees, no disciplinary or retaliatory action will ever be taken.

*Proposition 8: Consensus regarding what constitutes proper ethical behavior in a decision-making situation diminishes as the level of analysis proceeds from abstract to specific.* Put another way, it is easy to get a group of managers to agree *in general* that a practice is improper; however, casting that practice in a specific set of circumstances usually reduces consensus. For example, almost all

## "...younger, middle managers feel greater pressures to compromise their personal ethics."

businesspeople will agree that stealing by employees is wrong. But consider the following specific question: Is it alright for a manager to unwittingly take a few pens and pads of paper home for personal use? What about a stapler? A calculator? A typewriter? What if the pens will be used by orphans to play games at a charity picnic? Where does one draw the line?

Even a simplistic example like this can cause debate. The difficulty is compounded as the circumstances become more involved. In any event, Proposition 8 emphasizes the uncertain environment in which managers necessarily function as they attempt to make the ethically proper decision. Consider the following ethical precepts—with which all businesspeople would agree—along with the complication introduced by some hypothetical situation-specific examples.

• *Business has the obligation to honestly report financial progress and potential to holders of company debt and equity. Situation:* The annual report of the Columbia Railroad Co. reports that the firm has financially outperformed all its competitors. This was largely due to the sale of some highly appreciated Manhattan real estate. The income from this transaction is noted with only a footnote in the financial statement. Columbia avoided having the income classified as a special treatment "extraordinary item" because of some complex legal maneuvers and

because it has other real estate assets that might provide similar profits in the future. Should the income from the real estate be highlighted more clearly in the annual report?

• *Business has the obligation to treat potential, current, and past employees fairly. Situation:* Employee Harry Harris is apprehended stealing tools and equipment valued at $500 from the company. Company policy calls for dismissal in such instances. However, Harris is 63 years old—two years from pension—and has had a clean slate until this incident. Is it ethical for the company to fire him at this point in his career?

• *Business has the obligation to provide consumers with facts relevant to the informed purchase of a product or service. Situation:* The Doe Co. manufactures Clean & Gleem, an all-purpose cleaning concentrate that consumers mix with four parts water. Clean & Gleem has been sold this way for 25 years. A recent issue of *Consumer Reports* indicates that Clean & Gleem will clean just as effectively if mixed with eight parts water. Thus, consumers need only use half as much concentrate. Should the Doe Co. inform customers of this fact? Would it be unethical not to do so?

In summary, Proposition 8 and these examples of some specific "tough choice" cases provide some insight into the difficulty of steering an ethically proper course.

*Proposition 9: The moral tone of an organization is set by top management.* Stated another way, the organization is but a lengthened shadow of the morality of persons in charge. For instance, one study found that managers ranked the behavior of superiors as the strongest single factor in deterring unethical behavior.[7] Similar results are reported in more recent studies.[8]

The organizational implications of this proposition are clear. If employees take their cues concerning ethical behavior from top management, then the first line of responsibility for setting high ethical standards falls to these corporate executives. The following example partially embodies the proposition:

*An employee embezzled $20,000 over several years. When confronted with the incriminating evidence, the employee was not contrite and expressed the belief that he was just as entitled to the company's money as any member of top management. He pointed out that upper management dipped into petty cash for lunch money, used company stamps to mail Christmas cards, and had company personnel help with yard work at their personal residences.*

Numerous other real-world examples of this proposition abound. The J.C. Penney Co. is a classic illustration of a company with a reputation for high ethical standards along with a record unblemished by any major scandal. Much of the credit must go to the founder, who was so convinced that ethics and profit were compatible that the company's outlets were originally called the "Golden

Rule" stores. In contrast, many of the so-called "dirty tricks" and the political whip cracking of the Nixon administration can be explained by the win-at-all-costs philosophy of the men at the top.

*Proposition 10: The lower the organizational level of a manager, the greater the perceived pressure to act unethically.* At first glance, this proposition might seem contradictory to Proposition 9. After all, if the moral tone of an organization resides in top management, why the concern with the subsidiary levels of management? The answer lies in the fact that while a *general ethical climate* is established by an organization's superiors, many of the operational decisions that have ethical implications will actually be made at levels other than top management. Thus because the frequency of decision making is greater, the lower-level manager may simply have more opportunities to behave ethically or unethically. Furthermore, it may be that the areas of responsibility of middle management are treated as profit centers for purposes of evaluation. Consequently, anything that takes away from profit—including ethical behavior—is perceived by lower-level management as an impediment to organizational advancement and recognition.

Surveys of managers seem to confirm that ethical conflict is felt most strongly by lower-level managers.[9] Thus, top management's exhortations and policy regarding ethics will be a factor in ethical behavior at these levels of management, but only *one* factor. If organizational advancement and salary adjustments are made primarily by the rule of bottom-line unit performance, pressure will exist on middle managers to compromise ethical standards if profit can be served. In this sense, the "ethical buck" stops at the bottom rather than the top of the organization.

Top management should recognize that ethical pressure points will exist at all levels of the organization. Therefore, a sanctimonious statement of a manager's standards does not discharge a firm's duty to foster high ethical standards. Efforts should be made to communicate to all levels of management that ethical behavior will be monitored and will be rewarded accordingly. This proposition reminds business managers that they will be involved in potential ethical conflicts when they enter the organization. The proposition also implies that mechanisms, such as codes or policy statements, that could be used by top management to communicate an ethical commitment "down the line" should be examined for their usefulness to middle management.

Within the context of Proposition 10, it is interesting to note that some analysts have speculated that managers behave more ethically as they grow older—a kind of "mellowing" factor. Since managers in top management are usually older than those at the lower level, this might partially explain why the younger, middle managers feel greater pressures to compromise their personal ethics. Similarly, one can reason that top-level managers have attained career success already; thus they have the luxury

of subscribing to high ethical norms, while lower-level managers must still prove themselves, which perhaps requires a more aggressive (and likely less ethical) posture. This "mellowing" hypothesis is controversial and does not yet merit the status of a proposition.

# "...ethical propriety and legality do not necessarily coincide."

*Proposition 11: Individual managers perceive themselves as more ethical than their colleagues.* This postulate is the product of many studies of ethics in management. Typically, it evolves because of the following situation: An individual manager is interviewed by a researcher or reporter about a specific questionable practice, such as the use of invisible ink to track questionnaires after respondents have been promised confidentiality. The manager responds that X% of his colleagues would participate in such a practice but, of course, he or she would not. Thus, more than anything else, this proposition emphasizes the human tendency of managers to discuss ethics in a manner that will protect themselves from incrimination or to rationalize their own uprightness.

One implication of this proposition is that the actual ethical norms of businesspeople are probably more accurately reported in what they say their typical colleague would do in a situation than in what they report they themselves would do. The introduction of this proposition serves to remind the business manager of the difficulty of maintaining one's objectivity when one is involved in analyzing ethical questions that hold personal ramifications. Propositions 6 through 11 are limited in number but in fact establish some fundamental insights into the realm of business ethics. Namely:

● Multiple factors influence ethical decision making. Some are controllable, some are not. Ultimately, the final decision regarding an ethical question is strongly motivated by the manager's individual values.
● Consensus regarding ethical propriety is difficult to achieve when evaluating many specific situations; moreover, managers have a tendency to overstate their own ethical sensitivity.
● Ethical pressures are felt most acutely by lower- and middle-level managers who look to top management for behavioral cues but are themselves confronted with many difficult decisions.

## Proscriptive Propositions Concerning Ethics

Propositions regarding business ethics, while easy to postulate, are difficult to propose with the confidence that they will have a significant impact on the organization. One is reminded of the quip by Mark Twain, "To be good is noble. To tell people to be good is even nobler and much less trouble." Nevertheless, organizations with a reputation for impeccable ethical conduct have cultivated and enhanced their outstanding moral demeanor with organizational adjustments that have had an impact on ethical performance. The following propositions focus on such organizational strategies.

*Proposition 12: Effective codes of ethics should contain meaningful and clearly stated provisions along with enforced sanctions for noncompliance.* A code of ethics or some other formal statement of ethical concern is the minimum commitment to organizational social responsibility all firms should be expected to make. Unfortunately, the vast majority of executives have little confidence in the effectiveness of codes in improving morality because of their vagueness and the difficulty of enforcing them.[10] All too often such codes have become meaningless public relations gimmicks. Still, codes are not without value. They represent a public commitment regarding the prohibition of practices and can diffuse potential ethical problems. For example, consider the purchasing agent who wonders whether it is proper to accept a bottle of 12-year-old Scotch whiskey at Christmastime from a sales representative. He may reason that there is no explicit quid pro quo expected and that since the gift is given at holiday time, the practice is acceptable. Nevertheless, the manager makes this assessment half-heartedly, because he knows the sales representative's firm has several contracts pending and the practice looks suspicious. A specific code statement that prohibits the giving or receiving of gifts with a value of more than $5 would have eliminated the ethical question concerning the gift.

Successful codes tend to be those that are specific *and* enforced. To anticipate every ethical contingency that can arise in a business situation and to hope to include it in a code is both naive and unrealistic. However, certain specific ethical problems tend to arise in particular industries, and these problems require the special scrutiny of management. For instance:
• Producers of heavily sugared products must face the question of how ethical it is to advertise to children, given both the persuasibility of this group and their susceptibility to tooth decay.
• Companies selling whole life insurance must question the ethics of promoting a financial institution that can lock an individual into a low return on investment in perpetuity.

Almost every business environment suggests some relatively unique ethical questions.

The question of code enforcement is a matter of behavioral psychology. Unless members of the organization see a code of ethics monitored and subsequently enforced with visible sanctions, they will ascribe little organizational importance to the code. The implication of

Proposition 12 is that a code of ethics that is not enforced is a code of ethics without teeth, and it will be treated as such by personnel at all levels in an organization.

*Proposition 13: Employees must have a nonpunitive, failsafe mechanism for reporting ethical abuses in the organization.* This postulate raises the issue of "whistle blowing" and its role in the firm. On one hand, no corporation likes to have its dirty linen aired in public without an opportunity to examine internally its own transgressions. On the other hand, a real commitment to ethical propriety demands that clear abuses of organiza-

---

## "Successful codes tend to be those that are specific *and* enforced."

---

tional morality will be condemned and dealt with accordingly, no matter how they come to light. In recent years, too many corporate Serpicos have gone public with substantial abuses, only to be hounded by their own organizations. Organizations dedicated to high ethical standards should provide mechanisms that will assure channels of communication and subsequent protection for whistle blowers. Operationally, this sort of program requires the explicit support of high-level administrators. If top management might be involved in the transgressions, employees should be made aware of an audit committee of the board (chaired by a member independent of management, such as an outside director) to whom information can be given.

Admittedly, such a program can be difficult for management to accept. The possibility of undue negative publicity caused by an overzealous or alarmist employee is a risk. Some issues are difficult to resolve. For example, a financial auditor discovers a foreign payoff that was made several years ago by the now retired chief executive officer. Should this skeleton be allowed to leave the corporate closet? Yet, such dilemmas are the price of developing a climate of ethical responsibility in the organization.

*Proposition 14: Every organization should appoint a top-level manager or director to be responsible for acting as an ethical advocate in the organization.* In an organization committed to high moral standards, ethical responsibility falls into everyone's domain. But as with many things, unless someone is appointed to direct the effort the responsibility dissolves among the many. One researcher has insightfully proposed the concept of the ethics advocate—a top manager or director whose responsibility would be to elucidate the ethical implications of management's decisions.[11] For example, if a corporation is planning to shut down a plant in a particular community, the ethical advocate would seek to clarify what, if any, moral responsibility the company had to the community where the plant was located. Similarly, the representative would outline what ethical responsibilities the company has to the employees who might be discharged because of the plant shutdown. In short, the ethical advocate would serve as the verbal conscience of the corporation. Both Cummins Engine Co. and the Monsanto Corp. have introduced such positions into their organizations.

Notice that these three propositions—Propositions 12, 13, and 14—provide the business manager with a battery of questions that can be used to initially evaluate the ethical posture of an organization:

- Does the organization have a code of ethics? Is it specific? Is it enforced?
- Has the organization attempted to identify ethical concerns unique to its industry and operations?
- What is the organization's policy toward whistle blowers? What mechanisms are available to report ethical abuses? Internal channels? External channels?
- Has top management communicated its concern for a commitment to high ethical standards? How has this been practically demonstrated?
- Is there someone in the organization who serves as an ethical advocate or ombudsman? What are this person's specific responsibilities?

## Conclusion

Certainly, it can be said that there is not a great deal of definitive knowledge regarding the process that leads managers to behave ethically. It is also conceded that the precise philosophical perspective managers ought to use to make ethical decisions is open to debate. Whether it be moral intuition, a particular theory of distributive justice, utilitarianism, or some other framework, reasonable people can disagree on whether a particular decision is ethically proper or not. A few will also continue to maintain that such discussions and frameworks will never have a pragmatic influence on managerial behavior. In this sense the study of business ethics remains somewhat soft, relatively subjective, arguably superfluous, and prone to a soapbox mentality.

Nevertheless, the strength of such arguments is overstated. While business ethics may be an area that is relatively soft, certain solid propositions that are supported in multiple research studies and in the practices of progressive companies can be transmitted to current and future business managers. Rather than embodying a soapbox mentality, the purpose of these propositions is to sensitize the manager to some of the realities of ethics in the organization. The fact that ethical questions are unavoidable, that subordinates look to top management for behavioral cues, and so on, are bits of managerial acumen that should be well-ingrained in the future business executive. These propositions also describe some pragmatic mechanisms that have been utilized by organizations to develop a progressive ethical climate. Numerous executives testify to the worth of these propositions as an aide to moral responsibility. Thus one may realistically view business ethics as an area consisting of a limited number of solid, successfully adapted propositions that can sensitize managers to their ethical responsibility as organizational decision makers. On these propositions business practitioners can begin to build, supplement, and amplify the necessary discussion of ethics that must take place in the boardroom and beyond.

1. Raymond C. Baumhart, "How Ethical Are Businessmen?" *Harvard Business Review* (July-August 1961): 6.

2. Steven N. Brenner and Earl A. Molander, "Is the Ethics of Business Changing?" *Harvard Business Review* (January-February 1977): 52-71.

3. Archie B. Carroll, "A Survey of Managerial Ethics: Is Business Morality Watergate Morality?" *Business and Society Review* (Spring 1975).

4. Mary Susan Miller and Edward A. Miller, "It's Too Late for Ethics Courses in Business Schools," *Business and Society Review* (Spring 1976): 39-43.

5. Theodore V. Purcell, "Do Courses in Ethics Pay Off?" *California Management Review* (Summer 1977).

6. Richard A. Konrad, "Are Business Ethics Worth Studying?" *Business and Society Review* (Fall 1978): 54-57.

7. Baumhart, "How Ethical are Businessmen?" 6.

8. John W. Newstrom and William A. Ruch, "The Ethics of Management and the Management of Ethics," *MSU Business Topics* (Winter 1975): 29-37.

9. Carroll, "A Survey of Managerial Ethics"; Brenner and Molander, "Is the Ethics of Business Changing?" 52-71.

10. Brenner and Molander, "Is the Ethics of Business Changing?" 52-71.

11. Theodore V. Purcell, "A Practical Guide to Ethics in Business," *Business and Society Review* (Spring 1975): 43-50; "Electing an 'Angels Advocate' to the Board," *Management Review* (May 1976): 4-11.

## Ethics for Total Quality and Participation
# Developing an Ethical Climate for Excellence

**Dr. Joseph A. Petrick—Wright State University and Dr. George E. Manning—Northern Kentucky University**

*Joseph A. Petrick is an assistant professor of management at Wright State University in Dayton, Ohio. He is a management consultant to business, industry and government. He has served as an administrator and faculty member in a variety of public, private, and proprietary educational institutions.*

*George Manning is a professor of psychology at Northern Kentucky University. He is a consultant to business, industry, and government where his clients include AT&T, Sun Oil, IBM, Marriott Corporation, United Auto Workers, and the National Institutes of Health.*

*In today's global economy, the need to be internationally competitive in the work environment is an ongoing challenge for organizations. Part of that competitive edge is developing a reputation for superior productivity based on managing human resources with integrity.*

Organizational ethics is no longer an empty platitude, but a vital part of the business strategy, product quality, and service image of any firm that wants to be taken seriously in the marketplace. Bad ethical reputations have bankrupted firms. Good ethical reputa-tions have sustained customer, stockholder, employee, supplier, and creditor loyalty during turbulent market cycles.

In addition, since most careers are developed within an organizational context, the quality of an organization's ethical climate is of vital importance to most employees. Employees want to be treated fairly and rewarded justly for the contributions they make to an orga-nization's survival and growth. Few work conditions can be more fatal to morale, productivity, and loyalty than an unethical atmosphere.

While the literature on professional ethics, moral development, and organi-zational cultural values has become extensive, the literature on the pro-cesses of improving organizational ethical climates and its impact on qual-ity circle and employee involvement professionals is not nearly as volumi-nous. Our purpose here is twofold: to provide a theoretical model of profes-sional and organizational moral development, depicting its impact on quality/participation professionals, and to indicate five specific steps that can be taken to improve the ethical climate of any organization.

### Stages of Moral Development

Understanding the moral and ethical development of organizations is aided by using sound conceptual frameworks. The seminal frameworks of Lawrence Kohlberg and, with modifications, Ed-ward Stevens offer a working and practical start in this effort. (Please see Figure One.) The former conceptual framework was selected due to the ex-tensive empirical studies that support it; the latter framework was selected because of its organizational develop-ment compatibility with the Kohlberg model. Kohlberg proposes six stages of personal moral development, and Stevens' work indicates parallel stages of organizational moral development.

**Stages one and two: the lion and the fox**—In the first two stages of per-sonal moral development, fear and manipulation are the primary moral strategies used for survival. Their or-ganizational counterparts are Social Darwinism and Machiavellianism. In the organizational moral jungle, the lowest or first level of moral develop-ment can be described as a form of survival of the fittest. At this stage, the most powerful individual, coalition, or network determines what is right or wrong and punishes those who deviate from accepted behavior. The lion or lion prides are appropriate metaphors for forceful, ruling individuals and cliques that devise and monitor organi-zational policies and procedures.

At the next level of moral develop-ment is Machiavellianism, which entails organizational cleverness, indi-rectness, and deceit. Unlike the forceful lion, the Machiavellian fox is more likely to resort to rumor, cun-ning, and treachery to maximize personal gain. Organizations operating at the second stage of moral develop-ment are above the blood-baths of the first stage, but with every employee seeking personal gain, very few will risk venturing out on a limb to endorse a new idea or collaborate with untrust-worthy colleagues.

Organizations that operate at the

Reprinted with permission from *Journal of Quality and Participation*, March 1990, pp. 84-90. *Journal of Quality and Participation*, Association for Quality and Participation, Cincinnati, OH.

## Figure One: Models of Personal and Organizational Moral Development
**(examples of moral reasoning at each stage)**

| Personal Moral Development | Organizational Moral Development | Examples of Moral Reasoning |
|---|---|---|
| **Stage One:** Physical consequences determine behavior. Avoidance of punishment and deference to power are typical of this stage. *Threat* | **Social Darwinism:** Fear of extinction and the urgency of financial survival dictate moral conduct. The direct use of force is the accepted norm. | "I won't hit him, because he may hit me back." |
| **Stage Two:** Individual pleasure needs are the primary concern and dictate the rightness or wrongness of behavior. *lollipop* | **Machiavellianism:** Organizations' gain guides actions. Successfully attaining goals justifies the use of any effective means, including individual manipulation. | "I will help her, because she may help me in return." |
| **Stage Three:** The approval of others determines behavior. The good person is one who satisfies family, friends and associates. *good boy/girl* | **Popular conformity:** There is a tradition of standard operating procedures. Peer pressure to adhere to social norms dictates what is right or wrong behavior. | "I will go along with him, because I want him to like me." |
| **Stage Four:** Compliance with authority, upholding the social order and *doing one's duty* are primary ethical concerns. *laws & Rules* | **Allegiance to authority:** Directions from legitimate authority determine organizational moral standards. Right and wrong are based on the decisions of those with hierarchical power. | "I will comply with her order, because it is wrong to disobey her." |
| **Stage Five:** Tolerance for rational dissent and acceptance of majority rule become primary ethical concerns. *Best good* | **Democratic participation:** Participation in decision making and reliance on majority rule become organizational moral standards. | "Although I disagree with his views, I will uphold his right to have them." |
| **Stage Six:** What is right and good is a matter of individual conscience and responsibly chosen commitments. Morality is based on principled personal conviction. *Love* | **Organizational integrity:** Justice and individual rights are the moral ideals. Balanced judgment among competing interests forms organizational character, which in turn determines the rightness or wrongness of behavior. | "There is no external force that can compel me to perform an act I consider morally wrong."<br><br>**Sources:** See Resources list for Lawrence Kohlberg and Edward Stevens. |

first two stages are mired in a moral jungle and their predatory rewards are meager compared to the benefits that await them at higher levels.

**Stages three and four: peer pressure and fealty**—At the third and fourth stages of personal moral development, approval seeking and upholding authoritative order are the two leading moral strategies. Their organizational counterparts are popular conformity and allegiance to authority. At the third stage, an organization adopts conventional procedures to which it expects members to adhere if they are to be treated as part of the in-group. When an employee successfully appeals to standard operating procedures in order to counter an organizational lion or fox, a different dimension of moral discourse and or-

ganizational behavior serves to create a new ethical climate. It is a climate based on individual needs for belonging and the survival of the group.

At the fourth stage, organizational ethics is not based on a need for peer approval, but on authoritative command. The ethical climate is one in which employees do not think and act for themselves, but always check out the position of higher authorities before uttering an opinion. Compliance with authority is the behavioral norm in this process of hierarchical socialization. Whether it entails indoctrination processes detailed by William Whyte in the 1950s or powerful socialization pressures in organizational cultures delineated by Terrence Deal and Allan Kennedy in the 1980s, the absence of individual moral autonomy severely limits organizational ethical development.

ment. The group-centered mentality of stage three can blind the organization to environmental challenges, and uncritical subservience to organizational authority characteristic of stage four can institutionalize and perpetuate mediocrity. Both of these conditions can adversely affect an organization's survival and growth.

Recent moral development research on American business professionals and business school graduate students indicates that a preponderance of business practitioners seem to be reasoning at this level of conventional moral development.

At this level it is important for persons committed to participative quality processes to realize that the key motivators for moral conduct in many private sector organizations may well be conformity to existing organizational procedures, seeking recognition from others, and maintaining the existing social system.

**Stages five and six: participative management and principled conviction—**At the fifth and sixth stages of personal moral development, majority rule and principled conviction are the dominant moral strategies. Their organizational counterparts are democratic participation in decision making and principled choice on the basis of justice and individual rights.

Employees who work in organizations operating at the fifth stage are not guided by social approval-seeking or authoritative command typical of conventional organizational ethics. Instead, majority vote of individual members or their representatives ultimately determines policy and procedure.

Surveying majority trends is an important basis for organizational decision-making at this stage. An obvious defect in this stage is that just as a lion, fox, peer groups or heavy-handed authority figure can abuse power to the detriment of the organization, so can the tyranny of the majority. The majority can override the few and prematurely silence excellent contributors, thereby depriving the organization of potential benefits.

Nevertheless, the roots of participative management and quality circles are located in democratic ideals. A stage five organizational ethical climate, therefore, is most conducive to the growth of participative quality processes. Less developed ethical climates will normally constrain or inhibit the full implementation of participative quality processes. So, it is important for quality and participation advocates to be aware of an organization's ethical climate and to be prepared to utilize the five steps to improve organizational ethical climates that are mentioned at the end of this article.

The sixth and final stage of organizational moral development requires respect for justice and the minority rights of productive and creative individuals; searching for consensus rather than relying on a majority vote. Rewarding individuals justly and protecting key organizational contributors from democratic witch hunts (a la Socrates) become abiding features for employees working at the summit of organizational moral development. The

organization thrives by nurturing consensus rather than censoring independent-thinking employees, thereby gaining the valuable insights of the creative individuals who dare to go beyond the prevailing majority view at the time. It can be said that at this level an organization has achieved the highest stage of moral development and exhibits praiseworthy character.

*Continuous improvement . . .* Employees who work in organizations at the sixth stage of moral development cannot rest on their laurels. To sustain virtuous character, they must exercise ongoing and balanced judgment about the organizations' ultimate values. With slight modifications on James O'Toole's work, a concise model depicting the dynamic trade-offs among four ultimate values at the sixth stage of moral development can be easily envisaged. (See Figure Two) An organization's character can be determined by the relative emphasis it places on individual merit, economic equality, organizational growth and quality of life.

**Systemic impact of values—**The existence and relationship of these four ultimate values have systemic influence on organizational character formation. For example, if an airport wants to grow by adding another runway, it needs to address the environmental concerns over increased noise and air pollution from adjoining communities. By proceeding with the runway development and providing suitable compensation to the potentially damaged parties, the airport recognizes that quality of life is also an important moral concern.

Similarly, organizations must strike a balance between individual merit and group economic equality. For example, if a manager wants to distribute monetary rewards on the basis of individual merit, thee must also be a concern demonstrated for providing a minimum

living wage for each contributing group member. By implementing an individual merit raise and providing an equal group base salary increase, the manager recognizes that group economic equality is also a legitimate ultimate value.

Thus, organizations form praiseworthy characters and develop good reputations by maintaining commitment to and balance among all four ultimate values. This challenge requires an abundance of moral wisdom in addition to the technical, conceptual and human relations skills necessary for effective management.

### Identifying and Processing Organization-Specific Value Ideals

In addition to ongoing and balanced concern for the ultimate values of individual merit, economic equality, organizational growth, and quality of life, organizational integrity entails the articulation of and adherence to organization-specific value ideals. These value ideals must be modeled at the highest level of organizational leadership and reinforced in the resolution of moral dilemmas if the organization's public commitment to integrity is to be given credibility.

Examples include: "sanctity of human life" for health care organizations, "truth as discovered through science" for research institutions, "customer satisfaction through quality products and service" for business enterprises, "development of the human potential" for educational institutions, and "public service and trust" for governmental agencies. Value ideals that apply to most contemporary American organizations are respect for the individual (based on legal, political and moral foundations), commitment to service (based on the adage to "do unto others as you would have others do unto

*Stage 6*

---

**Figure Two: Balance of Ultimate Values for Organizational Character Formation**

| **Individual Merit** | **Organizational Growth** |
|---|---|
| **Quality of Life** | **Economic Equality** |

**Source:** See Resources list for James O'Toole.

you"), and performing with excellence (based on religious and secular work ethics).

*Ethics at IBM* . . . When asked to account for its enduring success as an economic enterprise, the founding leaders of IBM credit belief in and adherence to these three value ideals. "In any moral dilemma involving price, product, pay, people, or profit, these values have guided management action. Further, when failure occurred, it is because the organization strayed from or reduced its strength of commitment to respect for the individual, service to the customer, and performing with excellence."

In addition to organization–specific values, it is possible to formulate association and team-based value systems. Figure Three, for example, specifies the code of ethics of the International Association of Quality Circles (now the Association for Quality and Participation—AQP). It espouses the values of tolerance, fairness, respect,and honesty at the international level, which are characteristic of stages five and six of organizational moral development. In order for quality and participation practitioners to consistently implement the international code of ethics on a team basis, it is necessary to comply with the sample rules of conduct for quality teams, such as, respect for each person, sharing responsibility, criticizing ideas, not persons, keeping an open mind, attending all sessions, questioning and participating, and listening constructively.

Following the sample rules of conduct for quality teams insures value alignment or congruence between international groups and local teams, between organizational values and team values, and avoids any discrepancy between moral rhetoric and ethical behavior. When team members respect each other, keep an open mind, and listen constructively, it is more likely that persons will feel secure enough to propose novel, unconventional approaches to problems or formulate creative resolutions to work dilemmas. In effect, routinely following the conduct rules prevents the premature rejection of excellent quality and participation ideas simply because they are unusual or different from the normal operating procedures.

**The full moral cycle**—Figures Four and Five present a concept that can be used to assess the degree of integration of an organization's value ideals. This concept is called a full moral cycle. A full swing through this cycle in organizational ethics is comprised of the complete execution of the following six phases or points from start to finish:

*Point one is for the organization to know what it values.*

*Point two is for the organization to choose freely what it values.*

*Point three is for the organization to cherish what it values.*

*Point four is for the organization to declare what it values.*

*Point five is for the organization to act on its values.*

*Point six is for the organization to act habitually on its values.*

When an organization does not complete all six points in the morality cycle, it deprives itself of the power of moral strength and authority. In doing so it risks losing employee loyalty because employees correctly perceive a gap between organizational rhetoric and behavioral reality.

Consider the case of six business organizations, each facing a moral dilemma (e.g., how much to charge, how much to pay, how much quality to build into products):

Company A knows what it values, but has not examined other alternatives. It is running on the momentum of past value decisions without critically evaluating them, renewing its conscious allegiance to them, or freely choosing different values from viable alternatives. It is essentially an unthinking stance, which provides little or no moral strength.

Company B knows what it values and has chosen its values freely, but does not cherish them or feel a sense of internal organizational pride. It is functioning on the basis of bland operational efficiency without the benefit of group strength that comes from emotional commitment.

Company C knows what it values, has freely chosen its values, and cherishes its values, but has not declared them publicly. The organization possesses shared, but unproclaimed values. Without publicly acknowledging its values, the organization intentionally or unintentionally hides what it stands for and deprives itself of moral strength.

Company D knows what it values, has freely chosen its values, cherishes them, and publicly declares them, but does not act on its values. Its values are expressed in terms of theory, falling short of concrete action, and

## Figure Three: Code of Ethics

### Association Members' Code of Ethics

I recognize that every person, no matter where in the organization, desires to do quality work and be a respected and contributing citizen.

I will aid in the advancement of human welfare by helping to make people's lives more meaningful through enabling them to obtain maximum satisfaction from their work.

I will ensure that credit for the work of others is given to those to whom it is due.

I will not compete unfairly with others. I will assume responsibility for my own mistakes and refrain from shifting blame to others.

I will always keep an open mind and look for merit in the ideas of others.

I will maintain a reputation for good moral character, good citizenship, and honesty.

I will strive to keep informed of all the latest developments in the area of employee participation and will work toward implementing such advancements as appropriate to improve working conditions.

I will aid in the professional development and advancement of my colleagues, and those in my employ or under my supervision.

I will earnestly endeavor to aid the work of the Association and toe extend public knowledge of its purposes and activities.

**Source:** IAQC, *The Quality Circles Journal,* V. 1, N.1.

thereby falling short of internal and external moral credibility. Detecting, disclosing and correcting organizational moral hypocrisy is a sign of strong moral development.

Company E knows what it values, has freely chosen its values, cherishes them, publicly declares them, and has acted on its values but does not act habitually on its values. Its morality is based on occasional moral gestures without the follow-through of habitual ethical action that forms substantive virtuous character.

Company F knows what it values, has freely chosen its values, cherishes them, publicly declares them, acts on its values, and does so habitually to solidify its organizational character. Its internal and external constituencies know what it stands for and can count on the organizations' integrity. Company F exhibits an integrated moral cycle and demonstrates maximum commitment to its value ideals.

In his books, *In Search of Excellence* and *A Passion for Excellence,* Tom Peters goes to great lengths to demonstrate that customer service and commitment to quality yield great profits and enhance international competitiveness. The level of moral development achieved by the excellent organizations identified by Peters is the underlying foundation for the superior performance of these organizations. Superior performance is a side benefit, not an end in itself, of thoroughgoing moral respect for individuals typical of the level of moral development at stage six.

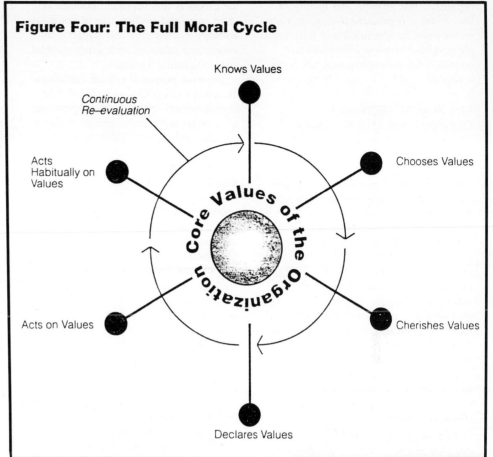

**Figure Four: The Full Moral Cycle**

Knows Values

Continuous Re-evaluation

Chooses Values

Acts Habitually on Values

Core Values of the Organization

Cherishes Values

Acts on Values

Declares Values

This high level of moral respect between leader and subordinate in successful Japanese organizations has been documented. The clear message is that international competitiveness in today's world requires continually improving organizational ethical climates, accomplished in part, by institutionalizing and implementing moral conduct codes.

To summarize, organizational integrity requires institutionalized moral reasoning at the sixth stage of moral development where right and wrong are determined by respect for justice and individual rights. In addition, an ongoing and balanced commitment must be maintained with four ultimate values as moral cornerstones: individual merit, economic equality,

## Figure Five: Full Moral Cycle

Persons and organizations process value ideals with different degrees of thoroughness when confronting specific moral dilemmas (e.g., for individuals: what to do about family or work moral issues, and for companies: what to do about prices, products, pay, people, and profits). Each person or organization experiences incomplete follow through at some point on the morality cycle, except Farah or Company F, which completes the cycle to maintain ethical integrity on an ongoing basis.

| Points on the Cycle | Anna/ Company A | Beth/ Company B | Cindy/ Company C | Donna/ Company D | Esther/ Company E | Farah/ Company F |
|---|---|---|---|---|---|---|
| Knows Values | X | X | X | X | X | X |
| Chooses Values | | X | X | X | X | X |
| Cherishes Values | | | X | X | X | X |
| Declares Values | | | | X | X | X |
| Acts on Values | | | | | X | X |
| Acts Habitually on Values | | | | | | X |

**Source:** Louis B. Raths, Merrill Harmin, and Sidney Simon, *Values and Teaching.* Columbus, Ohio: Charles E. Merrill Publishing, 1, 66, 27–36. AQP Graphics

organizational growth, and quality of life. Finally, organization–specific value ideals must be identified and fully implemented if employee loyalty and international competitiveness are to be achieved.

## Five Steps to Improving Organizational Ethical Climate

Given this model of organizational moral development, it is possible for quality practitioners to implement five specific steps to improve an organization's moral climate.

**Improve the quality of the leader–follower exchange**—This entails developing a nurturing, collaborative relationship where support for ethical conduct and initiative is regularly provided. The positive effects of increased performance, effective team work, and enhanced company competitiveness in Japanese organizations, where high quality leader–follower exchange and inspiration regularly occurs, has been thoroughly documented by Graen, Scandura, Wakabayashi, and Bass (please see Resources list)

**Reduce delays in enforcement of organizational ethical guidelines**—One way to do this is to devise an organizational code of ethics with value ideals identified and specific negative consequences mandated for unethical conduct, with decision timeframes explicitly stated. Organizational leaders should initiate this strategy, set up a task force on revising the code of ethics, and eventually solicit input from all organizational stakeholders. Third, increase the benefits of ethical behavior for employees of the organization. One way to do this is to recommend an ethical audit of each department in the organization and link managerial and team performance incentives with desirable ethical climate levels. An ethical audit may include a review of policies and procedures in the following areas: customer, vendor, and employee relations; quality standards

for products and services: policies on price, pay, and profits; use of company resources; environmental impact concerns; and relations with governmental and community agencies.

**Improve personal ethical conduct**—Two ways to do this are: (1) have an organizational ombudsman empowered to analyze and resolve ethical conflicts on site, and (2) provide systematic training to develop responsible ethical decision-making skills and full cycle morality. Organizational leaders need to actively educate followers to act responsibly, and in turn, the followers need to provide loyal support to deserving leaders.

**Leaders model behavior**—Most important, the formal and informal transformational leaders of the organization must personally exemplify and reinforce virtuous moral behavior. This means the actions of these influential individuals must reflect stage six moral reasoning, demonstrate balanced judgment among the four ultimate values of individual merit, economic equality, organizational growth, and quality of life, and model the full moral cycle in the processing and implementation of organization–specific value ideals.

## Final Note

This article has presented a theoretical model for professional and organizational moral development and five specific recommendations for improving an organization's ethical climate. Insofar as these facilitate participative quality processes and contribute to international competitiveness, these models of moral excellence warrant consideration by quality and participation professionals.

## Resources and References

### REFERENCES

Kenneth R. Andrews, ed. *Ethics in Practice: Managing the Moral Corporation* (Boston: Harvard University Press, 1989).

Tom L. Beauchamp and Norman E. Bowie, *Ethical Theory and Business,* Third Edition (Englewood Cliffs, NJ: Prentice—New York: Macmillan, 1990).

Terrence E. Deal and Allan Kennedy *Corporate Cultures: The Rites and Rituals of Corporate Life* (Reading, MA: Addison-Wesley, 1982).

R. Edward Freeman and Daniel R. Gilbert, Jr., *Corporate Strategy and the Search for Ethics* (Englewood Cliffs, NJ: Prentice Hall, 1988).

G. Graen and T. Scandura, "Moderating Effects of Initial Leader–Member Exchange Status on the Effects of a Leadership Intervention," *Journal of Applied Psychology,* 69, 1984, 428–436.

Lawrence Kohlberg, "Stages of Moral Development as a Basis for Moral Education," in *Moral Education: Interdisciplinary Approaches.* ed. C. M. Beck, B. S. Crittenden, and E. V. Sullivan (Toronto: University of Toronto Press, 1971).

James O'Toole, *Vanguard Management: Redesigning the Corporate Future* (New York: Doubleday & Company, 1985).

T. Peters and R. Waterman, *In Search of Excellence* (New York: Harper & Row, 1982).

T. Peters and N. Austin, *A Passion for Excellence* (New York: Random House, 1985).

Louis E. Raths, Merrill Harmin and Sidney Simon, *Values and Teaching* (Columbus, OH: Charles E. Merrill Publishing, 1966), 27–36.

Michael D. Smith, "The Virtuous Organization," in Albert Flores, ed., *Professional Ideals* (Belmont, CA: Wadsworth Publishing, 1988).

Edward Stevens, *Business Ethics* (New York: Paulist Press, 1981).

M. Wakabayashi, G. Graen, M. Graen, and M. Graen, "Japanese Management Progress: Mobility Into Middle Management" *Journal of Applied Psychology,* Vol. 73, No. 2, 1988, 217–227.

Doug Wallace and Julie B. White, "Building Integrity in Organizations," *New Management.* Vol. 6., No. 1., Summer, 1988, pp 30–35.

Thomas J. Watson, Jr., *A Business and Its Beliefs: The Ideas That Helped Build IBM* (New York: McGraw-Hill, 1963), 14.

Allan L. Wilkins. *Developing Corporate Character: How to Successfully Change an Organization Without Destroying It* (San Francisco: Jossey-Bass, 1989).

William H. Whyte, *The Organization Man* (New York: Simon & Schuster, 1956).

J. A. Wood and J. G. Longenecker, J. A. McKinney and C. W. Moore, "Ethical Attitudes of Students and Business Professionals: A Study of Moral Reasoning," *Journal of Business Ethics,* 7: 249–257, 1988.

# Ethics in Practice

*The values of a company's leaders are evident
in every strategic decision they make.*

## Kenneth R. Andrews

*Kenneth R. Andrews is the Donald K. David Professor of
Business Administration, Emeritus, at the Harvard Business School. He was editor of HBR from 1979 to 1985. This
article is adapted from his introduction to* Ethics in
Practice: Managing the Moral Corporation *(Harvard
Business School Press, 1989).*

As the 1990s overtake us, public interest in ethics is at
a historic high. While the press calls attention to
blatant derelictions on Wall Street, in the defense
industry, and in the Pentagon, and to questionable
activities in the White House, in the attorney general's office, and in Congress, observers wonder
whether our society is sicker than usual. Probably
not. The standards applied to corporate behavior
have risen over time, and that has raised the average
rectitude of businesspersons and politicians both. It
has been a long time since we could say with Mark
Twain that we have the best Senate money can buy or
agree with muckrakers like Upton Sinclair that our
large companies are the fiefdoms of robber barons.
But illegal and unethical behavior persists, even as
efforts to expose it often succeed in making its rewards short-lived.

Why is business ethics a problem that snares not
just a few mature criminals or crooks in the making
but a host of apparently good people who lead exemplary private lives while concealing information
about dangerous products or systematically falsifying costs? My observation suggests that the problem
of corporate ethics has three aspects: the development of the executive as a moral person; the influence
of the corporation as a moral environment; and the
actions needed to map a high road to economic and
ethical performance—and to mount guardrails to
keep corporate wayfarers on track.

Sometimes it is said that wrongdoing in business is an individual failure: a person of the
proper moral fiber, properly brought up, simply
would not cheat. Because of poor selection, a
few bad apples are bound to appear in any big barrel. But these corporate misfits can subsequently
be scooped out. Chief executive officers, we used to
think, have a right to rely on the character of individual employees without being distracted from business objectives. Moral character is shaped by family,
church, and education long before an individual joins
a company to make a living.

In an ideal world, we might end here. In the real
world, moral development is an unsolved problem at
home, at school, at church—and at work. Two-career
families, television, and the virtual disappearance of
the dinner table as a forum for discussing moral issues have clearly outmoded instruction in basic principles at Mother's knee—if that fabled tutorial was
ever as effective as folklore would have it. We cannot
expect our battered school systems to take over the
moral role of the family. Even religion is less help
than it once might have been when membership in a
distinct community promoted—or coerced—conventional moral behavior. Society's increasing secularization, the profusion of sects, the conservative
church's divergence from new lifestyles, pervasive
distrust of the religious right—all these mean that we
cannot depend on uniform religious instruction to
armor business recruits against temptation.

Nor does higher education take up the slack, even
in disciplines in which moral indoctrination once
flourished. Great literature can be a self-evident

## ▮ Why do so many good people get caught falsifying costs?

source of ethical instruction, for it informs the mind
and heart together about the complexities of moral
choice. Emotionally engaged with fictional or historic characters who must choose between death and
dishonor, integrity and personal advancement, power
and responsibility, self and others, we expand our
own moral imaginations as well. Yet professors of literature rarely offer guidance in ethical interpretation, preferring instead to stress technical, aesthetic,
or historical analysis.

# 1. ETHICS IN BUSINESS

Moral philosophy, which is the proper academic home for ethical instruction, is even more remote, with few professors choosing to teach applied ethics. When you add to that the discipline's studied disengagement from the world of practical affairs, it is not surprising that most students (or managers) find little in the subject to attract them.

What does attract students – in large numbers – is economics, with its theory of human behavior that relates all motivation to personal pleasure, satisfaction, and self-interest. And since self-interest is more easily served than not by muscling aside the self-interest of others, the Darwinian implications of conventional economic theory are essentially immoral. Competition produces and requires the will to win. Careerism focuses attention on advantage. Immature individuals of all ages are prey to the moral flabbiness that William James said attends exclusive service to the bitch goddess Success.

Spurred in part by recent notorious examples of such flabbiness, many business schools are making determined efforts to reintroduce ethics in elective and required courses. But even if these efforts were further along than they are, boards of directors and senior managers would be unwise to assume that recruits could enter the corporate environment without need for additional education. The role of any school is to prepare its graduates for a lifetime of learning from experience that will go better and faster than it would have done without formal education. No matter how much colleges and business schools expand their investment in moral instruction, most education in business ethics (as in all other aspects of business acumen) will occur in the organizations in which people spend their lives.

Making ethical decisions is easy when the facts are clear and the choices black and white. But it is a different story when the situation is clouded by ambiguity, incomplete information, multiple points of view, and conflicting responsibilities. In such situations – which managers experience all the time – ethical decisions depend on both the decision-making process itself and on the experience, intelligence, and integrity of the decision maker.

Responsible moral judgment cannot be transferred to decision makers ready-made. Developing it in business turns out to be partly an administrative process involving: recognition of a decision's ethical implications; discussion to expose different points of view; and testing the tentative decision's adequacy in balancing self-interest and consideration of others, its import for future policy, and its consonance with the company's traditional values. But after all this, if a clear consensus has not emerged, then the executive in charge must decide, drawing on his or her intuition and conviction. This being so, the caliber of the decision maker is decisive – especially when an immediate decision must arise from instinct rather than from discussion.

This existential resolution requires the would-be moral individual to be the final authority in a situation where conflicting ethical principles are joined. It does not rule out prior consultation with others or recognition that, in a hierarchical organization, you might be overruled.

Ethical decisions therefore require of individuals three qualities that can be identified and developed. The first is competence to recognize ethical issues and to think through the consequences of alternative resolutions. The second is self-confidence to seek out different points of view and then to decide what is right at a given time and place, in a particular set of relationships and circumstances. The third is what William James called tough-mindedness, which in management is the willingness to make decisions when all that needs to be known cannot be known and when the questions that press for answers have no established and incontrovertible solutions.

Unfortunately, moral individuals in the modern corporation are too often on their own. But these individuals cannot be expected to remain autonomous, no matter how well endowed they are, without positive organized support. The stubborn persistence of ethical problems obscures the simplicity of the solution—once the leaders of a company decide to do something about their ethical standards. Ethical dereliction, sleaziness, or inertia is not merely an individual failure but a management problem as well.

When they first come to work, individuals whose moral judgment may ultimately determine their company's ethical character enter a community whose values will influence their own. The economic function of the corporation is necessarily one of those values. But if it is the only value, ethical inquiry cannot flourish. If management believes that the invisible hand of the market adequately moderates the injury done by the pursuit of self-interest, ethical policy can be dismissed as irrelevant. And if what people see (while they are hearing about maximizing shareholder wealth) are managers dedicated to their own survival and compensation, they will naturally be more concerned about rewards than about fairness.

For the individual, the impact of the need to succeed is doubtless more direct than the influence of neoclassical economic theory. But just as the corporation itself is saddled with the need to establish competitive advantage over time (after reinvestment of what could otherwise be the immediate profit by which the financial community and many shareholders judge its performance), aspiring managers will also be influenced by the way they are judged. A highly moral and humane chief executive can preside over an amoral organization because the incentive system focuses attention on short-term quantifiable results.

Under pressures to get ahead, the individual (of whose native integrity we are hopeful) is tempted to pursue advancement at the expense of others, to cut corners, to seek to win at all cost, to make things seem better than they are – to take advantage, in sum, of a myopic evaluation of performance. People will do what they are rewarded for doing. The quantifiable results of managerial activity are always much more visible than the quality and future consequences of the means by which they are attained.

By contrast, when the corporation is defined as a socioeconomic institution with responsibilities to other constituencies (employees, customers, and communities, for example), policy can be established to regulate the single-minded pursuit of maximum immediate profit. The leaders of such a company speak of social responsibility, promulgate ethical policy, and make their personal values available for emulation by their juniors. They are respectful of neoclassical economic theory, but find it only partially useful as a management guide.

As the corporation grows beyond its leader's daily direct influence, the ethical consequences of size and geographical deployment come into play. Control and enforcement of all policy becomes more difficult, but this is especially true with regard to policy established for corporate ethics. Layers of responsibility bring communication problems. The possibility of penalty engenders a lack of candor. Distance from headquarters complicates the evaluation of performance, driving it to numbers. When operations are dispersed among different cultures and countries in which corruption assumes exotic guises, a consensus about moral values is hard to achieve and maintain.

Moreover, decentralization in and of itself has ethical consequences, not least because it absolutely requires trust and latitude for error. The inability to monitor the performance of executives assigned to tasks their superiors cannot know in detail results inexorably in delegation. Corporate leaders are accustomed to relying on the business acumen of profit-center managers, whose results the leaders watch with a practiced eye. Those concerned with maintaining their companies' ethical standards are just as dependent on the judgment and moral character of the managers to whom authority is delegated. Beyond keeping your fingers crossed, what can you do?

Fortunately for the future of the corporation, this microcosm of society can be, within limits, what its leadership and membership make it. The corporation is an organization in which people influence one another to establish accepted

values and ways of doing things. It is not a democracy, but to be fully effective, the authority of its leaders must be supported by their followers. Its leadership has more power than elected officials do to choose who will join or remain in the association. Its members expect direction to be proposed even as they threaten resistance to change. Careless or lazy managements let their organizations drift, continuing their economic performance along lines previously established and leaving their ethics to chance. Resolute managements find they can surmount the problems I have dwelt on – once they have separated these problems from their camouflage.

It is possible to carve out of our pluralistic, multicultured society a coherent community with a strategy that defines both its economic purposes and the standards of competence, quality, and humanity that govern its activities. The character of a corporation may well be more malleable than an individual's. Certainly its culture can be shaped. Intractable persons can be replaced or retired. Those committed to the company's goals can generate formal and informal sanctions to constrain and alienate those who are not.

Shaping such a community begins with the personal influence of the chief executive and that of the managers who are heads of business units, staff departments, or any other suborganizations to which authority is delegated. The determination of explicit ethical policy comes next, followed by the same management procedures that are used to execute any body of policy in effective organizations.

## ▌How can you tell whether managers merit your trust?

The way the chief executive exercises moral judgment is universally acknowledged to be more influential than written policy. The CEO who orders the immediate recall of a product, at the cost of millions of dollars in sales because of a quality defect affecting a limited number of untraceable shipments, sends one kind of message. The executive who suppresses information about a producer's actual or potential ill effects or, knowingly or not, condones overcharging, sends another.

Policy is implicit in behavior. The ethical aspects of product quality, personnel, advertising, and marketing decisions are immediately plain. CEOs say much more than they know in the most casual contacts with those who watch their every move. Pretense is futile. "Do not *say* things," Emerson once wrote. "What you *are* stands over you the while, and thunders so that I can not hear what you say to the contrary." It follows that "if you would not be known to do anything, never do it."

The modest person might respond to this attribution of transparency with a "who, me?" Self-confident sophisticates will refuse to consider themselves so easily read. Almost all executives underestimate their power and do not recognize deference in others. The import of this, of course, is that a CEO should be conscious of how the position amplifies his or her most casual judgments, jokes, and silences. But an even more important implication—given that people cannot hide their characters—is that the selection of a chief executive (indeed of any aspirant to management responsibility) should include an explicit estimate of his or her character. If you ask how to do that, Emerson would reply, "Just look."

Once a company's leaders have decided that its ethical intentions and performance will be managed, rather than left untended in the corrosive environment of unprincipled competition, they must determine their corporate policy and make it explicit much as they do in other areas. The need for written policy is especially urgent in companies without a strong tradition to draw on or where a new era must be launched—after a public scandal, say, or an internal investigation of questionable behavior. Codes of ethics are now commonplace. But in and of themselves they are not effective, and this is especially true when they are so broadly stated that they can be dismissed as merely cosmetic.

Internal policies specifically addressed to points of industry, company, and functional vulnerability make compliance easier to audit and training easier to conduct. Where particular practices are of major concern—price fixing, for example, or bribery of government officials or procurement—compliance can be made a condition of employment and certified annually by employees' signatures. Still, the most pervasive problems cannot be foreseen, nor can the proper procedures be so spelled out in advance as to tell the person on the line what to do. Unreasonably repressive rules undermine trust, which remains indispensable.

What executives can do is advance awareness of the kinds of problems that are foreseeable. Since policy cannot be effective unless it is understood, some companies use corporate training sessions to discuss the problems of applying their ethical standards. In difficult situations, judgment in making the leap from general policy statements to situationally specific action can be informed by discussion. Such discussion, if carefully conducted, can reveal the inadequacy or ambiguity of present policy, new areas in which the company must take a unified stand, and new ways to support individuals in making the right decisions.

As in all policy formulation and implementation, the deportment of the CEO, the development of relevant policy—and training in its meaning and application—are not enough. In companies determined to sustain or raise ethical standards, management expands the information system to illuminate pressure points—the rate of manufacturing defects, product returns and warranty claims, special instances of quality shortfalls, results of competitive benchmarking inquiries—whatever makes good sense in the special circumstances of the company.

Because trust is indispensable, ethical aspirations must be supported by information that serves not only to inform but also to control. Control need not be so much coercive as customary, representing not suspicion but a normal interest in the quality of operations. Experienced executives do not substitute trust for the awareness that policy is often distorted in practice. Ample information, like full visibility, is a powerful deterrent.

This is why purposely ethical organizations expand the traditional sphere of external and internal audits (which is wherever fraud may occur) to include compliance with corporate ethical standards. Even more important, such organizations pay attention to every kind of obstacle that limits performance and to problems needing ventilation so that help can be provided.

To obtain information that is deeply guarded to avoid penalty, internal auditors—long since taught not to prowl about as police or detectives—must be people with enough management experience to be sensitive to the manager's need for economically viable decisions. For example, they should have imagination enough to envision ethical outcomes from bread-and-butter profit and pricing decisions, equal opportunity and payoff dilemmas, or downsizing crunches. Establishing an audit and control climate that takes as a given an open exchange of information between the company's operating levels and policy-setting levels is not difficult—once, that is, the need to do so is recognized and persons of adequate experience and respect are assigned to the work.

But no matter how much empathy audit teams exhibit, discipline ultimately requires action. The secretary who steals petty cash, the successful salesman who falsifies his expense account, the accountant and her boss who alter cost records, and, more problematically, the chronically sleazy operator who never does anything actually illegal—all must be dealt with cleanly, with minimum attention to allegedly extenuating circumstances. It is true that hasty punishment may be unjust and absolve superiors improperly of their secondary responsibility for wrongdoing. But long delay or waffling in the effort to be humane obscures the message the organization requires whenever violations occur. Trying to conceal a major lapse or safeguarding the names of people who have been fired is kind to the offender but blunts the salutary impact of disclosure.

For the executive, the administration of discipline incurs one ethical dilemma after another: How do you weigh consideration for the offending individual, for example, and how do you weigh the future of the organization? A company dramatizes its uncompromising adherence to lawful and ethical behavior when it severs employees who commit offenses that were classified in advance as unforgivable. When such a decision is fair, the grapevine makes its equity clear even when more formal publicity is inappropriate. Tough decisions should not be postponed simply because they are painful. The steady support of corporate integrity is never without emotional cost.

In a large, decentralized organization, consistently ethical performance requires difficult decisions from not only the current CEO but also a succession of chief executives. Here the board of directors enters the scene. The board has the opportunity to provide a succession of CEOs whose personal values and characters are consistently adequate for sustaining and developing established traditions for ethical conduct. Once in place, chief executives must rely on two resources for getting done what they cannot do personally: the character of their associates and the influence of policy and the measures that are taken to make policy effective.

An adequate corporate strategy must include noneconomic goals. An economic strategy is the optimal match of a company's product and market opportunities with its resources and distinctive competence. (That both are continually changing is of course true.) But economic strategy is humanized and made attainable by deciding what kind of organization the company will be—its character, the values it espouses, its relationships to customers, employees, communities, and shareholders. The personal values and ethical aspirations of the company's leaders, though probably not specifically stated, are implicit in all strategic decisions. They show through the choices management makes and reveal themselves as the company goes about its business. That is why this communication should be deliberate and purposeful rather than random.

Although codes of ethics, ethical policy for specific vulnerabilities, and disciplined enforcement are important, they do not contain in themselves the final emotional power of commitment. Commitment to quality objectives—among them compliance with law and high ethical standards—is an organizational achievement. It is inspired by pride more than by the profit that rightful pride produces. Once the scope of strategic decisions is thus enlarged, their ethical

component is no longer at odds with a decision right for many reasons.

As former editor of HBR, I am acutely aware of how difficult it is to persuade businesspeople to write or speak about corporate ethics. I am not comfortable doing so myself. To generalize the ethical aspects of a business decision, leaving behind the concrete particulars that make it real, is too often to sermonize, to simplify, or to rationalize away the plain fact that many instances of competing ethical claims have no satisfactory solution. But we also hear little public comment from business leaders of integrity when incontestable breaches of conduct are made known—and silence suggests to cynics an absence of concern.

The impediments to explicit discussion of ethics in business are many, beginning with the chief executive's keen awareness that someday he or she may be betrayed by someone in his or her own organization. Moral exhortation and oral piety are offensive, especially when attended by hypocrisy or real vulnerability to criticism. Any successful or energetic individual will sometime encounter questions about his or her methods and motives, for even well-intentioned behavior may be judged unethical from some point of view. The need for cooperation among people with different beliefs diminishes discussion of religion and related ethical issues. That persons with management responsibility must find the principles to resolve conflicting ethical claims in their own minds and hearts is an unwelcome discovery. Most of us keep quiet about it.

In summary, my ideas are quite simple. Perhaps the most important is that management's total loyalty to the maximization of profit is the principal obstacle to achieving higher standards of ethical practice. Defining the purpose of the corporation as exclusively economic is a deadly oversimplification, which allows overemphasis on self-interest at the expense of consideration of others.

## Ultimately, executives resolve conflicting claims in their own minds and hearts.

The practice of management requires a prolonged play of judgment. Executives must find in their own will, experience, and intelligence the principles they apply in balancing conflicting claims. Wise men and women will submit their views to others, for open discussion of problems reveals unsuspected ethical dimensions and develops alternative viewpoints that should be taken into account. Ultimately, however, executives must make a decision, relying on their own judgment to settle infinitely debatable issues. Inquiry into character should therefore be part of all executive selection – as well as all executive development within the corporation.

And so it goes. That much and that little. The encouraging outcome is that promulgating and institutionalizing ethical policy are not so difficult as, for example, escaping the compulsion of greed. Once undertaken, the process can be as straightforward as the articulation and implementation of policy in any sphere. Any company has the opportunity to develop a unique corporate strategy summarizing its chief purposes and policies. That strategy can encompass not only the economic role it will play in national and international markets but also the kind of company it will be as a human organization. It will embrace as well, though perhaps not publicly, the nature and scope of the leadership to which the company is to be entrusted.

To be implemented successfully over time, any strategy must command the creativity, energy, and desire of the company's members. Strategic decisions that are economically or ethically unsound will not long sustain such commitment.

# A CEO Looks at Ethics

Vernon R. Loucks Jr., Guest Editor

*Vernon R. Loucks Jr. is president and chief executive officer of Baxter Travenol Laboratories, Inc., Deerfield, IL.*

This editorial is based on remarks to an Executive Forum on ethics and management, given at the Indiana University School of Business on November 7, 1986.

---

Ethics isn't a matter of law or public relations or religion. It's a matter of trust. Baxter Travenol's chief executive officer gives his thoughts on managing ethics and recommends four principles for managers.

---

I t's not often that a top executive gets to talk about ethics even though his company hasn't done anything wrong. My guess is that it's a lot easier to take a reasoned view of the subject without a bunch of TV cameras and subpoenas waving around in your face.

The topic of ethics is an important one. It's a part of management that balances ideals against reality. During a business career, every manager can be virtually certain that he or she will have to make some rugged ethical decisions.

## ETHICAL ISSUES: TIMELY AND TIMELESS

A s tempting as it might be to think that ethical issues are modern and exciting, they're really not all that new. It was about 560 B.C., for example, when the Greek thinker Chilon registered the opinion that a merchant does better to take a loss than to make a dishonest profit. His reasoning was that a loss may be painful for a while, but dishonesty hurts forever—and it's still true.

Others down through history (Greeley and Gandhi are two examples[1]) have talked about the immorality of taking money without earning it. And let's face it: When there's something going on that reasonable people would agree is unethical, there's usually an amount of cash on hand. There's nothing at all modern about that.

John Galbraith may have put it best. He once said: "There are no new forms of financial fraud; in the last several hundred years, there have only been small variations on a few classical designs."

But to say that ethics is an old subject is not to say that it's worn out. Much to the contrary, there seems to be a wave of interest in it lately—and I think that's healthy.

## 1. ETHICS IN BUSINESS

For one thing, there's a lineup of blue-chip companies that have been called on the carpet for some serious ethical flaws over the past year or two. G.E. was in the headlines for illegal billing and E.F. Hutton for wire fraud. The problems at Manville, General Dynamics, Union Carbide, and Morton-Thiokol have ranged from scandalous to shocking.

Those can't all be bad companies full of bad people. In a large company (and especially an international business), periodic ethical problems are all but predictable. It was reported in the *Harvard Business Review* recently that, over the past ten years, two-thirds of America's 500 largest corporations have been involved in some type of illegal behavior.[2]

So virtually no one is exempt from concerns about ethics—and some aspects of business today present added opportunities for unethical behavior. We have deregulation, merger mania, computerization, electronic transfer of funds, and growing international trade. Each of these presents opportunities for variations on Galbraith's classical designs.

Let's also not forget that it really isn't companies but people who are ethical or unethical. Corporate charters and bylaws take no action, right or wrong. They just sit there, leaving it to individual people to act properly or not. In this area as well, the record shows room for improvement. A survey of personnel vice-presidents across the country showed that one out every seven job candidates these days is likely to tell a lie about his or her background.[3]

People or companies are not necessarily less ethical than in the past. If anything, we work under a hotter spotlight than ever before. Mike Wallace, George Gallup, and the SEC are watching almost every move we make. So there is reason to care, and there is some good evidence that managers do care. The Conference Board is conducting a nationwide study about ethics as viewed by chief executive officers. Although the report won't be issued until later this year, the study has found a high level of concern among top executives for many current ethical issues: employee privacy, sexual harassment, product safety, and a host of others.

### WHAT IS ETHICS?

Ethics is a real concern. Though by no means new, it will be with us always, limited only by the imaginations of those inclined to be unethical. But what *is* ethics?

Ethics is not law. Nor is it public relations, with all the associated worries about corporate image. Nor is it religion or apple pie. It's not something you get from a consultant or from a course in business school.

So what is ethics? It somehow relates to law *and* to moral codes of conduct. For example, the dictionary defines ethics in terms of morality, and morality in terms of ethics. But if we as managers are to come to realistic grips with this subject, we need a more specific concept of just what it is.

In his book *Business and Society,* George Steiner defines business ethics as behavior "that is fair and just, over and above obedience to...laws...and regulations."[4] Steiner goes on to say:

> Corporations...have moral responsibilities which are not necessarily matters of law and which are not necessarily identical with the personal moral codes of the executives who run them. These may be internal (for instance, deciding matters connected with stockholders, customers, employees, creditors, and officers) or they may be external (such as matters affecting the interests of communities, competitors, government, and society).[5]

I like that definition for a number of reasons. It accurately points out that ethics relates to law but can also transcend the law. It's realistic in saying that collective ethics cannot satisfy everybody's views (although it seems to me that, in most cases, the majority should agree).

Perhaps most important, the definition reflects the fact that a corporation

"Corporate charters and bylaws take no action, right or wrong. They just sit there, leaving it to individual people to act properly or not."

needs to satisfy a diversity of groups: employees, customers, investors, and others. No one group ought to benefit while the others suffer. Therefore, corporate priorities—including ethics—must always consist of a balance of interests.

It's because of that need to balance the interests of various constituencies that business ethics is so vitally important. Ethics is simply and ultimately a matter of trust. People act in their economic self-interest. But a system based on that fact must also be grounded on mutual trust, among individuals and among organizations. A buyer needs to trust a manufacturer, a lender needs to trust a borrower, and so on.

The problem with a breach in ethics is not that it violates some natural or heavenly law—even though, in fact, it may do that. The practical problem is that an ethical violation makes continued trust difficult or even impossible. That formulation puts business ethics on a plane different from religion, philosophy, or politics. A view of ethics based on matters of trust also helps make the subject more practical and manageable.

> "Ethics is simply and ultimately a matter of trust. People act in their economic self-interest. But a system based on that fact must also be grounded on mutual trust, among individuals and among organizations."

## MANAGING ETHICS AT BAXTER TRAVENOL

Business ethics, after all, is a concern of management. It's something that managers, from the top on down, must properly deal with, every day in any organization.

Is ethics qualitative and philosophical and gray around the edges? It certainly is. It's impossible to computerize. You can't delegate accountability for it, if you intend to be a truly responsible and effective manager.

Of course, it's easier to say you *should* manage ethics than to tell *how* to manage it. I don't pretend to have a cookbook. The issues are far too interdependent for such an easy approach. I do have some thoughts on the matter, however, and some examples from within Baxter Travenol.

Baxter is a $5-billion manufacturer and marketer of health products. We have about 60,000 employees and operations around the world. We also work in a field where topics such as product safety can be matters of life and death.

We place a high priority on ethical behavior. We're among the many Fortune 500 companies that have definitive codes of conduct. Ours covers conflicts of interest, insider trading, and that sort of thing—and we take it very seriously.

But that's not enough. In fact, it's far from being enough.

When you start talking about ethics or anything else, the plain fact is that a few things happen among 60,000 employees and a few million transactions a year that the CEO doesn't know about. I'm sorry, but that's the way it is.

As an example, we have between three and four hundred issues pending at any given time in the area of product liability. It's far more than I should even try to track or monitor personally. The cases are extremely diverse, and they range from the serious to the ridiculous. I understand we have one now where a customer claims that he wrenched his back while unscrewing a bottlecap.

At the same time, we might also have 150 cases where employees say they've been aggrieved in some way. Although all of those cases don't deal with ethical matters, each of them needs to be taken seriously.

So how do we manage this? Beyond maintaining a large staff of lawyers, beyond spending millions every year in legal fees and regulatory activities, what can we do about managing properly in an area like product liability or employee relations or ethics in general?

We do what I've said already: We work to balance interests that often seem to be in conflict. We judge ideals against reality, and we realize that it's never easy. The issues are sensitive. There are few, if any, automatic answers.

# 1. ETHICS IN BUSINESS

## MORE QUESTIONS THAN ANSWERS

Think about a specific product, manufactured and marketed internationally by Baxter Travenol: the artificial heart valve. We make a range of valves with various designs. They're surgically implanted to replace patients' own natural valves when, for any number of reasons, they happen to fail. The artificial valve is truly a lifesaving device. It's been around for a couple of decades, and it's used almost routinely today.

Of course, heart valves present more critical tolerances than many other products—lawn chairs or donuts, for example. For that reason, they also present some hard ethical questions along several dimensions. Perhaps the most basic question is whether it's ethical to make a profit on such a product.

A debate has raged across our industry for some years about the emergence and great success of for-profit hospitals. Some say to leave them alone; they have the same right as anyone else to succeed or fail. Others say it's wrong to make a profit from human illness or injury.

There's not much of a logical leap from the hospital to the heart valve. Yes, the company supported the development of the product and shepherded it through eight or ten years of regulatory reviews. And, yes, the company runs all the risk of failure in a competitive market.

But what about it? It is right to make a profit when someone's survival is involved?

There are plenty of other questions. For example, if a profit is proper, then how much profit? And is it acceptable to increase the risk of the valve's malfunctioning by a tenth of one percent in order to reduce manufacturing costs (and maybe ultimately the price) by, say, 25 percent? Or is any increase in risk simply unconscionable?

This really gets at the issue of balancing interests. Certainly, the patient's interest is in the area of safety. But what is a reasonable level of safety when you consider a shareholder's legitimate interest in a reasonable return on investment?

The question that fascinates me is liability—for example, the patient whose artificial valve fails after five years' time. Does he (or do his survivors) have a legitimate grievance against Baxter Travenol? Many feel they do have a grievance, even with all the waivers that were signed before the operation and even with the realization that a new valve was necessary only because the valves that God makes tend to fail sometimes.

Heart valves are among 120,000 products that we market at Baxter Travenol. Not all of them are so critical, but many others carry just as much reason for concern. Our blood products, at a time of national concern about AIDS, are an excellent example.

The point is, it's not easy. To talk about business ethics with any degree of honesty means grappling with some tough issues in the real world.

Another example is not a product example but an issue we've shared with some big corporations, including IBM, GM, and Coca-Cola. The issue is whether to stay in business in South Africa.

On September 30, 1986, Baxter Travenol completed the sale of our operations in South Africa. We'd been there for almost 40 years, making lifesaving products. We were growing and highly profitable.

As to apartheid, we have nothing to debate. It's absolutely intolerable. As humans, as citizens of the world, and as businesspeople, we should do anything we can to wipe it out. But my question is whether running away is the best we can do.

Again, look at the balance of interests. Is the government in Pretoria harmed by the pullout of U.S. corporations? If so, who else is hurt? What about the customers who were relying on us? What about the people we were employing? And what about the investors in Baxter Travenol? Can and should a corporation fight a problem like apartheid on its own ground? Would that be more effective in the long run than trying to starve the problem by pulling out?

I realize that I'm providing questions without answers. But the problems

*"Is it acceptable to increase the risk of the valve's malfunctioning by a tenth of one percent in order to reduce manufacturing costs (and maybe ultimately the price) by, say, 25 percent? Or is any increase in risk simply unconscionable?"*

I've cited are real—and it's the job of management to solve them.

## FOUR PRINCIPLES FOR ETHICAL MANAGEMENT

I f I won't suggest easy answers to the questions I've raised, I will offer some principles that, in my experience, ought to guide our ethical decisions as managers. There are four of them.

*First, hire the right people.*

Employees who are inclined to be ethical are the best insurance you can have. They may be the only insurance. Look for people with principles. Let them know that those principles are an important part of their qualifications for the job.

*Second, set standards more than rules.*

You can't write a code of conduct airtight enough to cover every eventuality. A person inclined to fraud or misconduct isn't going to blink at signing your code anyway. So don't waste your time on heavy regulations. Instead, be clear about standards. Let people know the level of performance you expect—and that ethics are not negotiable.

*Third, don't let yourself get isolated.*

You know that managers can lose track of markets and competitors by moving into the ivory tower. But they also can lose sight of what's going on in their own operations. The only problem is that *you* are responsible for whatever happens in your office or department or corporation, whether you know about it or not.

*Fourth and most important, let your ethical example at all times be absolutely impeccable.*

This isn't just a matter of how you act in matters of accounting, competition, or interpersonal relationships. Be aware also of the signals you send to those around you. Steady harping on the importance of quarterly gains in earnings, for example, rather easily leads people to believe that you don't much care about how the results are achieved.

Mark Twain once said: "Always do the right thing. This will surprise some people and astonish the rest." I'm saying that it will also motivate them to do the right thing. Indeed, without a good example from the top, ethical problems (and all the costs that go with them) are probably inevitable within your organization.

H istory shows that, in the long run, the ethical course of action is the profitable course as well. That hasn't changed since 560 B.C. or so, and I don't believe it will. I also don't think we've ever really improved on the Golden Rule.

> "Hire the right people. Look for people with principles. Let them know that those principles are an important part of their qualifications for the job."

---

1.  Horace Greeley wrote, "The darker hour in the history of any young man is when he sits down to study how to get money without honestly earning it." "Wealth without labor" is one of Gandhi's seven sins.

2.  See Saul W. Gellerman, "Why 'Good' Managers Make Bad Ethical Choices," *Harvard Business Review*, July-August 1986: 85. Gellerman reports on the conclusions of Amitai Etzioni, a professor of sociology at George Washington University.

3.  According to a September 1986 survey reported by Robert Half International, New York. The findings were based on interviews with vice-presidents and personnel directors of one hundred of the nation's one thousand largest corporations.

4.  George A. Steiner, *Business and Society: Cases*, 2nd ed. (New York: Random House, 1972), p. 211

5.  Steiner (note 4): pp. 224-25.

# Corporate Responsibility

*Socially responsible corporate programs are critical strategic tools for sustaining competitive success in today's markets.*

## MARK ALBION

*Mark Albion, Ph.D., is chairperson of Apple Brook Farms in support of social causes, president of Children Against Drugs, author of three books on marketing, consultant to Fortune 500 companies developing strategic programs that address social needs, a member of the Social Venture Network, former faculty member at the Harvard Business School, and rated one of the top young business professors in America (617) 235-8923.*

T HE COST-BENEFIT ANALYSIS of business has been altered. Global economic imperatives, socio-demographic shifts, and the importance of human values to executives and consumers alike have created a new competitive climate — a shifting landscape of possibilities and opportunities for enlightened business leaders, but one with many pitfalls and traps as well.

Managing change may well be the executive's most important task. The definition of corporate responsibility is rapidly changing. It is no longer simply a question of wanting to do the right thing. Instead, an increasingly complex set of social imperatives are being generated by employees, consumers, investors, and interested communities.

Socially responsible actions play a critical role in creating competitive advantage, expressing corporate culture and improving the long-term bottom-line.

Making a profit no longer depends simply on traditional business strategies and management of resources. It also depends on paying close attention to your stake-holders. In their roles as your employees, consumers, investors, legislators, and the public at large, people are expressing their values in a changing marketplace. How is your company responding to the demographic and psychographic sea change in our society?

### Managing the Five E's

The marketplace of the 1990s will be about five Es: *Employees, Education, Ethics, Environment, and Externalities.*

• *Employee issues.* As reported in the *Wall Street Journal:* "Workplace shortages of the 1990s may accomplish what activism of the 1960s could not: getting corporations deeply involved in social issues." Social issues will be at the heart of a company doing well. Having focused on slashing the workforce in the 1980s, senior executives now must do an about face by recruiting, retaining, managing, and promoting the rapidly rising number of women and people of culturally diverse origins.

The aging workforce also consists of many two-career families (75 percent in the year 2000), some of the "sandwich" generation (adults taking care of their elders and children), whose values have evolved from those of ambition, acquisition, and accumulation to concern with fulfillment, family, and fun.

Those companies who recognize the Workforce 2000 imperatives, and are sensitive to the needs of these groups, will flourish. They will be better equipped to deal with problems of worker shortages, turnover, poor job skills, low morale and productivity. To date, most have not been so attentive. Why has readjustment been so slow? Says one workforce expert, "Senior executives (who are largely white males) still think like Ozzie and Harriet." *The price of insensitivity and discrimination will go up.*

• *Education.* To compete with the Japanese in business, we need better primary and secondary education. The extent of illiteracy (20 million functionally illiterate adults), the lack of basic reading and mathematics skills in new business recruits (expressed as a serious problem by 70 percent of firms surveyed in June 1990), and the shortage of skilled labor are threatening our competitive position in the global economy. Yet less than one percent of our major corporations spend 95 percent of the training

From *Executive Excellence*, Vol. 8, No. 4, April 1991, pp. 13-15. *Executive Excellence*, The Magazine of Personal Development, Managerial Effectiveness, and Organizational Productivity. Copyright © 1991 by The Institute for Principle-Centered Leadership.

dollars. Corporations who become involved in education can influence the quality of job candidates, protect and develop local talent, demonstrate community leadership, and improve the business climate in their own communities. *The price of poor education will go up.*

• *Ethics.* The aging or "maturing" of our society has seen the issues of life balance reappear. Time has become the cultural currency of the 1990s. Moreover, the 1980s values of Wall Street have turned into the 1990s values of Main Street, as we have gone from a mergers and acquisition era of the Boomtown to a return to the Hometown. The family is back. And with it, a return to a "kinder, gentler" age, nomered by *Good Housekeeping* as the "Decency Decade." The caring individual has replaced the rugged individual of the Right and the collective individual of the Left.

Companies that tap into those values can bond — not just brand — with employees and customers alike. Attracting and retaining workers and consumers, building corporate reputation, and sustaining corporate growth are functions of giving people what they want at a fair price. That price — if counted in terms of too much time away from the family or if in terms of fuzzy product/company images in a crowded marketplace — may be too high. *The price of this missed opportunity is going up.*

• *Environment.* If you doubt that corporate social responsibility is a requirement of being considered a good company, just look at the 180-degree change in approaching the environment. The return to our environmental concern followed naturally from our heightened concerns about our health (look at the meteoric sales trend of bottled water). Now, environmentally sensitive, "green" products are ready to become the "lite" products of the 1990s.

"An image as an environmentally responsible company is becoming an essential part of a competitive strategy," according to *Business Week*. In fact, their recent environmental section was 107 pages long, since so many CEOs wanted to have their company programs described. Environmental responsibility is now a key factor in making *Fortune's* Most Admired Company list. Some companies even include environmental measures in their compensation systems. Certainly, there are real costs associated with non-compliance (litigation, liability, imposed restrictions, fines, a damaged reputation). *And the costs of environmental irresponsiblity are going up.*

• *Externalities.* Externalities are behav-ioral outcomes not directly accounted for by the marketplace, such as the freedom to pollute at no direct cost to the polluter. These market failures need to be corrected by changing the "pricing" of the behavior, for example, by charging the polluter. We sometimes say that these behaviors have a "hidden subsidy" behind them. *Social and political forces are now working to remove certain subsidies.*

In many ways, externalities summarize the first four Es. The price of excessive time away from family, of a workplace that does not fit employees' values, of a poorly educated workforce, and of a polluted environment are not fully accounted for by the market system. *Companies will obtain competitive advantages by recognizing that these changes in values translate into changes in the economics of business.*

Will this broader definition of corporate responsibility evolve further? The westward shift in the population into more liberal states indicates that it will. (California will have 20 percent of the electoral votes by 1992.) And with skilled workers in demand, consumers offered more product choices than ever, and global competition increasing, social and business interests should continue to converge. *We are seeing no less than a redefinition of what constitutes good (and profitable) business practice.*

### Redefining Boundaries

Are you listening and responding to only your stockholders or to all your constituents? Everett Dirksen, former U.S. Senator, once said sagely, "Sometimes you have to realize that the people have spoken and that it's time to get on with it."

Has the definition of your corporate mission changed in the last three years? The last five years? If not, you might take another look. Does it pay attention to all those groups of people who can significantly influence your company's future?

Often, we concern ourselves with the financials and the investment community. When thinking about how we operate, we may say that "if we take care of our employees and they take care of our customers, the market will take care of us."

Today, more groups have a "stake" in how you do. The government can have a say through legislation; public interest groups, the media, and local communities may also influence your well-being. Their thinking on the role of the corporation in society has evolved. It is no longer just vague notions about corporate responsibilities — it involves a list of activities with direct bottom-line impact. To include the interests of these five stakeholders in your corporate activities requires a broader view of a corporation's role in society.

### Stakeholder Strategy

The essence of corporate strategy is to develop a broad formula for competing, based on corporate strengths and weaknesses within the context of the competitive environment. A successful strategy capitalizes on these strengths and anticipates important changes.

With a stakeholder view of the world, a firm will assess its competitive position, evaluate its strategies, and monitor changes with government, investors, consumers, employees, and society at large. To compete successfully, a firm must deal wisely with changes in the interests of its suppliers (investors and employees), its buyers (consumers), and the external forces of legislators and other societal groups. Few firms explicitly recognize, measure, and monitor their positions with each of these stakeholders.

Strategies that strengthen relationships with stakeholders create opportunities for sustainable competitive advantage and long-term profitability and dramatically improve the cost/benefit relationship of doing business.

• *Investors.* Economics catch up with social conscience. Rather than marching in the streets, private and institutional investors are using their dollars as market power. Securities invested according to various social standards exceeded $500 billion by the end of 1989, up from $31 billion in 1984. (These securities outperformed the *Standard and Poor's 500 Index* by 65 percent for the years 1984 through 1988.)

Other indicators: *The Domini Social Index* was created in April 1990. A socially responsible surrogate for the *S&P 500*, it includes 400 corporations that have passed multiple, broad-based social screens. In May 1990, NASDAQ ran a two-page ad in leading business magazines, declaring that social responsibility is a key indicator of the great companies of the 1990s (Ben & Jerry's was their example).

Individual examples of shareholder pressure on social issues, such as South African involvement and environmental responsibility, abound. Recently, a company was forced to rethink its marketing of plastic packaging because the institutional giant CALPERS called every couple of weeks to see "what are your environmental policies going to be." Divestment of tobacco company stocks by

# 1. ETHICS IN BUSINESS

Harvard University and the City University of New York have led Massachusetts to consider doing the same. *The cost of equity capital decreases for the socially responsible.*

• *Employees.* You do not need to be a fortune teller to know that diversity is the nature of tomorrow's workforce. If you can not attract the best minorities and women, and create a culture in which they are comfortable and productive, your costs from excessive recruiting, high turnover, and low productivity will skyrocket.

There is a real cost to not being on *Business Week's* list of the most "women-friendly" companies (August 8, 1990). For top MBAs of color, the third criteria for job choice was whether the company had a volunteer program to help educate minorities in the inner city. And if you are not involved in education and training, you will suffer from a skills shortage. The three things that bother business people the most at work are: lack of career purpose in life, little free time and high stress, and a poorly balanced professional and personal life. The employer that can help fulfill these needs will have a productive, innovative group of employees. *The cost of human resources decreases for the socially responsible.*

• *Consumers.* In a January 1990 Roper poll, more people than ever based their product choice on how a company rated on: pollution prevention efforts (12 percent; up from 6 percent); efforts to hire minorities (6 percent; up from 3 percent); and the kind of community events sponsored (4 percent). In the 1989 Chivas Regal poll, 45 percent said they are more loyal to a company's products if it gives substantially to charities and encourages volunteer efforts by employees.

The success of companies like The Body Shop, that are socially and environmentally responsible, testifies that consumers are looking for the good in companies as well. Responsibility leads to loyalty that goes beyond branding in a crowded marketplace. *The cost of marketing decreases for the socially responsible.*

• *Government.* The expanded rights given to the disabled, the new civil rights act, new clean air requirements, better food labeling, potential bans on cigarette machines, further restrictions on beer advertising, and potential diaper regulations — all indicate the growth in legislation to engender more responsible behavior. *The benefit of being ahead on these issues will increase for the socially responsible company.*

• *Society at large.* Business executives must monitor their constituencies to deal effectively with social issues and to enjoy good press and good community relations. Stories of corporate social "negligence" make good copy from the media's point of view. Public interest groups have grown stronger, with excellent publicists and established ties to city halls and regulatory agencies. And local communities where you do business are the homes of your employees and customers, and their families. *The benefits of addressing their needs increase for the socially responsible company.*

Corporate strategy should be set to address the needs of these corporate stakeholders and to create a corporate culture that is responsive to societal changes and can attract and retain qualified employees.

32

# Seven Reasons To Examine Workplace Ethics

*How to identify ethical problems in the workplace and do the right thing.*

## Alan Weiss

*Alan Weiss is the president of Summit Consulting Group Inc. based in East Greenwich, R.I. His most recent book is* Making It Work.

Is the attention being focused on ethics part of a cycle of fads which has included everything from transactional analysis to quality circles to fire walking, or are there pragmatic and sound underlying reasons for management to be concerned with the actions of employees? Here are seven factors that indicate why there is a legitimate perceived need to scrutinize ethical conduct now.

**1. There appears to be a widespread breakdown in ethical conduct among senior managers.** Many executives have labored under the assumption that workers would occasionally appropriate goods or services. They've also assumed that their colleagues deserve perquisites and special treatment. But the exposure of scandals among commodities traders and stock brokers; executives using inside information; the savings and loan

malfeasance; dishonesty in the U.S. Congress; and a host of similar instances has caused a reassessment. The double standard usually employed to allow senior people to take advantage of the system has been revealed to the general public for what it is: sanctioned illegal and unethical behavior. Too many managers are reading *How To Win No Matter What* and too few are reading *The Effective Executive.*

**2. Time and productivity can be "stolen" even more easily—and with more devastating effect—than goods and services.** Management has become increasingly aware that there's a distinct difference between an informal, low-stress organization and one that is simply not interested in producing. Accompanying one research and development director through dozens of near-empty labs and deserted of-

fices, I finally asked where everyone was.

"Funny," he said, genuinely puzzled, "I don't actually know. I mean they're probably on assignment someplace or at meetings, but I'll have to inquire."

I believe that the poorly-managed financial service organizations can usually cut 20 percent of management workers and not even notice a difference in productivity. White-collar moonlighting continues to plague organizational America, as managers with spare time run private businesses (ranging from consulting services to their spouse's private enterprise) right from their desks. Whose fault? The boss's.

**3. The traditional and primary conveyor of ethical values has diminished in availability and importance.** Many of us can still recall our family meals, where dinner wasn't

Reprinted with permission from *HRMagazine* (formerly *Personnel Administrator*), Vol. 36, No. 3, March 1991, pp. 69, 71-72, 74. *HRMagazine*, published by the Society for Human Resource Management, Alexandria, VA.

optional and our parents ran the show. This was the time to bring up difficulties in school ("My friends got a copy of the chemistry test and they want me to hide it in my locker.") and to hear of our parents' difficulties in the outside world ("Can you imagine? If I don't agree to contribute to the annual charity campaign it will hurt my chances for promotion!"). There were seldom absolute answers, and sometimes no answers at all. But there was usually discussion and the opportunity to hear how people we loved and trusted dealt with moral ambiguity.

Today, realities such as single-parent households, substance abuse, two-career families and the expanded extracurricular activities of the children mitigate against such daily discussions. As a result, a fundamental ethical "rudder" has not been set, and ethical influences are likely to originate in the media revelations of misplaced values.

**4. Virtually every business has become a people business.** Organizations from airlines to banks, from movie houses to health clubs, have sought to differentiate themselves in the market place through the quality of their service. In fact, service and customer-led support have usurped the traditional roles of price, convenience and status in creating consumer loyalty. Acura leads the polls in customer satisfaction, pointedly stressing that it ranks ahead of Mercedes-Benz in this category. Northwest Airlines is making a major investment to improve its service and image, largely through training personnel to better serve the customer and adding cabin attendants. Microsoft has a customer telephone technical-support system unexcelled in the industry and follows up diligently to ensure that its people are meeting customer needs. As the interaction with customers grows in importance, the appropriate behavior of those millions of company representatives takes on a critical dimension.

**5. A more sophisticated work force is increasingly sensitive to exemplars.** Organizations have learned that it's now difficult to fool any of the people any of the time. Employees are too well-educated and too well-versed in the realities of the workplace to accept management at its word if there is reason to distrust the word. People believe what they see. Conse-

> # P
> olicies are seldom reviewed and revised in light of changing conditions.
>
> ∎

quently, managers have to be more cognizant than ever of the unintended, inadvertent and almost subliminal messages they send to subordinates. You can't very well say "we're all in this together" when your top managers eat in a private executive dining room. Asking for labor concessions while awarding executive bonuses generates a militant response. Employees at all levels observe their superiors for clues regarding what constitutes acceptable and unacceptable behavior. Culture doesn't just create itself. It is the direct result of the tacit sanctioning or condemnation of individual actions.

**6. Organizational loyalty is declining sharply.** With the exception of those organizations known as excellent places to work, most employees have adopted much more strident "what's in it for me" attitudes. This is not, by and large, their fault. It is a natural outgrowth of a management that hasn't acted in a participative, honest manner unless forced to do so by adverse financial or competitive circumstances. Golden parachutes, leveraged buyouts, greenmail and an assortment of other legal chicaneries have demonstrated that the top-level people are intent on taking care of themselves. The message to the workers has been "them that has, gets." And the message management has started to hear back is, "We're going to look out for ourselves." Thus, management actions—even with the best intentions—are looked upon cynically.

Jumping ship for a better deal is considered the mark of an intelligent and upstanding person, and erstwhile dishonest acts (not to mention merely unethical acts) are seen as appropriate behavior if done in one's self-interest. A supervisor in New York was arrested recently for stealing computer lists of subscribers from her current employer with the intent of using them in her new position as circulation manager for a competitor. The competitor was not involved in the act. The individual was acting alone, even though she had already landed the new job on her merits.

**7. There is no quick fix that management can use.** Fortunately, there is no ethical grid or managing-the-value system or ethical-issues circles that management can throw money at and claim that the issue is being addressed by the latest intervention (read:fad). There are no black and white, simple responses to issues of ethics and behavior. Indeed, there is seldom more than varying shades of gray. If management is art and science, the study and resolution of ethical challenges lies solidly in the former. So, as the need to address ethical problems has arisen, the "easy answer" has been unavailable. Management has been forced to consider serious, specific and thoughtful responses.

## Current status

Many organizations have policies on ethical behavior and guidelines dealing with such things as accepting gifts from vendors, expense reporting and company property. Most are safely insulated in the three-ring binders on dusty shelves where such policy statements usually reside. But even those often do not cover the practical issues facing employees daily. Moreover, policies are seldom reviewed and revised in light of changing conditions.

Most organizations are well served by holding focus groups and/or classroom facilitated discussions just to learn what areas and topics are most appropriate to examine for ethical issues. There are no quick fixes, and each organization should examine its needs in this area by analyzing its people, practices, customers, products and services, competitors and current strategy.

Despite its high ratings, Merck & Co., the phamaceutical company based in New Jersey, realized that its very success might cause difficulties. For example, in expanding their U.S. field force by 50 percent, management carefully questioned whether they could guarantee the customary degree of selectivity for this key interface with the physician and pharmacist. In addition, their highly publicized excellence could attract people whose values were not commensurate with the traditional Merck employee. As a result, Merck has studied the best ways to communicate and reinforce its ethical posture, engages in ongoing surveys of its work force, and has held senior managers accountable for the management and leadership of this area.

Workshops, surveys, focus groups and other interventions have had a two-fold impact. First, they have gathered and communicated information, keeping management abreast of current and anticipated ethical challenges and keeping employees informed of company policy and support systems. Second, they have unequivocally demonstrated management's serious regard for identifying and constructively resolving ethical dilemmas.

Jim Burke, the recently retired CEO of Johnson and Johnson, is probably best known for his rapid and honest stance during the Tylenol-poisoning crisis and his solutions to the over-the-counter drug safety problem. His handling of that problem and his organization's superb response have found their places in the management text books. However, an important but overlooked fact is that anyone who worked for Burke at J&J will tell you that he had always placed a premium on values and ethics and had long been the top exemplar and reinforcer of the need to act ethically in all situations. He had made this a standard management tenet and practice and had held people accountable for adhering to it.

## A logical starting place

Senior management should make organizational-ethics assessment and management as serious and routine an undertaking as that of evaluating sales projections, financial status or product quality. "With that mentality, the

> C osts associated with an ethical study are relatively minor compared to financial or quality improvement efforts.
>
> ■

"how-to" becomes tangible and practical. How are those other areas organized and controlled? Usually, they are managed in meetings, on-site inspections, quality control procedures, planning processes and as an aspect of overall strategy. Leadership in the area of ethics requires no less of an investment in time, attention and money. Every senior officer should have an ethical dimension in his or her emphasis areas, and this should cascade downward.

In addition, just as you educate people in your products, services, customer relations and such, you should also provide for education in ethical challenges and their resolution—education, not training, because this isn't an issue that can be addressed through rote learning, forms or procedures. Rather, it requires reasoning, judgment and an open mind. This education is best accomplished internally (i.e., not in external seminars and stranger groups) so colleagues can share their wisdom and experience and management can ensure that its collective finger is on the pulse of its own organization.

Exploring and managing ethical issues involves several aspects:
● Validating that current practices are known (not the procedures, but what people are actually doing).
● Separating external ethical issues (i.e., the customer offers a kickback)

from internal ethical issues (i.e., the organization's own compensation system mitigates against performing certain quality procedures prior to a sale).
● Assessing what new ethical challenges may arise from accelerating change among customers, competitors, government regulation, vendors, the economy and so forth.
● Formulating guidelines for individuals to use in dealing with ethical issues and formalizing an easily accessible support system. For example, many organizations have a "hot line" available to report internal fraud, protecting the identify of the reporter. Others have an internal advisory board that determines what current issues require more comprehensive company response. Still others utilize an external "ombudsman" who provides a low-threat but powerful remedy for ethical problems.
● Assigning responsibility to management for the ongoing management and leadership of ethical behavior.

The costs associated with studying an organization's ethical stance and practices are relatively minor compared to activities such as financial audits or quality improvement efforts. Yet its return value may be unexceeded: a knowledge of the organization's current response to ethical challenge, an opportunity to proactively manage the process, and an unqualified message to employees about the organization's intent and values. It seems that the better organizations are attempting to do just that, the average ones are "sending their managers away" to learn how to do it, and the poorer ones are blissfully unaware of the need.

## The "do-as-I-say" phenomenon

Despite all the line management commitment, all the support in the world from human resources and even the finest external help obtainable, the ultimate question of whether such an effort will work can only be answered through senior management's active commitment and participation. Too many residents of the executive suite still feel that this is an issue that's "good for them" but "not necessary for us." One sales vice president, thoroughly exasperated with his sales force's cheating on expense reports, bemoaned the fact that even his sales managers seemed corrupted by the practice. However, it was his common—and well known—habit to buy first class tickets (as was his right), exchange them for coach and pocket the different.

Another executive, who complained that his people wouldn't listen and were, in his estimation, deliberately insubordinate, never let anyone question his decisions and vociferously shouted down even peers during meetings. And then there was the company president who said she needed testing assistance because the quality of new hires was abominable and turnover was ferocious. She read her mail and answered phone calls during interviews and meetings and her managers emulated their boss's behavior.

Are these ethical dilemmas? Absolutely. They are the very stuff and substance of the do-as-I-say-not-as-I-do mentality. People believe what they see, not what they hear or are told. They will do as you do.

Shortly after its launch, the new Lexus automobile suffered a potentially embarrassing recall. The Japanese manufacturer responded in a straightforward and symbolic manner: The defect was acknowledged, the company expressed its regret, and mechanics were dispatched to customers' homes wherever possible to fix the problem.

Managers in the truly excellent companies are constantly asking themselves "What's the right thing to do?" when confronted with ambiguous situations or, for that matter, unpleasant ones. And those excellent companies have created support systems, management beliefs and visible exemplars that reinforce such an attitude.

### Action points

Here is a summary or checklist to help determine whether your management team is doing everything possible to monitor and improve ethical standards of behavior:

● Are there regular ethical-conduct meetings between managers and subordinates and/or among worker teams? These meetings should be at least quarterly, priorities (they can't be missed for more "pressing matters") and extend from top management to front-line supervision.

● Do all key managers have an ethical component in their emphasis areas? Department heads and above should be held responsible for the ethical conduct of their people and their operation, which forces them to pro-actively manage these issues.

● Is there a mechanism to allow employees to report and/or explore suspected breaches of ethical conduct? Organizations need a "hot line," ombudsperson, ethical review board or some avenue that enables them to raise ethical questions or report ethical misconduct without fear of reprisal.

● Are employees rewarded for taking ethical stands even when loss of business or short-term discomfort results? The refusal to sink to a competitor's unethical tactics should be reinforced and recognized, not punished.

● Is ethical conduct built into every aspect of training and development? This is not a topic best dealt with in separate workshops (though these are also useful) but rather should be a part of courses in such areas as decision-making and negotiating, and in most on-the-job instruction.

● Is there active encouragement to "do the right thing" in the absence of policy and procedure and, sometimes, despite them? Employees should understand that their basic sense of decency is not discarded simply because the organization has certain rules, and their judgment in the absence of those rules is a valued part of their job performance.

It's time for all organizations to take their "ethical" temperature. For themselves, their employees, their customers and their future.

# Understanding Pressures That Cause Unethical Behavior in Business

## O. C. Ferrell, Ph.D. and John Fraedrich, Ph.D.

*O.C. Ferrell, Ph.D., is Distinguished Professor of Marketing and Business Ethics in The Fogelman College of Business and Economics at Memphis State University in Memphis, Tennessee. John Fraedrich, Ph.D., is an Assistant Professor of Marketing at Southern Illinois University in Carbondale, Illinois.*

## Abstract

This paper reviews how personal values, the competitive environment, organizational pressures and opportunity interact to determine ethical decisions in business. An ethically sensitive corporate culture, codes of ethics and enforced ethical policies in companies are seen as the best methods for improving ethical behavior.

## Introduction

Ethics in business is a major concern because of the lack of ethical behavior by some individuals and organizations in our society. Dennis Levine at the age of 32 was a managing director of Drexel Burnham Lambert, one of the country's top merger and acquisition specialists. His indictment for insider trading charges ignited the insider trading scandal of the 1980s, forever changing the landscape of American business. Levine was fined $362,000 and agreed to pay the federal government $11.6 million in illegal trading profits. He was sentenced to two years in prison and has since been paroled. Levine received a reduced sentence for helping the federal government in its investigation of insider trading. His testimony helped to implicate Ivan Boesky, who received a $100 million penalty, the biggest ever, for insider trading. Now Mr. Levine is being managed by a public relations agency and receives fees for speaking to MBA students on college campuses. Levine's message to college students is "Don't do it." "It's not worth it," he said of insider trading and other white collar transgressions (*Los Angeles Times,* 1989, part 4).

What causes people like Dennis Levine to behave unethically and even illegally in the business world? There are many scenarios to explain unethical behavior. One explanation is that the individual may be a "bad apple", with poor personal morals, in a good organization. Other explanations for unethical behavior include the nature of the competitive environment, organizational pressures, or even the opportunity to take advantage in the right situation. It is our purpose to explore how both personal and outside pressures on business people can increase the probability of ethical mistakes. In addition, we suggest several ways managers can improve ethical behavior and can avoid the destructive consequences of poor ethical decision making.

## Personal Values vs. Corporate Values

The personal dimension of ethics relates to an individual's values and moral philosophies. Individual values are learned from socialization through family, religion, school, and business experiences. These individual values are generally assumed to remain constant in both work and nonwork environments. However, doubt was first cast on this generalization by Carr (1968). He argued that business people have two ethical dimensions that include one ethical value system for home and one for business. Recently, support for Carr's statement has shown that most business persons use one moral philosophy at work and a completely different moral philosophy at home (Fraedrich 1988). This may explain why Dennis Levine says he has strong moral commitments today but could not explain to his five-year-old son a few years ago why he was going to prison. He was a good family man, yet cheated investors out of millions.

The personal value system combines with the corporate culture to affect behavior. In a study conducted by Frederick and Weber (1987) concerning the values of corporate managers and their critics, they concluded that personal values are involved in ethical decisions but are not the central component that guides the decisions, actions, and policies of the organization. They

From *Business Insights,* Spring/Summer 1990, pp. 1-4. *Business Insights,* published by the Center for Business Development and Research, College of Business Administration, The University of Southern Mississippi.

37

believe that personal values make up only one part of an organization's total value structure. Ethical behavior within the organization relates to the organization's values and traditions rather than solely upon individuals who actually make the decisions.

Consequently, ethical behavior may be a function of two different dimensions of an organization's value structure: the embedded organizational value system or corporate culture, and the personal value preferences of the organization's individual members. An individual member assumes some measure of moral responsibility by agreeing in general to abide by an organization's rules and standard operating procedures. When Dennis Levine stepped over the line into unethical and illegal behavior, it can be assumed that competitive pressures and organizational rewards provided the incentive.

### Competitive Pressures

Competition exerts pressure on business decision makers and is a key factor in influencing the ethical environment of the firm. In general, competition helps business and the economy to become more efficient and goal-oriented. However, when competition becomes so intense that business survival is threatened, then employees and managers may view once unacceptable alternatives as acceptable. In other words, pressured employees may engage in unethical practices for corporate survival. The culture of the corporation may encourage and reward unethical behavior because of fear of bankruptcy, possible loss of one's job, or the opportunity for promotion.

Corporate espionage and manipulation to gain insider information are often used in highly competitive industries. One example of such an act involved the acquisition of information on General Electric's turbine parts by a small manufacturing firm. GE employees were offered money in exchange for drawings. By acquiring these documents, the smaller company hoped to save millions of dollars in research and development and to capture a significant share of the more than $495 million turbine parts market (Carley 1988). As this example illustrates, some firms may approve corporate espionage, but society deems such actions as unethical and illegal.

As competition becomes intense and profit margins become smaller, pressures can build to substitute inferior materials or components to reduce costs. Often this is done without informing customers about changes in product quality that involve a form of dishonesty about the nature of the product. Beech-Nut Nutrition Corporation took this concept to an extreme when it changed the contents of its apple juice product. Instead of selling a product made from apples, the company substituted a chemical concoction which has the same taste, smell, and look of apple juice. However, the company continued to label and promote its product as being 100 percent apple juice. In fact, experts found it difficult to distinguish it from pure apple juice. Beech-Nut failed to inform consumers that its apple juice no longer was made from apples (Hall 1989). When companies do not inform consumers that product components are not of the same quality as promoted, ethical issues arise. In this case, Beech-Nut lost millions of dollars, and its executives were sentenced to prison terms.

Other questionable practices, such as increased EPA violations, mechanical devices that periodically increase assembly line speeds, bait-and-switch sales techniques, and bribery to obtain important customers, occur when a firm is in a highly competitive industry. These measures are used because managers are afraid that their company could not compete without using deception and manipulation.

### Organizational Pressures

While ethical decision making includes perceptions of how to act in terms of daily issues, success is determined by achievement of company goals. Pressure to perform and increase profits may be particularly intense in middle management. This internal organizational pressure is a major predictor of unethical behavior.

These organizational factors seem to have played a part in several recent scandals. Many insider traders in the Boesky scandal remain uncaught because trading of confidential information in investment banking circles is a routine way of doing business. The E.F. Hutton employees found guilty of 2,000 counts of mail and wire fraud did not understand their company's values. Some may have thought they were doing their company a favor (Dressang 1986). Robert Foman, former chairman of E.F. Hutton, states that, "I thought ethics was something you learned growing up at home, in school, and in church" (Moskowitz 1985, p. 63). Obviously, Foman was wrong in thinking that ethics is only developed at home, school and church. His managers were influenced by pressures to succeed, and by their peers and supervisors in the decision-making process.

The roles of top management and superiors are extremely important in developing the culture of an organization. Most experts agree that the chief executive officer and vice-president level executives set the ethical tone for the entire organization. For example, when Chrysler Corporation President Lee Iacocca learned that several executives of his company were driving new Chryslers with the odometers disconnected and then selling the cars as new, he admitted the company's unethical behavior in a national press conference and developed a program to compensate customers who had bought the pre-driven cars. Iacocca took out two-page advertisements in *USA Today, The Wall Street Journal,* and *The New York Times* to apologize for the ethical mistake and added, "The only thing we are recalling here is our integrity." Messages like this send a signal to all employees in the organization concerning what the firm stands for ethically (Schlesinger 1987). Lower-level superiors obtain their cues from these individuals, yet they too exert some of their personal value system on the company. This interplay between corporate culture and executive leadership helps determine the ethical value system of the firm.

## Opportunity Pressures

Opportunity to engage in unethical behavior provides another pressure that may determine whether or not a person will behave ethically. Opportunity is a favorable set of conditions to limit barriers or to provide rewards. Rewards may be internal or external. Internal rewards are those feelings of goodness and worth one feels after an altruistic action. External rewards are what people expect to receive from others in terms of values generated and provided on an exchange basis. External rewards are often received from peers and top management. Opportunity to engage in unethical behavior has been found to be a better predictor of such behavior than personal beliefs (Ferrell and Gresham, 1985). In a survey by Chonko and Hunt (1985), 56 percent of the managers indicated that there were many opportunities for managers in their industry to engage in unethical behaviors.

If an individual uses the opportunity afforded him/her to act unethically and is either rewarded or not penalized, that person becomes more likely to repeat such acts as the opportunity arises. For example, an accountant who receives a raise for preparing financial documents that he or she knows are not completely accurate is being rewarded for this behavior and, therefore, has an increased probability of continuing the behavior.

Several elements within the business environment help to create opportunities, including rewards and the absence of punishment. Professional codes of ethics and ethics-related corporate policy also influence opportunity. Enforcement of these codes and policies should generate the highest level of compliance to ethical standards. The greater the rewards and the less the punishment for unethical behavior, the greater the probability that unethical behavior will be practiced.

It is even suggested that the SEC contributed to the opportunity dimension of insider trading by allowing Ivan Boesky to reduce his partnership's liabilities by $1.3 billion by selling stocks or other securities before the government announced his crimes. This special treatment saved Boesky an additional $100 million in fines. In reality this cut his fines in half. In addition, Congress asked why, if New York Stock Exchange computers flagged 47 suspicious trades by Boesky—many before merger announcements—Boesky was not caught before Levine disclosed his actions. Even after being caught and punished, much opportunity exists for violators to profit from their success.

After being paroled early from his two-year prison sentence, Dennis Levine is being paid for public speaking and has started a new financial consulting practice in mergers and acquisitions. A *Barron's* article reports, "We're convinced the venture will be a great success. Mr. Levine's curriculum vita is sure to prove irresistible to any number of companies we can consider." (Abelson, 1989). Apparently, much opportunity continues for those convicted of unethical and illegal activity in the securities industry.

## Improving Ethical Decisions

Conflicts between personal values and corporate values, intense competition, organizational pressures and opportunity interact to create situations that can cause unethical behavior. Figure 1 illustrates the pressures that can influence ethical decision making. As discussed previously, both the individual and the organization can influence unethical behavior.

| Figure 1 |

**Pressures That Impact Ethical Decisions In Business**

| Personal Values | | Competition |
|---|---|---|
| | Ethical Decisions | |
| Organization | | Opportunity |

One way to sensitize personnel is to create codes of ethics. Trevino and Youngblood (1990) developed a "bad apple", "bad barrel" argument concerning this issue. The "bad apple" argument is that some people are basically bad and will do things in their own self interest regardless of organizational goals. Eliminating unethical behavior requires the elimination of the "bad apples" (individuals) within the corporation. This can be done through screening techniques and through the enforcement of ethics codes. The "bad barrel" argument is that corporate culture becomes unethical not because individuals are bad, but because the pressures to survive competition create conditions that reward unethical behavior. The solution to the "bad barrel" approach is to redesign the corporate image and culture such that it conforms to industry and societal norms of ethical behavior. Robin and Reidenbach (1987) suggest that ethics must be built into the corporate culture and corporate strategy. By sensitizing personnel in an organization to ethical issues and potential areas of conflict, one can eliminate or defuse some of the ethical pressures that occur in day-to-day business activities.

Codes of ethics can be established to help managers deal with ethical situations or dilemmas that develop in day-to-day operations. Top management should provide leadership to operationalize codes. Codes of ethics do not have to be so detailed they take into account every situation; rather codes should have general guidelines that operationalize the main goals and objectives.

If a company is to maintain ethical behavior, its policies, rules, and standards must be worked into its control system. When employees make unethical decisions, the company needs to determine why and to take corrective action through enforcement. Enforcement of standards is what makes codes of ethics effective. If codes are window dressing and do not relate to what is expected or what is rewarded in the corporate culture, then the codes serve no purpose other than to give the illusion that there is concern for ethical behavior.

## Conclusion

Ethical behavior in business must be based on a strong moral foundation, including personal moral development and an organizational structure that encourages and rewards desired ethical action. The pressures of competition must be understood and coped with to improve ethical behavior. The idea that ethics is learned at home, in school, and in church does not recognize the impact of the organization on ethical decision makers. Today there is an increasing need for professional associations and corporations to promote and to enforce codes of ethics and eliminate unethical conduct.

Codes of ethics and/or corporate policies on ethics must be established to control the opportunity factor in ethical decision making. Enforcement of corporate policies on ethics brings about more ethical behavior. The establishment of codes of ethics and corporate policies on ethics will enable company employees to better understand what is, and is not, expected of them. Understanding how a person chooses his or her own standards of ethics, and what prompts a person to engage in unethical behavior, may decrease the current trend toward unethical activity in the business world.

For a company to maintain ethical behavior, its ethical policies, rules, and standards must be worked into its control system, including activities related to target setting, measuring and monitoring performance. Increasing ethical behavior in a corporation is similar to increasing earnings. Ethical behavior will happen only after a strategic plan is developed and successfully implemented to achieve the desired results.

## References

Abelson, Alan (1989), "Up and Down Wall Street," *The Wall Street Journal,* July 24, p. 43.

Carley, William M. (1988), "Secrets War: GE Presses Campaign to Halt Rivals' Misuse of Turbine Parts Data," *The Wall Street Journal,* August 16, pp. 1, 10.

Carr, Albert Z. (1968), "Is Business Bluffing Ethical?" *Harvard Business Review,* (January-February), p. 145.

Chonko, Lawrence and Shelby Hunt (1985), "Ethics and Marketing Management: An Empirical Investigation," *Journal of Business Research,* 13, pp. 339-359.

Dressang, Joel (1986), "Companies Get Serious About Ethics," *USA Today,* (December), pp. 1-2B.

Ferrell, O. C. and Larry Gresham (1985), "A Contingency Framework for Understanding Ethical Decision Making in Marketing," *Journal of Marketing,* (Summer), pp. 87-96.

Fraedrich, John P. (1988), "Philosophy Type Interaction in the Ethical Decision Making Process of Retailers," Ph.D. Dissertation, Texas A&M University, College Station, TX.

Frederick, William C. and James Weber (1987), "The Value of Corporate Managers and Their Critics: An Empirical Description and Normative Implications," *Research in Corporate Social Performance and Social Responsibility* (9), William C. Frederick, ed., Greenwich, CT, pp. 149-150.

Hall, Mini (1989), "O.J. Wasn't 100% Pure, FDA Says," *USA Today,* July 26, p. A1.

Moskowitz, Daniel B. (1985), "Where Business Goes to Stock Up on Ethics," *Business Week,* (October 14), pp. 63-66.

Robin, Donald P. and R. Eric Reidenbach (1987), "Social Responsibility, Ethics and Marketing Strategy: Closing the Gap Between Concept and Application," *Journal of Marketing,* (January), pp. 44-58.

Schlesinger, Jacob (1987), "Chrysler Finds A Way To Settle Odometer Issue," *The Wall Street Journal,* December 10, p. 7.

Sing, Bill (1989), *Los Angeles Times,* May 24, part 4.

Trevino, Linda K. and Stuart Youngblood (1990), "Bad Apples in Bad Barrels: A Casual Analysis of Ethical Decision Making Behavior," *Journal of Applied Psychology,* forthcoming.

# Ethics and Profits Don't Always Go Hand in Hand

**DAVID VOGEL**

*David Vogel is a professor of business at UC Berkeley and the editor of California Management Review.*

In a recent survey of senior executives, deans of business schools and members of Congress, 63% said they believed that "a business enterprise actually strengthens its competitive position by maintaining high ethical standards." A century ago it was believed that good deeds would be rewarded and evil ones would be punished in the afterlife. In our more secular and impatient age, many people evidently are under the illusion that the market system—perhaps abetted by the Securities and Exchange Commission's enforcement division—is capable of meting out justice in this life.

The Business Roundtable earlier this year released a report, "Corporate Ethics: A Prime Business Asset," which says, "In the view of the top executives represented in this study, there is no conflict between ethical practices and acceptable profits. Indeed, the first is a necessary precondition for the second." Kenneth Blanchard, a co-author of "The One Minute Manager," writes in a special report on ethics in American business issued by Touche Ross that "successful companies over the long term tend to be ethical companies." In the same report, former SEC Chairman John Shad assures us, "Ethics pays: It's smart to be ethical." Others have suggested that restoring executive integrity is necessary to maintain public trust in the U.S. business system.

Does corporate social responsibility—or its current variant, "business ethics"—invariably pay? It is certainly possible to come up with some cases of virtue rewarded and vice punished. Johnson & Johnson is the most widely cited example of the former. Johnson & Johnson's management did the "right" thing by removing Tylenol from stores and medicine chests during a poisoning scare. And the company's customers rewarded it by again buying the product once the scare had passed.

Unfortunately, all stories about corporate social responsibility do not have such happy endings. During the 1960s and '70s, Cummins Engine, Levi Strauss, Polaroid, Control Data, Atlantic Richfield and Dayton-Hudson were commonly acknowledged to be firms that exhibited an unusually high degree of social commitment. Yet, over the last decade, each of these companies has experienced serious financial difficulties. With the possible exception of Control Data, the companies' social commitments did not cause their problems. But neither did they prevent them. Indeed, their experiences suggest that in many cases corporate responsibility, rather than being the cause of increased profitability, may instead be a consequence of it: A more profitable firm is better able to maintain some unprofitable facilities in economically depressed areas and contribute generously to cultural and civic activities.

The relationship between ethics and profits is a rather tenuous one, whether one defines corporate ethics narrowly in terms of obeying the law, or more broadly in terms of management's acceptance of responsibility for the welfare of the company's stockholders. Being "ethical" or "responsible" is no more, or less, likely to be rewarded in the marketplace than is investing heavily in research and development or having excellent labor relations. Ethics are certainly not a barrier to financial success, but neither are they a prerequisite to it.

While corporate codes of conduct and a strong corporate culture may improve the economic performance of some companies, it is naive to regard them or any other index of commitment to ethical standards as critical to the success of all companies. In fact, some of the companies profiled in the Roundtable's report will undoubtedly do poorly over the next decade, and other far less responsible firms will do extremely well. Some companies and individuals have suffered financially as a result of breaking the law or being insensitive to community concerns, but consider the enormous profits that are made selling illegal drugs and pornography. And for every insider trader who gets caught, one presumes that there are others who live happily ever after.

If good ethics are good business, then why do so many managers find themselves under financial pressures to cut corners? Moreover, to base the case for ethical conduct on economic self-interest is not only misleading, it trivializes the concept of ethics. Equating unethical conduct with errors in business judgment robs business decision-making of the element of moral choice. It also begs the more important and interesting question: What should managers do when there is a conflict between ethics and profits?

Ethics often pay, but sometimes they can be costly. The Roundtable and Touche Ross reports would be more credible if they cited examples of individuals and companies that did what they thought was right even though they lost money as a result. Have any of the firms in the Roundtable study ever rewarded an executive who cost the company a sale by following his or her conscience? Or refrained from entering a potentially profitable venture on the grounds that it was morally suspect? If not, are not the studies implying that one should be ethical only when it pays?

It is irresponsible to imply that acting responsibly is always costless, and it is unethical to base the case for ethics on economic self-interest. If we want executives to act more ethically, we need to be more honest with them and they need to be more honest with each other. The market has many worthwhile features, but setting an appropriate price on virtue is not among them.

# Ethics and Common Sense

**MINDA ZETLIN**

*Minda Zetlin is a New York-based business writer.*

Remember the Dark Ages, when managers believed that good business and good morals were mutually exclusive? Then came insider trading, and the downfall of companies like E.F. Hutton and Drexel Burnham Lambert. Suddenly it seemed obvious that a total disregard for ethics could be very bad business indeed. There were other forces too, though none quite as spectacular: New, tougher environmental laws meant even companies that had strictly obeyed the law could be forced to pay for expensive cleanups. The rising cost of using landfills made us see that recycling wasn't such a bad idea after all. A shrinking labor market and growing shareholder activism made a good public image a crucial asset.

Today, executives talk about treating ethics "proactively," rather than just with damage control. More and more companies have formal ethics policies, or even full-time ethics experts. The Harvard Business School is one of a number of B-schools that has an ethics program; there is a whole magazine devoted to business ethics. As one CEO remarked at a recent business conference, "Ethics is a hot topic."

Far from being at odds with business goals, ethics is actually good for the bottom line—at least in the long term. A study of 15 Fortune 500 companies that have adhered to written ethical principles over 20 years or more showed that these companies' profits grew nearly twice as fast as those of the rest of the Fortune 500 over a 30-year period. As business executives realize this, the phrase "doing well by doing good" is heard more and more often.

Time to go one step further. Time to stop focusing on bottom line benefits, at least as far as ethics is concerned. Time to start doing good for its own sake.

There's nothing wrong with making money off of ethical behavior. The fact that the most ethical companies have the highest-growing profits is one of the best indications that all is not wrong with the world. But it may be shortsighted to worry about corporate ethics *because* it's good for business, as many companies seem to be doing. Here's why:

□ *You'll want to see measurable results.* Good corporate ethics affect profitability over the long haul, and sometimes the greatest effect is the lawsuit or indictment that doesn't come. You won't be able to measure these benefits, so it's easy to grow frustrated and lose interest.

□ *You won't be fooling anyone.* Business ploys disguised as doing good have a way of backfiring with employees and the general public. Remember all those companies that promised to contribute "a portion" of the profits from certain products to various worthy causes? This was seen for what it frequently was.

□ *Eventually, you'll make the wrong decision.* Ethically wrong, that is. Not every ethical action can be justified by a bottom-line benefit.

□ *For all the above reasons, business-driven ethics often don't have much result.*

"But wait!" exclaimed one executive. "If all that businesses worry about is ethics, they'll go into bankruptcy and eliminate jobs, and that will be bad for everyone." It's not that all that businesses should worry about is ethics. This executive was so accustomed to thinking of ethical concerns and business concerns as natural adversaries that she couldn't imagine a company keeping its sights on both at once.

But it can. Consider Ben & Jerry's Homemade Inc., a corporation known for its commitment to ethics-for-its-own-sake. The company marketed a highly successful "Peace Pop"—then stood by its pro-peace position by making strong public statements against the Gulf war, which had strong American support. Nevertheless, Ben & Jerry's is very profitable, with net income growing more than 30 percent annually.

"Well, all right," the executive said, "but what about shareholders? Shouldn't they be our first priority?" Which shareholders? The ones who intend to sell at a quick profit, or the ones who plan to stick around for the long-term?

"Maximizing shareholder investment" is too often a code for "Let's make as much money as quickly as we can, no matter who gets hurt." Remember a CEO boasting back in 1983 about how much money his strategy had made for his shareholders? His name was William Agee, his company was Bendix, and his strategy had been to try a hostile takeover of Martin Marietta. Martin Marietta brought in Allied, which swallowed Bendix instead. Agee ended up with more valuable stock, but without a company to run.

And I don't think Agee is anyone's idea of a hero.

### INDUSTRY AND THE ENVIRONMENT

# A FAREWELL TO ARMS

Environmental concern is growing, and the debates are complicated. But industry can respond in a way that's environmentally and economically responsible.

THERESE R. WELTER

If you think the Clean Air Act amendments are going to force industry into action, brace yourself for even more.

Hardly a day goes by without another news report on global warming, ozone depletion, oil spills, the solid-waste glut, acid rain, pesticides in food, rain-forest depletion, endangered species, or pollution in Eastern Europe. Environmental legislation is sure to be a hallmark of the '90s.

The media and the government aren't the only ones calling industry to attention either. The Green revolution is building. It began in West Germany and has spread to other countries. "Greens" shun a formal organization, promoting grass-roots activism for social justice, democracy in politics and economics, peace and nonviolence, and environmental improvement.

Consequently, consumers, inspired by environmentalists, are buying or boycotting products according to advice from guides such as *Shopping For A Better World*, from the Council on Economic Priorities (CEP), New York, which rates companies according to social "screens," including environmental responsibility. Socially responsible investing is increasing, too, notes

Jonathan Schorsch, CEP's environmental research director.

Consumers' and investors' green dollars are luring many companies to try to be green themselves, by producing what have been dubbed "green products." Laundry-detergent bottles that contain recycled plastic, biodegradable household cleaners, and degradable plastic garbage bags now compete for attention on grocery shelves.

Behind the colorful marketing effort, however, is a grave danger: *Extremely* complicated environmental issues may be addressed too simply and with the wrong intentions.

It's not that green products are necessarily bad, but consumers may get the impression that if only they "buy right," environmental problems will be solved. And companies may view being green as a timely way to make money by selling products that are hitched to "environmentalism" in some small way.

"There's been enough demonstration that companies that leap to the fore with green labels, calling their products 'environmentally friendly,' can get in a lot of hot water," notes Dr. Robert Bringer, vice president of environmental engineering and pollution control at 3M Co., St. Paul.

Companies are willing to make small changes in the reformulations of products, says CEP's Mr. Schorsch. And, he notes, "they're willing to spend millions of dollars in advertising and public-relations campaigns that tell everyone how good they are environmentally . . . [but] that money is much better spent on solutions that may be a little quieter, but much more real."

First, and most important, a company should never market its products as "environmentally *friendly*," warns Gail Mayville, environmental program developer at Ben & Jerry's, Waterbury, Vt., ice-cream maker. "No product is 'friendly' in the sense that it always has some kind of impact on the environment."

Furthermore, says 3M's Dr. Bringer, "to look at a product and make a judgment whether it's environmentally sound, you have to look at the whole *process*," not just the packaging. The whole life cycle of that product should be considered—the raw material that is used, its manufacturing process, and its disposal or reuse.

"Pollution is a complex equation," agrees Dr. Bruce Piasecki, president of the American Hazard Control Group, consultants in Castleton, N. Y. It involves the number of people, the rate of consumption, and the toxic emission per unit of resource used. "If you want to call a product green," he says, "you have to measure that product in reference to that complex pollution equation rather than just according to marketing."

These caveats come to life in the controversy over degradable plastic garbage bags. They were originally thought to be better than nondegradables, since, theoretically, the material breaks down in landfills. They're being reassessed now. People are asking questions: "Does this material leach toxic substances into the environment when it breaks down? Is plastic safer left intact?" The debate isn't over.

Another danger arises when companies tell "little white lies" to appear green. To say that a product is made of recycled materials, simply because it contains scrap thrown back into the production process from the plant floor, is stretching the truth, for example. It's certainly economical and commendable for a company to recycle its own scrap. In fact, it's quite common. But it's not the same as the recycling that closes the product life-cycle loop by reusing materials that consumers have discarded.

Shallow or deceptive green marketing, angling for easy money, is not green at all. It's self-serving. And "ultimately, the consumers will find out the truth," Ben & Jerry's Ms. Mayville warns. "They're not going to trust anybody. And we're going to be back where we started. It's a matter of integrity."

In the wake of the "all-natural" and "low-cholesterol" marketing ploys, not to mention the catastrophes of Love Canal, *Exxon Valdez*, and Three Mile Island, neither government nor industry can afford the loss of credibility that comes from duping the public with misinformation on environmental issues.

Several private certification programs have been established to respond to the concerns about bogus green products. Similar to West Germany's "Blue Angel" labeling program, they plan to put a seal of approval on products that have met some standard environmental requirements.

For a product to receive full envi-ronmental certification from the Green Cross Certification Co., Oakland, for instance, it would have to undergo a total product assessment—of the product, the packaging, and the manufacturing process.

Additionally, the company itself would be under scrutiny. It would have to prove: that it has a maximum state-of-the-art percentage of sustainable resources and/or recycled materials; that it adheres to all government regulations; that it has no detectable residues of toxic effluents and emissions; that it has state-of-the-art solid-waste disposal and state-of-the-art solid- and toxic-waste reduction plans; and that it maximizes energy conservation.

Though trying to develop consistency to prevent false green-product claims is laudable—maybe even necessary—certifying all the products, all the processes, and all the companies that might apply for labels is obviously an enormous task.

In fact, since it can also detract from positive industry initiatives, Green Cross is moving away from a general environmental seal of approval. For now, it's focusing only on specific product claims—identifying the recycled-material content of products is one of them.

Clearly, part of being environmentally responsible is to refrain from being "driven by advertising agency concerns," says Dr. Margaret Maxey, professor of bioethics at the University of Texas, Austin. "The first principle is *truth*—truth in advertising because falsehoods will catch up with you." And the basis for truth for a product is scientific accuracy, which requires better comparisons and a better historical perspective, she says.

Yet, as the case of degradable plastic proves, the truth about being green is not always black and white.

Nearly every environmental issue being considered is fraught with factual uncertainties and debate. Science is based on conflicting opinion, notes Barbara Keating-Edh, president of Consumer Alert, Modesto, Calif. "I can give you 80 scientists at the drop of a hat who don't agree with the media trend on global warming," she says.

Furthermore, everyone knows that data can be manipulated to support any viewpoint. "The incineration industry has a record of covering up, of playing with the data," says CEP's Mr. Schorsch.

So, even with a dedication to researching the facts, the battles over the environment at some point boil down to matters of principle. It's essentially a moral issue.

"There are thousands of chemicals out there, and for most of them we have no clue what their toxicity is, what kind of impact they have, what kind of synergistic reaction they have with other chemicals," says Mr. Schorsch. "From our position of ignorance we've decided that it's not dangerous, instead of taking the equally logical position: 'We don't know very much, so we can assume that it *is* dangerous.'"

Many environmentalists, he continues, would simply like industry to change its attitude to the latter one. "That, in and of itself, would assuage many people that they're not on the receiving end of these decisions," Mr. Schorsch says. Echoing the same problem in the abortion debate, he says, it's a question of "who's going to decide?"

Of course the opportunity is there for industry to take the most politically expedient action—to succumb to the strongest pressure. What group would "win," though? Environmentalists fight for nature, industry argues for free enterprise, scientists value innovation, libertarians battle for unfettered civil rights. And their positions are not all mutually exclusive.

Being green involves being democratic about environmental decisions. "Multiple factors have to be taken into account and to focus on . . . supporting some kind of ideological bandwagon is not a responsible stance that any corporation should take," insists University of Texas' Dr. Maxey.

In fact, too narrow a focus may even turn out to be *less* environmentally responsible, as she thinks asbestos legislation illustrates. Asbestos removal in buildings releases fibers into the air. Regulations should be modified to differentiate between the two different kinds of asbestos: "white" and the much more hazardous "blue" fibers, she argues. And immobilization, rather than removal, should be encouraged more. These changes, she contends, would result in less environmental disruption and less cost.

Even environmental groups, which are still more trusted by people than are government and industry, are not without risk of losing popular support. Consumer Alert's Ms. Keating-Edh believes that some of these groups disseminate misleading, exaggerated information in order to perpetuate their own agendas and their own careers. If environmentalists seek to dominate their "opponents" more than to solve environmental problems equitably, their credibility *and* the environment may suffer.

"One of the ugliest things about modern industrial society is the notion that we are institutionalized people," says American Hazard's Dr. Piasecki, "that we have to represent a corporation, or we have to represent a governor, or we have to represent a radical environmental group. As a result, we become entrenched, and there's a logic to that entrenchment, so that while we're in that trench, our institution has only a finite amount of time and resources. This limits our perspective. It's difficult to consider the big picture, to make decisions that benefit the environment."

With his book *In Search of Environmental Excellence: Moving Beyond Blame* (Simon and Schuster, 1990), coauthored with Peter Asmus, Dr. Piasecki calls for peace among the combatants for the sake of all the constituents that make up planet Earth. "There isn't really a net environmental benefit when environmental groups and their corporate equivalents spend all their money in court and none of their money on process change," he says.

In light of what's finally happening now in Eastern Europe, those who care about the environment should recall what President Eisenhower said when the Cold War was still young: "Together, we must learn how to compose differences, not with arms, but with intellect and decent purpose."

Carrying that spirit to the world of the '90s, "the time is right to move beyond blame," Dr. Piasecki says. "It's now clear that there's a lot of environmental management improvement that can be made—and that should be made, cost-effectively—that is not being made because of so much wheelspinning in each of the trenches."

In fact, those in the trenches may not realize that there *is* common ground: opening up to people and considering their diverse concerns.

Consumer Alert's Ms. Keating-Edh, in arguing against radical environmentalism, says that "*people* matter, too," and her organization provides people with information they don't get from what she thinks is a sensationalist popular media.

The University of Texas' Dr. Maxey, calling for fairness and truthfulness in environmental assessments, points out that "the environmental movement is not some monolithic group that is holier than thou." It consists of many different *people*, with values that range from "good housekeeping" to dropping out of society to live off the land.

Grass-roots environmentalists recognize the importance of people too, a lesson that industry is learning in other areas: It is people on product-design teams, who bring amazingly creative and economic improvements to their companies, if only they're given information and are included in decision-making.

"What the labor-management people discovered in the 1930s and 1940s on the waterfront, the future managers in the 1990s and the year 2000 will need to discover concerning environmental decisions," says American Hazard's Dr. Piasecki, who is also a professor of environmental management in the School of Management at Rensselaer Polytechnic Institute, Troy, N. Y.

"What labor management discovered was that the workers have a part in the decisions," he says. "And what environmental managers will need to decide is that citizens have a right to participate in decisions—such as determining the scale of a facility in their community.

"If you simply make all of your decisions based on the gross aggregated economic model and you don't factor in the question of public concerns and public sensitivities, you are literally an economic fool," he warns.

The first step in avoiding that mistake is to always put the problem in historical perspective, he advises. "Leaders get paid a lot to evaluate the entrenched logic of the various camps." They have to understand the different streams of information—the industry perspective, the government perspective, and the citizens' perspectives.

The second step is to empathize with the logic of each position. "How else can you show your 'opponents' that you understand where they're coming from, if, instead, you call them idiots?" he asks.

Finally, when "you come to a point where you realize that all arguments falsify a little bit, and, as a result, you have to make a choice, the only way to make an equitable choice is to measure the consequences of that choice to each of the identified parties."

To begin to do this, industry must receive and share information with the public. Informed citizens ask the right questions, insists Dr. Piasecki. "It's only a suspicious, centralized, technocratic elite that comes to distrust people."

Indeed, being green is, in part, candor. "How does a company deal with the community?" asks CEP's Mr. Schorsch. "Sometimes you get the feeling [companies] are simply unwilling to relinquish control of the ability to make decisions."

Yet, he notes, "there are 60,000 chemicals out there, most of which we know nothing about. Someone's going to have to start sharing data. Someone's going to have to start dealing with some of these proprietary claims and claims that 'we need secrecy.'"

Polaroid Corp. is doing this, says William Schwalm, senior manager of environmental strategy for the Cambridge, Mass., company. In 1987 "we had to start keeping track of emissions through the [community right-to-know] reporting. At that time we made a decision that while we're doing that . . . it would make a lot of sense to educate the community about what it is we're emitting. Otherwise, how do people deal with these numbers?

"So we became very active," he continues. "We said, 'O.K., we're going to open our doors . . . We'll tell people what we're emitting' . . . with the idea that knowledge is better than ignorance."

Uniting to educate the public is what Consumer Alert's Ms. Keating-Edh urges industry to do to implement environmental solutions. Industry can't win the "war" she believes many environmentalists are waging against them by "simply being on the defensive. . . . You have to come up with a better winning position. . . . We *can* have industrial development and clean air and water," she argues. "We have the technology to do these things now. Let's get on with it."

Horst Rechelbacher, founder and chairman of Aveda Corp., a Minneapolis manufacturer of plant-molecular engineered products, is removing the classic veil of secrecy at his company. Commenting on environmental audits on a national videoconference produced by Governors State University, University Park, Ill., he said, "I'd really welcome the outside [environmental] audit. It's just another truth . . . another teacher. It's not controlling us, it's actually helping us."

Says American Hazard's Dr. Piasecki: "We have to remind ourselves that it is the American way to believe in a complex interaction between government, industry, and an informed citizenry."

This isn't only the American way, it's also green. If industry managers learn to truly appreciate the intrinsic value of people, not simply view them as consumers, investors, litigants, or laborers, "then maybe we can learn to look at nature a little more constructively," Dr. Piasecki says. "We could expand the return-on-investment equation so as to achieve social good as we achieve private profitability."

If, by accepting itself as part of a complex interaction, a company is

truly American, then Ben & Jerry's should make many U. S. executives turn green—at least in emulation.

This company's mission statement is three-fold: a product mission, a social mission, and an economic mission. The company's 1989 annual report (printed on recycled paper) reads, "Underlying the mission of Ben & Jerry's is the determination to seek new and creative ways of addressing all three parts, while holding a deep respect for individuals, inside and outside the company, and for the communities of which they are a part."

Similarly, a greener industrial economic philosophy is taking hold at 3M. Although major environmental improvements need to go through traditional cost-justification, "the environmental area is getting a bit like the safety area," says the company's Dr. Bringer. "Safety investments don't require any return at all. All someone has to do is come up and say, 'We don't think this is a safe enough operation; we want to invest this kind of money,' and that's it."

Unfortunately, environmentalists and industrialists have been battling for years, in part because "many managers and many engineers in America have been miseducated to think that the environment and the economy are in a vicious and direct conflict," says Dr. Piasecki.

Yet, if a manager "looks at three business indicators—the quality of the land where you could site a facility, the quality of the water that you use for your industrial process, and the kind of air that you need—you can see that there has been a pattern of environmental abuse that is so serious that we have distorted the return-on-investment equation in the way we finance manufacturing," says Dr. Piasecki.

Industry is actually incurring serious manufacturing costs upon itself, he says, noting that "we sometimes have to pretreat water, decontaminate real estate, and clean the air before we can manufacture high-quality products.

"If the real costs of polluting had been factored in from the start, America would not be facing these

environmental deficit challenges," he writes in his book.

End-of-the-pipe treatment and cleanup are indeed costly. Decontaminating Superfund toxic-waste sites could total $500 billion, reports Congress' Office of Technology Assessment. This compares to the savings-and-loan-industry debacle, notes CEP's Mr. Schorsch. The real issue, he says, is "to finally wake up and deal with it in a sound, sane, preventive manner, instead of too little, too late."

Therefore, being green also means adhering to efficiency in industry—protecting the environment by reducing or eliminating waste and its cleanup and treatment—in the first place.

"In order for us to seize this decade and make environmental progress, we have to transcend our entrenched positions and transact a more efficient kind of business," says Dr. Piasecki.

The goal he describes takes the form of an industrial-design triangle, with three corners: conserve energy, save materials, and reduce hazardous waste. This thrust comes from the insight about energy savings in the '70s, the lesson of hazardous-waste reduction in the '80s, and Europeans' experience with material scarcity in World War II, he explains.

It's a model that benefits both industry and the environment. And more and more companies are using it. A $1.3 million investment in a new process at Aeroscientific Corp., an Anaheim, Calif., printed-circuit-board manufacturer, reduced water consumption, reduced net energy consumption, eliminated sludge, and avoided a relocation. This project proves that by expanding the return-on-investment equation, it's industrially more competitive *in the long term* to make products without listed hazardous wastes, says Dr. Piasecki.

On a grander scale, 3M's Pollution Prevention Pays program has cut its pollution in half since 1975, and *saved* the company $500 million. Also, "there are some hidden benefits from doing environmentally positive things," says 3M's Dr. Bringer.

"We've been trying to tackle the

# SEARCH YOUR TRACKS

## Greener ways begin by asking questions.

When INDUSTRY WEEK challenged Jonathan Schorsch, environmental research director at the Council on Economic Priorities, to describe what companies can do to be environmentally responsible, he hesitated for only a moment. The answer he then gave was a list of questions for management to ask itself:

- Are we trying to reduce the volume of our packaging?
- How do we deal with disposal?
- Are we recycling in the office?
- Can we get beyond the concept of volume sales to build products that last?
- Are we reducing waste and substituting toxic substances with nontoxic ones?
- Are we reformulating waste for resale?
- Do we have a formal environmental policy?
- Do we go beyond compliance?
- Are we uniformly stringent environmentally in operations outside, as well as within, the U. S.?
- Do we educate employees about the hazards of working with toxic materials?
- Do we encourage employees to submit proposals on how to reduce waste?
- Do we conserve energy?
- Are we avoiding paying taxes, when those tax dollars might go to support environmental programs?
- How do our operations impact the communities they're in, including indigenous people in other countries?

hazardous-waste problem through end-of-the pipe regulation—with what I call 'half a pair of scissors,'" says Dr. Piasecki. "We have not sharpened the second half of the pair of scissors, which is the business-development approach."

In other words, "government must not only tell industry what it *shouldn't* do with the environment," he explains. "It must also stimulate innovation in energy and environmental products."

In coordination with such prodding, industry itself must create cleaner processes and products that contribute to profitability, rather than concentrate solely on pollution control. This requires someone inside a company, who, removed from market pressure, finds ways to pursue efficiency.

Dr. Piasecki calls that person a "risk-control manager": the person with corporate clearance to synthesize all the information—from the lawyers, the technical people, the public-relations people, the strategists, and from the community.

"The ultimate resource is information," he notes. "Can you get the best, real-time intelligence on what your choices are?" he asks. "The risk-control manager is the person who's given the time and staff to do that." Furthermore, he adds, this manager needs the authority to justify major operational changes to pursue efficiency beyond the normal return-on-investment equation.

The risk-control manager might also direct the company toward a more responsible future by identifying what Dr. Piasecki calls "environmental dead ends" in corporate strategy. "The petrochemical treadmill" tops his list.

"We've pursued a treadmill that is wearing out," he says. "The major present environmental predicament . . . is that the corporate manager can't discern the difference between the maintenance costs of using petroleum resources versus the opportunity costs of using nonpetroleum resources."

Aveda's Mr. Rechelbacher is an exception to those managers, however. His company is replacing all petroleum-derived materials in its products with plant-derived materials—a process to be completed no later than 1992.

The big dead end for industrialized nations in general might turn out to be the linear, throughput economy in which "the idea is to extract as many resources as possible, manufacture them, and get rid of them, so that you can then start the process all over again," CEP's Mr. Schorsch explains.

An alternative closed-loop economy is what Ben & Jerry's Ms. Mayville is pursuing in a small, but significant way. She plans to form a buying consortium with other companies to initiate group purchases of recycled materials. Ben & Jerry's is actually creating a market, while many others in industry are content to complain that the market doesn't exist and that the prices of recycled materials are too high.

Undoubtedly, in their quest to be more environmentally responsible, companies will stumble. Ms. Mayville forthrightly discusses a bruise Ben & Jerry's suffered. While the company was bringing a new treatment plant on-line, it temporarily violated its wastewater permit, obligingly paid a state fine, and promises to devote all necessary resources to improve.

"I'm not saying we're perfect," says Ms. Mayville. "We're not trying to pretend that we are. And we're not trying to pretend that we're experts in this field either. It's simply that we're doing what we can."

Finally, then, perfect green is unattainable, but, like any virtue, worthy of the reach. It's not a static condition. "It's not where you are—black or deep green or whatever," says Mr. Schorsch. "It's a process, an evolution. People like to see that companies are taking steps."

Having said that, he continues, "It becomes an issue of what does it take for a company to overcome its inertia and to take its blinders off?"

# The Corporate Ethics Test

*RONALD E. BERENBEIM*

Ronald E. Berenbeim is at The Conference Board. This article is adapted from *Corporate Ethics*, a Conference Board research report.

U.S. AND EUROPEAN CEOs and senior managers view corporate ethics as a subject to be dealt with at three levels, each more specific than the last: (1) the corporate mission, (2) constituency relations, and (3) policies and practices.

The most easily recognized and universally applicable category is the corporate mission. Executives interviewed say that the enterprise in which they are engaged, and the products or services that they market, ought to serve an inherently ethical purpose. They believe that a company's primary ethical responsibilities are defined by the nature of its corporate objectives. Thus, a pharmaceutical concern will see its objectives as serving ethical purposes—promoting better health and saving lives. Food companies see their ethical mission as improving nutritional standards while maintaining price levels that their poorest customers can afford.

Corporate managers speak of constituency relations in formulating their company's ethical standards. This effort usually entails statements of corporate responsibility to any or all of the following: employees, local communities, customers, suppliers, shareholders, home country and foreign governments, and in some cases the general public. The majority of the corporate codes of conduct examined describe the company's commitment to these groups rather than prescribe ethical conduct for specific situations.

The former chairman of a large Japanese company summarizes this view of constituency relations: "Our responsibility is not only to our stockholders, but to our clients, our employees and their families, our local community residents, and indeed all of society at large. Our profit comes about through our effort to promote the prosperity of the community as a whole."

There are significant differences of opinion in the role that ethics ought to play at the third level—in evaluating policies and practices. Ethics, as the vice president of public affairs of a Swiss multinational notes, can be "a key that opens all doors," the guiding principle behind every decision. But there is no widespread agreement among business leaders that this should always be the case. Some executives argue that ethical considerations are inappropriate for many management decisions and policies because, under certain circumstances, public commitments to ethical principles can give way to business and adminstrative priorities, or the potential connection between ethical commitments and broad social policies can make the company a target for pressure groups.

For example, while assigning ethics a place in business deliberations, an aerospace executive voices reservations: "The broad definition of ethics may permit the media, special interest groups, and the government to increase pressure on business to address areas that they are currently not equipped to handle. Companies should be concerned with business ethics in dealing with employees, suppliers and customers. They should not be involved in social, political or moral issues such as abortion, South Africa, sexual preference, and other personal moral issues."

Other executives are uneasy about the potential conflict between corporate ethics programs and management roles. The director of a corporate ethics program commented that among high-level executives, "discussion of the subject generates discomfort. The word suggests a mass confessional. It raises issues that are thought to be more relevant to philosophical discussions. People wonder what sort of new demands an ethics program will make on them. Will they be expected to act as judge, detective, guru, teacher, grand inquisitor, or guiding light to the employees whom they supervise? These roles and the tasks that go with them all imply new, difficult, and uncomfortable supervisory requirements for executives.

To get a sense of how CEOs of major companies would manage specific situations that might involve ethical issues, The Conference Board asked the executives to respond to four hypothetical cases and to indicate whether their decisions involved ethical as well as business considerations. Respondents were asked for their own views rather than for statements of company policy. Though the facts presented correspond to no individual company or occurrence, each case depicts

This article originally appeared in *Business and Society Review*, Fall 1987, pp. 22-25, 71. *Business and Society Review*, a quarterly journal of corporate social responsibility and ethics. Reprinted by permission.

# 1. ETHICS IN BUSINESS

## Ethical Issues?

The Conference Board asked executives at 300 companies worldwide whether the following constituted ethical issues for business. The percentage of affirmative responses is listed next to the issue.

| Issue | Percent |
|---|---|
| Employee conflicts of interest | 91 |
| Inappropriate gifts to corporate personnel | 91 |
| Sexual harassment | 91 |
| Unauthorized payments | 85 |
| Affirmative action | 84 |
| Employee privacy | 84 |
| Environmental issues | 82 |
| | |
| Employee health screening | 79 |
| Conflicts between company's ethics and foreign business practices | 77 |
| Security of company records | 76 |
| Workplace safety | 76 |
| Advertising content | 74 |
| Product safety standards | 74 |
| Corporate contributions | 68 |
| Shareholder interests | 68 |
| Corporate due process | 65 |
| Whistleblowing | 63 |
| Employment at will | 62 |
| Disinvestment | 59 |
| Government contract issues | 59 |
| Financial and cash management procedures | 55 |
| Plant/facility closures and downsizing | 55 |
| Political action committees | 55 |
| | |
| Social issues raised by religious organizations | 47 |
| Comparable worth | 43 |
| Product pricing | 42 |
| Executive salaries | 37 |

real issues encountered by managers and those who research business practices.

The four case studies and the ethical choices follow. The survey results are reported on the next page. See if your choices match those of the executives surveyed.

### CASE 1: BUSINESS MEETING OR VACATION?

For the last several years, Amberson Corporation has made occasional purchases of software packages from Hacker, Inc., a corporation located in Maui, Hawaii. Hacker produces a high-quality product which is generally more expensive than that of its competitors. Hacker has continued to press Amberson for business, because Amberson is very large and an industry leader.

Contrary to general practice in the software business, Hacker holds an annual four-day meeting in late February for important (and potentially important) customers at a popular local resort. Hacker's competitors complain that "these junkets are unfair and corrupt the purchasing process." Hacker argues that it uses this conference to explain its products and services and to learn more about the needs of its clients. A substantial amount of time is allocated for rest and recreation. All expenses (exclusive of transportation costs) are paid for by Hacker.

Amberson is reexamining many of its practices, and the policy of allowing corporate officials to attend the Hacker seminar has come under scrutiny. Under these circumstances:

**1. Amberson should:**
A. Continue to allow corporate officers to attend the meeting ☐
B. Discontinue attendance because Hacker's payment of expenses is a "gift" within the meaning of a credible corporate policy ☐

**2. Hacker should:**
A. Discontinue the meetings ☐
B. Take no action ☐

### CASE 2: TOXIC EMISSION STANDARDS AND A "WHISTLEBLOWER"

Brookfield Corporation operates a plant that conforms fully to local requirements for maximum emission of toxic substances, as established ten years ago. The facility is inspected annually and toxic emissions have always been and remain well below the acceptable level.

Relying on recently published research, one of the company's quality-control inspectors argues that the cumulative effects of the low level of pollution from the plant entail a possible risk to public health. He says that public officials would agree if they had known of these studies when the original figures were set.

Although there is some support for his views, most of the company's other quality-control inspectors disagree, and the community has not modified its requirements. Changing the manufacturing process would be costly—it would necessitate substantial layoffs and the plant is the largest single employer in the town.

**1. Brookfield should:**
A. Change the manufacturing process to achieve lower levels of toxic emissions ☐
B. Discuss the new data with local health officials, and agree to stricter standards if they determine that the data are persuasive ☐
C. Take no action ☐

The quality-control inspector is not satisfied with the company's decision and feels that it exposes the public to unacceptable risks. He has released company data to the press and his views are liberally quoted in local newspapers. He has worked for the company for fifteen years and his personnel record is exemplary.

**2. Brookfield should:**

A. Insist that he resign; if he refuses he should be fired. ☐

B. Insist that he accept reassignment as a condition of future employment ☐

C. Take no action ☐

### CASE 3: ACQUISITION AND LAYOFF

Corona Corporation's industrial facility in Smithville is unproductive because the organization has not modernized plant or equipment within the last twenty-five years. As the necessary changes would now be too costly, the company has purchased a local facility from Dexter Corporation, a competitor. Although many of the workers at Corona's and Dexter's other facilities are covered by collective bargaining provisions that provide benefits in the event of a shutdown, these two plants are nonunion. Neither company has a policy for non-union plant closures.

In announcing the deal, Corona's CEO told the press and community leaders that "we are going to keep the best people." In reviewing personnel records for the two plants, the human resources staff finds that they each have very different appraisal systems and there is no way to determine "who the best people are." A human resources staffer also says that due to the more advanced technology, the work in the new plant is organized very differently "from the way Corona employees are used to doing things. The most cost-effective solution is to lay off all the workers at the Corona plant." Under the circumstances:

**1. Corona should:**

A. Lay off all employees in the older plant ☐

B. Dovetail the seniority lists of both plants and retain the needed number of employees on the basis of seniority (this would give employees at Corona's plant a substantial advantage because the facility is older and has a higher proportion of workers with many years of service) ☐

C. Retain employees from both plants based on the ratio of revenues each facility generated in the prior business year (e.g., if revenues from both plants were the same, 50 percent of each workforce would be retained) ☐

**2. Dexter has:**

A. No responsibility for former employees whom Corona does not retain ☐

B. Responsibility for former employees whom Corona does not retain ☐

### CASE 4: INSIDE INFORMATION

Ellis and Finlay, the second and fourth largest companies in their industry, are discussing a merger. The resulting entity would be the largest company in the industry.

The CEO's staff assistant at Ellis, who has no knowledge of the impending transaction, tells his wife, a partner in an arbitrage firm, that "the boss has been asking for a lot of information about Finlay." She reasons that Ellis and Finlay may merge and that competitive pressures are likely to result in a merger of Gaston and Halyard, the first and third largest concerns.

Using this information, her firm invests heavily in Gaston and Halyard stock. Ellis and Finlay eventually merge. Gaston and Halyard stocks go up on speculation in the wake of the Ellis and Finlay merger. The arbitrageurs make a substantial profit.

**1. Upon learning of this transaction, the CEO of Ellis should**

A. Fire the staff assistant ☐

B. Take no action; he did not divulge true inside information ☐

**2. The arbitrage firm should:**

A. Demand the partner's resignation ☐

B. Take no action; the firm knew her source and took a substantial risk based on limited information ☐

Survey results appear below.

## Ethics Survey Results

The results from The Conference Board study on corporate ethics.

**CASE NUMBER 1:**

| | | | |
|---|---|---|---|
| 1A. | 29% | 2A. | 51% |
| 1B. | 71% | 2B. | 49% |

**CASE NUMBER 2:**

| | | | |
|---|---|---|---|
| 1A. | 6% | 2A. | 47% |
| 1B. | 76% | 2B. | 23% |
| 1C. | 18% | 2C. | 29% |

**CASE NUMBER 3:**

| | | | |
|---|---|---|---|
| 1A. | 19% | 2A. | 69% |
| 1B. | 24% | 2B. | 31% |
| 1C. | 41% | | |

**CASE NUMBER 4:**

| | | | |
|---|---|---|---|
| 1A. | 55% | 2A. | 34% |
| 1B. | 45% | 2B. | 66% |

# Ethical Issues and Dilemmas Involving Employees and the Workplace

- **Employee Rights and Duties (Articles 12–13)**
- **Employee Crime (Articles 14–15)**
- **Sexual Treatment of Employees (Articles 16–18)**
- **Discriminatory and Prejudicial Employment Practices (Articles 19–21)**
- **Downsizing of the Work Force (Articles 22–23)**
- **Whistleblowing in the Organization (Article 24)**
- **Handling Ethical Dilemmas at Work (Articles 25–27)**

LaRue Tone Hosmer, in *The Ethics of Management* (Homewood, Illinois: Irwin, 1987), lucidly states that ethical problems in business are truly managerial dilemmas because they represent a conflict, or at least the possibility of a conflict, between the *economic performance* of an organization and its *social performance*. Whereas the economic performance is measured by revenues, costs, and profits, the social performance is judged by the fulfillment of obligations to persons both within and outside the organization.

Units 2 to 4 discuss some of the critical ethical dilemmas that management faces in making decisions in the workplace, in the marketplace, and within the global society. This unit focuses on the relationships and obligations of employers and employees to each other.

Organizational decisionmakers are ethical when they act with equity, fairness, and impartiality, treating with respect the rights of their employees. An organization's hiring and firing practices, treatment of women and minorities, allowance of employees' privacy, and wages and working conditions are areas in which it has ethical responsibilities.

The employee also has ethical obligations in his or her relationship to the employer. A conflict of interest can occur when an employee allows a gratuity or favor to sway him or her in selecting a contract or purchasing a piece of equipment, making a choice that may not be in the best interests of the organization. Other possible ethical dilemmas for employees include espionage and the betrayal of secrets (especially to competitors), the theft of equipment, and the abuse of expense accounts.

The 16 articles in this unit are broken down into 7 subsections on different types of ethical dilemmas in the workplace. "An Employee's Right to Privacy" begins this subsection by revealing some of the ways companies delve into employee's personal lives—while the workers assert their right to be left alone. "Balanced Protection Policies" discusses the importance of employers reexamining the balance between employee and employer rights.

Following this, two articles explore white-collar crimes, employee theft, and destruction of company property and resources. Suggestions are provided on some ways to deal with these crimes.

The next three selections take a close look at the sexual treatment of employees in the workplace. The articles reveal some forms of sexual harassment and sexual abuse in office and business environments and provide ideas on how to stop and deal with sexual harassment.

The first article in the next subsection evaluates the tenability of affirmative action over the past 25 years and relates the ambivalence that many minorities have about affirmative action. The next article describes the prejudicial practices and discrimination against older people in the organizational arena. The last article in this subsection discusses how "hazing" often affects women, minorities, and some newcomers in crueler ways than other workers.

The first article in the subsection *Downsizing of the Work Force* supplies suggestions on how management can deal with employees' senses of security and justice during the downsizing process. The last article in this subsection, "Ethical Values Underlying the Termination Process," discloses how self-enlightened management can make socially responsible decisions in regard to employees' terminations.

The article "Changing Unethical Organizational Behavior" in the subsection *Whistleblowing in the Organization* analyzes the ethical dilemma and possible ramifications of whistleblowing.

The last three articles in this unit resonate the benefits of establishing a corporate culture that includes business ethics as an integral part of its ongoing organizational strategy. Some real-world ethical dilemmas for the reader to ponder are presented.

**Looking Ahead: Challenge Questions**

Ethical dilemmas occur when a manager or an employee is faced with two or more conflicting ethical choices. In your opinion, what ethical dilemmas do *managers* face most frequently? What ethical dilemmas do *employees* face most often?

In the article on "Silent Saboteurs," Frank Navran suggested that employees often become silent saboteurs out of their perceived needs for retaliation or self-preservation. What are some organizational environments or settings where you have seen this manifested?

What forms of sexual and minority discrimination are most prevalent in today's workplace? Do you think there are particular job situations or occupations where discrimination is more widespread and conspicuous? Why?

Whistleblowing occurs when an employee discloses illegal, immoral, or illegitimate organizational practices or activities. Under what circumstances do you believe whistleblowing is appropriate? Why?

As a condition of employment, does an organization have the right to subject its employees to lie detector, drug, or AIDS tests? Why or why not?

# An employee's right to privacy?

## Ted J. Rakstis

In April 1989, twenty-five-year-old Sibi Soroka applied for a position as a security guard with Target Stores, a discount retail chain based in Minneapolis, Minnesota.

As part of Target's pre-employment screening process, Soroka was required to take a 704-question pencil-and-paper "honesty test." He was instructed to answer "true" or "false" to such statements as: "I am very strongly attracted to members of my own sex," "I feel like jumping off when I am on a high place," and "I have no difficulty starting or holding my urine."

He got the job but was fired ten days later. In September 1989, Soroka filed a class-action suit against Target. The issue wasn't his loss of employment. It was the test forced upon him and other applicants.

Soroka told Parade magazine: "It made me physically sick. I asked some people familiar with employment how a company could ask such personal questions. I thought it was against the law."

In all but a few of the United States, pencil-and-paper "honesty" tests are legal. *(See "Catching Thieves on the Payroll,"* Kiwanis, *November/December 1989.)* And, to a large extent, so are most other tactics used to intrude upon employees' rights to privacy.

"Canada, all of Western Europe, Japan, and Australia have laws that protect workers' privacy," says Robert Ellis Smith, publisher of Privacy Journal, a newsletter with offices in Providence, Rhode Island, and Washington, DC.

"With some exceptions, that's not true in the US," he adds. "There's far more electronic surveillance in the American workplace. In general, employees have fewer privacy rights. For that reason, they're much less trusting than workers in other parts of the world."

David F. Linowes, a professor of political economy and public policy at the University of Illinois at Champaign, was head of the US Privacy Protection Commission in the mid-1970s. He also is the author of *Privacy in America: Is Your Private Life in the Public Eye?*

In the late 1980s, Linowes surveyed 126 Fortune 500 corporations with payroll totals of 3.7 million. Some of his findings from the study included:

• Although 87 percent of the companies studied allow workers to examine their personnel files, only 27 percent grant them access to their supervisors' performance appraisals.

> *Honesty tests, electronic surveillance, private investigations, and pure snooping: How far can employers go when "checking out" workers?*

• Fifty-seven percent retain private investigators to collect information on workers, and 42 percent do so without telling them.

• Thirty-eight percent have no policies that cover the release of employee data to US government agencies.

• Eighty percent supply information to workers' potential creditors without a subpoena, and 58 percent furnish such information to landlords.

The abuses of employee privacy rights are rampant. Business Week magazine, usually a strong supporter of management practices, observed in a 1990 editorial:

"Most major companies overtly or secretly videotape, eavesdrop, bug, tail, rifle through lockers or desks, or use computers to monitor employees on the job or off. Employers say that snooping isn't a choice anymore; it's a requirement.

"They must do it to protect themselves against negligence lawsuits, guard against theft, stop employees from sharing secrets with the competition, and make sure their workers don't have checkered life-styles.

"But all the appropriate reasons in the world won't make snooping palatable to workers. Right now, the legal scales weigh far too heavily in favor of employers."

In a news report in the same issue, Business Week pointed to some specific incidences:

"General Electric Company says it uses tiny, fish-eye lenses installed behind pinholes in walls and ceilings to watch employees suspected of crimes. DuPont Company says it uses hidden, long-distance cameras to monitor its loading docks around the clock.

"At airlines such as Delta, computers track who writes the most reservations. And Management Recruiters Inc. in Chicago says its bosses surreptitiously watch computerized schedules to see who interviews the most job candidates."

Employee privacy rights are among the most compelling of all workplace concerns. But for Americans at every job and economic level, privacy also has become all but nonexistent.

Three giant US credit bureaus maintain exhaustive records on an estimated *160 million* people. The organizations are TRW in Orange, California; Equifax in Atlanta, Georgia; and Chicago-based Trans Union Credit Information.

Through computer tie-ins with smaller local and regional credit bureaus, TRW, Equifax, and Trans Union have compiled massive electronic dossiers. They're crammed with information broken down according to age, sex, income, and numerous other categories.

Nearly anyone can buy the data, and there are some legitimate uses.

Lenders, for example, can slash their losses by securing the names of the 80,000 or so Americans who file for individual bankruptcies each year. They also can pinpoint the approximately 4 percent of US consumers who have a history of not paying their credit-card charges.

That, however, is but one use of the databases. Aside from valid credit investigations, TRW, Equifax, and Trans Union have created a marketing paradise.

William L. Edwards, an analyst for Volpe, Covington & Welty, an investment firm in San Francisco, California, says: "They have files on nearly every consumer in the largest consumer market in the free world."

The credit bureaus make possible the most sophisticated target marketing ever. As Business Week points out, companies can buy the names of Hispanics who earn $500,000 a year or those of every millionaire who lives within a fifty-mile radius of Dallas, Texas.

Robert S. Boyd, a writer for Knight-Ridder Newspapers, adds: "Personal information stored in business computers can be used in disturbing ways. An insurance company might like to check the names of people who bought cigarettes against a list of its clients in order to gauge their health risk.

"A proctologist might want to know who is buying Preparation H, and a pet-food salesman would relish the names and addresses of elderly women with cats."

Robert Ellis Smith, publisher of Privacy Journal, says 50,000 businesses obtain individual credit reports from Equifax alone. That gives millions of their employees potential access to personal credit information.

Smith defends the rights of businesses to buy database information for credit and marketing purposes. However, he says, it's not appropriate to purchase such data for intelligence-gathering about employees.

Even data collectors are becoming dismayed about misuses of their services.

In April 1990, Equifax released a voluminous report on consumer attitudes in the Information Age. It was compiled by Louis Harris and Associates and Alan F.

Westin, a professor at Columbia University in New York City.

Westin and the Harris organization worked on similar surveys for other corporate clients in 1978 and 1983. Their principal recent discovery was that 79 percent of the 2,254 adults whom they interviewed have serious concerns about their personal privacy. That's an increase from 64 percent in 1978.

Privacy Journal summarizes the study: "The public is particularly concerned about information practices related to certain industries, especially direct marketing. Direct marketers were singled out as untrustworthy in handling personal information. Only 34 percent of the general public gave direct marketers high or moderate levels of trust; no other industry or government organization received less than 50 percent.

"Next lowest were credit bureaus (59 percent) and auto-insurance companies (61 percent). Most trustworthy were hospitals and the (US) Census Bureau, each receiving the support of 81 percent of those polled."

Though both the boss and those whom he or she supervises are affected by credit-bureau investigations, the Equifax study also turned up some significant opinions about workplace privacy.

Eighty percent support the rights of an employer to learn whether a job applicant has a criminal record. Fifty-five percent say it's proper for a job candidate to submit to a written honesty test.

Further, 83 percent believe that employers should be able to conduct pre-employment tests to uncover drug users. And, 66 percent approve of random drug testing for those already on the payroll.

But several areas of employer scrutiny fared less well. Only 46 percent think that it's appropriate to test worker prospects for AIDS. In addition, a mere 12 percent endorse the rights of employers to pry into personal life-styles and political activities.

The Equifax pollsters also looked at Caller ID, a controversial new telephone technology.

Caller ID flashes the caller's number on a video display built into the phone receiving the call. With Caller ID, you can find out who's placing obscene or other unwanted calls. But if you want to make an anonymous business or per-

sonal call, the phone answerer also can obtain your number.

A Chicago Tribune editorial asserts: "This is an invasion of personal privacy and autonomy. Many individuals will be deterred from calling crisis centers that deal with suicide, rape, child abuse, or AIDS for fear of having their identities revealed.

"Psychiatrists, doctors, social workers, and lawyers will not be able to return emergency calls from home if they want to keep their numbers confidential. Victims of domestic violence will not be able to call spouses or their children without the possibility of giving away their location."

In a letter to Business Week, Christopher G. Scheck, president of Small World Paging Company in New York City, also points out a severe drawback for business users: "Every month, we are forced to call about 10 percent of our accounts to remind them to pay up. How many of those people will answer the phone if they know who's on the line?"

Fifty-five percent of the consumers surveyed by Equifax say Caller ID should be available but regulated by law. Twenty-five percent want it banned entirely, and 17 percent contend that it should be freely available.

Whether yours is a large or small organization, privacy issues are bound to affect your relationship with your employees. Let's examine each of them.

• Electronic surveillance. If you're monitoring your workers, do they know it?

Retailers and other businesses with high incidences of theft have found that the mere publicized presence of hidden cameras and recording equipment represents an effective deterrent.

Nation's Business magazine suggests that employers videotape their workers to assess their performances but advise them that they're doing so. It's a way to increase productivity and quality, the magazine claims.

But Privacy Journal's Robert Ellis Smith is skeptical of the notion that employee work habits will improve if they're aware of being videotaped. If anything, he says, it's likely to inhibit them.

---

## Many companies videotape, eavesdrop, bug, tail, rifle through lockers or desks, or use computers to monitor employees. They say snooping isn't a choice; it's a requirement

"Small businesses, in particular, should be wary of new electronic technology that can be used for spying," Smith says. "Without employee consent, serious violations of law may be involved."

In 1988, the US government made illegal the use of polygraph (lie detector) testing except for security personnel and others in extremely sensitive positions. Now, Industry Week magazine reports, there's a move to ban all hidden snooping devices.

• Honesty testing. After the polygraph prohibition went into effect, companies that produce pencil-and-paper tests to

be informed of any credit investigations being conducted for reasons of insurance or employment.

That sounds reassuring, but the law contains an enormous loophole. It allows the credit agencies to divulge information to anyone who has "a legitimate business need." The gates have been opened for the widespread sale of confidential data to almost anyone.

Americans supposedly also are protected by the Privacy Act of 1974, the Right to Financial Privacy Act of 1978, and the Computer Matching and Privacy Protection Act of 1988. Yet, various

can be used to build electronic files on present and future employees.

Says Robert Ellis Smith: "The most ethical, and perhaps most reliable, ways to get information on workers are the traditional ones. Get their references, and check them out carefully. And when you hire someone, put him or her under close supervision—by people, not electronic devices."

• Drug and AIDS testing. As noted earlier, most Americans surveyed in the Equifax poll favor both pre-employment and random testing for drugs. Fewer than half support the use of tests to detect AIDS.

US laws appear to mirror public opinion. According to federal legislation, it's illegal to fire or not hire a person because he or she has AIDS or the AIDS virus. It's also against the law to isolate workers who suffer from AIDS. Even so, abuses seem to be commonplace.

The rights of employers to conduct random drug tests were upheld in 1989 by the US Supreme Court. In 1990, however, the California Supreme Court ruled that such testing violates privacy protections guaranteed under the state constitution.

---

## "Small businesses should be very wary of new electronic technology that can be used for spying. Without employee consent, serious violations of law may be involved"

---

evaluate employee honesty saw their sales surge. Today, many defenders of privacy rights also would like to see the exams outlawed.

Alan M. Dershowitz, a law professor at Harvard University in Cambridge, Massachusetts, declares: "On the basis of such a test, which claims to predict whether you might steal something, you can be deprived of a job and a means of earning a living.

"This is 'Big Brother' at work. You can be penalized simply because a test says you may have a proclivity to be dishonest. In other words, you're guilty without a trial."

Pencil-and-paper honesty tests already are forbidden by the state governments of Rhode Island, Massachusetts, Maryland, Connecticut, and Minnesota.

Terrence Patterson, a psychologist for the US Public Health Service, also contends that they violate the standards of the American Psychological Association (APA).

"Honesty tests isolate one facet of the personality and offer no information on the complete personality constellation," Patterson argues. "Human beings don't perform one trait at a time. Any employer who hires or rejects an applicant on this basis does so at his own peril."

Furthermore, he points out, APA guidelines stipulate that a qualified psychologist must evaluate the results of such tests. In many organizations, Patterson says, people with no professional credentials assess the exams.

• Data collection. The US Fair Credit Reporting Act of 1970 prohibits credit agencies from sharing information with anyone other than authorized customers.

It also gives consumers the right to review their credit records, and they must

exceptions have made the laws almost meaningless.

The most advanced software package for the distribution of personal data made its debut in 1990. Known as Lotus MarketPlace, it originally sold for $695 in some 7,000 US computer stores.

The total software package contains names, addresses, and precise marketing information on 120 million American consumers, 80 million homes, and 7.5 million businesses.

Lotus MarketPlace runs on a Macintosh personal computer. The initial purchase price supplied the buyer with 5,000 names. Additional ones cost only eight cents each, and each name can be matched with those in other databases.

Marc Rotenberg, a Washington, DC, representative of Computer Profession-

als for Social Responsibility, told the US House Subcommittee on Government Information: "These new products pose a particular threat to personal privacy, because they place the actual data in the hands of individuals and beyond the control of even the responsible information brokers."

Lotus MarketPlace has been touted as a giant stride forward for small-business marketing. Like the other commercial databases, it may fill a reputable business need. Still, it's yet another tool that

Industry Week comments: "The California Supreme Court historically has been the impetus behind changes in employment laws across the nation. As a result, it may be only a matter of time before private employers nationwide begin to lose what has been a helpful—albeit controversial—means of curtailing drug-abuse problems in the workplace."

Arizona, New York, Florida, Montana, and Alaska also have explicit constitutional guarantees for the protection of privacy. At this writing, the clash between federal and state high-court rulings was

---

## With Caller ID, "every call to a business will enable (commercial operations) to place the caller's telephone number and address on a sales list without the person's consent"

---

unresolved.

Canada has taken an opposite position from that of the US Supreme Court. In his annual report for 1989-90, John W. Grace, then Canada's Privacy Commissioner, warned: "Urinalysis testing intrudes into private lives. It is scientifically unsuited to answering the questions of whether an individual engaged in safety sensitive activities is using, or is under the influence of, performance-altering substances."

In a special seventy-nine-page report,

*Drug Testing and Privacy*, the commissioner's office advised: "Testing programs should not distinguish between legal and illegal drugs that can impair." The document also listed a number of restrictions upon any form of drug testing.

• Caller ID. At the time of this writing, Caller ID telephone connections were legal in every US state except Pennsylvania.

Nevertheless, you should think twice before having such a system installed in your office. Caller ID almost certainly will restrict your workers' and your own need for confidentiality.

Besides the potential dangers already cited, Privacy Journal cautions: "Caller ID will be used by commercial operations to compile lists for phone solicitations.

"Every call to a business will enable them to place the caller's telephone number and address on a sales list without the person's consent. Instead of reducing junk mail and telemarketing, it more likely will increase them."

In Canada, former Privacy Commissioner John Grace originally advocated the use of a blocking device for those who don't want their phone numbers displayed to callers. Later he declared: "(Caller ID) would too greatly diminish the state of our personal privacy if every call we made to merchants, government departments, social agencies, or media outlets disclosed our identities. To prevent that loss of control, surely we are willing to tolerate the fact that some may abuse their ability to call anonymously."

Employees in every free land are entitled to perform their work in an environment devoid of suspicion and intrusion. When granted that, they probably will become more productive and loyal.

"The principal consideration is consent," publisher Robert Ellis Smith explains. "If employees agree to honesty tests, electronic surveillance, drug testing, and the like, there is no invasion of privacy. They have abrogated their rights.

"Otherwise, the burden falls upon the employer to adhere to the demands of laws and ethics. People in the workplace are highly vulnerable. It's in their interest, and that of business owners, to ensure that their rights are protected."

# For privacy loss, dial toll-free

While you're tending to your employees' privacy rights, you also should be concerned about your own.

If your business or practice is typical, you place many "800" and "900" area-code calls within or to the United States. And you probably also do so at home.

Most of the "800" calls are free, but you pay in other ways. The biggest price tag is your loss of privacy.

Have you heard of "Call Interactive"?

It's probably the world's most sophisticated telemarketing operation. Launched in 1989, Call Interactive is a joint venture between American Express and American Telephone & Telegraph.

The system has 10,000 continually operating long-distance phone lines in Omaha, Nebraska. Knight-Ridder Newspapers and the Chicago Tribune explain, step by step, how Call Interactive works:

First, you make a phone call to an "800" or "900" number to buy a product, obtain information, or express an opinion. You connect with a computer. In most instances, it's the monster unit in Omaha.

Using your phone number, the computer links you to a marketing service that secures your name and address. They're instantly displayed on a salesperson's computer screen. Call Interactive can search tens of millions of names in a second or two.

Next, the salesperson takes your order, answers questions, and may ask for more information.

If you've ordered something with a credit card, the computer checks an electronic credit-authorization bureau to verify your credit record. The three largest bureaus in the US are TRW, Equifax, and Trans Union Credit Information.

Whether you realize it or not, your call now is part of a permanent personal record. Through electronic means, the sponsoring company or organization has learned your name, address, phone number, and the purpose of your call. The data can be used for targeted mailing lists and telephone marketing campaigns.

Finally, the marketers analyze your life-style. By matching their information about you with that contained in other databases, you've become a prime sales prospect for thousands of companies.

Welcome to the world of electronic direct marketing. In the US alone, you have 160 million companions.

# Balanced Protection Policies

*Benson Rosen and*
*Catherine Schwoerer*

*Benson Rosen is professor of business administration at the University of North Carolina in Chapel Hill, N.C.*

*Catherine Schwoerer is assistant professor of business administration at the University of Kansas in Lawrence, Kan.*

Corporate human resource specialists currently face the challenge of shaping employment policies for the 21st century. In order to attract and retain the best and brightest workers, organizations must develop new personnel policies that recognize and protect individual rights. A critical element in future HR management policies is the guarantee of employee protection from what might be perceived as any form of arbitrary treatment by management.

Advocates for expanding employee rights warn that management policies that abridge free speech, privacy or due process will surely lead to more government regulation. There is already a movement toward drafting an employee rights law to set national standards for an implicit employment contract between managers and workers.

At the same time that human resource planners face pressures to protect individual rights, pressures are also mounting to maintain a lean, flexible, drug-free work force. Employers argue that to remain competitive, they must protect management's employment-at-will prerogatives, improve the quality of new hires and maintain work force productivity.

Growing international competition and rapid changes in the economy, coupled with increasing numbers of mergers and corporate downsizings,

---

Striking a balance between the rights of employers and employees is not easy. One study has dealt with this issue and reveals that common protection policies exist.

---

have made massive layoffs and terminations commonplace. In order to maintain efficiency, quality and productivity, organizations must have little tolerance for dead wood. Accordingly, HR specialists are particularly sensitive about protecting the traditional corporate right to dismiss employees under the employment-at-will doctrine.

Employment-at-will policies permit termination of employees for just cause, no cause or even bad cause at any time. In order to protect their rights under the termination-at-will doctrine, employers have been encouraged to reduce their vulnerability to charges of unjust dismissal resulting from an implied contract. For example, recruiters are warned not to describe employment opportunities as permanent or guaranteed.

Organizations are encouraged to require that job applicants sign a formal

statement acknowledging that their employment can be terminated by either party with or without cause or notice at any time. But, the consequences of adopting these protective measures are largely unknown.

A second approach to building a competitive work force centers on improving selection procedures. Growing concerns about the serious consequences of drug abuse and employee theft have compelled many organizations to adopt more stringent selection procedures. Comprehensive background investigations, pre-employment medical screening, drug testing and various psychological tests have been used to improve personnel selection. While acknowledging that some selection strategies risk potential invasion of privacy and violation of other employee rights, employers argue that such measures are necessary in order to screen out high-risk employees.

Finally, in order to improve quality and reduce employee theft, a few organizations have installed various types of electronic surveillance devices. Surveillance may include monitoring of telephone conversations, tapping into computer terminals and installing video cameras in certain work areas. Employers justify electronic surveillance as an important tool for monitoring individual performance and policy compliance.

Reprinted with permission from *HRMagazine* (formerly *Personnel Administrator*), February 1990, pp. 59-61, 63-64. *HRMagazine*, published by the Society for Human Resource Management, Alexandria, VA.

Clearly, human resource managers must walk a tightrope, balancing employees' rights of fair treatment and due process against employers' rights to manage the size, quality and productivity of their work forces without cumbersome restrictions. Surprisingly little research is available to help HR professionals evaluate where they stand in terms of employee and employer rights policies.

## Survey sample

To determine what policies currently exist, a survey was conducted by a random sampling of 3,800 names drawn from the SHRM national membership. Survey packages containing a cover letter, survey questionnaire and self-addressed, post-paid return envelope were mailed to selected members. By the survey deadline, 785 usable questionnaires had been returned from all regions of the country.

Organizations representing a diverse group of industries responded. Forty-five percent of the organizations employed less than 500 people, 19 percent employed between 500 and 999, and the remaining 36 percent had over 1,000 employees. Less than 30 percent of the organizations were unionized.

Respondents included an almost equal number of men (53 percent) and women (47 percent). The average age of participating human resource professionals was 42.1 and they had an average of 12.7 years of professional experience.

## Survey issues

A general question assessed whether organizations currently place greater emphasis on protecting employer or employee rights. Next, a series of specific questions probed what policies organizations currently have in place to protect both employee and employer rights. Participants evaluated the effectiveness of existing policies and reported on the need for additional policies. They also reported on the benefits and costs of existing policies. Finally, survey respondents shared their experiences on the effectiveness of various strategies for revising existing policies or implementing new ones.

The survey included fixed-alternative and open-ended questions. For the fixed-alternative questions, responses were recorded on five-point scales, ranging from 1 (unsuccessful or not needed) to 5 (extremely successful or extremely needed).

## Survey results

**The present balance.** Participants differ on whether their companies' employment policies put more emphasis on employee or employer rights. Slightly more than 44 percent of participating HR professionals characterized their organizations' policies as striking an even balance between employee and employer rights. Of the remaining 56 percent, almost twice as many characterized their organizations as emphasizing employer rights (37 percent) compared to employee rights (19 percent).

In open-ended comments, one participant noted that it may be counterproductive to consider employee and employer rights as mutually exclusive. Another participant pointed out that the challenge for human resource management is to define areas of mutual responsibility with respect to both employee and employer rights. In the next section, we examine specific policies designed to protect the rights of employees.

**Employee rights.** Experts argue that protecting the rights of employees is both socially responsible and good business. While it is difficult to document conclusively, protecting workers from arbitrary treatment and ensuring basic rights of privacy and free speech are widely believed to build organizational commitment. Moreover, resolving worker conflicts internally should reduce the threat of costly litigation.

Participants were asked to consider eight areas of employee rights. Four policies designed to protect employees from arbitrary treatment were:

- Access to grievance committees.
- Corporate ombudsman to investigate employee complaints.
- Impartial arbitrators for dispute resolution.
- Specific written disciplinary policies.

The remaining policies protected against violation of individual rights:

- Privacy protection with respect to performance, medical and financial information.
- Employee access to personnel records.
- Free-speech protection and safety information.

Respondents indicated whether their organizations currently followed each policy and evaluated the effectiveness of the existing policy. In the absence of a policy, respondents assessed the need for new policies. Findings with respect to employee rights are shown in Exhibit 1.

Survey results suggest a very mixed picture. In the critical area of protecting employees from arbitrary treatment, many organizations have taken a first step, but still appear to have a long way to go.

Written disciplinary policies have been implemented in more than 70 percent of participating companies. These policies guide the administration of discipline, contingent on specific rule infractions. Written disciplinary policies protect both the employee and the employer by ensuring that disciplinary actions are consistent and impartial.

Surprisingly few organizations, however, have taken the next step and supplemented their disciplinary policies with additional measures for resolving disputes between management and employees. Even fewer organizations report using management grievance committees or impartial arbitrators to resolve employment conflicts. Findings indicate that in a majority of organizations, employees have very limited access to internal dispute-resolution mechanisms. Accordingly, when disputes and grievances develop, employees in these organizations may see few alternatives to seeking redress through union grievance procedures or through the courts.

Developing policies to protect employees' rights to free speech is another area where organizations may be lagging. Given current concerns with corporate ethics, it is surprising how few organizations have formal policies protecting "whistle blowers," employees who criticize organizational policies, practices, products or services. Only 26 percent of organizations have implemented policies protecting employees' rights to free speech.

Our survey findings reveal that organizations have been considerably more responsive in protecting employee rights to ensure the accuracy and confidentiality of information contained in employee personnel files. Almost 90 percent of organizations in our sample allow employees to review their own personnel and medical files for accuracy. More than 83 percent have strict rules ensuring the privacy of performance, medical and financial information.

More than three-quarters of participating organizations have explicit policies governing disclosure of health and safety information. In most organizations these policies provide employees with information about potential risks associated with dangerous working conditions. The existence of these policies is no doubt driven in part by "right to know" laws which affect some industries.

**Business characteristics and employee rights policies.** Two business characteristics associated with the presence or absence of employee rights policies were industry and union status. Industries that were among the leaders in implementing employee rights policies included government, health and education, manufacturing and transportation. Disseminating health and safety information was significantly more likely in transportation, manufacturing and health industries. Government organizations were more likely to use arbitrators and to permit employees access to confidential records. Organizations in banking and finance trailed all other industries with respect to establishing formal grievance committees. Clearly, both the nature of the business and the industry's regulatory environment influence organizational posture on employee rights.

### Employer rights

In order to build a competitive, flexible work force, some organizations have implemented new human resource policies to improve personnel selection, monitor performance and preserve management's employment-at-will prerogatives.

We asked survey respondents to indicate which employer rights policies their companies have already implemented, to evaluate the success of existing policies and to indicate areas where new policies are needed (see Exhibit 1).

**Applicant screening policies.** Respondents reported a number of policies designed to screen applicants. The most frequently used approach to applicant screening is the background check (used by 80.9 percent). For most organizations, the background check included an investigation to verify education and work history. In other companies, an inquiry into financial background and criminal records was also conducted.

More than 40 percent of organizations in the sample require pre-employment medical examinations. Companies attempt to detect genetic traits that increase employee susceptibility to certain diseases and other pre-existing medical problems. There has been considerable debate over the potential for employment discrimination when genetic testing information is used to influence selection decisions. However, the use of pre-employment medical screening has been justified by some employers as necessary for containing health-care costs.

The survey findings indicate that drug-screening policies have been

---

EXHIBIT 1

## Status of Protection Policies
### (expressed in percentages)

**Employee Protection Policies**

| | Exist | Successful | Needed |
|---|---|---|---|
| 1. Access to records | 89.8 | 93 | 77 |
| 2. Privacy protection | 83.2 | 96 | 88 |
| 3. Health/safety information | 79.0 | 91 | 78 |
| 4. Disciplinary policy | 71.7 | 95 | 79 |
| 5. Company ombudsman | 39.8 | 91 | 54 |
| 6. Free speech protection | 26.3 | 85 | 45 |
| 7. Management grievance committee | 24.9 | 91 | 46 |
| 8. Impartial arbitrators | 23.3 | 87 | 31 |

**Employer Protection Policies**

| | Exist | Successful | Needed |
|---|---|---|---|
| 1. Background investigation | 80.9 | 89 | 91 |
| 2. Avoid "implied contract" | 79.7 | 95 | 87 |
| 3. Termination at will | 51.1 | 93 | 71 |
| 4. Medical screening | 40.6 | 88 | 56 |
| 5. Drug testing | 37.0 | 93 | 66 |
| 6. Non-competition agreement | 28.1 | 83 | 43 |
| 7. Psych/polygraph testing | 10.5 | 74 | 24 |
| 8. Electronic surveillance | 7.4 | 73 | 18 |

implemented by 37 percent of companies in the sample. All of the policies subject applicants to drug screening prior to employment. In addition, some organizations require periodic follow-up drug testing.

Only 10 percent of organizations reported using psychological testing or polygraph screening to identify "high-risk" applicants or employees. In past years, polygraph screening was used as a deterrent to employee theft. However, recent legislation has banned the use of polygraph testing in most employment situations. It appears that use of paper-and-pencil "honesty" tests has not yet been widely adopted in place of polygraph screening.

Electronic surveillance has been justified by some companies as an important tool for feedback, improving productivity and deterring employee theft. However, electronic monitoring and video surveillance have potential for increasing stress and invading employee privacy. Monitoring employee performance by means of computer, telephone or video surveillance is used in 7.4 percent of organizations in the sample. Survey data indicate that only 18 percent of organizations perceive a need for electronic surveillance. At present, the perceived psychological costs to employees scrutinized by electronic monitoring may far outweigh the organizational benefits.

**Employment-at-will rights.** The majority of organizations are very protective of their employment-at-will rights. Almost 80 percent have implemented new policies to avoid any indication of an "implied employment" contract. In many instances, organizations have deleted from company handbooks mention of permanent employment, promise of annual review or guarantee of a grievance and appeal procedure.

In addition, just over half of the organizations require employees to formally acknowledge that their employment may be terminated with or without cause at any time by either the company or the employee. Protecting against wrongful discharge or implied contract lawsuits and maintaining flexibility to adjust work force size are two frequently cited motivations for preserving management's employment-at-will prerogatives.

The majority of organizations are very protective of their employment-at-will rights.

**Non-competition agreements.** Non-competition agreements protect employers by prohibiting former employees from working for competitors. They are designed to curtail departing employees from taking valued customers or trade secrets to the competition. Such agreements may be particularly important in certain types of high-technology or sales organizations.

Employees, on the other hand, argue that non-competition agreements unfairly limit their re-employment opportunities. About 28 percent of companies require employees to sign non-competition agreements. Among companies that do not currently have such policies, 43 percent perceive a need to implement non-competition agreements in the future.

**Business characteristics and employer rights policies.** Industry, organizational size and union status were significantly related to the implementation of employer rights policies. Industries where employer rights policies were most frequently found included transportation, manufacturing and finance.

For example, organizations in the transportation industry were significantly more likely to use drug testing, medical screening and electronic surveillance. Similarly, manufacturing organizations conducted drug testing and medical screening and required non-competition agreements.

Financial institutions emphasized background checks and protected against employment-at-will litigation by revising company handbooks and requiring employees to sign statements acknowledging the termination-at-will principle. Organizations in the government and education sectors were least likely to develop policies surrounding non-competition or employment at will.

Organizational size also influenced employer rights policies. Relative to smaller organizations, the largest organizations in our sample (more than 1,000 employees) were significantly more likely to implement stringent pre-employment measures. The large organizations were most likely to require pre-employment psychological tests, drug tests and medical exams. Large organizations were more likely to monitor employee behavior through electronic surveillance.

Union status was associated with employer rights policies. Unionized organizations were more likely to conduct both drug testing and medical screening.

The most widely adopted organizational policies focus on ensuring the selection of quality employees and preserving organizations' employment-at-will rights. Comparing existing policies with perceptions of needs, the biggest gaps were found for drug testing and termination at will. In future years, more organizations will likely develop policies aimed at drug screening and reaffirming the employment-at-will doctrine.

## Implementing new policies

Organizations have long valued openness, trust, security and employee commitment. Accordingly, these organizations have implemented policies designed to protect employee rights to privacy, free speech and fair treatment. Yet to remain competitive and to ensure a safe work environment, management has also adopted policies and practices that represent potential invasions of employees' rights to privacy, security and due process.

Perhaps the secret for achieving harmony between employer and employee rights rests with the processes by which needs for new policies are identified and with the strategies used to implement these policies.

The majority of survey participants endorsed a strategy that provides education and training to help employees understand the reasons behind new policies. Education and training satisfy the need for communication of new policies in order to break down resistance to change.

Policy implementation based on consultants' advice was evaluated favorably by almost 80 percent of respondents. While this strategy has the potential for capitalizing on the experiences of other organizations, the strategy does not provide for employee input.

About two-thirds recommended policy implementation after negotiation and agreement with employees. Negotiation and agreement allow for modifying proposed policies to account for employee as well as employer needs.

The use of task forces to develop new policy recommendations was evaluated highly by 57 percent of par-participants. Waiting for a task force to reach consensus on new policy recommendations is clearly the most time-consuming approach. However, the task force ensures maximum involvement of those employees most likely to be affected by the new policies. Accordingly, the task force approach should be very effective in overcoming resistance to change.

In open-ended comments, many participants noted that a combination of approaches represents the most effective way to implement new policy. For example, one participant described an employee task force with management and legal experts serving in advisory capacities. Another participant stressed the importance of communication both before and after policy implementation in order to maintain trust and cooperation.

> The challenge is to find a common ground where good business practices do not limit basic employee freedoms.

As organizations strive to balance both employee and employer rights, the process of implementing new policies may be as important as the content of those policies. Our survey findings suggest that human resource professionals appreciate the value of effective communication. Results also suggest, however, that HR professionals may underestimate the importance of employee involvement and participation in overcoming resistance to policy changes.

## Implications for the future

The findings reveal that when employer and employee rights clash, many more organizations put the highest priority on preserving and protecting employer rights. The major conflicts between employee and employer rights center on issues of employee privacy and employment at will. The challenge for HR profes-

sionals in each of these areas is to find a common ground where good business practices do not limit basic employee freedoms.

In the future, resolving the conflict over employment at will requires that human resource managers accept the concept of an implied contract based on a clearly defined set of responsibilities and rights. Employee responsibilities must include adhering to high standards of honesty, safety, quality and productivity. Employee rights must include security from arbitrary dismissal, channels for dispute resolution and privacy protection. Statements of rights and responsibilities must also specify the mechanisms for settling wrongful discharge claims through binding arbitration before they reach litigation

Many organizations have already revised human resource management policies, often with the input of employees and outside experts. Other organizations have acknowledged the need for new policies, but have not yet taken action. We have offered some guidelines for resolving conflicts over privacy and employment at will. Past experiences in the areas of equal employment opportunity, occupational safety, and pension protection suggest that if companies fail to take the initiative in the area of employee rights, the courts and regulators will surely intervene.

***Editor's Note:** This study was funded by a grant from the Society for Human Resource Management. The interpretations, conclusions and recommendations are those of the authors and do not necessarily represent those of the Foundation.*

# Why Corporations Can't Lock the Rascals Out

**BANNING K. LARY**

*Banning K. Lary is executive director of Legal Development Resources, a research and education organization based in Austin, Tex.*

The problem of internal theft is big and getting bigger. This year alone, American businesses will lose upwards of $200 billion to thefts committed by employees. Fraud and embezzlement losses in financial institutions (banks, savings & loans, credit unions) have skyrocketed from $196 million in 1981 to $1.1 billion during 1986, according to the FBI, a 560 percent increase. When this loss is contrasted with losses from robberies, burglaries and larcenies during the same time period ($54 million in 1981 and $45 million in 1986), the enormity of the problem becomes crystal-clear: The thieves are not on the streets, they are working inside your company.

The Stanton Corp., an honesty testing firm in Charlotte, N.C., found in 1964 that of 25,000 prospective employees, 12 percent admitted they had stolen from a previous employer. In 1985, 21 years later, when asked "Have you ever stolen merchandise from a previous job?" an alarming 32 percent of more than 100,000 job applicants surveyed responded "Yes." The admitted value of the thefts ranged from $25 to $1500. But according to James Walls, senior vice president of Stanton: "If some-

one tells you they have stolen $100, we have found that you can safely multiply that figure by 10—they have actually stolen at least $1,000."

Employee theft is a far greater problem today than shoplifting, according to Judy L. Hoffmeister, senior in-store loss prevention agent with Ross Stores, a national clothing retailer. "Seven out of every 10 dollars we lose are not to thieves that come in off the street. Rather, [they are lost] to theft from inside the store."

## CORPORATE CRIME WAVE

A rule of thumb used by loss prevention analysts in the clothing industry is that 20 garments must be sold to generate enough profit to make up for the loss of one stolen garment. But employee theft of merchandise is only one way a company can lose. Indirect costs to inventory theft can add up to be a much larger total problem.

Is it stealing when an employee:
- ☐ Uses sick time when not sick?
- ☐ Gets paid for overtime not worked?
- ☐ Takes longer lunch and coffee breaks than authorized?
- ☐ Has a fellow employee punch his or her time card or punches a time card for a fellow employee?
- ☐ Comes in late to work or leaves early without approval?
- ☐ Does slow or sloppy work on purpose?

- ☐ Fakes injury to receive worker's compensation?
- ☐ Works while under the influence of drugs or alcohol?
- ☐ Takes care of personal business on company time?
- ☐ Actively helps another person remove company property or merchandise?
- ☐ Uses company copying machines or long-distance telephone for personal purposes?
- ☐ Appropriates stamps, pens or other supplies for personal use?
- ☐ Purposefully mistreats or breaks company property?
- ☐ Takes money from the petty cash drawer?
- ☐ Uses company vehicles or tools for own purposes?
- ☐ Purposefully damages merchandise so a cohort can purchase it at a discount?
- ☐ Underrings customer purchases and pockets the difference?
- ☐ Receives kickbacks from a supplier?

These activities, listed in *Theft by Employees* (Richard C. Hollinger & John P. Clark, Lexington Books), may seem petty, but all can be construed as illegal, unethical or irresponsible when perpetrated by an employee within the work environment. In all cases, losses tabulated from these activities are borne by the company and are translated on the bottom line into higher prices paid for goods, lower wages or business failures. The U.S. Chamber of Commerce estimates that 30 percent of all new business failures can be connected to some form of abuse by inside employees.

The problem is just as severe in financial institutions. Half the commercial bank failures in the last decade can be linked to some form of inside abuse, with the average bank fraud currently running about $120,000, according to the FBI.

## PROFILE OF THE WHITE-COLLAR BANDIT

A 1983 U.S. Department of Commerce study concluded that one-third of all employees steal from their companies. Other studies reveal that only 40 percent of the workforce is inherently honest, with 30 percent willing to steal and the remaining 30 percent capable of stealing given the right set of circumstances.

Minnesota sociologists Hollinger and Clark have conducted large-scale surveys to find out what proportion of employees had stolen on the job.

By industry, the results were:

| | |
|---|---|
| Hospital employees | 32.2 percent |
| Manufacturing employees | 26.2 percent |
| Retail store employees | 41.8 percent |

The studies also revealed that two-thirds of inside theft was by employees who had been on the job two years or less, and one-third by employees who had worked only six months or less. The young employee, age 16 to 22, was found to have committed 67 percent of all thefts.

Hollinger and Clark add that the highest levels of theft occur among young unmarried employees, and that job satisfaction plays a significant role. Satisfied employees are less likely to steal and the "high-theft" employee is one with a strong desire to achieve whose career aspirations are somehow blocked by the work environment. This can lead to frustration and then to stealing.

William Terris, Ph.D., chairman of London House, another honesty testing firm headquartered in Chicago, draws a distinction between the psychological profiles of the honest and dishonest employee. He says: "The honest person sees himself or herself as above all average and views the world as an honest, good place. Conversely, the employee who is prone to steal sees the world as a corrupt, dishonest place and himself as an average person in a dishonest world."

In an effort to locate a denominator common to inside thieves, Dr. Donald R. Cressey, cofounder of the Austin, Texas-based Institute for Financial Crime Prevention, analyzed thousands of criminal offenders, many of whom were confined inside prisons. He reduced his findings to three characteristics, all of which he claimed must be present in an individual before a theft would be committed. Cressey's employee theft formula is:

$$Motivation + Opportunity + Rationalization = Theft.$$

The motivation to steal comes from a real or perceived need for money, he postulated. Often, the need cannot be expressed because the money is needed for something illegal, immoral or otherwise unexplainable. Typical examples are drinking or drug habits, gambling debts, mistresses or other extravagances of lifestyle. Additional motivations could be the need to win approval from others who are also stealing from the company, or to "get even" with an employer for some real or imagined wrong. Even feeling challenged to "beat the system" can be a motivation to some individuals, Cressey says.

The opportunity can occur, according to Cressey, at the cash register or teller window, at the loading dock or the warehouse, on the sales floor or in the computer room—anywhere an employee has access to cash, inventory or merchandise.

But before an employee will steal, he or she will rationalize the behavior pattern to make it seem right, Cressey stresses. Rationalizations that employees might use to justify stealing from the company include:

☐ Feeling they are underpaid.
☐ Feeling the company "owes it to them."
☐ Considering it to be borrowing, or that they will pay it back later.
☐ Revenge—feeling they have been cheated by the company.

☐ Feeling that "everybody is doing it," so it must be alright.

Dr. W. Steve Albrecht, professor of accounting at Brigham Young University, uses a similar formula. He believes employee theft is caused by a combination of motive (usually stemming from personal financial pressures), opportunity (caused by poor accounting controls), and the personal integrity level of the employee. "Every person under enough financial pressure and with enough perceived opportunity will rationalize being dishonest in certain situations," Albrecht believes.

If the employee is under financial pressures but opportunities to steal are low, and the employee exhibits high integrity, no theft is likely to occur. But when severe financial pressures combine with high opportunity and low integrity, employee theft is much more likely, Albrecht says. The degree to which a business is at risk depends on the combination of these three factors.

## LOCKING THE DOOR

"By far the best way to prevent employee theft from occurring in your business is to screen out potential thieves before they are ever hired," says Joseph T. Wells, a former FBI special agent whose firm, Wells & Associates, investigates internal crime matters for *Fortune* 1000 companies. "Before a person is a trusted employee, the company should verify employment history and background. It is a lot easier to reject an applicant than to have to deal with him or her later as a disgruntled employee or someone who has stolen from the company."

And cheaper too. According to U.S. Department of Labor statistics, hiring an entry-level person and then firing him or her after three months costs $5,000 to $7,000. Mishiring a $20,000-per-year supervisor costs twice the annual salary. And mishiring a $100,000-per-year manager can cost the company $300,000. Losses include wasted salary, benefits, severance pay, headhunter fees, training costs and hiring time.

Personnel selection inventories (PSIs) available from London House, Reid, Stanton and others are designed to measure qualities including honesty, emotional stability, work habits and values, and whether or not an applicant is likely to steal on the job. Applicants can be classified as either low risk (no history of theft), borderline (some theft history), or high risk (history of repeated thefts). These profiles can form a powerful screening system to weed out the worst risks before they can get inside and poison the workforce.

In one London House study, 500 applicants for positions in a department store chain were given a PSI and hired without regard for their scores. When the PSI scores were later compared with employee terminations resulting from theft, the results were striking. Six months after being hired, of the 32 employees dismissed, 78 percent had failed the PSI and would have been rejected if the test had been used as a screening device.

In 1987 Arthur Young & Co.'s National Retail Group surveyed 115 retail companies responsible for a combined sales volume of $126 billion to find out where thefts are occurring and what is working in the area of prevention.

Stephanie Shern, who heads up the program, reports, "the retailers told us the most effective way to prevent theft is through training and awareness programs. Also, incentives and rewards for honest behavior helped promote company loyalty, which has been shown to further reduce insider theft."

According to London House's Bill Terris, people are not predisposed to steal from their family or friends. Getting employees involved in the company—both its successes and failures—creates a bond of identification between the employee and the company. Letting the employees in on the costs and ramifications of internal theft and soliciting their opinions on ways to help prevent it breaks down the erroneous concept of the "huge faceless corporation." Employees then begin to see the company differently, as an organization comprising fellow workers like them, and consequently they are less likely to steal.

Preventive video training is gaining in popularity among corporate trainers and security directors who realize the convenience and value of programs that hone in on a specific problem. "A lot of employees don't realize that they can get into real trouble by stealing from their companies," says Ted Hood of Western Merchandisers, based in Amarillo, Texas. "Showing them someone else whose life has been ruined by stealing is probably the most effective thing we've ever done to prevent internal theft."

Jim Walls of Stanton also believes that communicating with employees is essential. "When you ignore employees, they grow to believe the company doesn't care about them and they lose incentive. They then turn to other employees, often those with less virtue than management."

In many cases, these employees tend to be the ones who are actively engaged in stealing, rationalizing that their "faceless corporation" doesn't care about them.

This brings to light the value of an "open door" policy within a company. If supervisors and managers encourage communication and are attentive to the concerns of employees, employees will feel well cared for and will respect the company, its property and their own jobs.

## YOU TOO, BRUTUS?

Even though studies have shown that younger employees steal more than their seniors, potentially the most dangerous threat comes from older employees who have built trust through years on the job.

Kay Lemon, a Lincoln, Neb., bookkeeper, stole over $400,000 from a company where she had worked for eight years, according to court documents. A church-going grandmother, Lemon was in charge of both accounts payable and accounts receivable. Faced with personal financial pressures, she started writing checks to herself and disguised the disbursement by "piggybacking" it on a supplier's invoice. If her company owed an electrical distributor $40,000, she would write a $10,000 check to herself and enter a $50,000 disbursement in the books. When the statements came back from the bank, Lemon was there to intercept the checks and reconcile the accounts.

"Most of these crimes are deceptively simple," says Wells, who is also an Austin, Texas CPA, "and could have been prevented by a separation of accounting duties—custody over assets, recording of transactions, and reconciliation of accounts. Any time one person is responsible for two or more of these functions, you are leaving yourself open to trouble."

Inventory controls are similar to cash. If one person receives merchandise on the loading dock and is also responsible for off-loading deliveries, a company could be placing too much trust in a single employee. Employees are human beings susceptible to temptation, especially when confronted with the right set of circumstances.

Sometimes the physical layout of the firm makes theft easier. In one case, a manufacturer had trash dumpsters situated next to the loading dock. Instead of loading goods onto the truck, employees were dropping them into the dumpsters where they could be retrieved after office hours.

A valuable tool to help discover weaknesses in a physical layout that help to promote theft is a risk exposure inventory. These are questionnaires designed to collect data about the work environment, including ingress/egress, type of activity performed within an area, accessibility to tools, supplies or merchandise. After a risk exposure profile is drawn, potential theft problems can be spotted and corrected. The profile also correlates the type of employee who is best suited for the environment, and it separates candidates into low,

---

*Twenty garments must be sold to generate enough profit to make up for the loss of one stolen garment.*

borderline or high risk categories. This also helps security or management when making decisions on where to place employees.

### PROSECUTION AND HOT TIPS

With the cost, by some estimates, running as high as $33,000 to prosecute an incident of employee theft, some companies prefer simply to terminate the employee rather than bear the costs associated with prosecution. Other concerns, especially in the financial industry, about negative effects on the company image, unsympathetic juries and counter-lawsuits, make it easier to fire than prosecute. Unfortunately, this puts the criminal back on the street and into the job pool.

"There is no substitute for prosecution," says David Battle, a security consultant based in St. Louis. "In a lot of cases you have to create an atmosphere in the place of employment that will indicate to anyone who might have the notion to steal that if they are caught stealing, something will happen."

Corporate "hot tip" lines and reward programs that offer anonymity to the whistle-blower are proving more and more popular with employees concerned about stopping theft within their companies. At Marshall Field's & Co., a Chicago-based retailer with 14,000 employees, security personnel have apprehended nearly 500 persons guilty of inside theft since 1985. A $500 reward has been paid over 170 times to everyone from stock clerks to upper managers and trimmed inventory losses from 3.3 percent of sales in 1983 to 2.1 percent in 1986.

Another department store chain uses a special telephone line within the stores to alert employees to suspicious persons with a daily recording. If microwave ovens have been disappearing, the message mentions the items and any other known information about the suspected thieves. Employees who call in with a tip know that a reward is forthcoming, and the company pays promptly—usually within three days.

"When companies do not reward people for honest conscientious behavior, they are writing their own prescription for disaster," says Terris of London House. "The single most important person in an organization is the one at the top. The example set at the top cannot help but filter down through the ranks to every employee. Ethics start at the top."

As 'an ounce of prevention is worth a pound of cure,' more and more companies are realizing that locking doors and prosecuting employees is not enough. A company must establish clear guidelines about what is stealing and what is not. Is it okay to take paper clips and pencils but not envelopes? If a company manager or officer is seen loading steaks into his car, the freezer clerk is going to think it is all right to do it, also.

Everybody inherently knows what is right or wrong, but pressures—financial, personal, peer and other—often get in the way and cause people to steal. Part of the solution may be prosecution, but part of it is also setting an example and removing the barriers to good behavior.

# Silent Saboteurs

Employees are sabotaging their employers every day to get even for
perceived injustices or inequities.

## FRANK J. NAVRAN

*Frank J. Navran is president of Navran Associates in Atlanta,
GA. For more information on developing ethically congruent
leadership, call Navran Associates at (800) 635-9540, and ask
for the PACE program description.*

A CERTAIN CONSULTANT *was called into a lumber company.
Profits were slipping and management
couldn't figure out what was causing it. All
other performance measures were stable or
increasing. The consultant talked with
many employees and observed many things
about this company, including the fact that
working conditions were austere and that
the dominant leadership style was autocrat-
ic, almost abusive.*

*One day, the consultant asked an employ-
ee how it was that, given the difficult working conditions and harsh leadership style,
there wasn't more absenteeism, poor production or other symptoms of an organization
that was "hard" on its workers.*

*The employee answered, "Oh that's easy.
When we get frustrated or angry we just feed
the hog." Seeing the puzzled look on the consultant's face, the employee explained that
the "hog" was the big mechanical wood chip-
per at the back of the plant. All unusable
scrap was fed to the hog to make the wood
chips that go into particle board, one of the
least profitable products the company manufactured. "When we get upset," he explained,
"we take finished lumber and feed the hog."*

*The consultant was still puzzled. That
explained the slipping profits but not the
absence of the typical symptoms of an organization in distress. "I still don't see why
people don't just call in sick to avoid coming
to work." The employee explained. "We don't
really want to miss work. We all have hog
quotas. If we aren't here to feed the hog we are
fined $20. That money goes into the party
kitty and pays for our quarterly family picnic."*

People in every organization at all levels
"feed the hog," finding their own unique
way of punishing their employers for perceived wrongs. Feeding the hog is what
people do to get even, and getting even is
one of the two most powerful drivers
that cause good people to do bad things.
It is how people strike back when they
believe the organization is being unfair.

### Silent Saboteurs

Feeding the hog may sound funny, but
it is far from funny. Neither the actions
of the organization which stimulate that
degree of anger within an employee, nor
the unethical retaliations of the employees are at all funny.

We prefer to call the intentional, counterproductive behaviors of employees by
another name: *Silent Saboteurs. Silent*, because nobody talks about them and *Saboteurs*, because they undermine your business plans, creating failures, eating at your
effectiveness from the inside like a cancer.

People become Silent Saboteurs for
two reasons: 1) retaliation (when employees feel that they are being mistreated
and are getting even); and 2) self-preservation (where employees are attempting
to meet the perceived expectations or
requirements for success). Using the
word Saboteurs as a mnemonic, we can
look at a number of common practices
people use to meet requirements or
expectations for success at very high
costs to their employers.

**S***capegoating:* blaming failure on someone or something else.

**A***bdicating:* not accepting responsibility
for decision making.

**B***udgeteering:* manipulating budgets
and expenses.

**O***verpromising:* making commitments
one intends to ignore.

**T***urf guarding:* hoarding resources
and/or control.

**E***mpire building:* accumulating power
and control.

**U***nderachieving:* doing the minimum
needed to get by.

**R***isk avoiding:* taking the safe position
even when it is wrong.

**S***harp penciling:* making results look
better than they are.

Regardless of the form they take, Silent
Saboteurs are little more than sophisticated forms of lying, cheating and stealing.
And the costs are staggering. When people become Silent Saboteurs, there are
three costs: 1) direct tangible losses like
theft, fraud and destruction of company
property; 2) indirect tangible losses measured in terms of work load, productivity, product quality, and profitability; and
3) intangible losses of motivation, creativity and commitment, customer satisfaction and stress on employees and supervisors. According to a recent ABC News

## 2. EMPLOYEES AND THE WORKPLACE: Crime

Special, 1.86 percent of the Gross National Product goes to direct tangible losses like lying, cheating and stealing. That averages out to about $700 per employee per year. Dollar estimates range up to $5,000 per employee per year when you add in the costs associated with indirect tangible and intangible losses.

You may already know how people in your organization strike back. You may know how they protect themselves. If you came up through the ranks, you may know of the Silent Saboteurs. And, like many others, you may believe that there is nothing you can do about them. The good news is that you can do something about them. But before you can fix them, you have to find them.

### Finding Them

How can you find your Silent Saboteurs? How can you uncover the counter-productive behaviors that are silently undermining operational effectiveness?

Knowing to look for them is half the battle. But beware. It is easy to be lulled into thinking that everything is going well if the measurement systems are "in the green." The search requires that you use a variety of resources. We use three complimentary techniques: 1) examine the formal systems (ethics audit); 2) examine informal systems (review of the ethical climate); and 3) use diagnostic instruments (questionnaires).

All three techniques presume that human behavior is purposeful. Feeding the hog and the Silent Saboteurs are not random acts. If employees are being counterproductive, then there must be some perceived value in that behavior. To take action based on only one of these techniques is the organizational equivalent of prescribing a medical procedure without adequately diagnosing the patient. And we believe that *prescription without diagnosis is malpractice.*

What is needed is an integrated analysis applied to multiple functions and levels using internal resources with only minimal reliance on outsiders. To assume that the perceptions of a given function or level reflect the larger organization would risk missing the differences in perceptions across sub-populations.

The motivations behind Silent Saboteurs are forms of ethical conflict — the condition where the values of the organization, the values of the employees and the perceived criteria for success (as manifest in the formal and informal systems) are misaligned. That misalignment

results in people believing they must protect themselves from the organization, and it gives them justification to strike back. Ethical congruence is when values, behaviors and perceptions are aligned.

When we talk about lying, cheating and stealing, we are discussing the direct tangible symptoms of ethical conflict. When we talk about finding and fixing ethical conflict, we are discussing ways to increase ethical congruence. We also reduce indirect tangible and intangible costs because increasing ethical congruence reduces the motivation for counterproductive or retaliatory behavior.

### Fixing the Problem

Having completed an integrated analysis, we can now take a few steps to increase ethical congruence; however, these steps are not simple. We will never totally eliminate ethical conflict. Our best hope is to drastically reduce that conflict and increase congruence. Increased ethical congruence allows for increased employee commitment to organizational values and goals, resulting in increased ethical and organizational effectiveness.

We have developed a six-step action plan — the ABCs of ethical congruence.

*A - Admit it.* The diagnostic process uncovers the who, what, where, when and why of the Silent Saboteurs. Many leaders, when confronted with these data, experience the natural first reaction of denial. Before progress can be made, the leaders involved must admit that the data might be accurate, that they face ethical conflicts, that Silent Saboteurs are at work, and that your actions might be interpreted as unfair or inconsistent. Leaders must also recognize the risks inherent in increasing ethical effectiveness. Typically, any given leader has a vested interest in the status quo. Change threatens that stasis and represents a potential threat to one's power and position.

*B - Build ethical congruence.* While you

can take steps to build a higher level of ethical congruence, you must realize that these steps are not a one time fix. You don't increase ethical congruence with a single decision or action. The increases require change from past patterns, and those changes must be enduring.

*C - Communicate your values.* People act on what they believe. They can better understand your values if you make the effort to clarify what you want and expect, what is required for them to be successful, and the motives and intentions behind your decisions. People are more confident in your decisions and actions if they understand why you require them. Without your explanation, they will assume motives and values that may be less accurate and benevolent. And when people perceive hostile or conflicting motives, they revert back to Silent Saboteurs.

*D - Develop ethically congruent systems.* People not only need to hear you state your needs and requirements, they also need to see congruence between what you demand and how the formal systems support, monitor, measure and reward both compliance and non-compliance with those requirements. You must act in ways that are consistent with your rhetoric. Your words must match the message contained in the formal policies, procedures and practices that govern how work is performed and how employees are treated.

*E - Empower employees to excel.* Silent Saboteurs clearly demonstrate that employees are empowered. They have the power to cause the organization to fail through both retaliatory and defensive behaviors. Your job is to turn that empowerment toward increasing effectiveness. When people feel that they have some degree of control over their work, they are less inclined to strike back and less likely to misunderstand your motives. Empowerment does not mean giving up control. It means sharing information and helping employees develop increased commitment to organizational values and goals through increasing ethical effectiveness.

*F - Focus on ethically congruent leadership practices.* These are the decisions and actions which increase employee commitment to and trust in the organization. When leader behaviors are consistent with the organization's stated values (and the priorities implied by the formal systems) employee confidence increases. People know that the organization is serious about what it claims to believe in.

When organizational values are consistent with the individual's own beliefs, those values are perceived as being worthy of support, and employee commitment to those values and goals go up.

### Ethically Congruent Leadership

This factor is one of the most powerful forces for increasing ethical effectiveness. At the individual level, the question people have about their leaders is, *Can I trust you?* Ethical congruence is ultimately a matter of building individual trust. There are many ways a leader can build trust. Perhaps the simplest is keeping promises, both implied and explicit. Trust is the residue of promises fulfilled. At the organizational level, trust also means that the leaders' actions are consistent with the organization's values as well as the leaders' personal values. Ethically congruent leadership at the organizational level requires leaders to ethically apply the systems, policies and procedures of the organization. It presupposes knowledge of and respect for each employee's values.

Three preconditions exist for ethically congruent leadership: 1) a clear statement of operational values; 2) an ethics strategy; and 3) ethics policies, practices and procedures. If you do not have a clear statement of operational values, create one and communicate it. If you do not have an overall strategy for increasing the level of ethical and operational effectiveness, develop and implement one. If you do not have policies, practices and procedures that define the ethical conduct of business, then write them and train your people how to apply them.

If we, as leaders, are to stop people from silently sabotaging the organization, then we must understand why they feel motivated to seek retaliation or self-protection. What value or benefit do they derive from the behavior? We must discover the *What's In It For Me* behind the behavior and remove it. Rather than punishing the employee, consider removing the motivation behind the "punishable" behavior. Human behavior is not simple, but neither is it random. People act in ways that are productive according to some definition, even when that action is counterproductive from their employer's point of view.

Silent Saboteurs are not new. People have been silently and creatively beating the system since the first system was implemented. Unfortunately, these behaviors have either been ignored or misunderstood. Leaders have believed that there is nothing that can be done. Many have thought that it is human nature for people to resent having to work and those for whom they have to work. Elaborate controls have been installed to protect the organization from the unethical or uncommitted employee. We have measured and checked upon workers, always suspicious that they were beating the system. We made the systems tighter and tighter, squeezing out opportunities for employees to shirk their duty to the organization. We tried to make the systems foolproof. We lost sight of the intelligence and creativity our employees bring to work. We underestimated them and paid the price.

The answer is not in trying to make the systems foolproof. We have tried that for years and failed because the fools are smart enough to beat any system we can create. The answer lies in not treating our employees like fools. Take away the reasons for lying, cheating and stealing. Make the Silent Saboteurs an anachronism, and your organization will flourish. Find out what your employees are angry about. Identify which organizational requirements they view as conflicting with their personal values. Stimulate the necessary changes to achieve increased ethical congruence.

Ethical conflict is not the tell-tale sign of an unethical company. Ethical conflict occurs in ethical companies that do not fully appreciate its origins or impact in the workplace. It is the legacy of leaders who believe that such conflict is inevitable. It is symptomatic of organizations that fail to take advantage of the full set of human potential for which they are already paying. Ethical conflict represents perhaps our greatest opportunity to increase organizational effectiveness by doing something positive for (and with) employees.

We can achieve remarkable increases in productivity, quality and customer satisfaction when our employees are committed to organizational goals and objectives. And we can do that by reducing the ethical conflict they experience at work.

The people who chose to work for your organization do not awaken each morning looking forward to another day of internal turmoil and ethical conflict. They do not relish the struggle between their personal values and the pressures to succeed on the job. They are not thinking joyously of how they will beat the system yet another time. With few exceptions they are good people anxiously awaiting the chance to commit to the values and goals of an organization that values, respects and trusts them. An organization that is ethically congruent. An organization where there is no need for any person to resort to the Silent Saboteurs.

I challenge you to make that your organization.

# Stopping Sexual Harassment Before it Begins

**ROBERT K. McCALLA**

*Robert K. McCalla, a senior partner in the law firm McCalla, Thompson, Pyburn & Ridley in New Orleans, La., specializes in representing management in legal matters concerning employment and labor relations. He also serves as chairman of the Employment Law Committee of the 17,000-member Defense Research Institute, one of the largest associations of civil defense trial lawyers.*

Sexual harassment lawsuits have catapulted management's handling of harassment complaints into a position of considerable importance.

Today more than ever before, male and female employees work, travel, eat and socialize together. Thus, the pin-up pictures and obscene language that thrived in previously all-male domains must give way to the sensitivities of female coworkers. Managers must ask themselves this: Are sexual jokes, invitations for drinks after work or casual touching unwelcome or unlawful? And when an unwelcome incident occurs, managers and supervisors must know what to do to try to avoid legal consequences. The cases that follow illustrate how sexual harassment and sexual harassment lawsuits can be dealt with—and better yet, prevented.

□ *Dornhecker vs. Malibu Grand Prix Corp.* Three days after Marvelle Dornhecker took a job with Malibu, she and several coworkers, including outside consultant Robert Rockefeller, went on an out-of-town business trip.

During the first two days of the trip, Rockefeller put his hands on Dornhecker's hips in an airport ticket line and dropped his pants in front of the passengers while waiting to board the plane. Then he touched Dornhecker's breasts. Finally, at a business dinner, Rockefeller put his stockinged feet on a cocktail table in front of Dornhecker and "playfully choked" her when she complained.

Dornhecker ran to the ladies room and broke into tears. Dornhecker's female supervisor, who had not witnessed the choking incident, ran in to console her and then reported Rockefeller's conduct to the company president. The next morning, the president met with Dornhecker and told her she would not have to work with Rockefeller after the trip ended (it was to last another day and a half). In fact,

Rockefeller did not go to any of the remaining meetings which Dornhecker was scheduled to attend, and his contract with Malibu was not renewed.

However, Dornhecker did not wait for the company president to straighten matters out. Instead, she flew home after their meeting, leaving only a brief explanatory note for her supervisor, and resigned from the company. She then filed a sexual harassment suit, contending that she was forced to quit because the company was not sufficiently responsive to her complaints.

The court found that under the circumstances the company's actions were timely and effective. Moreover, it concluded that Dornhecker acted unreasonably in leaving town without any notice and before the president had a chance to remedy the situation.

Management's swift reaction in this case protected it in court. Other firms have behaved less prudently. The following cases demonstrate that an employer can suffer liability in two ways: by failing to take reasonable steps to prevent harassment or by failing to take reasonable steps to remedy it.

□ *Paroline vs. Unisys Corporation.* Elizabeth Paroline found herself stuck at the office without a car during a severe snowstorm. She accepted a ride home with her supervisor. En route to Paroline's apartment, the supervisor made sexually suggestive remarks. He kissed her and repeatedly tried to hold her hand during the drive. At the apartment, the supervisor insisted on coming in. He then grabbed Paroline and began kissing her, rubbing his hands up and down her back, and ignored her demands that he stop. Eventually, she persuaded him to leave.

Paroline reported the episode to her office manager and the company launched a formal investigation. Company officials warned the supervisor that any future offense would constitute grounds for immediate termination. The company also required him to seek counseling and limited his contact with female employees to situations involving official business.

Paroline learned, however, that she was not the first woman at the company to complain of harassment by this supervisor. He had been warned in the past.

Paroline resigned and filed suit against the company. She argued that the supervisor's prior conduct should have alerted the company to the likelihood that he would also try to harass her.

The court agreed, stating it would impute liability to an employer who anticipated—or should have anticipated—that a female employee would become a victim of sexual harassment, yet failed to take action reasonably calculated to prevent such harassment. The company knew the supervisor had previously harassed employees. Disciplining him after the fact was not enough to insulate the company from liability.

□ *Bennett vs. Corroon and Black Corp.* Bernice Bennett resigned from Corroon and Black after learning that obscene cartoons displayed in the men's room showed her engaged in sexual activities. The cartoons were labeled with her name. Other cartoons depicted male employees engaged in sexual activities. The cartoons of Bennett had been there about a week; the CEO had seen the cartoons but did not take any action to remove them until he learned that Bennett had quit.

Bennett sued, stating that "the realization that these cartoons had been visible to any male co-employee or client using the facility was extremely embarrassing and upsetting."

The parent company reacted by firing the CEO. The company paid Bennett's psychiatric counseling bills after the incident, and kept her on payroll until she began a new job. The company also asked her repeatedly to return to her job at Corroon and Black but she refused.

The court found in favor of the company and this was supported in appeals. But whereas the appellate court agreed that the company had provided reasonable relief, it disagreed sharply with most of the lower court's reasoning. It disagreed with the lower court's conclusion that the parent company should not be held liable because it took rapid remedial action by firing the CEO. The appellate court's view was that the company could be held liable for the CEO's failure to take prompt action after he had seen the offensive cartoons.

It also disagreed with the lower court's view that because there were cartoons of both men and women engaged in sexual activities, "the alleged harassment was not based upon the sex of the plaintiff."

The appeals court stated: "Any reasonable person would have to regard these cartoons as highly offensive to a woman who seeks to deal with her fellow employees and clients with professional dignity and without the barrier of sexual differentiation and abuse."

There is no question that preventive measures should have been in place at Corroon and Black to discourage this type of conduct in the first place. And the CEO or any other manager should have acted promptly to remove the drawings as soon as he saw or heard of them.

## DO THE RIGHT THING

The Equal Employment Opportunity Commission (EEOC) released its Policy Guidance on Current Issues of Sexual Harassment in March 1990, advising managers how to avoid lawsuits:

□ *Anti-harassment policies.* The most important thing is to adopt a policy against sexual harassment. Include procedures for employees who feel they have been harassed to come forward and develop a procedure for resolving their complaints.

Design the complaints procedure to encourage victims to come forward. Do not require a victim to complain first to the offending supervisor. It is critical to ensure confidentiality as much as possible and provide effective remedies, including protection of victims and witnesses from retaliation for speaking out.

Other steps include affirmatively raising the subject of harassment, expressing strong disapproval, developing appropriate sanctions, informing employees of their legal right to raise the issue of harassment under Title VII of the Civil Rights Act of 1964, and developing methods to sensitize all concerned. The following is a suggested policy:

*Sexual harassment of employees or applicants for employment will not be tolerated.*

*A knee-jerk decision to fire an alleged harasser before the facts are clear can lead to a claim of wrongful termination or defamation.*

*Any employee who feels that he or she is a victim of sexual harassment by a supervisor, coworker, or customer should bring the matter to the immediate attention of (the person's supervisor or a designated person in the personnel department). An employee who is uncomfortable for any reason about bringing the matter to the attention of his or her supervisor should report the matter to (the designated person in the personnel department).*

*Complaints of sexual harassment will receive prompt attention and be handled in a confidential manner to the extent possible. Prompt disciplinary action will be taken against persons who engage in sexual harassment.*

Of course, you need to tailor the policy to your company. But, at a minimum, it should set out in strong terms that the company prohibits sexual harassment and must describe what procedures the employee should follow to complain about harassment to company officials other than his or her immediate supervisor.

Next, communicate the policy to all supervisors and employees. Include the policy in the employee handbook, explain the policy at employee meetings and post it on bulletin boards. Videotapes are available to help educate employees and supervisors.

☐ *Handling complaints.* In handling sexual harassment complaints, you must guard against subsequent litigation by the complaining employee and by the subject of the complaint: First, the EEOC guidelines state you must investigate the complaint immediately and thoroughly.

Include in the investigation an interview of the complaining party by someone experienced in employee investigations. Ask the employee to sign a written statement of the facts. Since credibility is often an issue in these cases, it is advisable for two company representatives to attend all interviews.

Consider interviewing any witnesses to the alleged harassment. A word of caution here: Be very careful about what you reveal to coworkers about the investigation. For example, if you tell someone an explicit detail of the complaining party's charges, you may expose yourself to a subsequent claim by the accused on the grounds of libel or intentional infliction of emotional distress. This need for confidentiality applies throughout the investigation.

Second, the EEOC guidelines say to take immediate corrective action, "by doing whatever is necessary to end the harassment, make the victim whole by restoring lost employment benefits or opportunities, and prevent the misconduct from recurring. Disciplinary action against the offending supervisor or employee, ranging from reprimand to discharge, may be necessary....The employer should make follow-up inquiries to ensure that harassment has not resumed and the victim has not suffered retaliation."

If the investigation is inconclusive, you may nevertheless want to remind the supervisor of the company's policy on sexual harassment, and offer the complaining employee a transfer to another area or supervisor. But remember, a knee-jerk decision to discharge an alleged harasser before the facts are clear can lead to a claim of wrongful termination or defamation.

In an era in which men and women work closely together, claims of sexual harassment are more prevalent. A strong anti-harassment policy, supported by effective and well-planned preventive and/or corrective action, will go a long way to insulate your company from liability.

# DEALING WITH SEXUAL HARASSMENT

Smart companies are educating employees about what it is—not always an easy call—investigating allegations fast, protecting victims, and penalizing offenders.

*Alan Deutschman*

**W**HO COULD WATCH the controversy surrounding Clarence Thomas and Anita Hill without wondering how a case alleging sexual harassment might be handled in his or her own office? How to respond if you are preyed upon, or if you, as a manager, are charged to investigate an allegation? Says Labor Secretary Lynn Martin: "If any good comes from the Thomas situation, it will only be a wider discussion of the issue of harassment." That issue, always sensitive, has become increasingly subtle and confusing as legal definitions of harassment expand from obvious barbarities to encompass acts that over time create a "hostile work environment."

Business stands on the front line in the battle against harassment, pushed there by judicial decisions in the 1980s that hold employers financially liable for workers' transgressions unless the company actively strives to prevent offenses and responds effectively when they occur. As a result, corporations are getting tough about the subject: crafting intensive seminars for employees, such as those that take place at Honeywell and Corning; establishing 24-hour hotlines and providing security for victims fearful of reprisals, as Du Pont does; and initiating and completing inquiries swiftly, as AT&T strives to do.

The results? No big gains so far—it may be early, and there are precious few data from the past to compare with. But the experience of large organizations at work on change offers valuable lessons for any company or concerned employee.

While even a single case of harassment is one too many, the extent of the problem may be overblown, particularly in assertions that 75% or 90% of women have been victimized. The most authoritative data on the pervasiveness of harassment in its various guises come from the U.S. Merit Systems Protection Board, a federal agency. In 1980 it polled 20,000 federal employees about the

REPORTER ASSOCIATE *Sara Hammes*

incidence of sexual harassment in government offices. It repeated the survey in 1987, asking the same questions of another 8,500 government workers. The results of both polls were remarkably similar: 1% of female respondents claimed to be victims of actual or attempted rape or assault; 6% reported pressure for sexual favors.

Only a few incidents involved a boss demanding a quid pro quo from a subordinate—have sex with me if you want that promotion or want to keep your job. Most incidents occurred between peers or colleagues. In these cases job security isn't at stake, but the work environment can become abusive. Offensive conduct, according to the women polled, took the form of re-

marks (cited by 35% of women), suggestive looks (28%), touching (26%), pressure for dates (15%), and unwanted love letters and calls (12%). Men suffered all the same kinds of harassment, but the incidence was about a third that of women. Men were far less apt to talk about it or report it to supervisors.

Merit Systems found that the most likely victims—female or male—were single or divorced. Women were at above-average risk if they had college educations or graduate degrees; men, if they worked in clerical jobs. The risk was also higher for workers in places where the vast majority of their co-workers were of the opposite sex.

Harassment isn't just a matter of one employee's victimizing another. Clients

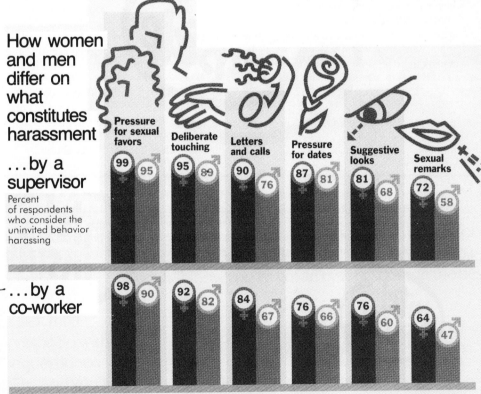

How women and men differ on what constitutes harassment

...by a supervisor

Percent of respondents who consider the uninvited behavior harassing

| | Pressure for sexual favors | Deliberate touching | Letters and calls | Pressure for dates | Suggestive looks | Sexual remarks |
|---|---|---|---|---|---|---|
| ♀ | 99 | 95 | 90 | 87 | 81 | 72 |
| ♂ | 95 | 89 | 76 | 81 | 68 | 58 |

...by a co-worker

| | Pressure for sexual favors | Deliberate touching | Letters and calls | Pressure for dates | Suggestive looks | Sexual remarks |
|---|---|---|---|---|---|---|
| ♀ | 98 | 92 | 84 | 76 | 76 | 64 |
| ♂ | 90 | 82 | 67 | 66 | 60 | 47 |

FORTUNE CHART / SOURCE: U.S. MERIT SYSTEMS PROTECTION BOARD, 1987

and customers can also use the power of their position—go along or I'll give the sale to somebody else—as a license for licentiousness, especially in such fields as law, consulting, and advertising. In a 1989 *National Law Journal* survey of 900 female attorneys, 10% said that clients exerted unwanted pressure for dates, 9% complained of touching, cornering, or pinching, and 4% cited pressure for sex, sometimes as a prerequisite for getting the client's business.

So what should a company do to keep its employees—and itself—safe? Educating employees is vital but not easy, because there is considerable uncertainty and disagreement about what harassment is (see table). Legal doctrine has evolved fitfully since the landmark 1986 Supreme Court decision *Meritor Savings Bank v. Vinson.* That case expanded the definition of harassment to include verbal or physical conduct that creates an intimidating, hostile, or offensive work environment or unreasonably interferes with an employee's job performance.

Unfortunately, men and women harbor different notions of what's intimidating, hostile, or offensive. A survey conducted in 1981 by sociologist Barbara Gutek of 1,200 people in Los Angeles County found that 67% of the men said they would feel flattered if a colleague of the opposite sex propositioned them, while 63% of women would be offended. Another survey by *Redbook* magazine and *Harvard Business Review* indicated that 24% of the women believed that a man giving a female worker a visual once-over was harassment, while only 8% of men thought so.

The best corporate practice calls for companies to create and publicize a forceful policy against sexual harassment. In 1989, Honeywell clarified its once obscure and legalistic harassment statement by distributing handbooks in plain English to every employee and putting up posters in conspicuous places. As a result the number of reported incidents has increased significantly, a good sign suggesting that more victims are seeking help.

Corporate education programs typically start out by sensitizing employees to the issue of harassment and then use role playing or other techniques to rehearse tactics to counter it. Du Pont's efforts are a worthy model. In 1988 the company began offering its employees a four-hour workshop on harassment called "A Matter of Respect." So far 65,000 workers have gone through it. Explains Dar Di Sabatino, a director of the workshop: "We were hearing about subtle situations of harassment. The individuals didn't know what they could do about it or if they should do anything about it." Each workshop is led by a specially trained man and woman; these teams are recruited from all areas of the company, not just from human relations. Small groups—always a balanced mix of men and women—watch videos portraying incidents that can be from real life, then discuss appropriate responses.

THE SIMPLEST and most effective way to put an end to harassment in most instances is to ask or tell the person to stop. This just-say-knock-it-off tactic worked for 61% of the women who tried it, according to the Merit Systems survey. Telling other colleagues, or simply threatening to do so, proved the second-best response, effective 55% of the time. Pretending to ignore the offensive behavior—a common ploy—usually doesn't work at all.

When employees can't resolve the situation on their own, or feel unsure about what to do, employers should make it easy and safe for them to seek help. Since 1985, Du Pont has run a unique 24-hour hotline that offers advice on personal security and sexual harassment. Callers need not identify themselves, calling does not constitute bringing charges, and confidentiality is assured. "The hotline is a real source of comfort," says Di Sabatino. "It gives people direction and helps them think the issues through before they take any action."

If a victim of or witness to harassment lodges an official complaint, there must be an immediate response. At Du Pont, the employee's supervisor usually handles the matter, but if he or she is the accused, or the employee feels uncomfortable talking to the supervisor, a personnel specialist can do the job. Sometimes a full-fledged investigation may be necessary. Alas, fact finding is often difficult or impossible, since there may not be any witnesses or physical evidence of harassment. Paula Winkler, who looks into charges for AT&T, which, like Du Pont, has a policy of immediate investigation, observes that another problem is proving the sexual attention was unwanted. "One of the first questions we ask the victim," she says, "is, 'Did you tell the person you didn't like it, and how many times?'"

Quick action is essential. In the early 1980s the federal government took an average of 482 days to resolve a harassment complaint filed by one of its employees. Not surprisingly, many victims said they lacked confidence in the system and didn't enlist its aid. Winkler says AT&T strives to complete its inquiries in three to 20 days. Even that period can seem nerve-rackingly long: Du Pont sometimes engages security guards to prevent retaliation against complainants during investigations.

If allegations are proved, companies must find an appropriate response—from warnings to reassignment to termination of the offender. Du Pont automatically reassigns the harasser unless the victim specifically requests a transfer.

Occasionally the accuser is the guilty party. Winkler estimates that some 5% of allegations at AT&T prove false. They are commonly the work of employees taking revenge against a boss—often following a disappointing performance review—or conniving to switch departments. AT&T suggests that these people go through counseling, and some companies subject them to penalties, such as demotion.

A final, and timely, word of warning: Sexual harassment tends to be less common in stable companies where employees feel some loyalty to the corporation and to one another. They realize they must treat everyone with respect and sensitivity, if only because they are all going to be working together a long time. One ugly consequence of restructuring and recession is that they may jeopardize that kind of stability, creating work environments more conducive to harassment.

# Companies Try a Variety of Approaches To Halt Sexual Harassment on the Job

## Joann S. Lublin

*Staff Reporter of* The Wall Street Journal

U.S. employers say they want to stamp out sexual harassment on the job, but they're struggling over how best to do it.

Many large companies have embraced policies denouncing sexual harassment and created training and internal grievance procedures. Critics, though, contend that most in-house programs lack real teeth. Few employers "fire the people who are good producers," contends Anne Vladeck, a sex-bias attorney in New York.

The sexual-harassment charges against Supreme Court nominee Clarence Thomas will undoubtedly heighten corporate America's policing of the explosive issue. "It raises attention to another level," says Barbara Jerich, **Honeywell** Inc.'s director of work-force diversity. Personnel officials "will dust off their books and say 'What should we do [differently]?'"

Honeywell, **Corning** Inc., **Du Pont** Co. and some other big concerns have beefed up their anti-harassment programs in recent years. In part, they were reacting to court rulings, which have broadened the definition of sexual harassment beyond job-related abuse to cover a "hostile" work environment—everything from love letters to pornographic pinups.

Last year, Honeywell revamped employees' training and replaced a vague policy manual with a detailed handbook. Possible "no-nos" spelled out in the handbook include catcalls, sexual jokes and staring. Nearly three-quarters of Du Pont's 90,000 U.S. staffers

have taken harassment-prevention training dubbed "A Matter of Respect" since the program started in 1988, and sexual-harassment suits involving the company have fallen off.

Corning is testing its first workshop devoted solely to the issue. "People who feel harassed in the workplace aren't productive employees," says Thomas McCullough, a human-resources manager. "It is a business issue for us."

**American Telephone & Telegraph** Co.'s efforts to combat sexual harassment aren't as far-reaching—and thus better illustrate what's happening at a lot of major corporations. The company's policy, discussed with employees annually, goes beyond barring hiring, firing or promotion decisions based on demands for sexual favors. AT&T warns its 279,000 U.S. staffers that they can be fired for repeated "unwelcome sexual flirtations," using sexually degrading words to describe someone or displaying "sexually suggestive" pictures or objects at work.

But the company no longer offers employees separate training about sexual harassment, as occurred in the late 1980s. Harassment is now among several topics covered in voluntary classes about workplace diversity. "We thought it would have more impact" this way, says Burke Stinson, an AT&T spokesman.

Employees can lodge their sexual-harassment complaints with a personnel officer and bypass their supervisors, who are often the alleged culprits. The company tries to assign both a man and a woman to investigate

charges involving opposite sexes. Both of these approaches win kudos from outside experts.

Men and women tend to see sexual harassment very differently—especially when it involves an offensive work environment, AT&T's most common complaint. For instance, sexually explicit language often doesn't offend men. But such talk "could give [a woman] 'the uh-oh' feeling," says Paula Winkler, an AT&T affirmative-action counselor who handles harassment complaints. "I have seen that happen" during investigations, she adds.

On the other hand, male counselors occasionally urge her "to look at this from the male point of view," Ms. Winkler says. They'll suggest "maybe there wasn't proper communication" because a complaining employee never clearly stated that she felt offended by sexual remarks.

"There's a lot of subtlety in what goes on with this," she says. It "can be very, very difficult" to decide whether someone is guilty of sexual harassment. At times, Ms. Winkler adds, no one witnessed the offensive behavior, but "there's that feeling in your heart" that harassment happened.

AT&T imposes penalties—from a mild reprimand to a transfer or dismissal—for infractions that might strike some men as trivial. Among them: demeaning comments about a woman's pregnancy or imminent menstrual period; a sign on a man's desk that reads, "beyond bitch"; and obscene messages on answering machines.

It's difficult to measure whether such efforts are making any difference

# How the Courts Define Harassment

By Arthur S. Hayes
*Staff Reporter of* The Wall Street Journal

Federal and state courts have ruled that sexual harassment covers conduct ranging from blatant grabbing and touching to subtle hints and suggestions. The U.S. Supreme Court ruled five years ago that a hostile environment exists when these actions unreasonably interfere with an employee's performance or create an intimidating work environment. Judges have recognized the following allegations as grounds for suits.

## Unwelcome Sexual Advances

An employee who is repeatedly propositioned by a supervisor or co-worker trying to establish an intimate relationship may sue for sexual harassment. The sexual advances can be made at the office or outside. A federal appeals court in California recently overturned a lower court and reinstated a suit filed by a female Internal Revenue Service employee against a co-worker. He had asked her for dates and written saccharine love letters but had not overtly threatened her. The case is pending.

## Coercion

In these cases, an employee alleges that a supervisor asked for a date or sexual favor with the stated or unstated understanding that a favor will be bestowed or a reprisal made. One federal court in Michigan found sexual harassment where a boss repeatedly asked a female employee to "do something nice." In one unusual case, a federal court in Rhode Island ruled that two male employees forced to engage in sexual activities with the boss's female secretary or lose their jobs were victims of sexual harassment.

## Favoritism

A company that allows intimate relationships between its executives and employees may be vulnerable to charges of creating a sexually hostile work environment. Courts have ruled that an employer is liable when employees who submit to sexual favors are rewarded while others who refuse are denied promotions or benefits. One federal court ruled that a female employee who wasn't asked for sexual favors while others were was a victim of sexual harassment.

## Indirect Harassment

A California state court decided that an employee who witnessed sexual harassment on the job could sue her employer even if the plaintiff wasn't a victim. In this case a nurse complained that a doctor grabbed other nurses in full view of her, causing an environment of sexual harassment.

## Physical Conduct

A female employee doesn't have to be touched to be harassed. Courts have ruled that unseemly gestures may constitute harassment and create a hostile work environment.

## Visual Harassment

Courts have ruled that graffiti written on men's bathroom walls about a female employee and pervasive displays of nude or pornographic pictures constituted sexual harassment.

---

in curbing sexual harassment at a company whose work force is 47% female. Officials decline to disclose both the number of internal complaints and the number of offenders punished.

The Communications Workers of America, a union representing about 100,000 AT&T workers, takes a dim view of the internal-grievance process. Union officers encourage sexually harassed members to take their complaints to outside agencies, such as the Equal Employment Opportunity Commission. The internal process "is run by management" and lacks objectivity, argues James Irvine, a CWA vice president who is the union's chief negotiator with AT&T. "I don't feel particularly safe with the fox guarding the chicken coop."

Unlike Du Pont, AT&T has yet to see any drop in sexual-harassment litigation. Staff members have sued AT&T about two dozen times over the issue in recent years, Mr. Stinson says. He emphasizes, however, that management has lost just one such case recently. It is appealing the $2 million award in the case, which a California state court granted to an ex-personnel manager in Los Angeles last year.

Shortcomings in AT&T's anti-harassment program may have helped to spark that manager's suit. The woman initially hesitated to gripe after a vice president made unwanted sexual advances. Some co-workers and supervisors had ostracized her for complaining internally about another boss's harassment years earlier, according to Lawrence Grassini, her attorney.

When she finally aired her charges, AT&T "failed her," Mr. Grassini contends, "because the investigation they did [was] a half-hearted investigation." He says "they never even wrote her a letter saying they were sorry it happened. They wrote her a letter saying 'nothing has occurred.' " Mr. Grassini believes that AT&T's grievance system broke down because the company didn't educate employees enough about why retaliation is wrong.

Says Mr. Stinson: "Despite the comments of her attorney, our track record is enviable."

# Many Minorities Feel Torn by Experience of Affirmative Action

## While Program Opens Doors, It Can Attach a Stigma That Affects Self-Esteem

### Firefighter: 'I'll Stick to Merit'

SONIA L. NAZARIO
*Staff Reporter of* THE WALL STREET JOURNAL

At first, Roland Lee was thrilled to be the newest lieutenant in the San Francisco Fire Department. Then he learned he had beaten out a close friend in the department for the promotion. Then he discovered that his friend had scored higher on the qualifying exam. Then his friend quit.

The son of Chinese immigrants, Mr. Lee welcomed being hired and promoted under affirmative action quotas at the department. Without them, he believes, minorities would have been barred from the fire station's doors. But he also says he is "disgusted" that race denied his white friend the promotion.

Mr. Lee is plagued by the stigma he feels is attached to affirmative action: white co-workers questioning his abilities and assuming he's not as qualified as they. He says that this has forced him "to work twice as hard" to prove others wrong, and that at times, his own self-esteem has been battered. "If I had to do it over again," he says with regret, "I would get my promotion" without using affirmative action preferences. "That would give me back my credibility."

### Ambivalent Beneficiaries

Such an overt rejection of affirmative action by one of its beneficiaries is uncommon. But as minorities look at the effects of affirmative action nearly a quarter-century after its inception, many feel torn by the policy's outcome.

Minorities say it has opened doors that would have remained shut, forced companies to look to employment groups they had ignored, and decreased racism by prodding workplace integration. But it has also brought unwelcome baggage: assumptions that minorities were hired only because of race, and what may be unwarranted skepticism about their abilities. This makes some minorities fear that even promotions and accomplishments they earn by working harder than their peers won't be respected.

Some minority employees believe racism—on the part of co-workers or employers—has a lot to do with their ambivalence. Others believe companies and government agencies approach affirmative action too much as a burden to be met as painlessly as possible rather than as something that can truly benefit the workplace. Still others, like Mr. Lee, believe the problem is inherent in affirmative action, part and parcel of a process that gives preference to people for reasons other than strictly merit.

"I don't know if promoting someone because they are Chinese is the way to do it," he says.

### The High Court

Several recent Supreme Court decisions have sparked a renewed debate over the legitimacy of affirmative action. Many now see an increasingly conservative court turning against the concept of setting quotas for hiring minorities.

First, the high court in January toughened the criteria under which a court could impose an affirmative action program on a business or municipality. Then earlier this month, the court made it easier for white workers to challenge affirmative action plans in court, and it also raised the difficulty for a plaintiff alleging racial discrimination in hiring.

Buoyed by the high court's recent decisions, conservatives are hoping they soon will be able to lessen what they see as "reverse" discrimination, while civil-rights activists are appalled at what they see as a chilling threat to years of progress in integrating the workplace.

Rarely heard in the debate, however, are the voices of those who actually have been hired or promoted under an affirmative action plan. In the workplace itself, lines that divide liberals and conservatives are blurred by the intrusion of a more complex reality. "I'm reluctantly appreciative of the affirmative action jobs I've had," says Migdia Chinea-Varela, a Hispanic Hollywood scriptwriter. "But at the same time, they made me really depressed."

### Employees Are Heard

The personal responses to affirmative action are diverse, as are the difficulties minorities have experienced using such programs. Mary Whitmore, a carpenter in Los Angeles who pried her way into the male-dominated construction business with the help of affirmative action, says her experience has been a wholly positive one. Co-workers "treat me equal. They let me use the saw. They give me the nails. They let me work."

Many minorities agree with William Mays, a black who now owns his own Indianapolis-based chemical-distribution company, and who got a graduate fellowship and several jobs through affirmative action. "I had to deal with the grief [affirmative action] brought," he says, "but it was well worth it."

Others argue that the emphasis of government-sponsored integration plans must change toward encouraging equal educational and hiring opportunities rather than setting numerical goals and timetables. And a small number believe affirmative action should be abolished. "Affirmative action robs us of our dignity. It says that somehow color, not our hard work, can bring us advancements," says Shelby Steele, a black associate professor of English at San Jose State University who says he no longer applies for affirmative-action-related research grants so he can shake the stigma that he somehow isn't as talented as a white professor.

All employers must by law provide equal hiring opportunities to people of all races, but affirmative action requires much more: specific goals and timetables for hiring and promoting underrepresented women and minorities. Since a 1965 executive order by President Johnson, all companies that do more than $50,000 in annual business with the federal government and have more than 50 employees have been required to institute affirmative action plans. Companies and government agencies are bound to more rigid quotas when they are sued for discrimination under the 1964 Civil Rights Act and either agree to or are ordered by the court to remedy it through hiring and promotions.

### The Need for Action

Interviews with scores of affirmative action employees reveal that despite their individual impressions of specific programs, all cite a strong need for some effort to combat racism and purposefully open jobs to minorities that they might have held, absent past discrimination. Louis Winston, a black who is the affirmative action officer for Stockham Valves & Fittings Inc. in Birmingham, Ala., recalls the days when that company had two entry gates—one for whites, one for blacks—and a divided cafeteria. When he began in the 1960s, blacks were forced to work in the sweltering heat of the foundry, while only whites could qualify for training programs to become machinists or electricians.

In part because of a 1969 lawsuit he helped initiate that then led to an affirmative action plan, he became the first black electrician trained at Stockham in 1975; now there are many, and blacks hold 60% of Stockham's jobs. Affirmative action, he says, has "put some blacks in higher jobs, and shown the company that we aren't ignorant. We can do the job, if given the chance."

It has also helped reduce racial tensions by forcing blacks and whites to work together, he says. "Without affirmative action, Stockham may have come around, but I wouldn't swear on it," he says. More important, he says, there are still no blacks among the company's 35 managers.

### Breaking the Ranks

Diane Joyce believes that without affirmative action, she couldn't have advanced in the male-dominated Santa Clara County, Calif., road-maintenance department. A road worker for six years, she took an oral test to become a dispatcher in 1980 and was ranked fourth of those who took the test.

County rules allowed the supervisors to give the job to any one of the seven highest-scoring candidates, and she knew that one wouldn't be her; she claims the men who administered her test told her they didn't like her. So she phoned the county affirmative action officer, and got the job. A man who scored second on the test and was about to get the job sued the county in a case that went all the way to the Supreme Court. He lost.

Three years later, Ms. Joyce scored first in a written and oral test to become a road foreman. A man who ranked fifth got the job. This time, she didn't challenge it, even though she again felt unfairly treated. "I'm tired of fighting," she says.

One reason she and some others weary of the fight is the way their accelerated promotions or even their hiring are received by co-workers. Take, for example, the Birmingham, Ala., fire department.

### Problems in Birmingham

When Carl Cook applied to be a firefighter in 1964, a city clerk took one look at his face and refused to even hand over an application to the young black man, he says. In 1976, two years after Mr. Cook finally was hired, only 1.4% of firefighters were black. Attorney Susan Reeves, who helped file a suit for blacks against the city, says a Birmingham official once explained that "blacks congenitally don't like to fight fires."

Now the department is divided by a court-imposed affirmative action plan: Some white and black firefighters don't

even speak to each other. Some whites refer to promoted minorities as "welfare captains." In a highly publicized case, the Supreme Court last month gave Birmingham's white firefighters the right to challenge the affirmative action plan initiated by the lower court.

Mr. Cook, who was both hired and promoted under affirmative action, says, "I feel I am under a microscope." He won't ask white supervisors for advice or information for fear they are looking for an excuse to label him incompetent, he says. Battalion chief Tony Jackson, the city's highest-ranking black firefighter, says a white colleague once approached him and said, "Well, it sure is nice to be black. If I were black, I could have been promoted."

A white firefighter in Birmingham, David Morton, believes such suspicions will continue as long as some minorities are given special treatment—promoted over whites who rank higher in the test scores and experience. "If you take an airplane, do you want a pilot who was ranked No. 1, or one who is ranked No. 50 but is black?" he asks.

Ms. Chinea-Varela, the scriptwriter, says she has participated in four programs to encourage ethnic writers at four different production companies. No show she worked on was ever produced, she says. In one of the programs, sponsored by CBS Inc., a secretary explained to Ms. Chinea-Varela that she was just part of the network's minority headcount, the scriptwriter says.

As part of the CBS program, Ms. Chinea-Varela says she developed a situation comedy involving a young Hispanic woman who, trying to make ends meet after the death of her husband, takes in a white male boarder. "Because I came through the affirmative action door," she says, "there was no seriousness to the project."

A CBS spokeswoman says that this specific minority program no longer exists, and that the company has a strong commitment to affirmative action.

Regardless of the reaction of employers and co-workers, the mere fact that affirmative action involves special treatment has the potential to damage one's self-confidence, some minorities say. "Sometimes I wonder: Did I get this job because of my abilities, or because they needed to fill a quota?" says Caridad Dominguez, a Hispanic who is director of special studies for Bank of America, and who nonetheless says her own self-esteem carries her through such situations. "I consider myself a good contributor," she says.

### Questioning Quotas

The perception that affirmative-action hires sometimes aren't as good as other workers is perpetuated in some respects by employers so bound by court-ordered quotas that the measurable qualifications of minorities hired fall far below white

counterparts. "We hire 60% Hispanics here, regardless of qualifications," says Freddie Hernandez, a Hispanic lieutenant in the Miami fire department. "The fire department doesn't go to schools in other cities to recruit for minorities. They just have people take a test, and they pick minorities [even] from the bottom of the list." Fire Chief C.H. Duke says that a city ordinance requires his hires to be 80% women and minorities, and that this does require passing up whites with higher test scores for minorities, although anyone considered must pass the test.

Theodore Edwards, a black division manager at Ameritech Corp.'s Illinois Bell Telephone and an affirmative-action hire, says, "I think affirmative action is necessary, but I don't think it should be administered so that we say we have to have X number of minorities regardless of qualifications." He sees a need for more active recruiting so that firms can find minorities who are as qualified as other workers.

Whether they blame bosses, co-workers or simply human nature for their dissatisfaction with affirmative action, some minorities have been led by years of experience to call for major changes in government's approach to integrating the workplace.

The scriptwriter, Ms. Chinea-Varela, argues that hiring based on quotas should be done only in entry-level jobs, and that thereafter, a pure merit system should be used. She and others note that any hiring may at times be based less on merit than such factors as whom you know, ties to the appropriate Ivy League college, or nepotism. Still, she says that "there's a point where affirmative action should stop: I'd like to by now be considered on my own merits," having been in the business 10 years.

A Hispanic scriptwriter friend of hers, Julio Vera, is opposed to affirmative action altogether and will no longer apply for minority writing programs. "Martin Luther King's dream was to erase color lines; affirmative action hasn't done that," he says. Mr. Vera advocates spending more to redress the legacy of unequal education for minorities so they have a better chance of being equally qualified when they apply for a job. Affirmative action, he says, "is a handout."

Mr. Hernandez, the 34-year-old Hispanic firefighter from Miami, agrees. He turned down an affirmative-action promotion to lieutenant six years ago, waiting three years until he had the seniority and test scores to qualify for the promotion under normal procedures.

By doing so, he passed up $4,500 a year in extra pay and had to undergo 900 hours of extra study time. But "it was a self-pride thing," he says. "I knew I could make it on my own." Mr. Hernandez plans to take the exam for fire chief soon, but says he'll accept the job only if he wins it on paper. "I will stick to merit," he says.

They won't take it anymore.

# Older Workers Face Age-Old Problem

## IRENE PAVE

Irene Pave is head of Irene Pave Associates, a management consulting firm specializing in social issues. This article is reprinted from *Across the Board*; The Conference Board, 845 Third Avenue, New York, NY 10022.

AFTER A DECADE of mergers, acquisitions, and downsizing, American business has thousands of former employees, many of them older people. And it has something else: a spate of age discrimination cases that currently costs companies almost three times as much as their race and sex bias cases combined.

According to the U.S. Equal Employment Opportunity Commission (EEOC), in fiscal 1989 employers paid out about $9 million in back compensation and damages in EEOC cases brought under Title VII of the Civil Rights Act, which bars job bias on the basis of race or sex. During the same period, employers paid out about $25 million in EEOC cases brought under the less-publicized Age Discrimination in Employment Act. The same ratio holds true for bias suits brought by private attorneys, experts believe. Since 1980, the number of all age discrimination cases has risen steadily, and the process is likely to accelerate as older workers become more familiar with the law. Only three years ago, half the members polled by the Washington, D.C.-based American Association of Retired Persons (AARP) did not know that the age discrimination act existed. "Now people are learning," says John A. Rother, chairman of legislation, research, and public policy for AARP, a service and advocacy organization for people over age 50. AARP is actively working to educate its 32 million members, a third of whom hold jobs.

As companies prune their work forces to become more competitive, they typically target older workers for layoff or retirement. The salaries of these longtime employees tend to be higher than average, so companies save more money. There is also a perception that older workers may be slowing down. The attitude of many companies seems to be that, after all, those workers are approaching the customary, if no longer mandatory, retirement age, so why not get rid of them first. All this reflects a shift in corporate culture. Not too long ago, the seasoned veteran was highly prized by companies. Today, however, firms glorify the young tiger. For older employees, this adds up to bad news.

The cuts are frequently deepest in middle management, an area often considered "fat" by corporate executives. This area is also the one that supplies the typical age discrimination plaintiff. "Who files charges? Disproportionately, managerial or professional white males," says Charles A. Shanor, the recently resigned general counsel of the EEOC. "They understand the law, and they have the financial and psychological resources to hold out during a long process." They are also usually men in their 50s, says AARP's Rother. "They have limited job opportunities, but they're not ready to retire, financially or emotionally."

### DOUBLE DAMAGES

In one well-known age discrimination suit, three white male former vice presidents of the Chase Manhattan Bank sought compensation for lost pay, profit sharing, and other benefits. The plaintiffs, all of whom were between the ages of 49 and 55 at the time of their dismissal in 1980 and 1981, won damages of $588,000 in a case that dragged on until 1986. The award represented double damages for willful violation of the act; the jury found that the men had been set up for replacement by "younger, lower-salaried workers" when, among other ploys, a new supervisor had set unrealistic performance goals that they could not possibly meet.

The Chase Manhattan case was atypical in one respect: It went to court. Nine out of ten age bias cases are settled out of court, primarily because, unlike Title VII, the age discrimination act permits a trial. (This difference may change; the proposed Civil Rights Act would provide for jury trials with limited damage under Title VII.) A jury is more likely to be composed of employees than employers, a fact that gives companies a powerful incentive to settle. It also explains in part the large sums paid out in age bias cases compared with Title VII cases. Another factor: The higher salaries earned by many age-discrimination complainants lead to higher compensation when damages are awarded.

When the EEOC settled with Joseph E. Seagram & Sons in 1988, for example, fifty-nine former sales, administrative, and clerical employees shared $2.1 million in back pay, pension credits, and damages. Some of the higher-level employees received more than $100,000 apiece. The EEOC charge here was that a 1985 "reorganization" had intentionally reorganized these older workers out of their jobs.

Typically, none of the plaintiffs in the Seagram case — or the Chase Manhattan case — sought reinstatement. "After the second deposition, there's too much acrimony for reinstatement to be a real option," says Ira A. Turret, the New York City lawyer who represented the plaintiffs in the Chase Manhattan suit.

### NO RETURN

In many instances, the acrimony precedes the depositions. Firing an older employee or persuading him to take early retirement while trying to avoid an age bias suit frequently involves building a record of incompetence — an experience that generates enormous bitterness. The former employee generally does not want to return.

This record of incompetence is often the main point of dispute in cases brought against companies. Last year, Deere & Company paid $4.3 million in settlement costs to 116 salary-exempt former employees after the EEOC charged that a 1984 performance-related layoff showed a strong correlation between high pay and low performance.

The company's executives are not always at fault. "Sometimes top management tells all departments to cut 10 percent of their budget, and some department

heads find it easier to cut one high-priced older employee than two younger, lower-paid ones," says Burton Fretz, executive director of the National Senior Citizens Law Center in Washington, D.C. When early retirement is the goal, the company usually offers enhanced benefits — say, additional pension credits or continued health insurance — and asks employees who accept the offer to waive their right to bring age discrimination suits. But signed waivers are binding only if they are obtained without coercion. "The EEOC looks at the circumstances," says Shanor. "It asks, 'Did you consult a lawyer, did you understand what the waiver meant, were you in such a bind that you had no choice?' If the boss said, 'You're going to be eliminated, so this is your best bet, you have three days to decide,' that's coercion."

---

> "To avoid age bias lawsuits, companies try to build a record of incompetence."

---

The EEOC also examines the case law in the circuit court with jurisdiction. At present, legal definitions of coercion vary from circuit to circuit. A single definition of a legal waiver is part of the Older Workers Benefit Protection Act of 1990.

Coercion may raise its ugly head even if the offer is refused, says David Field, a New York City lawyer who handles age bias suits. He cites a current case: "Jim is a middle manager who had been with the company for twenty-eight years. Two years ago, when he was age 55, the corporation declared his job surplus and offered him early retirement with an enhanced pension. But even with the enhancement, that would drop his income from $75,000 to $30,000 a year, and he had a kid at college. So he turned it down. He was bypassed, ignored, given bad performance appraisals for the first time in his life, and eventually was demoted. He wound up sitting in an office with no staff and no responsibilities."

At that point, says Field, Jim talked things over with his lawyer, quit, and came to him. If Jim had gone to the EEOC instead, it would have investigated his charge for an average of six to eight months. If it found the charge had merit, the commission would have tried to settle the case by conciliation — perhaps for a year or more — before taking legal action.

The possibility of a two-year delay before going to court accounts in part for the increasing number of private suits — although the plaintiff must first file a charge with the EEOC in any case, usually within 180 days of the alleged violation. The popularity of private suits is also a result of the fact that the EEOC

## Same Old Story

The American Association of Retired Persons receives dozens of calls each week from members who believe they may have been dismissed or forced to retire from their job because of their age. These statements are from actual letters received by the organization:

● I would like to file an age discrimination complaint against my supervisor. I am 62 years old and would like to work until I am 65. She is trying to prevent me from accomplishing this goal by action based upon contrived information. She asks me to submit reports and data. The data and reports disappear from my desk. I have lost information from my residence.

● I am 58 years of age and have worked for my current employer since August 1961. I was given my performance evaluation for the year 1988 in September 1989 after the corporation had announced a restructuring and a significant lay-off. My performance was rated as unsatisfactory and was already signed by my manager's manager when it was presented to me. I was told there was no room for any discussion on the rating. This was the first time I have ever been poorly rated.

● I am 55 years of age and was employed by company X from 1963 until 1989 as an accountant. My last position with company X was being eliminated as a result of the consolidation of the accounting function for all the corporation's wholly owned subsidiaries. A younger accountant, trained by myself, is still

with the company. In my opinion, it was never the intent of company X to eliminate the position but only to change the title of the employee performing this function.

● I am 56 years old. I have been employed by the same company for the last thirty-five years. Two-and-one-half years ago, the company, although very profitable, introduced a new reporting structure that I believe was aimed at the older employees. I had been a senior analyst for the preceding fourteen or so years, having joined after college as a clerk and working my way up. The company reduced me to an analyst along with several other predominately middle-aged employees.

Six months later I got my first unsatisfactory review under the new regime. I have gotten two more similar reviews since. Therefore, no raise; in fact, I was told I was lucky to have a job.

Several weeks ago I was called into my supervisor's office and berated. Then I was told to consider early retirement. I was offered three options: one year at full pay, two years at half pay, or agree to take a demotion down one level. I currently make $45,000; this demotion would reduce [my salary] to $30,000-35,000.

---

is limited to seeking damages under the age discrimination act; private lawyers, however, may sue and win damages under various state and federal laws. Jim, for instance, is suing for pain and suffering under state law as well as the age discrimination act. Any money won on these grounds carries a bonus, Field notes: Back wages are taxable, but compensation for pain and suffering is tax-free under Internal Revenue Service rules. To date, suits brought by the EEOC that involved large numbers of older workers tended to win in court or achieve a favorable settlement, says Don Livingston, acting general counsel of the EEOC. EEOC suits involving one or two plaintiffs have gone either way. No won-lost record exists for private suits.

Originally, the U.S. Department of Labor was mandated with enforcing the age discrimination act, passed in 1967 to ban job discrimination against persons over age 40. Its caseload was small because ageism drew little notice in the 1960s and early 1970s, and the department litigated only precedent-setting cases. In 1978, when Congress banned mandatory retirement at age 65 and moved the

permissible age to 70, jurisdiction for the age discrimination act was shifted to the EEOC. Unlike the Labor Department, the EEOC is strictly in the antidiscrimination business. Given these changes, Congress' 1987 ban on any fixed retirement age made little practical difference — age bias had already become a hot issue for employers and employees alike.

---

"AARP now has more than 32 million members — up from 11 million in 1980."

---

Contributing to the heat was the phenomenal growth during the 1980s of the AARP, which started the decade with 11 million members and ended it with more than 32 million. AARP's worker equity department gets fifty to sixty letters and phone calls weekly, most frequently about dismissal or forced retirement, says Cathy Ventrall-Monsees, head of the department's advocacy program. Writers and callers receive advice, copies of a booklet on the age discrimination act, and — if they like — the names of home-state lawyers who handle antibias suits. If a case shows promise of setting a precedent, the AARP may participate as a friend of the court.

### NEW PROTECTIONS

In the face of all this, in a country with 24 million persons over age 50 in its population, how can a company avoid age bias when it implements a layoff or early retirement offer? There's no guarantee, but some general rules apply.

The employer need not worry, says Shanor, the former general counsel of the EEOC, if the layoff includes only a proportionate number of older workers. If there is a disproportionately high number, the employer must have a good reason — for example, the older employees worked on a product line that is being discontinued.

An early retirement offer to employees above a set age is legal, according to Shanor, if it is in fact an offer and not a demand. Employees should get at least several weeks to consider the early retirement offer and should be encouraged to consult an attorney. The offer should be free of threats, direct or implied, about what will happen if someone turns it down and free of reprisals if someone does. As for the content of the early retirement offer, much of what is permissible has been clarified by the Older Workers Benefit Protection Act of 1990.

The recent act stems from the Supreme Court's June 1989 decision in the *Betts* case. In that case, an Ohio county agency denied disability benefits to an employee who had been laid off at age 61 because its disability plan cut off at age 60. The Supreme Court upset twenty years of case law by ruling that the agency had not violated the Age Discrimination in Employment Act because, it said, the law did not cover benefits (pension, severance pay, and the like), just hirings, firings, and promotions.

Originally a bipartisan measure designed to restore benefits coverage, the older workers bill acquired additional clauses that tied it up in committee for more than a year. The restoration act that finally emerged last fall won congressional passage by compromising on the touchiest issue involved, integration of benefits. It barred the most controversial form, integration of pensions and severance pay, but permitted three other forms.

Under the new rules, employers may "integrate" disability pay and a pension (in other words, offset one against the other) by paying the retiree the higher of the two; integrate retiree health insurance and severance pay by deducting the former from the latter; and, in cases of plant closings or mass layoffs, integrate pension subsidies and severance pay by deducting from the severance pay the amount added to the pension. Formerly, a company that laid off an older employee who was eligible for a pension sometimes integrated the worker's pension and severance pay by canceling some or all of the severance pay. Most pre-*Betts* court decisions went against this practice, but some did not.

The new act also gives employees time to consider the company's early retirement package — twenty-one days if an individual is involved, forty-five days if a group. Employees get another seven days to change their mind after signing waivers of the right to sue.

Finally, the act specifically permits so-called bridge payments — higher pension payments for the years before Social Security kicks in. Although parts of many early retirement offers, bridge payments never had their legality tested. Formally approving them helped reconcile business representatives to retaining a clause dear to AARP: that early retirement offers not part of a permanent personnel program must "further the purposes of the Age Discrimination in Employment Act." Many employers had feared that the vague language of the clause would enable AARP, which dislikes one-shot retirement offers, to challenge their offers in court, with bridge payments and pension subsidies two likely targets. The new act legalizes both.

# Hazing: Uncovering One of the Best-Kept Secrets of the Workplace

Many people think of hazing as a ritual limited to college campuses. But the workplace has its own form that can run off even the best worker.

## Natasha Josefowitz and Herman Gadon

**Natasha Josefowitz** is a syndicated columnist and adjunct professor in the School of Social Work, San Diego State University. **Herman Gadon** is Director of Executive Programs at the University of California-San Diego.

K athryn, the newly promoted supervisor of a large supermarket, is asked to check something in the meat freezer. As she does so, she hears the door lock behind her. It is closing time and she knows that everyone leaves promptly. Will she spend the next 12 hours in the freezer, only to be found frozen solid in the morning? Twelve hours at these temperatures would mean certain death, but Kathryn does not panic. Why? Her manager had let her know that new supervisors in the store are commonly subjected to being locked in the freezer for five minutes. Kathryn remained calm because she had been prepared for this practice. Otherwise she might have "freaked out" at the thought of dying, and even after she had been "rescued," she probably would have angrily concluded that she was working with a bunch of savages and quit the job. But Kathryn knew she was being hazed, and therefore could go along with the gag.

Practical jokes, intentionally meaningless or humiliating tasks, and unnecessary assignments are all forms of hazing. The language is explicit: learning the ropes, paying your dues, passing muster, and earning your stripes

are all terms referring to the rites of passage from outsider to insider.

Newcomers are hazed to test them for potential membership. Will they fit in, be loyal to the group, be reliable, have a sense of humor? The tests for compatibility are varied: new to the job, a counter clerk at McDonald's is told to inventory pickle slices; a hospital orderly is asked to look for the fallopian tube; a bank teller has her keys hidden; an engineer is given cleaning jobs; and a new lawyer gets the most boring cases.

### THE PURPOSE OF HAZING

H azing accomplishes a number of goals for a group. It gives senior members a way of establishing their seniority and dominance; it ensures that formal work rules will be respected and that unwritten practices, known as norms, will be followed; it pushes newcomers into letting go of their old identities with and loyalties to former groups and organizations and taking on new identities; it ensures continuity of the existing ways of relating and of working; and it makes membership in new systems something to be valued.

A new employee coming into a work group creates uncertainty. As an unpredictable voice, a person who has no loyalty to the group, the newcomer implicitly threatens to diminish the power and influence of some older members. In order to prevent newcom-

ers from rocking the boat by participating too soon, group members will often try to put them in their place at the bottom of the ladder. A recent college graduate who had just been hired as a salesperson at Procter & Gamble was given a map of the company's territories and some crayons and told to color the different territories. The message was clear—although he may have been accomplished in many respects, he was still in kindergarten as far as what he knew about Procter & Gamble.

We differ little from other animals that align themselves in a definite pecking order. It is always the same chicken that gets to peck first, the same cow that leads the others to pasture, the same lion that has the largest pride, until a younger, stronger lion challenges the patriarch to a fight and wins that next step on the ladder. This step, however, does not come easily.

Group membership is valued more if becoming a member is a privilege that must be earned. The group will temporarily keep the newcomer on the outside because the longer he or she stays there, the more appealing membership becomes. In interviewing people who had been severely hazed in their new jobs, we asked if they would be easy on other newcomers in the future. By far the majority answered, "Why should they have it any easier than I did?" Apparently membership would be devalued by less demanding entry, and the struggle members experienced in seeking acceptance would then lose its meaning. As people remember their hazing experiences, they feel a sense of mastery. Those who had "made it" felt that their stripes were well earned, were proud of getting through the ordeals, and wanted to retain the exclusiveness they had earned by not making it easy on newcomers.

Hazing is a device protecting tightly knit groups against intrusion by strangers until the group is assured that the newcomer values the group and that he or she will fit in. Acceptance is usually not marked by a specific event but by the person's inclusion in informal get-togethers after work, casual sharing of information and gossip, and implicit assumptions that the new member will take part in the hazing of other newcomers.

## THE AFRICAN BUSH AND MADISON AVENUE

Primitive tribes in Africa, medieval guilds in Europe, and corporate offices in the United States all have rites of passage for their new members. And the rites of passage from outsider to member are surprisingly similar whether in the African bush or on Wall Street.

The difference between the African bush and Madison Avenue is that the rites of passage in primitive tribes are public. The terms and conditions are clearly spelled out; the initiates know more or less what to expect; the rules of behavior are understood; and, above all, initiates know that the rite is common practice, that they are not the first or the only ones subjected to the ordeal, and that the reward of the humiliation is membership and acceptance. Not so for today's employees newly entering an organization. Here the initiation rites are covert; criteria for membership are unknown; tests are unpredictable; correct behavior is not spelled out; and more often than not the new people believe they are being singled out because of something they have done wrong or because of some unacceptable trait. If they don't blame themselves for what is happening, they blame their coworkers, and will sometimes quit rather than continue to suffer, ignorant of the causes behind the pain.

Initiation rites must be considered not as isolated events, but as a function of the human need to maintain social order. Newcomers arouse anxiety until the members of an established group are sure that the social order of their group will not be threatened. Rites of passage are thus a necessary practice that eases the transition from newcomer to group member. Putting hazing in this context may help reduce the level of stress.

## WHO NEEDS TO KNOW?

We believe that managers, policymakers, and anyone entering a new group must understand the practices of hazing, the reasons behind them, and the responses that work. Though not widely recognized, hazing at work is indeed a common practice and takes many forms. Making new employees aware of this phenomenon is managers' responsibility, since responses by newcomers to hazing can greatly influence the way in which it progresses.

Most women seem to be unfamiliar with the practice of hazing and therefore react more negatively to it than men. Hazing has traditionally been mostly a male experience associated with neighborhood groups, team sports, fraternities, and military academies. Most men know from experience as youngsters that such pranks are inflicted on new people, so they expect them and take them in stride. Women, however, have little experience with hazing and may take the acts personally, believing they are being singled out. Knowing they are being hazed, men accept it as a part of the ritual for all newcomers; women, on the other hand, may see it as harassment.

In fact, people at work are hazed in places as diverse as corporate offices, professional associations, factories, laboratories, construction sites, athletic practices, and service organizations. A judge recently told us that new judges are given the chambers without a jury box, the worst clerks, and all the cases no one else wants. Hazing or rites of passage rituals are found in all sectors of the economy; they may be subtle and hardly noticeable or severe and even painful.

## RESEARCH FINDINGS

More than 300 students interviewed more than 1,000 people in depth, from different fields and at different job levels, about their experiences either of being new themselves (which could include a new job, a transfer, or a promotion) or being the manager of a new employee. In three-fourths of the cases, wherever we found groups of employees we found that entry into those groups consisted of identifiable stages from outsider to insider. Contrary to expectations, people and organizations made it anything but easy for newcomers to become part of a work team. Many barriers to achieving membership were thrown up by coworkers, supervisors, and organizational norms and policies. The costs in wasted recruitment dollars are real and considerable. Fully 10 percent of our sample quit their jobs because of hazing, and most said that they would not have done so had they known what to expect.

The unpleasantness and the duration of hazing depend on three factors: the cohesiveness of the group, the individual's fit into the group, and the newcomer's response to hazing. Our research shows that the tighter the group, the more difficult it is for new members to be accepted. The looser the group, the less resistance they encounter. When a newcomer faces not a group but an agglomeration of individuals who happen to work in the same place at the same time, then membership is not an issue and hazing does not occur.

How different the individual is from the other members of the group is also a large factor in the severity and duration of hazing. The greater the perceived difference (gender, race, background, age, education, religion), the more the newcomer's competence and personality fit are tested.

In addition, the assumptions made by newcomers about hazing influence how they react to it. We discovered in our research that men and women not only had different responses to hazing, but assumed that there were different reasons for it. Three times as many men as women mentioned that power was the overriding reason. They said that because new persons threaten the status

# "To distinguish hazing from harassment, one should view the circumstances with these questions in mind: are most new employees treated the same way, or at least similarly?"

quo, they need to be shown their place in the hierarchy. Perhaps men more often than women see newcomers as a possible threat to their power or position, or perhaps they are just more aware of power politics than women are.

Women, on the other hand, assumed that membership was the reason for hazing. Five times as many women as men cited it as the purpose for hazing, mentioning relationships and inclusion/exclusion as the real issue. Who will be accepted? Who will be kept out?

## WHO IS HAZING WHOM?

Men are usually hazed by other men. Women are hazed by men and sometimes by other women. We have seen very few examples of women hazing men except as part of a group joke. This may be due to the fact that women are socialized to defer to men, or perhaps they fear an aggressive response.

Occasionally even executives can be hazed by their staff. The more tightly knit the group, the more likely will be the hazing of the new boss, testing him or her for flexibility and good humor.

Even though we claim to value rugged individualism, there tends to be little tolerance for it in groups. Deviation from the norm is not looked upon favorably. This is why individuals who are seen as different in any way are often hazed harder. Although more obvious than others, race and gender are not the only differences that attract attention. An accent, a different background, or even unaccustomed behavior may generate extra hazing.

The more the person differs from the majority, the greater the need to test

for compatibility and reliability. Therefore, women and members of minority groups are hazed differently from white males. However, even white males who are seen by other members as different—effeminate in a macho environment, or macho in a more feminine environment—will be a threat to the norm and therefore hazed more. We have also noted cases where the most successful or skilled members are hazed more severely because their perceived differences are threatening to the status quo.

A woman who chooses to work in a traditionally male environment is often pushed to the limit in every possible requirement to see if she can pull her own weight. If she gets upset and makes a fuss, she may get the response: "Well, she's just a typical woman; she wants a man's job, but can't take the pressure." In all—or almost all—male environments, women usually do undergo more hazing than men or else they are protected from hazing and thereby are not given a chance to prove themselves and thus gain true membership.

If going through hazing earns membership, then being protected from it may spell continued exclusion and indicate that membership is not possible. If a new worker is not hazed when all other newcomers are, this may be a form of discrimination. Of course, temporary workers are not hazed because it is not expected that they will be included in the informal groupings at work.

We must be cautious, however, not to conclude that lack of hazing is necessarily exclusionary. About a quarter of the working population have not recognized any hazing and say that they

were easily incorporated into their work groups without any special rites of passage. Some people say that they never felt excluded, others that they were not teased, and a few report that they were not asked to do the more menial tasks at the beginning. The way in which newcomers behave, as the new kids on the block, can influence the type and length of hazing they will be made to endure. Knowing ahead of time what to expect will help them respond more appropriately.

## WHEN DOES HAZING TURN INTO HARASSMENT?

As long as hazing is done more or less equally to all newcomers and has an end whose goal is membership, then it is not harassment. Whereas the objective of hazing is inclusion, the goal of harassment is exclusion.

To distinguish hazing from harassment, one should view the circumstances with these questions in mind: are most new employees treated the same way, or at least similarly? If the new person reacts acceptably by going along, not reporting his or her treatment to the boss, not getting angry or upset, learning needed skills, and deferring to senior people, does the treatment stop? Are the people who cope successfully with the way they are treated then accepted as part of the group?

We have noted that women, minorities, and other newcomers who are different from members of an established work group are often hazed more harshly. Though the purpose of differential treatment may still be inclusion through testing for acceptability, it is clearly discriminatory, probably illegal, and cannot be tolerated by organizational policy or the organization's managers. It ought to be reported and sanctions applied to perpetrators.

An example of such discrimination was experienced by the only woman in an all-male factory. Her coworkers subjected her to severe tests of her acceptability. Her response was, "Hey, listen. I don't care what you say. I've got a job to do and if you want to joke, if you want to say dirty stuff, if you want to put naked ladies in the tool box, it's not going to do nothing to me. Because I've got my job and you're not going to make me quit if you keep on doing those things." This confrontation not only stopped the hazing but gained her respect and acceptance from her colleagues. Thereafter she was treated as "one of the guys." Although she was successful in coping with this abuse, neither she nor any other woman should have to endure it. The hazing was unacceptable and should have been stopped.

## COPING

Responses to hazing range from feeling hurt, embarrassed, frustrated, and outraged to hiding distress, pretending not to notice, and thinking the whole thing funny. If hazing is meant to test whether the newcomer's personality will fit in with the rest of the group, then the new employee has to accept being the butt of jokes, have a relaxed, low-key response, accept the temporary humiliation by seeing it as "paying your dues," and simply laugh along with the rest. Patience and going along with the hazing seem to be the best ways of coping.

To ignore the hazing or the feelings it provokes or to pretend total indifference does not work because the hazers expect a reaction. Robbing them of that

pleasure will drive them to invent something else—possibly even worse—until they get an acceptable response. One response that is definitely unacceptable to hazers is the reporting of the incident to a supervisor. The newcomer who does so will flunk the test for loyalty to the group.

We found some interesting differences in males and females involving supervisors. Only 9 percent of the men in our sample would tell their supervisor about the hazing incident, whereas 24 percent of the women said they would do so. Women were more likely to seek out an authority figure to solve the problem for them, thus relinquishing control of the situation rather than relying on their own solutions. Men in the study seldom went to their supervisors first. They found other means of dealing with the incidents. Only when the perpetrators continued their actions for a long time did the men request help from a superior. Indeed, involving a supervisor would cause the coworkers to resent the newcomer and possibly create permanent alienation from the group.

By far the most successful resolution to hazing seems to be to go along with it good-humoredly or to confront the hazers. A new deputy at a downtown jail was told to get a prisoner named Meoff, Jack. He yelled over the loudspeaker "Jack Meoff," realizing too late what he was saying. He was embarrassed but laughed along with his perpetrators and was accepted for his good humor.

Bob, a construction worker, had a successful solution to his hazing. He was excluded from the after-work beer-drinking sessions for two weeks, having been told that there was not enough beer to go around. Finally Bob brought beer for everyone. Henceforth he was included in the group. There are many creative ways to deal with hazing and to gain acceptance into the desired

group. The keys seem to be patience and tolerance.

Keeping a cool head while seeing this whole experience in perspective, maintaining a sense of humor, and generally being low key are all successful outward responses to hazing. However, the single most important way of coping with hazing is being forewarned by one's manager. Assigning a "buddy" to the newcomer, someone with credibility in the work group, may ease the transition. This person will be placed temporarily in charge of the newcomer to answer questions and help integrate him or her into the group more quickly.

Hazing evidently is here to stay. As long as we have human groups, we will have membership issues and rites of passage. If hazing is mild and neither slows integration of new employees nor causes undue pain, then the manager should leave well enough alone. When it creates unreasonable stress, causes delays in learning the new job by hindering training, and leads to unnecessary turnover, absenteeism, tardiness, or even depression, it should not be tolerated. The cost in dollars and human discomfort is too high. An unhappy worker is an ineffective worker. Few employees can be high producers in an atmosphere that leaves them feeling alienated. When the hazing is harmless, the manager should explain to the newcomer that it is typical, that he or she is not being singled out, that it can be endured, and that membership will eventually follow. Being forewarned will make the hazing bearable, perhaps even fun. All managers should be alert to hazing so it will become a function they monitor and control, instead of a repetition of old rituals that they accept uncritically as a matter of habit.

# After the Downsizing

*When an organization reduces its workforce, managers face
violated senses of security and justice in the employees who remain.
Here's some advice for helping the survivors survive.*

## Dan Rice
## and Craig Dreilinger

**Rice** *and* **Dreilinger** *are with the Dreiford
Group, 6917 Arlington Road, Suite 227,
Bethesda, MD, 20814.*

Managers in organizations that are downsizing face many difficult tasks. One of the most difficult is helping survivors (those employees who are chosen to remain with the organization) overcome their reactions to the situation and recommit to being productive and motivated.

Survivors often display several reactions:

■ **They have low morale.** Survivors tend to become depressed when their friends and associates have to leave the organization. They are not sure what they can or should do to save their own jobs and may want to maintain low profiles for fear that they might be seen in an unfavorable light.

■ **They become less productive.** Survivors frequently face work overload because fewer employees must handle what needs to be done. They may be unsure about their responsibilities and confused about what management expects of them. "Who's supposed to take care of this now that Joe is gone? Is it me?" is an all-too-common reaction.

■ **They distrust management.** Survivors have seen that competent performance no longer guarantees continued employment in their organization. Their bargain with management has been canceled unilaterally; they wonder whether management can be trusted to keep its word about anything.

■ **They become excessively cautious.** Given the atmosphere of uncertainty, no one wants to make mistakes—survivors don't want to be on the top of the list when the next downsizing comes along. Risk taking and innovation are likely to disappear; playing it safe and passing the buck may become the activities of choice. During a downsizing, such responses are the least desirable for the organization.

To help their organizations downsize successfully, managers must understand such reactions thoroughly and learn ways to help survivors survive.

One of the reasons that downsizing has such a profound effect on survivors is that it violates two fundamental human precepts—the need for security and the desire for justice.

## The need for security

Theorists (notably Abraham Maslow) have stated that a sense of security is one of the most basic human motivating forces. When that need is not met, a person's efforts focus almost entirely on gaining that sense of security.

Clearly, downsizing poses a threat to survivors' feelings of security. They are likely to believe that they may be the next ones who are dismissed: "If it happened once, it can happen again; if it happened to Alice, it can happen to me."

Most survivors don't know what they can or should do to protect themselves. The lack of power to ensure their own futures simply compounds the insecurity they experience.

Survivors often concentrate, then, on doing whatever they feel is necessary to secure their futures with the organization. That may mean that they spend their time politicking rather than producing. They may be unwilling to take risks or to operate using anything other than traditional methods, in order to avoid blame should anything go wrong. They are likely to focus completely on what they can do for themselves and feel little concern about what is good for the organization.

Especially during times of change, such behaviors can be highly counterproductive. To ensure a successful transition, people in changing situations need to be open to new ways of

# "If it happened once, it can happen again; if it happened to Alice, it can happen to me"

doing things. They need to be outwardly focused so that they can contribute to the team effort.

## The desire for justice

A desire for justice is another fundamental human characteristic. People want to believe that the world operates on the principles of fairness; they react strongly when that belief is violated.

When they see what they believe is injustice, people side with either the victim or the perpetrator, according to how strongly they identify with one or the other. For the most part, survivors identify with downsizing's victims—the outgoing employees—and distance themselves from the organization, which they consider the perpetrator of the injustice.

Another aspect of the desire for justice is a demand for equity: in any relationship, a person should receive benefits that are in proportion to the value of his or her contributions to the relationship. Part of the relationship contract between employees and the organization is that employee contributions of loyalty should result in the benefit of job security.

When that contract is broken through downsizing, employees perceive a state of inequity. They may react in one of two ways to rebalance the relationship:

■ They try to increase the benefits they derive from the relationship (by demanding more pay, promotions, increased recognition, and so forth).
■ They reduce the contributions they make to the relationship (by performing less work, putting in shorter hours, reducing the quality of their work, and so forth).

Downsizing usually is a result of cost-consciousness, so the first reaction tends to be unsuccessful. So the survivors of downsizing most often react by reducing their contributions to the organization.

Such a reaction does not always

come in the form of decreased task-productivity—that would leave survivors open to retaliation, which would further threaten their sense of security. More likely to occur are absenteeism, complaints, resistance to suggestions and ideas from management, unwillingness to put in extra hours, strict adherence to job descriptions, and similar subtle but disruptive types of behavior.

If you, as a manager or human resource specialist, are to help employees function effectively after downsizing, you must re-establish employees' feelings of security and their belief that they can still count on the organization for fairness and justice. There are three important ways to do that:
■ Provide information.
■ Give survivors personal attention.
■ Attend to your own personal well-being.

## Provide information

When survivors feel well informed about what is going on, their feelings of security increase. When they receive rational explanations for the downsizing, their sense of justice is less likely to be violated.

Attend to rumors. Employees will talk about what they think is going on in the organization; if they do not have real information, they will create and pass on rumors. They can spend so much time talking about and trying to interpret the latest rumor, that they neglect their work. And because rumors are more likely to be dire than upbeat, they cause anxiety that further interferes with productivity.

One corporation that was secretive about its downsizing plans discovered that its salespeople were spending all their road time on the telephone, checking out the latest news from headquarters. Not only were they not doing their jobs, but they were also costing the company a small fortune in phone charges.

One creative manager at a downsizing company developed a "rumor board." Any employee who heard a rumor about what was going on wrote it up and posted it on the rumor board outside the manager's office. Within 24 hours, the manager posted next to the rumor the real facts pertaining to the issue.

Provide employees with all available information; admit when answers are not yet obtainable. That openness reassures employees that they know what is occurring. It also allows them to get on with their jobs.

Make employees aware of the organization's goals. A major step in helping employees understand what is happening is to make them fully aware of what the new, downsized organization expects to accomplish. You must convey not only the reasons for downsizing, but also the specific results the organization expects.

For example: "We streamlined the organization with the intent of being able to respond to user requests on the day they are made, rather than allowing a week's lag time. Here's how we expect that to work. . . ."

People are more willing to accept immediate injustices if they can see how the actions will contribute to long-term benefits for themselves and others. Your task is to provide employees with a sense of how the organization's mission eventually will lead to a more equitable situation for themselves, their peers, and others involved.

Moreover, knowing the organization's intent and the benefits it expects to gain from downsizing helps survivors feel more secure about their own jobs.

Clarify what the company expects from employees. Many survivors are worried about increased workloads and unfamiliar responsibilities. Explain to each employee exactly what he or she will be expected to do, how

# Help survivors understand that there were reasons for choosing them to remain

he or she will do it, and with whom he or she will interact.

Let employees know how you will help them adapt to new tasks and functions (for example, with training or mentoring). Tell them how rewards will correlate with performance. Connect job responsibilities to organizational goals: How does what they do benefit the organization and contribute to its success and to their own success?

Educate the survivors about the responsibilities and functions of those with whom they will now interact. To a certain extent, employees are entering a new organization. You want to give them an orientation, just as you would with newly hired employees.

## Give survivors personal attention

Survivors of downsizing need a great deal of TLC from their managers. If providing TLC does not fit your personal management style, you must make some short-term adjustments—personal attention is vital in order to help survivors regain a sense of inclusion in the organization.

Recognize employees' specific values. Tell them why they are valued personally by you and the organization. Let them know what their unique contributions are. Discuss your own vision of the future of the organization, their places in it, and the ways in which they can expect to benefit.

Such recognition builds up sur-

vivors' feelings of self-worth and security, and helps them understand that there were reasons for choosing them to remain while dismissing others.

Stay in touch with employees' feelings. On a regular basis, spend some unstructured time with employees—individually if possible, but in groups if necessary. Use the time to talk about their feelings rather than about work. Be aware that some employees will be defensive or will feel uncomfortable about opening up. Be sensitive to and accommodate their individual tendencies.

In any meeting that is work-oriented, ask how employees feel about the discussion at hand. Encourage openness and honesty. You may want to talk about how you are feeling about something in order to encourage them to do the same.

Attention to survivors' feelings demonstrates concern for their well-being. Your sincere concern for employees will be reciprocated by their increased concern for the welfare of the organization.

Allow time for grieving. Downsizing disrupts relationships; one of the reactions to such change is grief. Survivors grieve over what has occurred. You must allow them the time to do so. Empathy and patience are necessary: encouraging employees to talk about their feelings helps them put their grief behind them and come to terms with what has happened.

## Help yourself

Finally, you need to attend to your

own personal well-being. After all, you, too, are a survivor and may have reactions similar to those of your employees. But remember that they will be watching you for cues as to how they should react to the situations that arise. If your morale is low, if you are afraid to take risks or make mistakes, or if you are distrustful of your bosses, then you certainly won't be able to help survivors overcome their own negative reactions.

Go out and get the information you need to feel comfortable with what is going on and to re-establish your own sense of security. Talk to your boss, your peers, and your family about how the downsizing has affected you. If your boss does not offer the personal attention you need, solicit it. Ask why you were chosen to remain with the organization, what the future is likely to hold for you, and what the organization expects of you.

Acknowledge your own feelings and grief. Give yourself some time to get over them. Take advantage of others' support.

## The goal: recommitment

Taking the steps necessary to help survivors survive involves restoring their sense of security and their belief in the justice of the organization. By keeping the basic reasons for survivors' reactions in mind, you will find more ways to help them continue to be productive workers. You will help them escape self-interest, end withdrawal, and recommit to the organization.

# Ethical Values Underlying The Termination Process

**ROBERT E. KARP**
Professor of Marketing
Jackson State University

**NELL M. WEAVER**
Director of Marketing
Vickers, Inc.

The 1980's have been hard on the job security of managers and professionals. In industry after industry, companies are responding to economic downturns, market shifts, competitive pressures, and the need to cut costs through massive layoffs in their work forces and "early retirement" plans.[1] Companies with a long history of "no layoff" policies are taking aim at broad sections of their employee populations and wielding the axe with little regard for tenure, experience, performance, or previous investments in management training and development. Here are some examples of such cutbacks:

1. When the Stroh Brewery, in Detroit, acquired the Joseph Schlitz Brewing Company in the 1980's, the twenty year old Detroit facility became expendable. In 1985, the decision was made to close the landmark Detroit plant, and more than 1100 jobs, including sixty (60) management positions, were scheduled to disappear.

2. The Kemper Insurance Company had a long history of no layoffs. At the end of 1982, ten (10) percent of Kemper's employees were released. Thousands of white collar workers were cut in the insurance industry when the recession reduced purchases and lower interest rates reduced incomes.

3. Hoffman-LaRoche, Inc. gave nine (9) percent of its U.S. work force less than one weeks' notice in early 1985. It dismissed 1,000 employees at two New Jersey locations for reasons that included the strength of the U.S. dollar and the imminent expiration of patents on several best-selling drugs, including Valium.

4. Even in Japan, the nation of lifetime employment appears to be on the way out. Such companies as Kobe steel, Mitsui Engineering and Shipbuilding and Sumitomo Metal Industries are being overwhelmed by excess managers in their 40's and 50's.

Clearly, we are entering an era when, for a variety of reasons, corporations are forced into situations where they must layoff large numbers of employees.[2] Also, very clearly, there are different ways to handle the problem of cutbacks. Why does

From *Business & Society*, Spring 1991, pp. 1-6. *Business & Society* is a publication of the Walter E. Heller College of Business Administration, Roosevelt University.

one corporation respond in a proactive, socially responsible manner, and another corporation hands out a pink slip late on Friday afternoon? What are the alternatives for the modern corporation? What are the costs involved? What are the benefits to modern corporations? These issues will be explored in this paper. First, let us examine some models of Corporate Social Responsibility to see where the concept of outplacement might fit.

## Models of Corporate Social Responsibility

There are several models of corporate social responsibility which could be listed and described in this manner:[3]

1. **The Austere Model:** This is the classical model in which the stockholders either are the managers or exert a complete and immediate control over managers and the means of production. In this model, of course, there is no room for philanthropy, since it is only the self-interest of the shareholders that matters. This is a socially responsible way to act and, in so doing, society as a whole benefits.

2. **The Household Model:** Managers in this model feel that their employees (managers and other workers) are their most precious asset and that they have a claim equal, if not superior to, that of any stockholders. In this view, the company is a team, a family, a social organization; it stresses the importance of the dignity, growth, fulfillment, and abilities of employees. It recognizes a management responsibility to employees, going considerably beyond legal obligations to meet their interests and demands.

3. **The Vendor Model:** This model focuses attention on the consumer. Over a period of years, we have built a substantial body of laws to protect the consumer, but this model goes further in seeking to determine his wants and to favor his interests.

4. **The Investment Model:** Here, the focus is on long-term profits and the survival of the firm. This model incorporates the idea that if the corporation is to enlarge its mission, it must expand its donative power in order to serve its own long-run, enlightened, self-interest by strengthening those private sectors of the economy which, in turn, will ensure the survival and vitality of the corporation. Therefore, each company should formulate its giving in terms of its own self-interest, circumstances, and responsibility. This philosophy captures the older idea of self-interest and recognizes the professionalization of today's managements in large companies as well as the importance of taking the longer view.

5. **The Civic Model:** In this model, executives recognize a responsibility to the industrial and political system which not only gives them their franchise, but also provides the means for their growth and prosperity. The managers in this model recognize responsibilities to the community and seek to help the community fulfill its objectives. These managers work with government in conducting the business of the country, contribute substantially to public requests, respond to joint industry-government projects like Comsat and, in all their activities, display the social consciousness and public spiritedness of a civic-minded citizen.

6. **The Artistic Model:** This model is still in the process of emerging. There is, according to Professor Richard Eells, an inevitable convergence between corporate enterprises and the arts. Business has, and will have, an even deeper interest in supporting the arts in the future because a flowering of the arts is essential to the development of a higher-quality life for the people of a society.

7. **The Eclectic Model:** This final model incorporates two or more of the preceding models. For many companies, the eclectic model is probably a more realistic one than the single-purpose models.

The household model of corporate social responsibility (Number 2) places a good deal of emphasis on companionship in the organization. The household model accepts, as its first proposition, the fact that human resources are a firm's most valuable asset. Therefore, anything that depersonalizes an employee, or assigns to him or her a low rating in the corporation's list of priorities, is to be rejected as unsound. All employees have a claim that is equal, if not superior, to that exercised by stockholders.

As people are the most important resource of any organization, let's take a look at a relatively new program for terminated employees and see how it operated in socially responsible corporation.

## Outplacement As Corporate Social Responsibility

For most people, termination is one of life's major stresses. Research indicates that it ranks with divorce and death in terms of its disruptive impact on an individual. [4] All of these involve a great sense of loss. Termination brings a loss of sense of purpose and structure and the abrupt severance of gratifying interpersonal relationships that have been formed on the job.

There is growing recognition of the fact that the manager who has to initiate a termination is also adversely affected. These executives see themselves as the "bearers of bad news" and experience a considerable amount of stress. As one executive put it, "being out of work is not easy, but making the decision to put people out of work may even be harder." A growing number of corporations are beginning to help terminated employees with the more practical aspects of career change by providing outplacement services.

## Outplacement Counseling

Termination of a person, executive or non-executive, is not only a traumatic experience for the individual handling the termination, it is also a potentially hazardous situation for the organization.

Because people are proud and sensitive, terminated employees feel rejected, shocked and bitter - no matter how much they may have anticipated the termination. Also for: the person doing the terminating, it is a painful experience And, for the corporation, there is always the risk that the termination act will be poorly handled. If this is the case, the corporation's public image and legal stability may be adversely affected. In addition, there can be great erosion of the sense of security of the other employees. Outplacement Counseling (OPC), a proven concept in human resource management, softens these traumatic experiences. Specifically, OPC is a systemic process designed to assist the displaced person in finding the right position within a short period of time and with a minimum of trauma. With the consultation of a third party before and after the termination session, the transition of a terminated person from the employment of one company to another can be positive and mutually rewarding for all concerned.

## Reasons For Providing Outplacement

There are six (6) basic reasons why organizations provide outplacement counseling. They are as follows:[5]

1. **Organizational Growth vs Organizational Stagnation**
   An effective outplacement counseling program frees up the management of an organization to make decisions in a more timely manner about individuals who are not working out within the organization. From an organization's point of view, and from an individual's career development point of view, early identification and severance of the poor performer can save organizations unlimited dollars and a great deal of trauma. Unfortunately, most companies still wait until the individual is 40-50 years old and has 15-30 years with the company, and than place the individual in a shelved position that only provides a stumbling block to the rest of the organization's personnel growth.

2. **Conscience**
   Organizations do have consciences, and management realizes that often it is not the individual's fault that he or she is not successful within the organization.

3. **Morale**

   People who are poorly treated in the act of termination do affect internal morale of others who stay with the organization. Once a company has the image of treating people poorly, it becomes extremely difficult to retain current talent and to obtain new talent.

4. **External Image**

   Persons who are treated fairly when being terminated do not usually speak in public or to various forms of media about how bad the company was to them. In addition, many people who are forced to leave organizations end up in positions of influence which can affect sales and inter-company relationships in their new endeavors.

5. **Legal Risks**

   People who are speaking with outplacement counselors about future career opportunities are not speaking with their lawyers about how unfairly they were treated.

6. **Saves Money**

   Finally, an effective outplacement program can save severance monies because individuals tend to move to new jobs faster if they are properly counseled.

## Outplacement At Stroh's Brewery

The family-owned Stroh Brewery, in Detroit, always had an outstanding reputation for being a secure place to work, but when The Stroh Brewing Company acquired the Joseph Schlitz Brewing Company in the early 1980's, its 70-year old Detroit facility became expendable.[6]

In 1985, the decision was made to close the Detroit plant, and more than 1,000 jobs, including 60 management positions were scheduled to disappear. Eighty-five percent of the hourly employees and 22 percent of the salaried employees had been at Stroh's for more than twenty years. From these numbers, it was apparent that the people who had gone to work at Stroh's had plans to stay.

But, at this point, a decision was made at Stroh's that separated the "here is your pink slip on Friday afternoon one week before Christmas" from those corporations that function at the highest levels of corporate social responsibility. Stroh's decided that they wanted to develop an aggressive program that would assist those former employees in a new beginning, be that a new career, their own business, retirement, a job at another Stroh's plant, or whatever their goal might be.

To help the terminated employees achieve goals, Stroh's eventually selected an outplacement firm from Chicago, Illinois - Janotta, Bray Group Services. What happened after that is one of the classic outplacement success stories in business. Janotta, Bray Group Services provided an outplacement service that included the following elements:

1. Orientation sessions to explain the overall concept and give employees ample opportunity to ask questions.

2. Individual skills testing and assessment.

3. Development of an individual job-search strategy.

4. A job-development effort and a computerized job bank.

5. Individual job-search counseling.

6. Job-search skills workshop.

7. Counseling sessions on financial planning, retirement planning relocation, and starting a new business.

8. Available psychological counseling.

9. A research library, free phones, and secretarial facilities.

10. Extended health and severance benefits.

These professional counseling services were very rewarding. Approximately 35 percent of the 125 salaries employees who participated in the program were transferring work at corporate headquarters in Detroit or were relocated to other Stroh facilities. A year after the plant closed, 100 percent of the salaried employees and 98 percent of the hourly employees had found new jobs!

The outplacement program was not inexpensive. Stroh spent more than $1.5 million, exclusive of the cost of severance pay and benefit continuation; and government funding contributed another $600,000 to the cost of more than $2 million. The cost saving and the benefits to the 1,100 employees are nearly impossible to measure.

## Outplacement Services

A recent survey was completed in 1985 and summarized some of the important findings in regard to the prevalence of outplacement services.[7] About half (51 percent) out of a total of 191 companies surveyed have provided outplacement services to terminated or laid off employees. Other important findings from the survey are as follows:

1. Providing outplacement services appears to be more prevalent in manufacturing companies (54 percent) and non-business organizations (57 percent) than in non-manufacturing firms (42 percent).

2. By company size, 55 percent of large organizations have provided outplacement services, while 47 percent of smaller organizations have ever provided such services.

3. Although over half of the respondents have provided outplacement services to employees, only 9 percent have formal written policies concerning these services.

4. The few firms that have formal policies have adopted them fairly recently; more than 80 percent formulated their policies since 1980.

5. Eighty-seven percent of companies that provide outplacement services do so when employees are discharged or permanently laid off for economic reasons.

6. When outplacement services are provided, the majority of companies (53 percent) provide assistance to all employees who will be terminated.

7. In terms of the types of outplacement services provided, nearly nine out of ten (89 percent) provided for individual counseling and/or job search assistance to terminated employees.

8. More than half (57 percent) of the 60 companies that utilize outside consultants for outplacement services do so when key executives have been terminated.

While outplacement is a relatively new management tool (within the past ten years), the results of this survey indicate that it has already achieved widespread use and acceptance. As we have seen, the results of such programs can be impressive.

## Summary and Conclusions

This article has attempted to show how self-enlightened, modern corporations and organizations are making socially responsible decisions in regard to employees terminations. By helping employees to re-enter the work force as soon as possible, corporations are saving themselves millions of dollars in direct and indirect costs. The savings, in terms of humanistic results for both the employee and his or her family, make it nearly impossible to measure in any quantitative way.

The essential ingredient of this type of corporate social responsibility is the degree of voluntary action as opposed to a coercive type of government action. This newer version of corporate social responsibility would argue that the corporation is not required to invest in higher education, sponsor artists, and actors, or endow the poet with pensions. However, while the modern corporation needs to do these things, it may not be compelled to do them.

Those corporate and organization leaders who are today developing outplacement programs for terminated employees and managers are revealing a sense of voluntary social responsibility of the highest order. They are investing in the most valuable management resource that any economy can have - the corporations invisible capital - its managers and employees.

## Postscript

**Item:** The General Electric Corporation has decided to close one of its manufacturing plants in Jackson, Mississippi. It is anticipated that 1,000 people will be terminated as a result of the decision. The plant closing comes two weeks prior to the Christmas season.

**Item:** E.F. Hutton has announced it will be cutting back on its work force twelve percent. The cutbacks come on the r. news of Hutton's recent merger.

**Item:** Chase Manhattan Bank will begin trimming its mid-management after the first of the year. The original announcement calls for cutbacks in the neighborhood of eight percent.

These events, some very real, some fictitious, testify that normative (that is, ethical) issues are alive and well is corporate America. In a thought provoking article, Professor William C. Fredrick has pointed out that today, when scholars investigate the relationships between business and other institutions in society, they realize that they must ultimately deal with normative or ethical matters.[8] The "normative" reference here refers to what happens when business comes into contact with other parts of society a result of this inherently normative character of their work, ethical scholars incur a threefold responsibility:

1. To make clear the values that are at stake as business and society interact with one another.

2. Be able to identify where one stands with respect to these values.

3. To use one's scholarly knowledge to point out to business practitioners the moral consequences of pursuing the values they and their companies hold.

It is because business and society have the power to affect each other in a profound way that the relationship between the two is unavoidably normative and laden with value issues. When a single firm (such as Stroh's) can, through a plant closure decision, cause widespread distress for an entire community, and many individual lives within it, an act of profound normative significance has occurred. It is certainly worth the scholar raising some questions about how it is handled.

## The First and Second Waves: CRS$_1$ and CRS$_2$

The first wave about a corporation's interactions with society will be referred to as CSR$_1$. Its main focus was on corporate social responsibility. Much of it was really pioneering work with little attempt to relate it to important moral principles that were there.

The second wave, or CSR$_2$, focused upon the individual firm as ways were sought to enhance the skill and effectiveness with which corporations could cope with social pressures. There was a lot of emphasis to concentrate-on the very pragmatic matters of responding effectively to environmental pressures.

The third wave, CSR$_3$, is what this paper is all about. For convenience, it may be referred to as corporate social rectitude. In this sense, rectitude embodies the notion of moral correctness (or incorrectness - as the case may be) in corporate actions taken, and policies formulated. We recognize corporate rectitude, the sense of moral goodness, when a corporation like Johnson and Johnson immediately takes steps to remove possibly tainted Tylenol capsules from store shelves. By the same token, we recognize the sense of moral goodness (corporate rectitude) when a Stroh's corporation assists 1,100 terminated employees to successfully regain productive employment!

The normative alterations in which business operations have some visible impact upon the human community are among the most central concerns of all mankind. This paper has dealt with just such an alteration-the fact that people, human resources, are still the most important resources that any management can have.

## NOTES

1.  Hoban, Richard, "The Outplacement Option: Everybody Wins! ", *Personnel Administration*, June 1987, pp. 184-193.

2.  Greenberg, Karen, and Mary Zippi, "How Companies Feel About Outplacement Services,"*Personnel Administration*, June 1983, pp. 55-57.

3 . Karp, Robert E., "Corporate Social Responsibility," *Corporate Morality and Executive Ethics*, Ginn Publishing Company, Lexington, MA, 1985, pp. 133-136.

4.  Kirkland, Ropp, "Downsizing Strategies," *Personnel Administration,* February, 1987, pp. 61-64.

5.  Morin, William J., "Outplacement Counseling, " Pamphlet by Drake Beam Morin, Inc., 1987, p. 4

6.  Jannotta, Joseph, "Strohs Outplacement Success," *Management Review*, January 1987, pp. 52-53.

7 . "Severance Benefits and Outplacement Services," *Personnel Policies Forum*, The Bureau of National Affairs, Inc., Washington, D.C., 1986 , pp. 12-16.

8 . Fredrick , William C., "Toward CSR3: Why Ethical Analysis is Indispensable and Unavoidable in Corporate Affairs," *California Management Review*, Vol. 28, No. 2, Winter 1986, pp 126-140.

## REFERENCES

Fredrick, William C., "Toward CSR3: Why Ethical Analysis is Indispensable and Unavoidable in Corporate Affairs," *California Management Review*, Vol. 28, No. 2, Winter 1986, pp. 126-140.

Greenberg, Karen and Mary Zippi, "How Companies Feel About Outplacement Services," *Personnel Administration*, June 1983, pp. 55-57.

Hoban, Richard, "The Outplacement Option: Everybody Wins!", *Personnel Administration*, June 1987, pp. 184-193.

Jannotta, Joseph, "Strohs Outplacement Success," *Management Review*, January 1987, pp. 52-53.

Karp, Robert E., "Corporate Social Responsibility," *Corporate Morality and Executive Ethics*, Ginn Publishing Company, Lexington, MA, 1985, pp. 133-136.

Kirkland, Ropp, "Downsizing Strategies," *Personnel Administration*, February, 1987, pp. 61-64.

Morin, William J.,"Outplacement Counseling," Pamphlet by Drake Beam Morin, Inc.,1987, p. 4

"Severance Benefits and Outplacement Services," *Personnel Policies Forum*, The Bureau of National Affairs, Inc., Washington, D.C., 1986, pp. 12-16.

# Changing Unethical Organizational Behavior

*Richard P. Nielsen*
*Boston College*

*Richard P. Nielsen is an associate professor in the Department of Organizational Studies, School of Management, Boston College. He has been a faculty member at Boston College since 1980. He has served as a speaker and taught seminars and management development courses in France, Germany, Holland, Indonesia, Mexico, Pakistan, and Switzerland. He has also served as a consultant and presented management development progams to such organizations as Citicorp, GSX/Genstar, IBM, Arthur D. Little, the Society of Friends and the American Friends Service Committee, the United Nations, the U.S. Agency for International Development, the U.S. Office of Education, and the WGBH Educational Foundation.*

*His research, teaching, and consulting interests are in the areas of ethics practice and cooperative change management. He serves as an editorial board member and referee for the Journal of Business Ethics. Some of his related recent publications include "Limitations of Reasoning as an Ethics Action Strategy" (Journal of Business Ethics, 1988), "Arendt's Action Philosophy and the Manager as Eichmann, Richard III, Faust or Institution Citizen (California Management Review, 1984), and "Cooperative Strategy" (Strategic Management Journal, 1988).*

> *"To be, or not to be: that is the question:*
> *Whether 'tis nobler in the mind to suffer*
> *The slings and arrows of outrageous fortune,*
> *Or to take arms against a sea of troubles,*
> *And by opposing end them?"*
>
> William Shakespeare, *Hamlet*

What are the implications of Hamlet's question in the context of organizational ethics? What does it mean to be ethical in an organizational context? Should one suffer the slings and arrows of unethical organizational behavior? Should one try to take arms against unethical behaviors and by opposing, end them?

The consequences of addressing organizational ethics issues can be unpleasant. One can be punished or fired; one's career can suffer, or one can be disliked, considered an outsider. It may take courage to oppose unethical and lead ethical organizational behavior.

How can one address organizational ethics issues? Paul Tillich, in his book *The Courage to Be*, recognized, as

Hamlet did, that dire consequences can result from standing up to and opposing unethical behavior. Tillich identified two approaches: *being* as an individual and *being* as a part of a group.[1]

In an organizational context, these two approaches can be interpreted as follows: (1) Being as an individual can mean intervening to end unethical organizational behaviors by working against others and the organizations performing the unethical behaviors; and (2) being as a part can mean leading an ethical organizational change by working with others and the organization. These approaches are not mutually exclusive; rather, depending on the individual, the organization, the relationships, and the situation, one or both of these approaches may be appropriate for addressing ethical issues.

## Being as an Individual

According to Tillich, the courage to be as an individual is the courage to follow one's conscience and defy unethical and/or unreasonable authority. It can even mean staging a revolutionary attack on that authority. Such an act can entail great risk and require great courage. As Tillich explains, "The anxiety conquered in the courage to be . . . in the productive process is considerable, because the threat of being excluded from such a participation by unemployment or the loss of an economic basis is what, above all, fate means today. . . ."[2]

According to David Ewing, retired executive editor of the *Harvard Business Review*, this type of anxiety is not without foundation.

> "There is very little protection in industry for employees who object to carrying out immoral, unethical or illegal orders from their superiors. If the employee doesn't like what he or she is asked to do, the remedy is to pack up and leave. This remedy seems to presuppose an ideal economy, where there is another company down the street with openings for jobs just like the one the employee left."[3]

How can one *be* as an individual, intervening against unethical organizational behavior? Intervention strategies an individual can use to change unethical behavior include: (1) secretly blowing the whistle within the organization; (2) quietly blowing the whistle, informing a responsible higher-level manager; (3) secretly threatening the offender with blowing the whistle; (4) secretly threatening a responsible manager with blowing the whistle outside the organization; (5) publicly threatening a responsible manager with blowing the whistle; (6) sabotaging the implementation of the unethical behavior; (7) quietly refraining from implementing an unethical order or policy; (8) publicly blowing the whistle within the organization; (9) conscientiously objecting to an unethical policy or refusing to implement the policy; (10) indicating uncertainty about or refusing to support a cover-up in the event that the individual and/or organization gets caught; (11) secretly blowing the whistle outside the organization; or (12) publicly blowing the whistle outside the organization. Cases of each strategy are considered below.

*Cases*

1. *Secretly blowing the whistle within the organization.* A purchasing manager for General Electric secretly wrote a letter to an upper-level manager about his boss, who was soliciting and accepting bribes from subcontractors. The boss was investigated and eventually fired. He was also sentenced to six months' imprisonment for taking $100,000 in bribes, in exchange for which he granted favorable treatment on defense contracts.[4]

2. *Quietly blowing the whistle to a responsible higher-level manager.* When Evelyn Grant was first hired by the company with which she is now a personnel manager, her job included administering a battery of tests that, in part, determined which employees were promoted to supervisory positions. Grant explained:

*"There have been cases where people will do something wrong because they think they have no choice. Their boss tells them to do it, and so they do it, knowing it's wrong. They don't realize there are ways around the boss. . . . When I went over his [the chief psychologist's] data and analysis, I found errors in assumptions as well as actual errors of computation . . . . I had two choices: I could do nothing or I could report my findings to my supervisor. If I did nothing, the only persons probably hurt were the ones who 'failed' the test. To report my findings, on the other hand, could hurt several people, possibly myself."*

She quietly spoke to her boss, who quietly arranged for a meeting to discuss the discrepancies with the chief psychologist. The chief psychologist did not show up for the meeting; however, the test battery was dropped.[5]

3. *Secretly threatening the offender with blowing the whistle.* A salesman for a Boston-area insurance company attended a weekly sales meeting during which the sales manager instructed the salespeople, both verbally and in writing, to use a sales technique that the salesman considered unethical. The salesman anonymously wrote the sales manager a letter threatening to send a copy of the unethical sales instructions to the Massachusetts insurance commissioner and the *Boston Globe* newspaper unless the sales manager retracted his instructions at the next sales meeting. The sales manager did retract the instructions. The salesman still works for the insurance company.[6]

4. *Secretly threatening a responsible manager with blowing the whistle outside the organization.* A recently hired manager with a San Francisco Real Estate Development Company found that the construction company his firm had contracted with was systematically not giving minorities opportunities to learn construction management. This new manager wrote an anonymous letter to a higher-level real estate manager threatening to blow the whistle to the press and local government about the contractor unless the company corrected the situation. The real estate manager intervened, and the contractor began to hire minorities for foremen-training positions.[7]

5. *Publicly threatening a responsible manager with blowing the whistle.* A woman in the business office of a large Boston-area university observed that one middle-level male manager was sexually harassing several women in the office. She tried to reason with the office manager to do something about the offensive behavior, but the manager would not do anything. She then told the manager and several other people in the office that if the manager did not do something about the behavior, she would blow the whistle to the personnel office. The manager then told the offender that if he did not stop the harassment, the personnel office would be brought in. He did stop the behavior, but he and several other employees refused to talk to the woman who initiated the actions. She eventually left the university.[8]

6. *Sabotaging the implementation of the unethical behavior.* A program manager for a Boston-area local social welfare organization was told by her superior to replace a significant percentage of her clients who received disability benefits with refugee Soviet Jews. She wanted to help both the refugees and her current clients; however, she thought it was unethical to drop current clients, in part because she believed such an action could result in unnecessary deaths. Previously, a person who had lost benefits because of what the program manager considered unethical "bumping" had committed suicide: He had not wanted to force his family to sell their home in order to pay for the medical care he needed and qualify for poverty programs. After her attempts to reason with her boss failed, she instituted a paperwork chain with a partially funded federal agency that prevented her own agency from dropping clients for nine months, after which time they would be eligible for a different funding program. Her old clients received benefits and the new refugees also received benefits. In discussions with her boss, she blamed the federal agency for making it impossible to drop people quickly. Her boss, a political appointee who did not understand the system, also blamed the federal agency office.[9]

7. *Publicly blowing the whistle within the organization.* John W. Young, the chief of NASA's astronaut office, wrote a 12-page internal memorandum to 97 people after the Challenger explosion that killed seven crew members. The memo listed a large number of safety-related problems that Young said had endangered crews since October 1984. According to Young, "If the management system is not big enough to stop the space shuttle program whenever necessary to make flight safety corrections, it will not survive and neither will our three space shuttles or their flight crews." The memo was instrumental in the decision to broaden safety investigations throughout the total NASA system.[10]

8. *Quietly refraining from implementing an unethical order/policy.* Frank Ladwig was a top salesman and branch manager with a large computer company for more than 40 years. At times, he had trouble balancing his respon-

sibilities. For instance, he was trained to sell solutions to customer problems, yet he had order and revenue quotas that sometimes made it difficult for him to concentrate on solving problems. He was responsible for signing and keeping important customers with annual revenues of between $250,000 and $500,000 and for aggressively and conscientiously representing new products that had required large R&D investments. He was required to sell the full line of products and services, and sometimes he had sales quotas for products that he believed were not a good match for the customer or appeared to perform marginally. Ladwig would quietly not sell those products, concentrating on selling the products he believed in. He would quietly explain the characteristics of the questionable products to his knowledgeable customers and get their reactions, rather than making an all-out sales effort. When he was asked by his sales manager why a certain product was not moving, he explained what the customers objected to and why. However, Ladwig thought that a salesman or manager with an average or poor performance record would have a difficult time getting away with this type of solution to an ethical dilemma.[11]

9. *Conscientiously objecting to an unethical policy or refusing to implement it.* Francis O'Brien was a research director for the pharmaceutical company Searle & Co. O'Brien conscientiously objected to what he believed were exaggerated claims for the Searle Copper 7 intrauterine contraceptive. When reasoning with upper-level management failed, O'Brien wrote them the following:

> *"Their continued use, in my opinion, is both misleading and a thinly disguised attempt to make claims which are not FDA approved. . . . Because of personal reasons I do not consent to have my name used in any press release or in connection with any press release. In addition, I will not participate in any press conferences."*

O'Brien left the company ten years later. Currently, several lawsuits are pending against Searle, charging that its IUD caused infection and sterility.[12]

10. *Indicating uncertainty about or refusing to support a cover-up in the event that the individual and/or organization gets caught.* In the Boston office of Bear Stearns, four brokers informally work together as a group. One of the brokers had been successfully trading on insider information, and he invited the other three to do the same. One of the three told the others that such trading was not worth the risk of getting caught, and if an investigation ever occurred, he was not sure he would be able to participate in a cover-up. The other two brokers decided not to trade on the insider information, and the first broker stopped at least that type of insider trading.

11. *Secretly blowing the whistle outside the corporation.* William Schwartzkopf of the Commonwealth Electric Company secretly and anonymously wrote a letter to the Justice Department alleging large-scale, long-time bid rigging among many of the largest U.S. electrical contractors. The secret letter accused the contractors of raising bids and conspiring to divide billions of dollars of contracts. Companies in the industry have already paid more than $20 million in fines to the government in part as a result of this letter, and they face millions of dollars more in losses when the victims sue.[14]

12. *Publicly blowing the whistle outside the organization.* A. Earnest Fitzgerald, a former high-level manager in the U.S. Air Force and Lockheed CEO, revealed to Congress and the press that the Air Force and Lockheed systematically practiced a strategy of underbidding in order to gain Air Force contracts for Lockheed, which then billed the Air Force and received payments for cost overruns on the contracts. Fitzgerald was fired for his trouble, but eventually received his job back. The underbidding/cost overruns, on at least the C-5/A cargo plane, were stopped.[15]

*Limitations of Intervention*

The intervention strategies described above can be very effective, but they also have some important limitations.

1. <u>*The individual can be wrong about the organization's actions.*</u> Lower-level employees commonly do not have as much or as good information about ethical situations and issues as higher-level managers. Similarly, they may not be as experienced as higher-level managers in dealing with specific ethical issues. The quality of experience and information an individual has can influence the quality of his or her ethical judgments. To the extent that this is true in any given situation, the use of intervention may or may not be warranted. In Case 9, for example, if Frank Ladwig had had limited computer experience, he could have been wrong about some of the products he thought would not produce the promised results.

2. *Relationships can be damaged.* Suppose that instead of identifying with the individuals who want an organization to change its ethical behavior, we look at these situations from another perspective. How do we feel when we are forced to change our behavior? Further, how would we feel if we were forced by a subordinate to change, even though we thought that we had the position, quality of information, and/or quality of experience to make the correct decisions? Relationships would probably be, at the least, strained, particularly if we made an ethical decision and were nevertheless forced to change. If we are wrong, it may be that we do not recognize it at the time. If we know we are wrong, we still may not like being forced to change. However, it is possible that the individual forcing us to change may justify his or her behavior to us, and our relationship may actually be strengthened.

3. *The organization can be hurt unnecessarily.* If an individual is wrong in believing that the organization is unethical, the organization can be hurt unnecessarily by his or her actions. Even if the individual is right, the organization can still be unnecessarily hurt by intervention strategies.

4. *Intervention strategies can encourage "might makes right" climates.* If we want "wrong" people, who might be more powerful now or in the future than we are, to exercise self-restraint, then we may need to exercise self-restraint even when we are "right." A problem with using force is that the other side may use more powerful or effective force now or later. Many people have been punished for trying to act ethically both when they were right and when they were wrong. By using force, one may also contribute to the belief that the only way to get things done in a particular organization is through force. People who are wrong can and do use force, and win. Do we want to build an organization culture in which force plays an important role? Gandhi's

response to "an eye for an eye" was that if we all followed that principle, eventually everyone would be blind.

---

*Being as a Part*

While the intervention strategies discussed above can be very effective, they can also be destructive. Therefore, it may be appropriate to consider the advantages of leading an ethical change effort (being as a part) as well as intervening against unethical behaviors (being as an individual).

Tillich maintains that the courage to be as a part is the courage to affirm one's own being through participation with others. He writes,

"The self affirms itself as participant in the power of a group, of a movement . . . . Self-affirmation within a group includes the courage to accept guilt and its consequences as public guilt, whether one is oneself responsible or whether somebody else is. It is a problem of the group which has to be expiated for the sake of the group, and the methods of punishment and satisfaction . . . are accepted by the individual . . . . In every human community, there are outstanding members, the bearers of the traditions and leaders of the future. They must have sufficient distance in order to judge and to change. They must take responsibility and ask questions. This unavoidably produces individual doubt and personal guilt. Nevertheless, the predominant pattern is the courage to be a part in all members of the . . . group . . . . The difference between the genuine Stoic and the neocollectivist is that the latter is bound in the first place to the collective and in the second place to the universe, while the Stoic was first of all related to the universal Logos and secondly to possible human groups. . . . The democratic-conformist type of the courage to be as a part was in an outspoken way tied up with the idea of progress. The courage to be as a part in the progress of the group to which one belongs . . . ."[16]

*Leading Ethical Change*

A good cross-cultural conceptualization of leadership is offered by Yoshino and Lifson: "The essence of leadership is the influential increment over and above mechanical compliance with routine directives of the organization."[17] This definition permits comparisons between and facilitates an understanding of different leadership styles through its use of a single variable: created incremental performance. Of course, different types of leadership may be more or less effective in different types of situations; yet, it is helpful to understand the "essence" of leadership in its many different cultural forms as the creation of incremental change beyond the routine.

For example, Yoshino and Lifson compare generalizations (actually overgeneralizations) about Japanese and American leadership styles:

"In the United States, a leader is often thought of as one who blazes new trails, a virtuoso whose example inspires awe, respect, and emulation. If any individual characterizes this pattern, it is surely John Wayne, whose image reached epic proportions in his own lifetime as an embodiment of something uniquely American. A Japanese leader, rather than being an authority, is more of a communications channel, a mediator, a facilitator, and most of all, a symbol and embodiment of group unity. Consensus building is necessary in decision making, and this requires patience and an ability to use carefully cultivated relationships to get all to agree for the good of the unit. A John Wayne in this situation might succeed temporarily by virtue of charisma, but eventually the inability to build strong emotion-laden relationships and use these as a tool of motivation and consensus building would prove fatal."[18]

A charismatic, "John Wayne type" leader can inspire and/or frighten people into diverting from the routine. A consensus-building, Japanese-style leader can get people to agree to divert from the routine. In both cases, the leader creates incremental behavior change beyond the routine. How does leadership (being as a part) in its various cultural forms differ from the various intervention (being as an individual) strategies and cases discussed above? Some case data may be revealing.

*Cases*

*1. Roger Boisjoly and the Challenger launch.*[19] In January 1985, after the postflight hardware inspection of Flight 52C, Roger Boisjoly strongly suspected that unusually low temperatures had compromised the performance effectiveness of the O-ring seals on two field joints. Such a performance compromise could cause an explosion. In March 1985, laboratory tests confirmed that low temperatures did negatively affect the ability of the O-rings to perform this sealing function. In June 1985, the postflight inspection of Flight 51B revealed serious erosion of both primary and backup seals that, had it continued, could have caused an explosion.

These events convinced Boisjoly that a serious and very dangerous problem existed with the O-rings. Instead of acting as an individual against his supervisors and the organization, for example, by blowing the whistle to the press, he tried to lead a change to stop the launching of flights with unsafe O-rings. He worked with his immediate supervisor, the director of engineering, and the organization in leading this change. He wrote a draft of a memo to Bob Lund, vice-president of engineering, which he first showed and discussed with his immediate supervisor to "maintain good relationships." Boisjoly and others developed potential win-win solutions, such as investigating remedies to fix the O-rings and refraining from launching flights at too-low temperatures. He effectively established a team to study the matter, and participated in a teleconference with 130 technical experts.

On the day before the Challenger launch, Boisjoly and other team members were successful in leading company executives to reverse their tentative recommendation to launch because the overnight temperatures were predicted to be too low. The company recommendation was to launch only when temperatures were above 53 degrees. To this point, Boisjoly was very effective in leading a change toward what he and other engineering and management people believed was a safe and ethical decision.

However, according to testimony from Boisjoly and others to Congress, the top managers of Morton Thiokol, under pressure from NASA, reversed their earlier recommendation not to launch. The next day, Challenger was launched and exploded, causing the deaths of all the crew members. While Boisjoly was very effective in leading a change within his own organization, he was not able to counteract subsequent pressure from the customer, NASA.

*2. Dan Phillips and Genco, Inc.*[20] Dan Phillips was a paper products group division manager for Genco, whose upper-level management adopted a strategy whereby several mills, including the Elkhorn Mill, would either have to reduce costs or close down. Phillips was concerned that cost cutting at Elkhorn would prevent the mill from meeting government pollution-control requirements, and that closing the mill could seriously hurt the local community. If he reduced costs, he would not meet pollution-control requirements; if he did not reduce costs, the mill would close and the community would suffer.

Phillips did not secretly or publicly blow the whistle, nor did he sabotage, conscientiously object, quietly refrain from implementing the plan, or quit; however, he did lead a change in the organization's ethical behavior. He asked research and development people in his division to investigate how the plant could both become more cost efficient and create less pollution. He then asked operations people in his division to estimate how long it would take to put such a new plant design on line, and how much it would cost. He asked cost accounting and financial people within his division to estimate when such a new operation would achieve a breakeven payback. Once he found a plan that would work, he negotiated a win-win solution with upper-level management: in exchange for not closing the plant and increasing its investment in his division, the organization would over time benefit from lower costs and higher profitability. Phillips thus worked with others and the organization to lead an inquiry and adopt an alternative ethical and cost-effective plan.

*3. Lotus and Brazilian Software Importing.*[21] Lotus, a software manufacturer, found that in spite of restrictions on the importing of much of its software to Brazil, many people there were buying and using Lotus software. On further investigation, the company discovered that Brazilian businessmen, in alliance with a Brazilian general, were violating the law by buying Lotus software in Cambridge, Massachusetts and bringing it into Brazil.

Instead of blowing the whistle on the illegal behavior, sabotaging it, or leaving Brazil, Lotus negotiated a solution: In exchange for the Brazilians' agreement to stop illegal importing, Lotus helped set them up as legitimate licensed manufacturers and distributors of Lotus products in Brazil. Instead of working against them and the Lotus salespeople supplying them, the Lotus managers worked with these people to develop an ethical, legal, and economically sound solution to the importing problem.

And in at least a limited sense, the importers may have been transformed into ethical managers and business peo-ple. This case may remind you of the legendary "Old West," where government officials sometimes negotiated win-win solutions with "outlaw gunfighters," who agreed to become somewhat more ethical as appointed sheriffs. The gunfighters needed to make a living, and many were not interested in or qualified for such other professions as farming or shopkeeping. In some cases, ethical behavior may take place before ethical beliefs are assumed.

*4. Insurance company office/sales manager and discrimination.*[22] The sales-office manager of a very large Boston-area insurance company tried to hire female salespeople several times, but his boss refused to permit the hires. The manager could have acted against his boss and the organization by secretly threatening to blow the whistle or actually blowing the whistle, publicly or secretly. Instead, he decided to try to lead a change in the implicit hiring policy of the organization.

The manager asked his boss why he was not permitted to hire a woman. He learned that his boss did not believe women made good salespeople and had never worked with a female salesperson. He found that reasoning with his boss about the capabilities of women and the ethics and legality of refusing to hire women was ineffective.

He inquired within the company about whether being a woman could be an advantage in any insurance sales areas. He negotiated with his boss a six-month experiment whereby he hired on a trial basis one woman to sell life insurance to married women who contributed large portions of their salaries to their home mortgages. The woman he hired was not only very successful in selling this type of life insurance, but became one of the office's top salespeople. After this experience, the boss reversed his policy of not hiring female salespeople.

### Limitations to Leading Ethical Organizational Change

In the four cases described above, the individuals did not attack the organization or people within the organization, nor did they intervene against individuals and/or the organization to stop an unethical practice. Instead, they worked with people in the organization to build a more ethical organization. As a result of their leadership, the organizations used more ethical behaviors. The strategy of leading an organization toward more ethical behavior, however, does have some limitations. These are described below.

1. In some organizational situations, ethical win-win solutions or compromises may not be possible. For example, in 1975 a pharmaceutical company in Raritan, New Jersey decided to enter a new market with a new product.[23] Grace Pierce, who was then in charge of medical testing of new products, refused to test a new diarrhea drug product on infants and elderly consumers because it contained high levels of saccharin, which was feared by many at the time to be a carcinogen. When Pierce was transferred, she resigned. The drug was tested on infant and elderly consumers. In this case, Pierce may have been faced with an either-or situation that left her little room to lead a change in organizational behavior.

Similarly, Errol Marshall, with Hydraulic Parts and Components, Inc.,[24] helped negotiate the sale of a subcontract to sell heavy equipment to the U.S. Navy while giving $70,000 in kickbacks to two materials managers of Brown &

Root, Inc., the project's prime contractor. According to Marshall, the prime contractor "demanded the kickbacks. . . . It was cut and dried. We would not get the business otherwise." While Marshall was not charged with any crime, one of the upper-level Brown & Root managers, William Callan, was convicted in 1985 of extorting kickbacks, and another manager, Frank DiDomenico, pleaded guilty to extorting kickbacks from Hydraulic Parts & Components, Inc. Marshall has left the company. In this case, it seems that Marshall had no win-win alternative to paying the bribe. In some situations it may not be possible to lead a win-win ethical change.

2. Some people do not understand how leadership can be applied to situations that involve organizational-ethics issues. Also, some people — particularly those in analytical or technical professions, which may not offer much opportunity for gaining leadership experience — may not know how to lead very well in any situation. Some people may be good leaders in the course of their normal work lives, but do not try to lead or do not lead very well when ethical issues are involved. Some people avoid discussing ethical, religious, and political issues at work.

For example, John Geary was a salesman for U.S. Steel when the company decided to enter a new market with what he and others considered an unsafe new product.[25] As a leading salesman for U.S. Steel, Geary normally was very good at leading the way toward changes that satisfied customer and organizational needs. A good salesman frequently needs to coordinate and spearhead modifications in operations, engineering, logistics, product design, financing, and billing/payment that are necessary for a company to maintain good customer relationships and sales. Apparently, however, he did not try to lead the organization in developing a win-win solution, such as soliciting current orders for a later delivery of a corrected product. He tried only reasoning against selling the unsafe product and protested its sale to several groups of upper-level engineers and managers. He noted that he believed the product had a failure rate of 3.6% and was therefore both unsafe and potentially damaging to U.S. Steel's longer-term strategy of entering higher technology/profit margin businesses. According to Geary, even though many upper-level managers, engineers, and salesmen understood and believed him, "the only desire of everyone associated with the project was to satisfy the instructions of Henry Wallace [the sales vice-president]. No one was about to buck this man for fear of his job."[26] The sales vice-president fired Geary, apparently because he continued to protest against sale of the product.

Similarly, William Schwartzkopf of Commonwealth Electric Co.[27] did not think he could either ethically reason against or lead an end to the large-scale, long-time bid rigging between his own company and many of the largest U.S. electrical contractors. Even though he was an attorney and had extensive experience in leading organizational changes, he did not try to lead his company toward an ethical solution. He waited until he retired from the company, then wrote a secret letter to the Justice Department accusing the contractors of raising bids and conspiring to divide billions of dollars of contracts among themselves.

Many people — both experienced and inexperienced in leadership — do not try to lead their companies toward developing solutions to ethical problems. Often, they do not understand that it is possible to lead such a change; therefore, they do not try to do so — even though, as the cases here show, many succeed when they do try.

3. Some organizational environments — in both consensus-building and authoritarian types of cultures — discourage leadership that is nonconforming. For example, as Robert E. Wood, former CEO of the giant international retailer Sears, Roebuck, has observed, "We stress the advantages of the free enterprise system, we complain about the totalitarian state, but in our individual organizations we have created more or less a totalitarian system in industry, particularly in large industry."[28] Similarly, Charles W. Summers, in a *Harvard Business Review* article, observes, "Corporate executives may argue that . . . they recognize and protect . . . against arbitrary termination through their own internal procedures. The simple fact is that most companies have not recognized and protected that right."[29]

David Ewing concludes that "It [the pressure to obey unethical and illegal orders] is probably most dangerous, however, as a low-level infection. When it slowly bleeds the individual conscience dry and metastasizes insidiously, it is most difficult to defend against. There are no spectacular firings or purges in the ranks. There are no epic blunders. Under constant and insistent pressure, employees simply give in and conform. They become good 'organization people.'"[30]

Similar pressures can exist in participative, consensus-building types of cultures. For example, as mentioned above, Yoshino and Lifson write, "A Japanese leader, rather than being an authority, is more of a communications channel, a mediator, a facilitator, and most of all, a symbol and embodiment of group unity. Consensus building is necessary to decision making, and this requires patience and an ability to use carefully cultivated relationships to get all to agree for the good of the unit."[31]

The importance of the group and the position of the group leaders as a symbol of the group are revealed in the very popular true story, "Tale of the Forty-Seven Ronin." The tale is about 47 warriors whose lord is unjustly killed. The Ronin spend years sacrificing everything, including their families, in order to kill the person responsible for their leader's death. Then all those who survive the assault killed themselves.

Just as authoritarian top-down organizational cultures can produce unethical behaviors, so can participative, consensus-building cultures. The Japanese novelist Shusaku Endo, in his *The Sea and Poison*, describes the true story of such a problem.[32] It concerns an experiment cooperatively performed by the Japanese Army, a medical hospital, and a consensus-building team of doctors on American prisoners of war. The purpose of the experiment was to determine scientifically how much blood people can lose before they die.

Endo describes the reasoning and feelings of one of the doctors as he looked back at this behavior:

*"At the time nothing could be done. . . . If I were caught in the same way, I might, I might just do the same thing again. . . . We feel that getting on good terms ourselves with the Western Command medical people, with whom Second [section] is so cosy, wouldn't be a bad idea at all. Therefore we feel there's no need to ill-temperedly refuse their friendly proposal and*

*hurt their feelings. . . . Five doctors from Kando's section most likely will be glad to get the chance. . . . For me the pangs of conscience . . . were from childhood equivalent to the fear of disapproval in the eyes of others — fear of the punishment which society would bring to bear. . . . To put it quite bluntly, I am able to remain quite undisturbed in the face of someone else's terrible suffering and death. . . . I am not writing about these experiences as one driven to do so by his conscience . . . all these memories are distasteful to me. But looking upon them as distasteful and suffering because of them are two different matters. Then why do I bother writing? Because I'm strangely ill at ease. I, who fear only the eyes of others and the punishment of society, and whose fears disappear when I am secure from these, am now disturbed. . . . I have no conscience, I suppose. Not just me, though. None of them feel anything at all about what they did here.' The only emotion in his heart was a sense of having fallen as low as one can fall."[33]*

## What to Do and How to Be

In light of the discussion of the two approaches to addressing organizational ethics issues and their limitations, what should we do as individuals and members of organizations? To some extent that depends on the circumstances and our own abilities. If we know how to lead, if there's time for it, if the key people in authority are reasonable, and if a win-win solution is possible, one should probably try leading an organizational change.

If, on the other hand, one does not know how to lead, time is limited, the authority figures are unreasonable, a culture of strong conformity exists, and the situation is not likely to produce a win-win outcome, then the chances of success with a leadership approach are much lower. This may leave one with only the choice of using one of the intervention strategies discussed above. If an individual wishes to remain an effective member of the organization, then one of the more secretive strategies may be safer.

But what about the more common, middle range of problems? Here there is no easy prescription. The more win-win potential the situation has, the more time there is, the more leadership skills one has, and the more reasonable the authority figures and organizational cultures are, the more likely a leadership approach is to succeed. If the opposite conditions exist, then forcing change in the organization is the likely alternative.

To a large extent, the choice depends on an individual's courage. In my opinion, in all but the most extreme and unusual circumstances, one should first try to lead a change toward ethical behavior. If that does not succeed, then mustering the courage to act against others and the organization may be necessary. For example, the course of action that might have saved the Challenger crew was for Boisjoly or someone else to act against Morton Thiokol, its top managers, and NASA by blowing the whistle to the press.

If there is an implicitly characteristic American ontology, perhaps it is some version of William James' 1907 *Pragmatism*, which, for better or worse, sees through a lens of interactions the ontologies of being as an individual and being as a part. James explains our situation as follows:

*"What we were discussing was the idea of a world growing not integrally but piecemeal by the contributions of its several parts. Take the hypothesis seriously and as a live one. Suppose that the world's author put the case to you before creation, saying: 'If I am going to make a world not certain to be saved, a world the perfection of which shall be conditional merely, the condition being that each several agent does its own 'level best.' I offer you the chance of taking part in such a world. Its safety, you see, is unwarranted. It is a real adventure, with real danger, yet it may win through. It is a social scheme of co-operative work genuinely to be done. Will you join the procession? Will you trust yourself and trust the other agents enough to face the risk? . . . Then it is perfectly possible to accept sincerely a drastic kind of a universe from which the element of 'seriousness' is not to be expelled. Who so does so is, it seems to me, a genuine pragmatist. He is willing to live on a scheme of uncertified possibilities which he trusts; willing to pay with his own person, if need be, for the realization of the ideals which he frames. What now actually are the other forces which he trusts to co-operate with him, in a universe of such a type? They are at least his fellow men, in the stage of being which our actual universe has reached."[34]*

In conclusion, there are realistic ethics leadership and intervention action strategies. We can act effectively concerning organizational ethics issues. Depending upon the circumstances including our own courage, we can choose to act and be ethical both as individuals and as leaders. Being as a part and leading ethical change is the more constructive approach generally. However, being as an individual intervening against others and organizations can sometimes be the only short or medium term effective approach.

### Acknowledgements

I would like to acknowledge and thank the following people for their help with ideas presented in this article: the members of the Works in Progress Seminar of Boston College particularly Dalmar Fisher, James Gips, John Neuhauser, William Torbert, and the late James Waters; Kenneth Boulding of the University of Colorado; Robert Greenleaf; and, Douglas Steere of Haverford College.

### Endnotes

1. Paul Tillich, *The Courage to Be.* New Haven, CT: Yale University Press, 1950.

2. See Endnote 1, page 159.

3. David Ewing, *Freedom Inside the Organization.* New York: McGraw-Hill, 1977.

4. The person blowing the whistle in this case wishes to remain anonymous. See also Elizabeth Neuffer, "GE Managers Sentenced for Bribery," *The Boston Globe,* July 26, 1988, p. 67.

5. Barbara Ley Toffler, *Tough Choices: Managers Talk Ethics.* New York: John Wiley, 1986, pp. 153-169.

6. Richard P. Nielsen, "What Can Managers Do About Unethical Management?" *Journal of Business Ethics*, 6, 1987, 153-161. See also Nielsen's "Limitations of Ethical Reasoning as an Action Strategy," *Journal of Business Ethics*, 7, 1988, pp. 725-733, and "Arendt's Action Philosophy and the Manager as Eichmann, Richard III, Faust or Institution Citizen," *California Management Review*, 26, 3, Spring 1984, pp. 191-201.

7. The person involved wishes to remain anonymous.

8. The person involved wishes to remain anonymous.

9. See Endnote 6.

10. R. Reinhold, "Astronauts Chief Says NASA Risked Life for Schedule," *The New York Times*, 36, 1986, p. 1.

11. Personal conversation and letter with Frank Ladwig,1986. See also Frank Ladwig and Associates' *Advanced Consultative Selling for Professionals.* Stonington, CT.

12. W. G. Glaberson, "Did Searle Lose Its Eyes to a Health Hazard?" *Business Week*, October 14, 1985, pp. 120-122.

13. The person involved wishes to remain anonymous.

14. Andy Pasztor, "Electrical Contractors Reel Under Charges that They Rigged Bids," *The Wall Street Journal*, November 29, 1985, pp. 1, 14.

15. A. Ernest Fitzgerald, *The High Priests of Waste*. New York: McGraw-Hill, 1977.

16. See Endnote 1, pp. 89, 93.

17. M. Y. Yoshino and T. B. Lifson, *The Invisible Link: Japan's Saga Shosha and the Organization of Trade.* Cambridge, MA: MIT Press, 1986.

18. See Endnote 17, p. 178.

19. Roger Boisjoly, address given at Massachusetts Institute of Technology on January 7, 1987. Reprinted in *Books and Religion*, March/April 1987, 3-4, 12-13. See also Caroline Whitbeck, "Moral Responsibility and the Working Engineer," *Books and Religion*, March/April 1987, 3, 22-23.

20. Personal conversation with Ray Bauer, Harvard Business School, 1975. See also R. Ackerman and Ray Bauer, *Corporate Social Responsiveness.* Reston, VA: Reston Publishing, 1976.

21. The person involved wishes to remain anonymous.

22. The person involved wishes to remain anonymous.

23. David Ewing, *Do It My Way or You're Fired.* New York: John Wiley, 1983.

24. E. T. Pound, "Investigators Detect Pattern of Kickbacks for Defense Business," *The Wall Street Journal*, November 14, 1985, pp. 1, 25.

25. See Endnote 23. See also Geary vs. U.S. Steel Corporation, 319 A. 2nd 174, Supreme Court of Pa.

26. See Endnote 23, p. 86.

27. See Endnote 14.

28. See Endnote 3, p. 21.

29. C. W. Summers, "Protecting All Employees Against Unjust Dismissal," *Harvard Business Review*, 58, 1980, pp. 132-139.

30. See Endnote 3, pp. 216-217.

31. See Endnote 17, p. 187.

32. Shusaku Endo, *The Sea and Poison.* New York: Taplinger Publishing Company, 1972. See also Y. Yasuda, *Old Tales of Japan.* Tokyo: Charles Tuttle Company, 1947.

33. See Endnote 32.

34. William James, *Pragmatism: A New Name for Some Old Ways of Thinking.* New York: Longmans, Green and Co., 1907, p. 290, 297-298.

# Implementing Business Ethics

*Patrick E. Murphy*

*Patrick E. Murphy is an Associate Professor of Marketing in the College of Business Administration at the University of Notre Dame. He is coeditor of* Marketing Ethics: Guidelines for Managers, *Lexington Books, 1985 (with G. R. Laczniak). His articles on ethics have appeared in* Journal of Marketing, Review of Marketing *and* Advances in Marketing and Public Policy. *Professor Murphy currently serves as editor of the* Journal of Public Policy and Marketing.

ABSTRACT. This article outlines an approach for *implementing* business ethics. A company should both organize for ethical business policies and execute them. The organizational dimension refers to structural components including codes of ethics, conferences and training programs and an ethical audit. The corporate culture must support these structural elements with top management playing a central role in implementing ethics.

The execution of ethical business policies includes implementation responsibilities and tasks. These responsibilities are leadership in ethics, delegation, communication and motivation of the company's ethical position to employees. Execution tasks are delineated for the marketing function. Although many company examples are provided, a program in place at McDonnell Douglas is highlighted as a model of ethics implementation.

## Introduction

Most organizations have learned that it is not enough to have a well designed corporate strategy in place. Equally important is to be able to *implement* this strategy. In fact, one projection is that only about ten percent of all strategies are effectively implemented. If implementation is to succeed, the entire organization must be committed to the strategy and even the smallest detail should not be overlooked. The same is true with ethics. Implementing ethics is not just a concern of managers setting the firm's overall strategic direction, but should pervade all levels of the business.

Recent events concerning unethical business practices not only on Wall Street, but also in many other places, appear to highlight the lack of attention to implementation of ethical policies. The existence of a carefully defined ethical code does not guarantee ethical behavior. A good example is General Electric (GE). The company has long had a formal, written code of conduct that is communicated to employees and perceives itself as a leader in subscribing to ethical business practices. Yet, GE ran into trouble in 1985 for having time cards forged at a Pennsylvania defense plant. This situation caused a suspension of new defense contracts for a time and much embarrassment for the firm. More recently, their Kidder Peabody subsidiary was implicated in the insider trading scandal even though GE was assured before their June, 1986 acquisition of Kidder that the firm faced no major problems with the SEC or Justice Department. These events lead to a management shake-up at Kidder. GE found that it is quite difficult to implement ethics in their far flung range of businesses.

What can be done to make sure that ethical policies are implemented and that the firm will steer clear of wrongdoings that result in legal problems and/or bad press? The answer is not an easy one. This article outlines steps that companies might use in carrying out ethical business practices. Implementing business ethics involves organizing for and executing ethical policies.[1] The organizational aspects of implementation are covered initially and then we will turn our attention to executing ethical strategies.

This paper takes a pragmatic, rather than a philosophical, approach to examining ethics. The manager is pulled from several directions — personal, organizational and market — in reconciling ethical dilemmas.[2] Making good moral judgments requires frank discussions and ethical sensitivity. This point was well articulated by B. H. McCoy (1983): "In contrast to philosophy, business involves action and implementation — getting things done. Managers must come up with answers to problems based on what they see and what they allow to influence their decision making process."

## Organizing for ethical business policies

Figure 1 lists the organizational dimensions of business ethics and procedures that will bring about the implementation of ethical company practices. _Structure_ refers to formal organizational mechanisms that foster ethical decisions. _Culture_ pertains to the informal organizational climate.

### Structure

Corporate codes have long been viewed as the major organizational structure in which to implement ethical policy. Research indicates that approximately 90 percent of _Fortune 500_ firms and almost half of all companies have codes in place (Center for Business Ethics, 1986; Murphy, 1986). Several writers, the first being the late Ted Purcell, S. J. (1978), have viewed ethical codes as the cornerstone to "institutionalizing" ethics. However, codes of conduct continue to be criticized as being too general, containing too many platitudes, serving purely as public relations ploys or being designed strictly to avoid legal problems (Berenbeim, 1987; Wartzman, 1987). Cressey and

---

*Organizing for Ethical Business Policies*

Structure: the formal organization

    Corporate codes
        Specific
        Public documents
        Blunt and realistic
        Revised periodically

    Committees, conferences
    and training

    Ethical audit
    questions

Culture: the informal organization

    Open and candid

    Management role

- - - - - - - - - - - - - - - - - - - - - - - - - - - - - - - - - - -

*Executing Ethical Business Policies*

Implementation responsibilities

    Leadership
    Delegation
    Communication
    Motivation

Implementation tasks

    Product alteration
    Price negotiation
    Place determination
    Promotion presentation

Fig. 1. Implementing business ethics.

Moore (1983) found that codes give more attention to unethical conduct likely to decrease firm's profits than to conduct that might increase profits. After closely examining over 50 corporate codes of ethics, several observations can be offered.

If codes, are to serve as a foundation for implementation, they should possess the characteristics listed in the Figure 1. Corporate codes should be *specific*. Employees need guidance in interpreting their actions. Motorola gives specific examples (i.e., A Motorolan traveling on Motorola business may accept the courtesy of free lodging in a customer facility so long as properly noted on the Motorolan's expense records) after each of the sections of its code. IBM lists three types of activities — mandatory, acceptable and unacceptable — in its Business Conduct Guidelines.

An area needing specificity is gifts and entertainment. Several companies state that employees can give or receive gifts of "nominal," "token" or "modest" value. However, it is very difficult to determine what is nominal or token and when a gift becomes a bribe. A number of companies have made their codes more specific in this area. Ford and GM stipulate that employees cannot give or receive gifts exceeding $25. Waste Management defines nominal value as "not exceeding $100 in aggregate annual value." Donnelly Mirrors gives the following guidelines: "If you can't eat it, drink it or use it up in one day, don't give it or anything else of greater value."

Second, codes should be *public documents*. Some corporate codes are exclusively for internal corporate use. If a code is worth developing, it should demonstrate to customers, suppliers, stockholders and others interested in the company the organization's commitment to fair and ethical practice.

Corporate codes should also be *blunt and realistic about violations*. For example, Baxter's code states that violators will be terminated. Gellerman (1986) indicated that the most effective deterrent is not to increase the severity of the punishment, but to "heighten the perceived probability of being caught." Therefore, active enforcement of existing codes should enhance compliance. Firms also need to consider how employees should react when confronted with violations of the code. Several codes instruct them to talk to their supervisor. Difficulties arise when the supervisor is the violator. Marriott tells employees to "see your manager or department head" if the issue cannot be resolved with the immediate supervisor.

Finally, codes should be *revised periodically*. That is, they should be living documents and updated to reflect current ethical problems. Caterpillar has revised its code three times since 1974. Investment banking firms likely would want to revise their codes in light of recent events. Specifically, Goldman Sachs now lists fourteen business principles and the last one states: "Integrity and honesty are at the heart of our business. We expect our people to maintain high ethical standards in everything they do, both at work for the firm and in their personal lives." This point probably should be placed much higher on the list and given greater emphasis in future revisions.

Ethics committees, training and conferences are a second structural method for implementing ethical business policies (see Figure 1). Only 15 percent of firms have ethics modules in their training programs and about 30 percent discuss ethics in management or policy sessions (Murphy, 1986). Motorola has a Business Ethics Compliance Committee that is charged with interpreting, clarifying, communicating and ajudicating the company's code. Some firms have used ethical consultants or speakers at dealer meetings on ethics. Cummins Engine for a time had an in-house ethicist. Polaroid held day long in-house conferences on ethics in '83 and '84 as part of a major ethics program.[3]

The Drackett Company, a subsidiary of Bristol Myers, recently implemented an ethics module in their 1987 Market Research Conference. Attendees at the meeting submitted in advance their responses to sixteen ethical scenarios. During the meeting small groups met to discuss three of the eleven scenarios where there was the greatest disagreement. According to the manager who led this activity, it was enthusiastically received. Many of the participants were surprised by their colleagues' judgments, but enjoyed the interchange in analyzing these issues.

Another structural suggestion for implementing business ethics listed in Figure 1 is an ethical audit. Just as financial and marketing audits seek to gain information about these functions, an ethical audit would pose questions about manufacturing practices, personnel policies, dealings with suppliers, financial reporting and sales techniques to find out if ethical abuses may be occurring. It might be argued that the answers to such questions are less important than raising and grappling with the issues.

Dow Corning instituted a face-to-face audit in their firm over ten years ago at company locations throughout the world. The agenda has shifted over the years from a standard one of 8–10 items for each site to a tailored discussion of specific questions about functional areas. At sales offices, issues such as kickbacks, unusual requests from customers and special pricing terms are examined. John Swanson, who heads this effort as Manager of the Corporate Internal and Management Communications Division, explained that the benefit of their innovative audit approach is "to make it virtually impossible for employees to consciously make an unethical decision."[4] Swanson (1987) indicated that twenty-one meetings were led by one of the four Business Conduct Committee members in '86–'87 and a report was prepared for the Audit Committee of the Board. He emphasized that there are no shortcuts to implementing this program and it requires time and extensive interaction of the people involved.

### Culture

The informal organization or corporate culture is the second component of the organizational dimension of ethics implementation (see Figure 1). Some commentators have indicated that the informal organization is much more important in the development of the firm's ethical posture than the formal organization. The informal organization creates the culture and formal policies are then a reflection of that culture. It works well at Hewlett-Packard, where the firm follows policies of liberal health benefits and no layoffs, because Bill Hewlett and David Packard want to remain true to the ideals on which the firm was founded. On the negative side, the recent revelations of nepotism and bribe taking by executives at Anheuser Busch was at least partially explained by observers who criticized the Busch family for perpetuating a corporate culture that condoned these activities. Therefore, the informal organization must reward ethical activities and give signals to managers that the company is committed to integrity in all business dealings.

A candid and ethical culture is one where communication freely flows within the organization (Serpa, 1985). This type of culture can help to reduce "moral stress" (Waters and Bird, 1987) and achieve "moral excellence" (Hoffman, 1986). A number of individuals including a CEO of a Big Eight accounting firm have advocated this approach to dealing with ethical problems. A climate where ethical issues can be openly discussed can lead to this type of culture. Spending time in management meetings is one avenue that has been used effectively. This sort of ethical training should ideally occur before problems arise and not after the fact such as the instance of E. F. Hutton and General Dynamics

contracting with the Ethics Resource Center for ethics training after running into serious problems.

The role of top management is crucial in creating the culture of an organization. The tone starts at the top. The CEO and other Vice-President level executives are extremely important in setting the ethical tenor of the firm.

## Executing ethical business policies

Figure 1 also shows the two components of the executing phase of business ethics implementation. It is not enough to have the structure and culture that support ethical decision making. These organizational dimensions must be combined with implementation responsibilities and tasks so that a firm is ethical in its execution of strategies.

### Implementation responsibilities

Although there are four execution responsibilities listed in the Figure, the over-arching one is leadership. As Bennis and Nanus (1986) have stated: American corporations are over-managed and under-led. Leadership is important in all aspects of the business, but it is critical in the ethics area.[5] Horton (1986) examined characteristics of CEOs and listed integrity as an "indispensible ingredient." A good example is James Burke of Johnson & Johnson who had managers evaluate the J & J Credo (which is often given as the reason for the swift and ethical reaction to the Tylenol poisonings). Basically, they reaffirmed the company's longstanding commitment to ethical business practice. A recent illustration is Lee Iacocca's stance regarding Chrysler's questionable practice of disconnecting odometers during testing by executives. He admitted that the company made mistakes in judgment and set forth a program to rectify them and promised that they would not happen again in a two page national ad. Mr. Iacocca did not view this as a product recall, but added "the only thing we're recalling here is our integrity."

Delegation follows from leadership, but is an essential responsibility for effective implementation to occur. Middle and lower level managers are sometimes placed in difficult ethical situations because high level executives are unclear in their delegation of ethical responsibilities. Statements such as "I don't care how you do it, just meet or beat your quota" or "Ship more to that customer this month than you did last" or "Find a way to fire that person" often give subordinates the impression that any tactic can be used to reach organizational objectives. Several years ago managers in a truck plant installed a secret control box to override the speed of the assembly line because they felt it was the only way to achieve production objectives set by upper management. If the delegation responsibility is to be dispatched properly, executives must be more explicit about what are acceptable and ethical practices.

Communication is an essential responsibility if ethical policies are to be executed in any organization. Formally, this communication can happen in many ways through the ethical code and seminars/ training programs that deal with ethical issues. New employees of most companies are asked to read and sign the ethical code upon their employment. In many instances, however, little communication follows the initial exposure. To overcome this potential problem, Caterpillar requires its managers to report annually about its implementation of the code within the division/department. Similarly, Michigan National Bank requires that employees sign off on the ethical code every year.

Informal communication is also a potentially effective implementation responsibility. The grapevine can disseminate information that formal vehicles cannot. For instance, the fact that a salesperson lost his/her commission for padding the expense account may not lend itself to discussion in the company newsletter. However, the word can get through informal channels and consequently influence future behavior.

The last, but certainly the not the least important, implementation responsibility is motivation. If companies are to be successful in executing ethical marketing policies, individuals must be motivated to do the right thing. This means that higher level executives must look closely at how performance is measured. Managers who engage in exorbitant entertaining of clients or informally practice discrimination should not be rewarded for these activities. One of the problems with the Wall Street scandal was that top managers did not look closely at the large profits their firms were earning. How did these large returns happen? Unfortunately, we know the answer in many cases. Employees are motivated by higher level executives and their expectations regarding ethical business practices.

*Implementation tasks*

Implementation tasks relate to specific functional areas within the firm. One area that has received much attention in the academic and popular press is marketing implementation (Bonoma, 1984; Enis and Murphy, 1987; Peters and Waterman, 1982). Since marketing is charged with external relations with customers where many ethical issues arise, it will serve as the focal point for this discussion. Other functional areas could be treated similarly. For example, if human resources were the focus, tasks relating to hiring, training and promoting employees would be relevant.

Figure 1 lists the relevant implementation tasks for the marketing mix variables of product, price, channel and promotion. Product alteration is intended to get the consumer to make the intended exchange. Ethical issues result when minor adjustments are promoted as being significant changes to the product. Furthermore, the development of me-too products could be questioned from an ethical standpoint. One other product alteration issue relates to the product manager. Does this person, who is usually on the fast-track, make needed modifications to a brand to insure its long-term marketplace staying power or only perform cosmetic changes to improve next quarter's market share or profit picture?

Price negotiation is often at the heart of marketing implementation. Those sales executives and marketing managers who can effectively negotiate on price win many contracts. An ethical problem occurs in this process when one of the participants has much more power than the other. An example is a large Midwestern department store chain which dealt with a small candy producer and told the company that they would pay 70 percent of the negotiated price and the small firm could keep the account or pay 100 percent and they would lose the account. These types of practices are unethical, but not illegal. They possibly might be curbed by the small firm taking its case to the top echelon of the larger company.

Place determination refers to getting the product to the place it is demanded in an expeditious manner. Here marketers often promise more than they can deliver. It becomes an ethical issue when there is economic or psychological harm to the client/consumer. In health care or other life threatening situations, execution of place determination is critical. Greater emphasis on marketing by these organizations may heighten the ethical problems they face. Furthermore, large retailers may coerce other members of the channel to achieve their objectives in getting products to the market.

Promotion presentation is often viewed as a

crucial function of marketing. Both selling and advertising have persuasive, informative and re-minding components. The persuasive area is most often associated with ethical abuses. In selling, ethical problems often arise when persuasion is too intense or competitors are unscrupulous in their appeals. What the ethical salesperson should do is to insure that the buyers are making decisions on what he/she believes are the most important evaluative criteria. If the unethical marketer cannot deliver on their promises, the ethical firm has a good chance to gain the business. Even if the business is lost once, there is sometimes an opportunity to gain it later. For example, a communications firm sought a contract with a defense contractor, but found the defense company only wanted entree to newspaper editors. The consultant indicated that he could not meet these unrealistic goals and ". . . walked out. Several months later he got a $50,000 contract" (Davidson, 1986).

Some companies even identify the types of sales tactics that are acceptable in their firm's code of ethics. For instance, ADP, a computer software company, states: "Aggressive selling should not include defamation of competition, malicious rumors or unsupportable promises." IBM's code makes a similar point: "It has long been the company's policy to provide customers the best possible products and services. Sell them on their merits, not by disparaging competitors."

The advertising area is one where persuasion is often criticized for being unethical. If the message includes puffery, but not deception (which is illegal), then it falls into an ethical gray area. One type of advertising that is receiving growing criticism is advertising to children, especially for war toys and highly sugared products. Furthermore, the current debate about advertising beer and wine on television centers on free speech vs. potential negative effects of product usage on consumers, especially teenagers who find the lifestyles portrayed in these commercials to be rather desirable.

In examining a number of codes of conduct, it was surprising to find that very few list a specific posture with respect to advertising. An exception is Ford which provides explicit policies for the use of comparative advertising. This might be an area where consumer products marketers consider developing explicit guidelines. Some have ad hoc policies regarding sponsorship of shows dealing with sensitive subjects or containing large amounts of sex/violence. It appears that thought should be given to appropriate advertising messages and possibly even

media in implementing the ethical policies of the firm.

## An illustration of business ethics implementation

In 1987 one firm, McDonnell Douglas, has engaged in an extensive business ethics implementation program.[6] Their effort even has a theme — "Always take the high road." The corporate code has been revised for the third time in the 1980s. A series of three ethics books were distributed to all employees at their home address in June. The "Code of Ethics" book features ethical decision making guidelines, a short version of their code and the ethical decision making checklist. The latter two are also available in pocket size cards and are shown in Figure 2.

The "Standards of Business Conduct" book lists five overriding standards and several areas pertaining to each of them. Discussion of these standards is treated in three sections — *In General* (states the overall principle), *Specifically* (contains specific rules, laws and requirements applicable to each standard) and *Where to Go* (where to turn to for help). This book concludes with a section on procedures for reporting possible violations including employees' obligation to report, confidentiality and absence of reprisals.

The third book, "Questions and Answers," shows how selected standards apply in potentially difficult work situations through a question and detailed answer format. This publication is written in layman's terms and cross referenced to the longer standards book. The company also has a corporation-wide ethics training program that all management and blue collar employees attend. A seven person ethics committee is formally charged with implementing all facets of the program.

The informal organization is involved in several ways. An extensive ombudsman program is operational as well as a number of instructions to employees to openly discuss and air ethical abuses they see occurring. At the end of the "Questions and Answers" book, employees are asked for their comments or questions on ethical issues. These informal responses are to be returned directly to the Corporate Ethics Committee. Another alternative for responding about ethical problems and violations is a hotline number used exclusively for reports to this committee.

The role of top management is instrumental in making the program work. S. N. "Sandy" McDonnell,

## McDONNELL DOUGLAS CODE OF ETHICS

Integrity and ethics exist in the individual or they do not exist at all. They must be upheld by individuals or they are not upheld at all. In order for integrity and ethics to be characteristics of McDonnell Douglas, we who make up the Corporation must strive to be:

- *Honest and trustworthy in all our relationships;*

- *Reliable in carrying out assignments and responsibilities;*

- *Truthful and accurate in what we say and write;*

- *Cooperative and constructive in all work undertaken;*

- *Fair and considerate in our treatment of fellow employees, customers, and all other persons;*

- *Law abiding in all our activities;*

- *Committed to accomplishing all tasks in a superior way;*

- *Economical in utilizing company resources; and*

- *Dedicated in service to our company and to improvement of the quality of life in the world in which we live.*

Integrity and high standards of ethics require hard work, courage, and difficult choices. Consultation among employees, top management, and the Board of Directors will sometimes be necessary to determine a proper course of action. Integrity and ethics may sometimes require us to forgo business opportunities. In the long run, however, we will be better served by doing what is right rather than what is expedient. (From MDC Policy 2, *MDC Policy Manual*).

## ETHICAL DECISION MAKING CHECKLIST

### Analysis

- *What are the facts?*

- *Who is responsible to act?*

- *What are the consequences of action? (Benefit-Harm Analysis)*

- *What and whose rights are involved? (Rights/Principles Analysis)*

- *What is fair treatment in this case? (Social Justice Analysis)*

### Solution development

- *What solutions are available to me?*

- *Have I considered all of the creative solutions which might permit me to reduce harm, maximize benefits, respect more rights, or be fair to more parties?*

### Select the optimum solution

- *What are the potential consequences of my solutions?*

- *Which of the options I have considered does the most to maximize benefits, reduce harm, respect rights and increase fairness?*

- *Are all parties treated fairly in my proposed decision?*

### Implementation

- *Who should be consulted and informed?*

- *What actions will assure that my decision achieves its intended outcome?*

- *Implement.*

### Follow up

- *Was the decision implemented correctly?*

- *Did the decision maximize benefits, reduce harm, respect rights and treat all parties fairly?*

Fig. 2. McDonnell Douglas ethical code and check list.

the former CEO, has been on the forefront in advocating ethical practices in the aerospace industry. He has taken a leadership role as evidenced by the following comment made in 1984:

A company has to go beyond just tacking an ethics code up on the wall. You have to make sure that everyone

knows and understands it — from the chairman on down through supervision (Miller 1984);

and this statement which appeared in a 1987 company publication describing his commitment to the current ethics program:

What I hope all this will lead to is a business environment in which the issue of ethics remains in the forefront of everything we do. If we always make the ethical choice, if we always take the high road, we will be doing not only what is right, but also what is best for McDonnell Douglas and ourselves as individuals.

A procedure is delegated and communicated throughout the organization in the form of the company's "ethical decision making" check list in Figure 2. The steps outlined are analysis, solution development, selection of the optimum solution, implementation and follow-up parallel closely those advocated by Nash (1981) several years ago. These mechanisms have motivated employees to become more active in providing comments and suggestions on how ethics can be improved in the firm. This complete ethics implementation program can serve as a model for other companies.[7]

## Conclusion

The major premise articulated here is that firms can ethically implement their business strategies. Several conclusions can be drawn.

1. Codes of ethics must be more than legal or public relations documents. They must provide specific and useful guidance to employees. Firms are urged to rethink their codes to make them more viable by including specific practices, examples or answers to often asked ethical questions.

2. Visible signs must exist that ethics matters to the firm. This can be accomplished by spending time in formal meetings discussing ethical issues and working through the corporate culture. Both the carrot and stick methods should be used. Employees should be rewarded for making ethical choices and at the same time the code must be enforced. These actions must be communicated throughout the firm, so that the commitment is understood.

3. Top management must pay attention to detail on how results are accomplished. The same scrutiny should be employed when examining profits as costs. Similarly, management should not give vague or unrealistic goals to subordinates without some explanation of how they are to be attained.

4. Ethics implementation needs a champion. Someone must make it happen. It is essential that the CEO be in support of it, but in companies like McDonnell Douglas and Polaroid the ethics cause had a champion. This is likely most effective if the job title in not solely related to this task.

In implementing business ethics, attention must be paid to both the organizing and executing components (see Figure 1). Only if managers and top executives are consciously committed to carrying out ethical policies will implementation actually occur. Tough questions must be asked and appropriate answers should be given at all levels of the organization. We can improve the ethical posture of business, but everyone must be committed to it.

## Notes

The author would like to thank Gerald Cavanagh, S. J., Stephen Greyser, Gene Laczniak, Lee Tavis, Clarence Walton and Oliver Williams, C. S. C. for their helpful comments on an earlier version of this article.

[1] This definition and format of the article are partially adapted from "Marketing Implementation," in Murphy and Enis (1985).
[2] The following discussion of implementing business ethics relies primarily on structural or organization procedures. An alternative approach which focuses on individual responsibilities is outlined by Nielsen (1986).
[3] For a discussion of Polaroid's program, see Godfrey (1987) and Godfrey and Williams (1985).
[4] For more detail on this program, see Swanson (1984) and ("Dow Corning" . . . 1986).
[5] A recent in-depth examination of the ethical leadership issue appeared in Enderle (1987).
[6] McDonnell Douglas is a participant in the eighteen point voluntary industry agreement, "The Defense Industry Initiatives on Business Ethics and Conduct." The company's commitment to ethics is the driving force for this program, not industry or governmental pressure.
[7] Although McDonnell Douglas was implicated in recent U.S. Defense Department contract problems, the company feels that its policies are sound and set up a high level task force to determine whether additional guidelines are needed. The CEO stated: "We want to leave no doubt that McDonnell Douglas believes in and acts in accordance with the highest ethical standards" (Schachter 1988).

## References

Bennis, Warren and Bert Nanus: 1985, *Leaders*, New York: Harper & Row.

Berenbeim, Ronald E.: 1987, *Corporate Ethics*, New York: The Conference Board.

Bonoma, Thomas V.: 1984, 'Making Your Marketing Strategy Work', *Harvard Business Review* (March–April), 69–76.

Center for Business Ethics: 1986, 'Are Corporations Institutionalizing Ethics?', *Journal of Business Ethics* **5**, 85–91.

Cressey, Donald R. and Charles A. Moore: (1983), 'Managerial Values and Corporate Codes of Ethics', *California Management Review* (Summer), 53—77.

Davidson, Jeffrey P.: 1986, 'The Elusive Nature of Integrity', *Marketing News* (November 7), 24.

'Dow Corning Corporation: Ethics, "Face-to-Face" ': 1986, *Ethics Resource Center Report* (Winter), 4—7.

Enderle, Georges: 1987, 'Some Perspectives of Managerial Ethical Leadership', *Journal of Business Ethics* **6**, 657—663.

Enis, Ben M. and Patrick E. Murphy: 1987, 'Marketing Strategy Implementation', in G. L. Frazier and J. N. Sheth (eds.), *Contemporary Views on Marketing Practice*, Lexington, MA: Lexington Books, pp. 159—173.

Gellerman, Saul W.: 1986, 'Why "Good" Managers Make Bad Ethical Choices', *Harvard Business Review* (July—August), 85—90.

Godfrey, Joline: 1987, 'Ethics as an Entrepreneurial Venture', *Training News* (June).

Godfrey, Joline and R. Williams: 1985, 'Leadership and Values at Polaroid Corporation', unpublished paper.

Hoffman, W. Michael: 1986, 'What Is Necessary for Corporate Moral Excellence?', *Journal of Business Ethics* **5**, 233—242.

Horton, Thomas R.: 1986, *What Works for Me: 16 CEOs Talk About Their Careers and Commitments*, New York: Random House.

McCoy, Bowen H.: 1983, 'The Parable of the Sadhu', *Harvard Business Review* (September—October), 103—108.

Miller, William H.: 1984, 'Business' New Link: Ethics and the Bottom Line', *Industry Week* (October 29), 49—53.

Murphy, Patrick E.: 1986, 'Marketing VPs Views Toward Marketing Ethics', Working Paper, University of Notre Dame.

Murphy, Patrick E. and Ben M. Enis: 1985, *Marketing*, Glenview, IL: Scott-Foresman.

Nash, Laura: 1981, 'Ethics Without the Sermon', *Harvard Business Review*, (November—December), 79—90.

Nielsen, Richard P.: 1987, 'What Can Managers Do about Unethical Management?', *Journal of Business Ethics* **6**, 309—320.

Peters, Thomas J. and Robert H. Waterman, Jr.: 1982, *In Search of Excellence*, New York: Harper & Row.

Purcell, Theodore V., Jr.: 1978, 'Institutionalizing Ethics on Corporate Boards', *Review of Social Economy*, December, 41—53.

Schachter, Jim: 1988, 'McDonnell Douglas to Probe Use of Defense Officials as Consultants', *Los Angeles Times* (August 5, 1988), Part IV, 3.

Serpa, Roy: 1985, 'Creating a Candid Corporate Culture', *Journal of Business Ethics* **4**, 425—430.

Swanson, John E.: 1984, 'Developing a Workable Corporate Ethic', in W. M. Hoffman, J. M. Moore, and D. A. Fedo (eds.), *Corporate Governance and Institutionalizing Ethics*, Lexington, MA: Lexington Books, pp. 209—215.

Swanson, John E.: 1987, Personal communication with the author, June 21.

Wartzman, Rick: 1987, 'Nature or Nurture? Study Blames Ethical Lapses on Corporate Goals', *The Wall Street Journal* (October 9), 21.

Waters, James A. and Frederick Bird: 1987, 'The Moral Dimension of Organizational Culture', *Journal of Business Ethics* **6**, 15—22.

# Take the Pap Out of Ethics

*Ethics is a hot business topic. And while that is a potential boon to us all, dealing with the realities is not easy.*

## Tom Peters

*Tom Peters is founder of The Tom Peters Group, four training and communications companies in Palo Alto, CA (415) 326-5400. He is the coauthor of the bestsellers* In Search of Excellence *and* A Passion for Excellence *and author of* Thriving on Chaos. *Tom is now writing a book about the end of hierarchy and the futility of most corporate renewal efforts [to be published Spring 1992]. He has an MBA and Ph.D. from Stanford and BCE and MCE degrees from Cornell.*

THE HEIGHTENED AWARENESS of ethics has spawned an industry of mindless, "do good, be good" writings. But dealing with ethics isn't so easy. The point was driven home after I accepted an invitation to speak about ethics. I spent many a restless night grappling with the easy simplifications that ignore messy reality.

### 15 Observations

This set of somewhat disjointed observations is one byproduct.

• *Ethics is not principally about headline issues* — responding to the Tylenol poisoning or handling insider information. Ethical concerns surround us all the time, on parade whenever we deal with people in the course of the average day. How we work out the "little stuff" will determine our response, if called upon, to a Tylenol-sized crisis. When disaster strikes, it's far too late to seek out ethical touchstones.

• *High ethical standards* — business or otherwise — are, above all, about treating people decently. To me (as a person, businessperson and business owner) that means respect for a person's privacy, dignity, opinions and natural desire to grow; and people's respect for (and by) coworkers.

• *Diversity must be honored.* To be sure, it is important to be clear about your own compass heading; but don't ever forget that other people have profoundly different — and equally decent — ethical guidance mechanisms.

• *People, even the saints, are egocentric and selfish.* We were designed "wrong" in part from the start. Any ethical framework in action had best take into account the troublesome but immutable fact of man's inherently flawed character.

• *Corporations are created and exist to serve people* — insiders and outsiders — period.

• *By their very nature, organizations run roughshod over people.* Organizations produce powerlessness and humiliation for most participants with more skill than they produce widgets.

• *Though all men and women are created equal, some surely have more power than others.* Thus, a central ethical issue in the workplace (and beyond) is the protection of and support for the unempowered — especially the front-line worker and the customer.

• *For employees and managers alike, fighting the impersonal "they"/"them" (every bureaucratic institution) is almost always justified on ethical grounds.*

• *While one can point to ethically superior (and profitable) firms, such as Herman Miller, most of us will spend most of our working life in compromised — i.e., politicized — organizations.* Dealing with office politics is a perpetual ethical morass. A "pure" ethical stance in the face of most firms' political behavior will lead you out the door in short order, with only the convent, monastery or ashram as alternatives. The line between ethical purity and arrogant egocentricism (i.e., a holier-than-thou stance toward the tumult of everyday life) is a fine one.

• *Though I sing the praises of an "action bias," ethical behavior demands that we tread somewhat softly in all of our affairs.* Unintended consequences and the secondary

From *Executive Excellence*, Vol. 8, No. 4, April 1991, p. 8. *Executive Excellence*, The Magazine of Personal Development, Managerial Effectiveness, and Organizational Productivity. Copyright © 1989 by TPG Communications.

and tertiary effects of most actions and policies far outnumber intended and first-order effects. I sometimes think — as a manager, as a "change agent" — that dropping out is the only decent/ethical path; our best-intended plans so often cause more harm than good. (Think about it: Leaving the world no worse off than when you arrived is no mean feat.)

• *The pursuit of high ethical standards in business might well be served by the elimination of many business schools.* The implicit thrust of most MBA programs is that great systems and great techniques win out over great people.

• *Can we live up to the spirit of the Bill of Rights in our work places?* Can "good business ethics" and "good real-life ethics" — and profit — coincide on a routine basis? One would hope that the answer is yes, although respect for the individual has hardly been the cornerstone of American industry's traditional approach to its work force.

• *Capitalism and democracy in society are messy.* But I believe that they have far fewer downsides and far more upsides than any alternative so far concocted. The same can be said for capitalism and democracy inside the firm — e.g., wholesale participation, widespread ownership.

• *Great novels, not management books, might help.* There are no easy answers, but there are fertile fields for gathering ideas. If you wish to be appropriately humbled about life and relationships and the possibility of ethical behavior, read Dostoyevsky, Forster or Garcia Marquez instead of Drucker, Blanchard or Peters. Then reconsider your latest magisterial proclamation.

• *Each of us is ultimately lonely.* In the end, it's up to each of us and each of us alone to figure out who we are, who you are not, and to act more or less consistently on those conclusions.

### A Good Start

In my view, anyone who is not very confused all the time about ethical issues is out of touch with the frightful (and joyous) richness of the world. But at least being actively confused means that we are actively considering our ethical stance and that of the institutions we associate with. That's a good start.

# The Ethics Game

## Karin Ireland

*Karin Ireland is senior editor.*

Citicorp developed a game that teaches ethics by asking employees to confront difficult scenarios.

Citicorp has developed a sophisticated board game to communicate corporate ethics to its 90,000 employees worldwide.

Ethics is more complicated than labeling some things right and other things wrong. In many cases, whether a behavior is right or wrong depends on the circumstances. But a company that allows each employee to make decisions based solely on his or her complex background of beliefs and training is asking for trouble and one doesn't have to look far to find evidence that this is true.

Citicorp has communicated its ethics policies to employees for years in speeches, training sessions and its thick policy manual. A 60-page booklet describing the company's ethical standards is distributed every three years to officers worldwide.

In 1985, senior management asked corporate communications to develop a program to provide even more exposure to the integrity issue. The goal was two-fold: teach the company's ethical culture and encourage compliance through the subtle peer pressure that would come from continuing dialog.

The result was a game that challenges employees to think, gives them permission to question and trains them to develop insights into dealing with issues beyond the obvious right and wrong.

"At Citicorp we've found that one of the best training methods on ethics is the case study approach," says Kate Nelson, head of communication for corporate human resources. "We think one of the reasons this approach is so effective is that it creates a dialog on ethics — it makes it OK to talk about ethics out loud with peers and management."

*The Work Ethic* is a board and card game that presents ethical dilemmas. Each dilemma and its possible solution were discussed by management and tested extensively during the six months the game was being developed.

The playing board is divided into four levels: entry-level, supervisor, manager or senior manager. The points a team can win or lose are different at each level — not because the underlying ethical choices are different, but because as one rises in an organization the consequences of a decision have increasingly serious implications and that behavior sets an example for a greater number of junior employees.

Each card presents an ethical dilemma that deals with situations including insider trading, customer confidentiality, conflicts of interest or sexual harassment.

Four solutions are offered for each dilemma, although none of them is perfect. No changes may be made to make any of the choices more acceptable. Based on the answers chosen, participants can win or lose points, end up in the penalty box (losing a turn), or get fired for just cause, which means they're out of the game. Small teams of employees work together to try to identify the answers management feels most nearly reflect the ethical way to resolve the dilemma.

Ready to try one? A vice president in your organization asks you, as corporate recruiter, to find a career opportunity for a manager in his area. You know this manager is a poor performer, although the vice president hasn't reflected any performance issues on the manager's performance reviews. The VP tells you he wants this manager out of his area within three months. Your rapport with this VP is critical to success in your job.

You:

A) Insist that the manager be counseled on his performance before any transfer process begins

B) Present the manager to your fellow recruiters with the performance review and say nothing about the performance

C) Refuse to help in this transfer

D) Present the candidate to your fellow recruiters, but are frank about the performance issues.

Players feel the most correct answer to some dilemmas is obvious until team members add their points of view. How does a corporate recruiter tell a vice president or manager that that manager must undergo performance counseling before a transfer will be arranged? Notice that the most comfortable solution, taking the problem to the recruiter's supervisor, is not an option. Teams that choose A) receive 20 points; B) -10; C) 0; and D) 10.

Because the game can generate tremendous disagreements, there's an appeals process built into it, again, to encourage dialog. A trained facilitator and an appeals board of three or four members of senior management sit in on each orientation, training session or off-site conference where the game is played. Players who disagree with a printed answer can challenge it; the appeals board can support or override the printed scoring, but only if their vote is unanimous.

Nelson feels the appeals board concept accomplishes a number of important goals: It gives participants the very clear message that ethics is important because senior management is taking time to talk about it; players have the opportunity to see how management works to resolve an ethical problem; and it gives senior management the opportunity to interpret corporate policy for their own business.

This kind of openness reaffirms the company's position on encouraging employees to speak up without fear of censure. It also identifies management as approachable in case any of the players need future advice.

During the game, employees are reminded that the company's ethical ombudsman provides confidential advice and is a method for going around their chain of command, if necessary.

Since the first game was developed there have been new questions created for lawyers, traders, private bankers, recruiters, international money managers and credit card collectors, and for geographic regions such as the Far East and South America.

Nelson began pilot testing *The Work Ethic* in 1987 and since then 30,000 to 40,000 Citicorp staff have played it in at least 54 countries. The game has been translated into Spanish, Portuguese, French, German, Flemish and Japanese.

As a result of observing an ongoing ethics dialog for more than four years, Nelson says she's learned a valuable lesson. "You can't overstate the importance of talking about ethics," she says, "whether it's in a corporation or in our personal lives. Without training, even well-meaning employees can make bad decisions.

"As the IRS will tell you, laws don't deter people. And neither do fines, the threat of imprisonment, a spouse's wrath, or the prospect of ruining a career. What does influence behavior is the expectations of our peers. Talking about ethics can change behavior; we reinforce our own commitment to integrity and we can deter other people from behaving unethically."

# Business and Society: Contemporary Ethical, Social, and Environmental Issues

- **Changing Perspectives in Business and Society (Articles 28–32)**
- **Major Contemporary Dilemmas (Articles 33–35)**
- **Global Ethics (Articles 36–37)**

Both at home and abroad there are social and environmental issues that have potential ethical consequences for management. Incidents of insider trading, deaths resulting from unsafe products or work environments, AIDS in the workplace, and the adoption of policies for involvement in the global market are a few of the issues that need to be seriously addressed by management.

This section will investigate the nature and ramifications of some of the salient ethical, social, and environmental issues facing management today. The 10 articles are grouped into 3 subsections. The first article in this subsection emphasizes that while the level of business ethics appears to be edging upward, ethical abuses still clearly abound. "The Parable of the Sadhu" is a thought-provoking parable exemplifying the consequences of the breakdown between the individual ethic and the corporate ethic. The next article asserts that, although from outward appearances Americans seemingly claim to be environmentalists, actual purchase decisions reveal that many are not the environmentalists they claim to be. "New Trends in Relocation" discloses the importance of management's understanding how changing attitudes about work and family can affect future relocation strategies. The last article in this subsection reveals the barriers that women executives face and experience in attempting to break the "glass ceiling" in many organizations.

The second subsection addresses some of the major dilemmas that contemporary business has recently been forced to reckon with. The first articles in this subsection consider the impact of drugs and AIDS in the workplace and suggest ways to establish sensitive policies and ongoing programs to help deal with each. The last article, "The Untouchables," analyzes the dilemmas surrounding the drafting of an integrity code for a South African company.

The last subsection, *Global Ethics*, includes two articles that provide helpful insight on ethical issues and dilemmas inherent in multinational operations, discuss the problem of money laundering, and offer guidelines for helping management deal with ethical issues in international markets.

### Looking Ahead: Challenge Questions

In "The Parable of the Sadhu," a major problem was the lack of a mechanism for developing a consensus on dealing with the Sadhu. Given the complexities of an organization where an ethical dilemma often cannot be optimally resolved by one person alone, how can an individual secure the support of the group and help it to reach a consensus?

Is it fair to bring criminal charges against corporations and executives for unsafe products, dangerous working conditions, or industrial pollution?

How do you feel management should deal with AIDS in the workplace? Should management deal with drugs in the same way? Why or why not?

What types of ethical dilemmas is management likely to face when conducting business in foreign environments? How can management best deal with these dilemmas?

# Unit 3

# INDUSTRY ETHICS EDGE UPWARD

After the decade of anything goes, U. S. companies are
taking a closer look at their ethical standards.

TRACY E. BENSON

To hear it from INDUSTRY WEEK readers, the ethical climate in U. S. companies appears to be on the rise. Even so, the issue is as much of a hot button today as it was four years ago when IW first undertook a poll on the subject.

For every positive comment received ("Doing business in an honest and fair manner is the only way!"), there were piles of scrawlings from skeptics. One reader laments, "They don't seem to teach ethics in business school anymore—just profits and ambition."

Another charges: "Business ethics is an oxymoron."

Roughly half the respondents to IW's recent survey on ethics report that not much has changed compared with two years ago. However, the ranks of those who claim ethics are now *higher* than they were two years ago—28.8%—are up 5.6 percentage points from 1987.

Perhaps it is the increase in companies that put codes of ethics into writing—58.3% compared with 48.6% four years ago—that has nudged the level of ethical awareness upward.

However, many readers caution that while their companies do boast such written codes, the documents are often overlooked or ignored. An unidentified reader complains, "Emphasis on ethics in this company appears to be 'eyewash.'" A senior systems engineer calls his company's written code "just a piece of paper with no relationship to actuality."

In the face of such cynicism, it is not surprising that although written codes of ethics are cropping up more often, fewer employees are reading them. The number of those who claim to have read their company's codes dropped from 95.5% in '87 to 91.5% this year.

Perceived management hypocrisy is a common culprit. Business ethics, says a Midwestern senior programmer, "is the corporate version of 'Do as I say, not as I do.'" One reader notes that "the higher the officer, the bigger the problem." And a Wisconsin-based purchasing manager takes his complaint all the way to the top: "I think CEO multi-million-dollar incomes are immoral and related to business ethics."

On the more positive side, three in four readers claim their company's code of ethics—or ethics in general—means something to them

in their day-to-day work. That figure is up 2.3 points from IW's earlier survey. Ethics means so much to one Southern chief engineer that he left a division and eventually the company because he was expected to behave in what he considered to be an unethical way.

Clearly, managers and executives send powerful messages about the priority of business ethics through their own behavior and their expectations of those who work for them. Thus it is good news indeed that the ranks of those who have been asked to behave unethically by a supervisor have shrunk from 30.6% in '87 to 24.9% this year. On the other hand, of those who have been asked to behave unethically, an overwhelming majority—63.8%—felt the alternative was to lose their job.

The role of management in promoting—or degrading—ethics is not lost on workers. "Ethics, like quality, starts as the vision of top management," a quality-assurance director aptly writes. A Georgia-based reader notes, "When leaders are very clear about their personal values (and ethics) and how those

# WHERE HAVE OUR ETHICS GONE?

### As markets constrict, ethics takes the heat.

Sixty-four percent of respondents to IW's business-ethics survey claim to have witnessed unethical behavior by others at their companies.

Here are some reasons our readers—and your colleagues, customers, and suppliers—cite for poor ethical choices:

#### Cultural Pervasiveness

- "Business ethics are a reflection of overall ethics in a society. The U. S. is currently seeing a general decline in personal ethics."
- "America lacks enforcement of standards—TV, Congress, professional sports, criminal justice, business, you, me. No fear of punishment."

#### The Bottom Line

- "Around here anything is ethical if it improves the bottom line."
- "The problem is keeping stockholders happy. Morita [of Sony] is

right about American business—we think only as far as the next dividend check."

#### Lack Of Ethics Training

- "Ninety-five percent of top executives never had any training or education in the subject."
- "Why aren't we teaching ethics in all grades—K through 12? Very few people understand ethics and leadership."
- "They don't seem to teach ethics in business school anymore—just profits and ambition."

#### Team Pressures

- "The 'yes-man/team player' concept cultivates and rewards unethical behavior."

#### Foreign Competition

- "The influence of Pacific Rim companies has negatively impacted U. S. corporate ethics. Their acceptance of unethical behavior as 'O.K.' hurts."

*Compared with two years ago, are ethics in your company:*

Higher
Lower
Unchanged

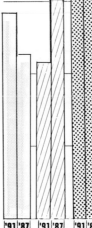

'91 '87  '91 '87  '91 '87

and only 1.9% dared to discuss the abuse with the person involved.

**Factors contributing** to the state of business ethics vary as widely as the individuals who make up IW's readership. Several respondents note that the factors listed in our survey all imply a negative sense of ethics: ambition, personal financial gain, competition, job pressure, corporate financial gain, and peer pressure. Some point out that factors such as upbringing, traditional or "Christian" morals, and education all affect the development of business ethics as well.

Interestingly, the motivation for unethical behavior seems to have shifted significantly during the last four years. Only half of this year's respondents credited ambition as a contributing factor, while ambition was the unanimous choice in the earlier survey. Likewise, personal financial gain seems to have fallen out of favor (checked by 95% in 1987 and only 50.4% this year). Surprisingly, competition was granted less influence, from 87% four years ago to just 36.9% this year. And, finally, job pressure was cited by 85% in '87 and only 34.2% this year. Corporate financial gain made a strong showing at 32.7%, followed by peer pressure, with 14.7%.

While the level of business ethics appears to be edging upward, ethical abuses clearly abound. Moral conscience may not be enough to turn the tide. But perhaps those encouraging, causing, and tolerating these abuses will heed the wise words of a chief engineer whose concern is U. S. industry: "The lack of a strong ethical backbone is the single most debilitating problem in American management."

are expected to be played out in the business world, with few exceptions, they will be."

An alarming 63.9% of respondents report having witnessed unethical behavior in their companies. And while that number is down slightly from four years ago (when it was 70%), the insidious fact is that far fewer witnesses have confided in their bosses—29.7% as opposed to roughly half in 1987.

Among the startling reasons for keeping a tight lip: "If you complain, you get sent for two weeks of

counseling, then fired." One reader describes a co-worker who was operating his own business on the job. When a report was made, the witness was brought into a closed-door meeting with the accused and the supervisor. "I was told that I had two problems—a lack of trust and a lack of loyalty. Then I was basically told they would find something to fire me for if I pursued the issue any further."

One in five IW readers admits ignoring ethical abuses, 13.7% to feeding the perennial grapevine,

# The parable of the sadhu

*After encountering
a dying pilgrim
on a climbing trip in the
Himalayas,
a businessman ponders
the differences between
individual and
corporate ethics*

## Bowen H. McCoy

*Mr. McCoy is a managing director of Morgan Stanley & Co., Inc., and president of Morgan Stanley Realty, Inc. He is also an ordained ruling elder of the United Presbyterian Church.*

*It was early in the morning before the sun rose, which gave them time to climb the treacherous slope to the pass at 18,000 feet before the ice steps melted. They were also concerned about their stamina and altitude sickness, and felt the need to press on. Into this chance collection of climbers on that Himalayan slope an ethical dilemma arose in the guise of an unconscious, almost naked sadhu, an Indian holy man. Each climber gave the sadhu help but none made sure he would be safe. Should somebody have stopped to help the sadhu to safety? Would it have done any good? Was the group responsible? Since leaving the sadhu on the mountain slope, the author, who was one of the climbers, has pondered these issues. He sees many parallels for business people as they face ethical decisions at work.*

Last year, as the first participant in the new six-month sabbatical program that Morgan Stanley has adopted, I enjoyed a rare opportunity to collect my thoughts as well as do some traveling. I spent the first three months in Nepal, walking 600 miles through 200 villages in the Himalayas and climbing some 120,000 vertical feet. On the trip my sole Western companion was an anthropologist who shed light on the cultural patterns of the villages we passed through.

During the Nepal hike, something occurred that has had a powerful impact on my thinking about corporate ethics. Although some might argue that the experience has no relevance to business, it was a situation in which a basic ethical dilemma suddenly intruded into the lives of a group of individuals. How the group responded I think holds a lesson for all organizations no matter how defined.

### The sadhu

The Nepal experience was more rugged and adventuresome than I had anticipated. Most commercial treks last two or three weeks and cover a quarter of the distance we traveled.

My friend Stephen, the anthropologist, and I were halfway through the 60-day Himalayan part of the trip when we reached the high point, an 18,000-foot pass over a crest that we'd have to traverse to reach to the village of Muklinath, an ancient holy place for pilgrims.

Six years earlier I had suffered pulmonary edema, an acute form of altitude sickness, at 16,500 feet in the vicinity of Everest base camp, so we were understandably concerned about what would happen at 18,000 feet. Moreover, the Himalayas were having their wettest spring in 20 years; hip-deep powder and ice had already driven us off one ridge. If we failed to cross the pass, I feared that the last half of our "once in a lifetime" trip would be ruined.

The night before we would try the pass, we camped at a hut at 14,500 feet. In the photos taken at that camp, my face appears wan. The last village we'd passed through was a sturdy two-day walk below us, and I was tired.

During the late afternoon, four backpackers from New Zealand joined us, and we spent most of the night awake, anticipating the climb. Below we could see the fires of two other parties, which turned out to be two Swiss couples and a Japanese hiking club.

To get over the steep part of the climb before the sun melted the steps cut in the ice, we departed at 3:30 A.M. The New Zealanders left first, followed by Stephen and myself, our porters and Sherpas, and then the Swiss. The Japanese lingered in their camp. The sky was clear, and we were confident that no spring storm would erupt that day to close the pass.

At 15,500 feet, it looked to me as if Stephen were shuffling and staggering a bit, which are symptoms of altitude sickness. (The initial stage of altitude sickness brings a headache and nausea. As the condition worsens, a climber may encounter difficult breathing, disorientation, aphasia, and paralysis.) I felt strong, my adrenaline was flowing, but I was very concerned about my ultimate ability to get across. A couple of our porters were also suffering from the height, and Pasang, our Sherpa sirdar (leader), was worried.

Just after daybreak, while we rested at 15,500 feet, one of the New Zealanders, who had gone ahead, came staggering down toward us with a body slung across his shoulders. He dumped the almost naked, barefoot body of an Indian holy man—a sadhu—at my feet. He had found the pilgrim lying on the ice, shivering and suffering from hypothermia. I cradled the sadhu's head and laid him out on the rocks. The New Zealander was angry. He wanted to get across the pass before the bright sun melted the snow. He said, "Look, I've done what I can. You have porters and Sherpa guides. You care for him. We're going on!" He turned and went back up the mountain to join his friends.

I took a carotid pulse and found that the sadhu was still alive. We figured he had probably visited the holy shrines at Muklinath and was on his way home. It was fruitless to question why he had chosen this desperately high route instead of the safe, heavily traveled caravan route through the Kali Gandaki gorge. Or why he was almost naked and with no shoes, or how long he had been lying in the pass. The answers weren't going to solve our problem.

Stephen and the four Swiss began stripping off outer clothing and opening their packs. The sadhu was soon clothed from head to foot. He was not able to walk, but he was very much alive. I looked down the mountain and spotted below the Japanese climbers marching up with a horse.

Without a great deal of thought, I told Stephen and Pasang that I was concerned about withstanding the heights to come and wanted to get over the pass. I took off after several of our porters who had gone ahead.

On the steep part of the ascent where, if the ice steps had given way, I would have slid down about 3,000 feet, I felt vertigo. I stopped for a breather, allowing the Swiss to catch up with me. I inquired about the sadhu and Stephen. They said that the sadhu was fine and that Stephen was just behind. I set off again for the summit.

Stephen arrived at the summit an hour after I did. Still exhilarated by victory, I ran down the snow slope to congratulate him. He was suffering from altitude sickness, walking 15 steps, then stopping, walking 15 steps, then stopping. Pasang accompanied him all the way up. When I reached them, Stephen glared at me and said: "How do you feel about contributing to the death of a fellow man?"

I did not fully comprehend what he meant.

"Is the sadhu dead?" I inquired.

"No," replied Stephen, "but he surely will be!"

After I had gone, and the Swiss had departed not long after, Stephen had remained with the sadhu. When the Japanese had arrived, Stephen had asked to use their horse to transport the sadhu down to the hut. They had refused. He had then asked Pasang to have a group of our porters carry the sadhu. Pasang had resisted the idea, saying that the porters would have to exert all their energy to get themselves over the pass. He had thought they could not carry a man down 1,000 feet to the hut, reclimb the slope, and get across safely before the snow melted. Pasang had pressed Stephen not to delay any longer.

The Sherpas had carried the sadhu down to a rock in the sun at about 15,000 feet and had pointed out the hut another 500 feet below. The Japanese had given him food and drink. When they had last seen him he was listlessly throwing rocks at the Japanese party's dog, which had frightened him.

We do not know if the sadhu lived or died.

For many of the following days and evenings Stephen and I discussed and debated our behavior toward the sadhu. Stephen is a committed Quaker with deep moral vision. He said, "I feel that what happened with the sadhu is a good example of the breakdown between the individual ethic and the corporate ethic. No one person was willing to assume ultimate responsibility for the sadhu. Each was willing to do his bit just so long as it was not too inconvenient. When it got to be a bother, everyone just passed the buck to someone else and took off. Jesus was relevant to a more individualistic stage of society, but how do we interpret his teaching today in a world filled with large, impersonal organizations and groups?"

I defended the larger group, saying, "Look, we all cared. We all stopped and gave aid and comfort. Everyone did his bit. The New Zealander carried him down below the snow line. I took his pulse and suggested we treat him for hypothermia. You and the Swiss gave him clothing and got him warmed up. The Japanese gave him food and water. The Sherpas carried him down to the sun and pointed out the easy trail toward the hut. He was well enough to throw rocks at a dog. What more could we do?"

"You have just described the typical affluent Westerner's response to a problem. Throwing money—in this case food and sweaters—at it, but not solving the fundamentals!" Stephen retorted.

"What would satisfy you?" I said. "Here we are, a group of New Zealanders, Swiss, Americans, and Japanese who have never met before and who are at the apex of one of the most powerful experiences of our lives. Some years the pass is so bad no one gets over it. What right does an almost naked pilgrim who chooses the wrong trail have to disrupt our lives? Even the Sherpas had no interest in risking the trip to help him beyond a certain point."

Stephen calmly rebutted, "I wonder what the Sherpas would have done if the sadhu had been a well-dressed Nepali, or what the Japanese would have done if the sadhu had been a well-dressed Asian, or what you would have done, Buzz, if the sadhu had been a well-dressed Western woman?"

"Where, in your opinion," I asked instead, "is the limit of our responsibility in a situation like this? We had our own well-being to worry about. Our Sherpa guides were unwilling to jeopardize us or the porters for the sadhu. No one else on the mountain was willing to commit himself beyond certain self-imposed limits."

Stephen said, "As individual Christians or people with a Western ethical tradition, we can fulfill our obligations in such a situation only if (1) the sadhu dies in our care, (2) the sadhu demonstrates to us that he could undertake the two-day walk down to the village, or (3) we carry the sadhu for two days down to the village and convince someone there to care for him."

"Leaving the sadhu in the sun with food and clothing, while he demonstrated hand-eye coordination by throwing a rock at a dog, comes close to fulfilling items one and two," I answered. "And it wouldn't have made sense to take him to the village where the people appeared to be far less caring than the Sherpas, so the third condition is impractical. Are you

really saying that, no matter what the implications, we should, at the drop of a hat, have changed our entire plan?"

## The individual vs. the group ethic

Despite my arguments, I felt and continue to feel guilt about the sadhu. I had literally walked through a classic moral dilemma without fully thinking through the consequences. My excuses for my actions include a high adrenaline flow, a superordinate goal, and a once-in-a-lifetime opportunity—factors in the usual corporate situation, especially when one is under stress.

Real moral dilemmas are ambiguous, and many of us hike right through them, unaware that they exist. When, usually after the fact, someone makes an issue of them, we tend to resent his or her bringing it up. Often, when the full import of what we have done (or not done) falls on us, we dig into a defensive position from which it is very difficult to emerge. In rare circumstances we may contemplate what we have done from inside a prison.

Had we mountaineers been free of physical and mental stress caused by the effort and the high altitude, we might have treated the sadhu differently. Yet isn't stress the real test of personal and corporate values? The instant decisions executives make under pressure reveal the most about personal and corporate character.

Among the many questions that occur to me when pondering my experience are: What are the practical limits of moral imagination and vision? Is there a collective or institutional ethic beyond the ethics of the individual? At what level of effort or commitment can one discharge one's ethical responsibilities?

Not every ethical dilemma has a right solution. Reasonable people often disagree; otherwise there would be no dilemma. In a business context, however, it is essential that managers agree on a process for dealing with dilemmas.

The sadhu experience offers an interesting parallel to business situations. An immediate response was mandatory. Failure to act was a decision in itself. Up on the mountain we could not resign and submit our résumés to a headhunter. In contrast to philosophy, business involves action and implementation—getting things done. Managers must come up with answers to problems based on what they see and what they allow to influence their decision-making processes. On the mountain, none of us but

Stephen realized the true dimensions of the situation we were facing.

One of our problems was that as a group we had no process for developing a consensus. We had no sense of purpose or plan. The difficulties of dealing with the sadhu were so complex that no one person could handle it. Because it did not have a set of preconditions that could guide its action to an acceptable resolution, the group reacted instinctively as individuals. The cross-cultural nature of the group added a further layer of complexity. We had no leader with whom we could all identify and in whose purpose we believed. Only Stephen was willing to take charge, but he could not gain adequate support to care for the sadhu.

Some organizations do have a value system that transcends the personal values of the managers. Such values, which go beyond profitability, are usually revealed when the organization is under stress. People throughout the organization generally accept its values, which, because they are not presented as a rigid list of commandments, may be somewhat ambiguous. The stories people tell, rather than printed materials, transmit these conceptions of what is proper behavior.

For 20 years I have been exposed at senior levels to a variety of corporations and organizations. It is amazing how quickly an outsider can sense the tone and style of an organization and the degree of tolerated openness and freedom to challenge management.

Organizations that do not have a heritage of mutually accepted, shared values tend to become unhinged during stress, with each individual bailing out for himself. In the great takeover battles we have witnessed during past years, companies that had strong cultures drew the wagons around them and fought it out, while other companies saw executives supported by their golden parachutes, bail out of the struggles.

Because corporations and their members are interdependent, for the corporation to be strong the members need to share a preconceived notion of what is correct behavior, a "business ethic," and think of it as a positive force, not a constraint.

As an investment banker I am continually warned by well-meaning lawyers, clients, and associates to be wary of conflicts of interest. Yet if I were to run away from every difficult situation, I wouldn't be an effective investment banker. I have to feel my way through conflicts. An effective manager can't run from risk either; he or she has to confront and deal with risk. To feel "safe" in doing this, managers need the guidelines of an agreed-on process and set of values within the organization.

After my three months in Nepal, I spent three months as an executive-in-residence at both Stanford Business School and the Center for Ethics and Social Policy at the Graduate Theological Union at Berkeley. These six months away from my job gave me time to assimilate 20 years of business experience. My thoughts turned often to the meaning of the leadership role in any large organization. Students at the seminary thought of themselves as antibusiness. But when I questioned them they agreed that they distrusted all large organizations, including the church. They perceived all large organizations as impersonal and opposed to individual values and needs. Yet we all know of organizations where peoples' values and beliefs are respected and their expressions encouraged. What makes the difference? Can we identify the difference and, as a result, manage more effectively?

The word "ethics" turns off many and confuses more. Yet the notions of shared values and an agreed-on process for dealing with adversity and change – what many people mean when they talk about corporate culture – seem to be at the heart of the ethical issue. People who are in touch with their own core beliefs and the beliefs of others and are sustained by them can be more comfortable living on the cutting edge. At times, taking a tough line or a decisive stand in a muddle of ambiguity is the only ethical thing to do. If a manager is indecisive and spends time trying to figure out the "good" thing to do, the enterprise may be lost.

Business ethics, then, has to do with the authenticity and integrity of the enterprise. To be ethical is to follow the business as well as the cultural goals of the corporation, its owners, its employees, and its customers. Those who cannot serve the corporate vision are not authentic business people and, therefore, are not ethical in the business sense.

At this stage of my own business experience I have a strong interest in organizational behavior. Sociologists are keenly studying what they call corporate stories, legends, and heroes as a way organizations have of transmitting the value system. Corporations such as Arco have even hired consultants to perform an audit of their corporate culture. In a company, the leader is the person who understands, interprets, and manages the corporate value system. Effective managers are then action-oriented people who resolve conflict, are tolerant of ambiguity, stress, and change, and have a strong sense of purpose for themselves and their organizations.

If all this is true, I wonder about the role of the professional manager who moves from company to company. How can he or she quickly absorb the values and culture of different organizations? Or is there, indeed, an art of management that is totally transportable? Assuming such fungible managers do exist, is it proper for them to manipulate the values of others?

What would have happened had Stephen and I carried the sadhu for two days back to the village and become involved with the villagers in his care? In four trips to Nepal my most interesting experiences occurred in 1975 when I lived in a Sherpa home in the Khumbu for five days recovering from altitude sickness. The high point of Stephen's trip was an invitation to participate in a family funeral ceremony in Manang. Neither experience had to do with climbing the high passes of the Himalayas. Why were we so reluctant to try the lower path, the ambiguous trail? Perhaps because we did not have a leader who could reveal the greater purpose of the trip to us.

Why didn't Stephen with his moral vision opt to take the sadhu under his personal care? The answer is because, in part, Stephen was hard-stressed physically himself, and because, in part, without some support system that involved our involuntary and episodic community on the mountain, it was beyond his individual capacity to do so.

I see the current interest in corporate culture and corporate value systems as a positive response to Stephen's pessimism about the decline of the role of the individual in large organizations. Individuals who operate from a thoughtful set of personal values provide the foundation for a corporate culture. A corporate tradition that encourages freedom of inquiry, supports personal values, and reinforces a focused sense of direction can fulfill the need for individuality along with the prosperity and success of the group. Without such corporate support, the individual is lost.

That is the lesson of the sadhu. In a complex corporate situation, the individual requires and deserves the support of the group. If people cannot find such support from their organization, they don't know how to act. If such support is forthcoming, a person has a stake in the success of the group, and can add much to the process of establishing and maintaining a corporate culture. It is management's challenge to be sensitive to individual needs, to shape them, and to direct and focus them for the benefit of the group as a whole.

For each of us the sadhu lives. Should we stop what we are doing and comfort him; or should we keep trudging up toward the high pass? Should I pause to help the derelict I pass on the street each night as I walk by the Yale Club en route to Grand Central Station? Am I his brother? What is the nature of our responsibility if we consider ourselves to be ethical persons? Perhaps it is to change the values of the group so that it can, with all its resources, take the other road.

# Shades of Green

## Eight of 10 Americans Are Environmentalists, At Least So They Say

## But Poll Finds Many Are Torn By Wish for Convenience In Their Buying Decisions

## Guilt Over Disposable Diapers

### Rose Gutfeld

*Staff Reporter of* The Wall Street Journal

Michelle Thompson, a 26-year-old receptionist at a Traverse City, Mich., plastics plant, tries to buy biodegradable detergents and paper products made from recycled paper. But she adds, "If there's something else on sale, I'll go for it."

She considers herself environmentally sensitive—but drives 80 miles round trip a day to her job because she can't find work closer to home. After experimenting with cloth diapers for her 11-month-old son, she is using disposable ones. "I'm not happy with it, but it's my only alternative," she says.

Mrs. Thompson is far from the only American who feels torn between conscience and necessity on the question of the environment. A new nationwide Wall Street Journal/NBC News poll shows that concern and awareness of environmental problems are all but universal: Eight in 10 Americans regard themselves as "environmentalists" and half of those say they are "strong" ones. Further, most aren't content to wait for future technological fixes to solve problems: They recognize the need for substantial, and in some cases profound, shifts in their own life styles.

This and earlier polls indicate that Americans *say* they are willing to make sacrifices for a better environment. But what they *do* is another story. When it comes to making concrete buying decisions, many aren't the environmentalists they claim to be. While overwhelming majorities say the environmental reputation of a product or manufacturer is important to them in deciding what to purchase, the margin narrows sharply

when asked whether such concerns have actually led them to buy something—or not buy it—in the last six months.

What emerges from the poll and from interviews with individual consumers across the country is the fact that environmental concerns have become a significant factor in buying decisions—but one factor out of several more traditional concerns, such as price and convenience, that still weigh heavily with consumers.

"Overall, interest and concern about the environment is definitely on the rise," says Judith Langer, president of Langer Associates Inc., a New York market research firm. "But my impression is that there is a minority who are passionately concerned and will inconvenience themselves to do good environmentally—paying more or changing habits or giving more thought to daily practices."

#### A Stagnant Market

Gary Stible, who runs New England Consulting Group in Westport, Conn., adds that "people are saying they're doing an awful lot. But the market share of environmentally friendly products has not grown that much."

Still, Mr. Stibel predicts it's going to be very difficult to sell a product that isn't "environmentally friendly" in the year 2000. And the Journal/NBC poll makes clear just how embedded environmentalism has already become in the national psyche.

For one thing, voters don't expect technology to bail the nation out of its problems. By 53% to 34%, they say it will take fundamental changes in life

style, rather than scientific advances, to bring about dramatic changes in the environment. "Changing the way we live is a little more sure, the way I see it," says Walter Hrozenchik, a 60-year-old engineering designer from Ridgefield, Conn. The risk of depending on technology, he says, is that "we'll come up with something new, and it's not as great as people think."

This same sentiment shows up as well when voters are asked to choose between technological and life-style fixes to specific environmental issues. For instance, nearly seven in 10 voters say the best way to deal with the nation's trash crisis is to require manufacturers to use less packaging and consumers to do more recycling. Fewer than one in five thinks a better way of dealing with the problem would be to develop less polluting ways of burning trash.

Underscoring their willingness to sacrifice, more than eight out of 10 voters say protecting the environment is generally more important than keeping prices down; 67% of those polled say they would be willing to pay 15 to 20 cents a gallon more for gasoline that causes much less pollution than current blends. (At least one major refiner says it has developed such a blend.) "People had to switch from leaded to unleaded gas," points out Irma Gawboy, a retired social worker in Sun City West, Ariz. "Our health is more important than the price of gas."

Moreover, three out of four people say the government should mandate the use of such fuel despite the added cost. "It would be frustrating if you were the only one on your block doing it," says 40-year-old Gary Campbell, of St.

Peter, Minn., who works at a telecommunications firm while looking for work as an art teacher.

Jim Pascoe, a 37-year-old claims manager at a Traverse City insurance company, says he probably wouldn't voluntarily buy the gasoline because he wouldn't be able to make much of a difference if other people continued to buy the polluting kind. "But if they passed a law, I wouldn't mind it," he says. "I just don't like that feeling of futility."

Yet while most motorists are willing to pay more for cleaner gasoline, the poll found a sharply different answer when they were asked whether they would favor a 25-cent gasoline tax increase to encourage less driving, more conservation and less dependence on foreign energy sources. On that subject, 69% oppose such a tax increase, while only 27% support it.

"The commitment to cleaning up the environment is there," say Democratic pollster Peter Hart and Republican pollster Robert Teeter, who conducted the survey for the Journal and NBC. "But Americans are unwilling to fork over this additional money to the government or to endorse a policy that might mean they could drive less."

### The Environmental President?

One reason for their mistrust of government may stem from their general dissatisfaction with how political leaders are handling the issue. Despite President Bush's campaign pledge to be "the environmental president," voters show a growing disapproval of his handling of the issue.

And while Democrats are seen as the party better able to handle the issue by 24% to 6% over the GOP, nearly two-thirds of all voters see no difference between the two parties on the issue. In general, voters seem more willing than does the political process to embrace some far-reaching steps.

Of those polled, 85% would require cars to be more fuel-efficient and less polluting even if that made them more expensive; by a narrower 51% to 42% margin, they are even willing to see cars made "smaller and less safe" in the name of protecting the environment.

In people's day-to-day lives, though, this strong environmental streak becomes somewhat tempered. While three-fourths of those surveyed say a product's or manufacturer's environmental reputation is important to them in deciding what to buy, 46% say they have actually bought any item for those

reasons within the last six months, while 45% say they haven't. Fifty-four percent say they have bought a more expensive product rather than a less expensive one because of environmental concerns, while 53% say they have avoided buying something because of environmental fears about the product.

Those numbers remain considerable, analysts say, and marketers ignore them at their own peril. "It's a mistake to say that 'only' half have done something," say Mr. Hart and Mr. Teeter. "Half is still a huge number; there is tremendous mileage in having the green label." But the numbers suggest the complexity of people's buying decisions, and the fact that even very environmentally correct people sometimes find themselves compelled to be environmentally incorrect.

### Caught in the Act

Consider, for example, the reaction of Maggie Galbraith, a 36-year-old Cragsmoor, N.Y., housewife. When a reporter notes the disposable diapers and juice boxes in her shopping cart, she looks startled and tries to cover the offending items with her hands.

"Normally, you would never see these things in my basket—never!" she exclaims. "The only reason is that we're going on a six-hour trip. I don't know what to expect on the road, or what to expect when I get there."

Many more people would be more willing to do the environmentally correct thing if it were made easier. Mr. Pascoe, the claims manager, says he doesn't bother to recycle much now but is looking forward to the day in 1995 when his county plans to make recycling mandatory. He figures that means there will be more, and more convenient, drop-off locations.

Gordon Lingbeck, 50, a Mankato, Minn., auto-parts wholesaler, says he recycles aluminum cans only because he can get money for them. He isn't willing to pay for more environmentally safe products unless he has to. "I think the only way you're going to get people to change their life styles as far as the environment goes is you're going to have to make it law," he says. "People don't volunteer to do those things."

But many consumers report another factor pushing them toward environmentalism: social pressure, especially from the young. Leaving a takeout restaurant with her food in a plastic-foam container, 41-year-old Traverse City teacher Jane Boerema admits that if her nine-year-old son were with her, "he

wouldn't let me walk out with this." Ms. Boerema says she has been forced to become more environmentally aware in response to her son's pressure; he insists on paper rather than plastic bags at the checkout counter and has even questioned his 75-year-old grandmother's shopping habits.

### The Age Gap

John Wilkes, a 49-year-old Live Oak, Calif., resident who lectures at the University of California, Santa Cruz, says that if he were talking to somebody over 40 he wouldn't be embarrassed to admit that he uses disposable diapers. But "if I'm talking to a person under 30, I wouldn't mention it."

Even Barb and Dan Hoeft, two 29-year-olds in Blue Earth, Minn., who are so avid that they haul trash 20 miles to be recycled, still use disposable diapers for their one-year-old son. "We've had long arguments about diapers," says Dan, who works for a processing firm. "If we weren't both working full-time, he'd be in cloth diapers." But Barb, a teacher, adds that cloth diapers are no panacea either, considering the detergents and energy needed to wash them.

This difficulty of figuring out where to draw the line on environmentalism recurs throughout the Journal/NBC poll. One place the line is drawn has to do with jobs. By 51% to 34%, for instance, voters think the need to protect jobs in the Northwest is more important than the need to protect the endangered spotted owl. In addition, slim majorities think it might be worth it to allow more oil exploration of wilderness areas and to delay new power-plant emissions rules if those steps would lessen the nation's dependence on foreign oil.

But a plurality also believes it wouldn't be worth it to loosen rules on offshore drilling for the same reason. And, on the anniversary of the Iraqi invasion of Kuwait, Americans say by 45% to 36% that the nation should put the goal of protecting the environment above that of reducing the nation's dependence on foreign sources of energy.

*—Additional reporting for this article was provided by the following Dow Jones Ottaway Newspapers: The News-Times, Danbury, Conn.; The Free Press, Mankato, Minn.; The Times Herald-Record, Middletown, N.Y.; Owatonna People's Press, Owatonna, Minn.; Santa Cruz Sentinel, Santa Cruz, Calif.; Daily News-Sun, Sun City, Ariz.; Traverse City Record-Eagle, Traverse City, Mich.*

# New Trends in Relocation

*Linda K. Stroh, Anne H. Reilly
and Jeanne M. Brett*

*Linda K. Stroh is assistant research professor
and director of relocation study, Department
of Organization Behavior, Kellogg Graduate
School of Management, Northwestern University in Evanston, Ill.*

*Jeanne M. Brett is a Dewitt W. Buchannan
Jr. professor of organization behavior,
Department of Organization Behavior,
Kellogg Graduate School of Management,
Northwestern University.*

*Anne H. Reilly is assistant professor of
management, Department of Management,
School of Business Administration of Loyola
University of Chicago, Ill.*

Commentators have been saying for years that traditional families are disappearing and that increasing numbers of employees will turn down transfers, primarily because of their spouse's job or other family considerations. Some predict that by the year 2000, the number of dual-career couples in the labor force will double, from 32 to 64 percent.

For those interested in relocation, that statistic is not the end of the story. Research and demographic trends suggest that corporate employees of the 1990s will bring with them a set of family responsibilities that will involve not only working spouses, but also children, stepchildren, custodial children, non-custodial children — and elderly parents.

The American workplace itself is changing. The U.S. corporate world has undergone an unprecedented period of restructuring during the past 10 years. Managers and scholars alike believe that this turbulent corporate environment will have significant negative effects on employees' loyalty to their companies.

Employees' desire to relocate for a company position is dwindling. The rise in dual-career couples as well as vanishing employee loyalty are the main reasons for the drop in relocation. As companies prepare for the '90s, flexibility should be part of their revamped relocation strategies.

Place all of these changes in the context of a shrinking skilled labor force that will give employees increased bargaining power, continued merger and acquisition activity that has forced many to reassess their loyalty to the company, and the end result is that corporate relocation officers will face an ever more challenging task: relocating employees who are less willing to relocate and who have more special needs. Two factors may explain this increased resistance to moving: the changing character of the American family and the changing character of the workplace.

## Changes in the family

In a 1978 study of the effect of corporate relocation on families, typical transferred employees were almost entirely male, married, and worked in sales or marketing. These were not families dependent on two paychecks.

Most of the wives studied were not career-oriented. Most of those who were working did not have the psychological involvement with their jobs or commitment to their companies exhibited by today's female employees. But even in 1978, some wives did have this commitment, and their husbands were more likely to turn down transfers.

Today, more than 50 percent of America's women work, and only about 10 percent of middle-class families follow a traditional pattern of husband as breadwinner and wife as homemaker. Data support the view that resistance to moving will increase in the 1990s. The problems associated with a more diverse work force and with corporate relocation are real.

One woman interviewed for a study of relocation commented:

> Our company is really slow to address these [family] issues. We are really not a very progressive company. When I was a single employee I had a better opportunity for relocation and promotions. Married women, especially women with children, are viewed as less committed and have less opportunity for relocation [than men]. When men marry and have children, they are viewed as settling down and becoming more desirable employees — while the opposite is true for women.

The demographic trend toward dual-career couples also has significant implications for relocation. American companies have been hir-

Reprinted with permission from *HRMagazine* (formerly *Personnel Administrator*), February 1990, pp. 42-44. *HRMagazine,*
published by the Society for Human Resource Management, Alexandria, VA.

ing large numbers of women into entry-level sales, marketing and professional positions. The bright, single, career-oriented young women that companies began hiring a few years ago will become valued employees, and they may marry (or be married to) bright, career-oriented men and have bright children. These couples' lifestyles will reflect the two paychecks in their households, they will share in child-care responsibilities and they will also understand each other's career aspirations.

These dual-career couples entered marriage committed to two careers, not just one. Both husband and wife expect periodic sacrifices in their own or the other's career as part of the marriage contract or to avoid uprooting spouse or children. Logically, this may mean a less loyal and committed company employee, whether male or female.

Male managers whose wives are also employed earn less on average than male managers whose wives do not work. To tell which comes first — the men's relatively low income or the wives' working — is impossible, but dual-career couples make family/work decisions based on the demands of two careers, not one.

## Effects of moving

A man whose wife was recently relocated told a story that reflects our societal biases and the unique issues facing a male vs. a female "trailing" spouse. The setting is a men-only barber shop in a smaller community. Several men are reading the morning newspaper, waiting their turn in the barber's chair. This husband explained:

I went to the barber shop last Saturday and while I was getting my hair trimmed, the barber asked me what brought me to this city. (I 'kinda' squirmed in my chair and debated whether to make something up or bite the bullet. I decided, "what the hell," and said:) "My wife got a promotion." (There was dead silence for a few seconds, then, the rustling of paper as everyone in the room peered over his newspaper to examine the characteristics of a man who would MOVE FOR HIS WIFE'S JOB.)

I was a little self-conscious, but I really don't care. We work together and make decisions together. My father made the mobility decisions in our household, because it benefitted the company, but he had no consideration for the effects on the rest of the family.

Another attitudinal trend that may serve to increase resistance to moving is the impact on children. While children adjust to moving with little negative impact and some positive effects (especially with respect to social development), parents remain concerned about the short-term dislocation caused by moving, particularly the effect on teenagers.

This concern is not new, but it is getting more complicated. As noted earlier, employees and companies must now face the "yours, mine and ours" syndrome.

One dual-career couple, both in their second marriage, attempted to resolve the issue of having left the husband's non-custodial teen-age child behind. The husband explained:

It really was a hard decision. Naturally I wanted to be with my son. Before we moved, I didn't think being divorced affected my son negatively at all. I saw him all the time. He thought of our house as his house too. I could be there when he needed me. Now, it's real formal and awkward when he comes out to see us. His friends aren't here, and I feel he resents that I've abandoned him and chosen to move with my wife, not his mother, to a community hundreds of miles away. I can't tell you the sadness I feel to think I've lost that relationship with my son. If I had the decision to make all over again, I don't think I would make the same choice. But, I thought it would work. I was wrong.

Clearly, employees must face some difficult choices where relocation is concerned.

## Changes in the workplace

Managers and researchers alike question the effect of the restructuring of American business on corporate loyalty and organizational commitment. America's mightiest firms are firing thousands of talented employees. Between 1980 and 1990 as many as one

million managers may have lost their jobs due to buyouts, sell-offs, mergers, acquisitions and liquidations. Not surprisingly, for many employees the psychological work contract — loyal service for good pay and job security — has been broken.

The merger mania began in earnest in the 1970s when corporate raiders started collecting conglomerates of companies. Beatrice Foods is a good example. At one time, Beatrice owned firms as varied as Dannon Yogurt and Morgan Yachts. Conglomerate-building was primarily a financial phenomenon at that time; current management was typically left in place. While the holding company scooped up profits, employment levels were rarely affected.

But then things changed. The investment bankers discovered how much money could be made putting together deals; the Reagan administration relaxed antitrust prohibitions and encouraged deregulation of such industries as banking and the airlines. Strategists began to see the potential in synergistic deals where acquisitions married one company's brand name to another's distribution channels, or one company's capital to another's technological know-how.

This new wave of mergers and acquisitions has significant effects on employment. Corporate America is caught up in a frantic drive to reduce its work force, mostly to save money, but also to slim down into what top management hopes will be a more responsive structure. A newly merged company does not need two corporate headquarters, nor does it need two corporate staffs.

For example, whole departments were wiped out when Beatrice acquired Esmark in 1984. When Quaker acquired Stokley Van Camp, what it really wanted was Gatorade; Quaker sold all Stokley's real estate and its industrial oil division and terminated large numbers of employees.

Furthermore, in response to the threat of takeovers, some tradition-bound managers, intent on saving their companies, have been restructuring voluntarily. "Downsize, dismantle and debt" are the new strategies to fend off takeovers. How do companies do this? Sell off some divisions and cut employment across the board.

## Impact of restructuring

These corporate restructuring actions are affecting the careers of managers throughout America. Employees who grew up in the 1950s and '60s often lived in traditional families, in which fathers worked for a single corporation, perhaps for the duration of their careers, and mothers were housewives. Women no longer automatically expect to be housewives. And employees working for large corporations no longer expect to spend their entire career in one company.

Paul Hirsch, perhaps the most outspoken commentator on the effect of what he calls "the dismantling of the Fortune 500," says that many corporations' commitment to their own people at every level has fallen so quickly that it is still catching managers off guard. They see older mentors and talented coworkers — the rising stars of several years ago — being moved down and out. The lesson for those who are left is that "hard work/good work" is no protection. Prudent managers will begin to spend more time planning their own future and less time concerned about the company's.

This phenomenon may be especially true for the growing number of dual-career couples, who have grown up in a competitive corporate environment in which employees have grown increasingly less loyal to one company and one job. Chances are good that these younger dual-career employees will work for several firms.

Add all of these changes to the concern about the effect of a move on a spouse's career, and transfers may not seem quite as desirable as they once were. One employee said:

I work with several long-time employees who were big performers and who were demoted or let go because the company was forced to make cutbacks. They now have very little company loyalty, and regret the many times they moved their families and children all over the country at the company's beck and call. These kinds of stories affect younger employees. Our mentors dissuade us from making the same mistakes, and their influence is felt on all employees.

Another noted:

To give you an idea of the magnitude of this problem, I started [at this company] five years ago with 45 other employees. It cost $30,000 per employee to train us. Today only two of those employees are still with the company. This high rate of turnover and other problems associated with potential takeovers are forcing more employees to say no to company moves. A company no longer protects your job. While it used to be guaranteed that if you performed well you would have a job, now other factors come into play, and they affect what you will do for the company.

## Implications of change

Relocation managers and human resource strategists have been preparing for resistance to moving due to changes in the American family. They also need to be prepared for the resistance to moving that may result from the wholesale violation of the psychological contract between company and employee and, by extension, the family. Changes in families and changes in corporations will have significant implications for employee relocation. Some of these are:

● Corporations can no longer count on employees' commitment and loyalty to move to a job that does not directly develop their careers, or to move when a child has just one more year of high school, or to ask a spouse to give up an exciting job. Employees will think hard before agreeing to move to a subsidiary that the corporation might decide to sell the next day. Why move to a division that just might be folded into another, and half of its managers folded out?

● In merged or acquired companies, compensation packages may need to be adjusted to reflect commitments made before the merger or acquisition. Promotion opportunities may also have to be re-evaluated. At a minimum, new post-merger/acquisition policies must be made perfectly clear to employees involved in relocation.

● Companies increasingly will have to consider employees in context of their family unit. Are there elderly parents? Non-custodial children? Companies must expect either more exceptions to existing policy or new policies for these changing families, such as policies on job assistance for spouses.

● Relocation policies in general may need to be reviewed more frequently than in the past to keep up with the rapidly changing environment of both family and workplace. The most pertinent question might be: Do all of these employees really need to be relocated? Given rapid advancement in communications and information transfer, can both company needs and employee career development be accomplished without a relocation?

# A New Look at Women Executives

*To bring down glass ceiling barriers, we need strategies for change in attitudes, development and work-family balance.*

## JEAN R. HASKELL

*Jean R. Haskell, Ed.D., is chairman of Haskell Associates in Philadelphia, PA (215) 735-3348.*

WOMEN ARE MAKING A BIG DENT in the formerly all-male world of business by occupying key executive positions. Many women who aspire to executive positions, however, seem to meet impenetrable barriers as they move up the corporate ladder. Their mobility seems to stop two-thirds of the way up — almost as if there is an invisible "glass ceiling" that they can see above yet cannot crack.

### Six Barriers to Promotion

In a series of extensive interviews with high level executives, we found six barriers that create the glass ceiling. These barriers are built by traditional practices, assumptions and attitudes of corporate men and by women who do not understand the rules or try to change them too quickly. I will discuss these six barriers in order of frequency.

• *Good Old Boys*. This continues to be the major stumbling block for women. Often called the Old Boys' Network, this barrier encompasses *stereotyping, social discomfort*, and *exclusivity*.

Stereotyping seems to be a fact of life in the male-dominated work world, where men — accustomed to working with other men, and having wives, daughters and mothers at home — tend to believe that the only role for women is as a wife, mother or secretary. Thus, in the workplace, women tend to be treated by men as sex objects, little girls, or

mothers, and those women who step outside of the expected roles and interact as peers are perceived as "not okay" women.

As a result of their traditional attitudes, men feel uncomfortable working with women as peers. They are not accustomed to seeing women as competent business people, are afraid to give women accurate feedback or tough assignments, and tend not to trust that women can do the job. Male managers are not comfortable managing women's careers or disciplining women, and feel they must take extra care not to be misunderstood in their actions with women.

Men tend to have their own way of relating to and dealing with each other (male bonding), from which women are excluded and which creates exclusivity and separation. The Old Boys' Network, often comprised of men who have served together in the military or attended the same schools, provides a major source of help and support to younger men coming up in the organization. However, there is no such support for women, who have a difficult time gaining acceptance in this "macho" culture. "We consider the young men to be an extension of ourselves," said one male executive, "but it's quite difficult to see a woman in that way."

• *Pioneer's Pain*. This a barrier created by the dilemmas that women face in balancing career, personal, and family life and being the first of their gender to attempt to gain acceptance by the good old boys. As more women establish themselves as competent professionals, there is more conflict of interest between career and family and more pain around being the *first* or the *only*. Moreover, expecta-

tions for those women who do succeed are much higher than for most men, and a woman who fails not only has a personal failure, but, in the eyes of men, fails for all of her gender. As men hang on to stereotyped perceptions of where women should be spending their time and what they can do, pioneers encounter strong elements in uncharted territory!

• *Back to Basics*. This encompasses issues related to 1) lack of expertise, training, experience, and knowledge of the business; 2) internal systems; and 3) the economy. Five years ago, the perception was that women lacked experience, and did not know the business. Also, the changing economy restricted available positions, often limiting promotional opportunities to men who had seniority, and making it more difficult for men as well as women to move up.

Back to Basics appears somewhat less frequently now, with the major concern being that women lack technical expertise or engineering degrees, rather than business knowledge in general, or that the number of women with technical degrees is relatively small. It also suggests that as more women move up through the pipeline and prove themselves, the lack of experience and expertise becomes less of a problem.

• *What Problem?* This category of barriers reflects the view that there is no problem in relation to women moving up the corporate ladder, or even that women are seen as assets.

In the past, we were unwilling to see the problem; we denied that it existed. Today, responses reflect a more honest indication that barriers have either disap-

From *Executive Excellence*, Vol. 8, No. 1, January 1991, pp. 13-14. *Executive Excellence*, The Magazine of Personal Development, Managerial Effectiveness, and Organizational Productivity. Copyright © 1991 by The Institute for Principle-Centered Leadership.

peared or were never there, particularly in the financial services industry where the trend is to move women into high level positions. Comments from the banking industry indicate that there are more women than men in banking, and that in some cases, notable women have been extraordinarily instrumental in implementing organizational improvements.

• *Political Savvy.* This category of barriers includes interpersonal communication styles, group and social behavior, and the ability to build alliances and support. It often reflects a lack of fit with a particular company's culture and can be elusive for men as well as for women.

Political Savvy carries with it extensive advice to women about how they should talk, walk, interact and "play the game". In the past, women were advised to talk faster, learn team playing, think globally, put the company first, and "fake it".

The fact that these issues are less important in 1991 seems to reflect the perception that as women prove to be competent in high level positions, the lack of political savvy becomes less of an issue, or that women are preceived as having it.

• *Backlash.* This is the phenomenon of retaliation or punishment against women who become successful by men who may have been supportive at a previous time. A man may withdraw support when a woman gets a high level promotion; a husband may leave the marriage when a wife brings home a bigger pay check than his.

The Backlash phenomenon is described as The New Old Boy, referring to the younger male manager who will be supportive until he feels threatened, then colludes with the older generation of "old boys" at the top and will use any weapon in his arsenal to fight back.

### Strategies for Change

Of major importance in the effort to shatter the glass ceiling are strategies for change — what men and women can do to enable women to succeed at the executive level, and what organizations can do to create environments in which both men and women can contribute their full range of talents. Organizations must focus strategies for change in three areas:

1) *Attitudes at the top.* As in any cultural change effort, cracking the glass ceiling must begin at the top by understanding

and working to change those traditional attitudes, perceptions and assumptions about women that have long been held by generations of corporate men.

This change is being approached by training on gender bias and sex role stereotyping. Executives and managers attend workshops and seminars to better understand stereotyping and exclusionary behavior, learn how to give women constructive feedback without being afraid that the women will cry, and understand the importance of offering women the same challenging assignments they give to men.

In some companies, the influx of women as well as minorities has become so great that the training includes gender as well as race/color bias and is generally referred to as Diversity Training. To have meaningful impact, such training should be highly interactive and experiential, extend over time, be shared with groups of peers, and provide opportunities for on-the-job follow-up.

2) *Developing women.* Along with attitude change is the need to develop women through technical and management training, constructive feedback and evaluation, targeting women for challenging work assignments and developmental opportunities, job rotation, giving women the high-risk/high-visibility assignments traditionally reserved for men, mentoring, and rewarding managers for developing talent.

Mentoring, rewarding managers, and risk-taking appear to be most critical to the success of the change effort. In some organizations, performance appraisals include an assessment of the extent to which managers develop women; in others, bonus pay is linked to a manager's record on promoting women and minorities.

3) *Sensitivity to work and family needs.* The key to creating a work environment that enables women to maximize their potential at work while also raising a family is sensitivity to work and family issues.

With a work force that is 50 percent women, most of whom are part of two-career families, single parents, or the family's sole breadwinner, organizations that hope to retain women must develop policies and programs that enable women to pursue both career and family. Such efforts include educational benefits, pay equity, child care and maternity benefits, on-site child care, flex time, part-

time work, paid maternity and paternity leave, sabbatical leave, clear non-discriminatory and sexual harassment policies as well as re-structuring of promotions so careers are not derailed by a few months' absences or unwillingness to relocate.

Changes women can make. In the past, women were told to modify their behaviors so as to fit into the corporate culture — play the game, learn team sports, be more assertive, put the company first, and don't be too emotional. To crack the glass ceiling in the 1990s, women are encouraged to take personal risks, be more proactive, create visibility and develop a network. Survey comments include:

• *Continue to push for change in attitudes about stereotypes and the old boy network.*
• *Be honest, be yourselves, be wary of accommodating men — trying to be one of the boys doesn't work.*
• *Broaden exposure to include more than one discipline; press for varied functional assignments. Develop skills other than those needed in present position.*

***Changes men can make.*** Men are urged to deal with their own gender biases, mentor women, give women more opportunities, and take risks by promoting women to the high level positions. Comments from our survey include:

• *Be trained to deal with stereotypes; stop condescending.*
• *Sit and walk beside women, not in front of them.*
• *Correct the assumption that a female in a job will be a problem, but a man won't. Drop the stereotype that women can't travel; some men can't travel.*
• *Don't deny discrimination and work to eliminate it.*
• *Give women more opportunities; be more objective in making recommendations for promotion.*
• *Mentor women with potential.*
• *Judge by a track record.*

The challenge for the 1990s is to move beyond providing the trappings of what looks like support for women to intensive work with both men and women to break down internal barriers, open up honest dialogue, support women's efforts to learn, grow, and market themselves, and build a collaborative New Person's Network to move productively and competitively into the next century.

# Combating Drugs In the Workplace

**MINDA ZETLIN**

*Minda Zetlin is a New York-based writer.*

George was one of the owners of a small, family-run business in the Midwest. One day, while walking around his manufacturing plant, he found a package of suspicious-looking white powder.

Bewildered, he summoned the local police; their investigation turned up an entire cocaine-dealing ring operating on his premises. In fact, the drug was being transported inside the stuffed animals his company manufactured.

Although names and identifying details have been changed, the above story is true. The point is a simple one: No matter who you are or what your company does, your workplace can be affected by drug abuse. And if your image of the typical drug abuser is a minority, inner-city teenager, think again. "Sixty-eight percent of drug users are currently employed," says Lee Dogoloff, executive director, American Council for Drug Education. "Seventy-six percent are white, which you would never know by watching the evening news." This, he says, explains the current concern with drugs in the workplace: "That's where they are."

Corporate America is beginning to think so too. Five years ago, an American Management Association survey of human resources managers showed that less than half their companies had addressed the issue of drugs at all; this year, the same survey showed 85 percent had established specific drug-abuse policies. Sixty-three percent were conducting some form of drug testing. (The possibilities include random testing of all employees, testing for "cause," as when an employee presents suspicious behavior or is recovering from a drug problem, testing as a routine part of post-accident investigation, or as a condition of hire.)

"Most major corporations now do pre-employment testing," Dogoloff says. Some managers only began such testing because most other companies in their communities were doing it. "They started thinking, 'Gee, what kind of candidates are coming to us?'"

Though most human resources managers believe testing is an effective weapon against workplace drug abuse, it does have passionate opponents. "Drug testing is an invasion of privacy," says Shelly Ginenthal, director of human resources at Macworld Communications Inc. "Besides, the accuracy is often in question, and a false positive can do a lot of damage to a person's reputation."

Whether or not you are in favor of it, drug testing alone is not enough, experts say. That belief is echoed by respondents of the AMA survey: Less than 9 percent of its survey respondents depend on testing alone to combat drug abuse. Most also provide drug education, supervisory training, employee assistance programs, or some combination of these.

Drug education is particularly effective, many companies have found. According to the survey, those companies that conducted drug education had a 55 percent lower test-positive rate than those that didn't. "A person who understands how a drug like marijuana interferes with coordination will have a different view of the crane operator's pot break—especially if he or she is on the receiving end of a bucket of concrete," Dogoloff explains.

## PROCESS OUTWEIGHS POLICY

The foundation of an effective anti-drug program, experts agree, is a clear and coherent drug policy. "The first thing a company's management needs to do is figure out why drug use is unacceptable in its workplace and what it's going to do about it," Dogoloff explains. "To me, the process by which you figure your policy out is more important than what the policy is at the end. The thing not to do is hire some expert to come sit alone in a room and write up a policy for your company."

Instead, he suggests bringing together those areas of the company that must deal directly with drug problems: human resources, legal, safety, an EAP or a health department, and a representative who can speak for employees—whether or not they're represented by a union.

For one thing, he adds, you're more likely to create a policy that fits your company's philosophy, corporate culture and the industry it's in. Besides, "these are the same people who will have to live with the policy and implement it when it's done."

Whatever drug program or policy you wind up with, experts caution against ignoring the most common workplace drug: alcohol. Most do not make a distinction between alcohol abuse and illegal drug abuse—since drug abusers often use both at once.

"Alcohol is the overwhelming drug of choice," notes Jim Kelley, a partner in the Washington, D.C., law office of Morgan, Lewis & Bockius. Unfortunately, he says, many companies see alcoholism as a "run-of-the-mill" addiction. And because the media focus has been on illegal drugs, many companies have had a tendency to overlook alcohol abuse.

## THE CORPORATE QUANDARY

Whatever you do, when faced with a drug abuse problem, "the first rule is: don't do nothing," Dogoloff says. "If you leave it alone, it's going to get worse."

## MANAGED CARE— DOES IT WORK?

Talk to employee assistance program (EAP) professionals about drug rehabilitation, and you'll often hear the same complaint: a substance abuser comes to them for help and they recommend treatment—only to find the company's insurance won't pay for it.

At issue is the concept of managed care: reducing medical expenses, and thus insurance premiums, by ensuring that employees receive only such treatment that is deemed medically necessary. The idea has spawned an industry: Most major companies now have managed care companies overseeing employees' medical expenses and ruling out those seen as inappropriate; many of these managed care companies are subsidiaries of insurance firms. HMOs, though fundamentally different, operate on managed care principles, as well.

Managed care's detractors claim that this kind of care serves to treat employees only when they're really ill, and refuses treatment earlier, when illness might be prevented. Further, they point to the fact that both managed care companies and HMOs profit most by denying treatment. (HMOs can cut expenses, and thus raise profits, by denying treatment. And, although managed care companies may not gain directly by denying treatment, every time they do, they save money for the company that hired them.)

Managed care providers argue that it is the complete lack of control on medical spending that has driven insurance premiums into the stratosphere. Further, they claim, each individual case is evaluated according to the patient's needs and *not* the bottom line. So how can they produce these savings that companies hire them to create? "If you're making decisions based on the client's needs, you're going to save money, because there's been a lot of inappropriate hospitalizations, people staying in the hospital longer than they need to, and that type of thing," says Jeff St. Romain, national account manager consultant for Human Affairs International, a managed care company and subsidiary of Aetna.

Whether good or bad, managed care has a profound effect on the treatments available to drug abusers. Most often at issue is an EAP's recommendation of inpatient treatment, which is frequently turned down in favor of much less expensive outpatient sessions. Frustrated EAP professionals are left scrambling for free beds at government-sponsored facilities, or finagling free beds from programs they've sent paying clients to in the past. In extreme cases, some have even doubled as social workers, counseling substance abusers themselves after coverage was turned down.

"The whole idea is to deny treatment," says Tom Ruggieri, LCSW, coordinator of the faculty-staff assistance program at the University of Maryland in College Park. "We've had employees who stay at home detoxing, in withdrawal for three or four days because we can't get inpatient treatment approved."

"HMOs, in particular, want the financially easy way out," says Valetta Evans, EAP manager for the American Red Cross. "Some have programs that don't do much at all, with only one meeting a week. Others will say: 'Okay, even if the person needs inpatient treatment, they have to fail at outpatient treatment first.' This is a tragedy. It just doesn't make sense."

Another EAP manager described one employee receiving drugs at home from a live-in boyfriend who was also physically abusing her. An insurance company denied inpatient treatment. Here was one case, he claimed, where inpatient treatment was clearly needed to get her out of a home environment in which going straight would be all but impossible.

But managed care professionals question this assessment. "You don't put someone in an inpatient program for housing reasons," St. Romain says. "What is insurance for? It's for medical conditions, not for housing. Companies can't afford to take on these kinds of situations."

Further, they argue, inpatient programs, especially ones of fixed duration, too often have been used as a rather costly panacea. "The idea is to go in for 28 days to straighten out—as if there were something magic about that length of time," St. Romain says. "I guess the magic is that insurance companies usually cover about 30 days of treatment."

"HMOs invariably want to manage treatment case by case," notes Glenn Young, chief operating officer of Health New England, an HMO in Springfield, Mass. "A program that automatically runs 28 or 21 days is not managing case by case."

And, he adds. "There's another aspect to this that EAP managers don't always talk about. The same company that instituted the EAP also decided to offer healthcare through an HMO or another managed care program. When the company's executives contracted for it, they knew what it meant. Often the two programs clash."

*—M.Z.*

---

As an employer, you are in a good position to help a drug abuser face reality, adds Ginenthal. "A lot of companies are quick to fire a drug abuser, but once that person is at large, the chances that he or she will get treatment diminish greatly." Often, the threat of dismissal will get a drug user into treatment when nothing else can, she adds. "So much of your identity and self-worth is tied to your job."

What's more, says Tom Ruggieri, LCSW, coordinator of the faculty-staff assistance program at the University of Maryland in College Park, "There are plenty of studies that show it's cheaper to rehabilitate someone than recruit, hire and train a new person."

Some job-related drug problems have straightforward solutions. Let's say an employee comes to work drug-impaired and relapses several times despite repeated rehabilitation treatment. You'd probably fire him: You'd have little choice. Or let's say someone stopped by your office to tell you she'd seen one of your employees smoking a joint at a private party Saturday night. You'd probably ignore this rumor without further substantiation.

But some drug-abuse incidents are not so clear-cut, presenting problems not only of good management, but also of good ethics. Following are five such dilemmas, each drawn from real life, though names and identifying details have been changed. *Management Review* asked for comments from four experts: a corporate manager (**Norm Bush,** president and chief operating officer at ENSCO Inc., a Virginia-based research and development company), a human resources executive (**Shelly Ginenthal,** director of human resources at Macworld Communications Inc., located in San Francisco), an employee assistance program professional (**Dale Masi,** D.S.W., professor at the University of Maryland School of Social Work and president of Masi Research Consultants Inc.) and an attorney who specializes in this area (**Jim Kelley** of Morgan, Lewis & Bockius). Their answers illustrate the conflicting concerns of safety, fairness, productivity and compassion that confront managers when dealing with this difficult issue.

*Charles operates heavy equipment for a power company. One evening, on his own time and away from company premises, he is arrested for driving while intoxicated. A search of his car turns up packets of cocaine, a loaded gun and drug paraphernalia. Under police questioning, he admits he's been dealing drugs. Without Charles' arrest and confession, the company would have no knowledge of his dealing, and there was no evidence that he has been using or selling drugs at work. But the power company has recently instituted a drug-abuse policy forbidding employees to sell drugs. The policy does not specify whether this stricture applies only to the workplace, or to outside locations as well. Charles promises to go straight and offers to subject himself to drug testing. Should he be allowed to keep his job?*

**NORM BUSH:**

Although this is a serious charge, I would hate to condemn him on his first incidence without understanding what history was involved. A lot would depend on *how* we learned about the problem: If he was hiding it and we found out through other means, it would indicate that he wasn't trying to correct the situation.

If he came forward, though, and I felt he was being honest, I would want to give him a chance through drug testing—which would be reasonable in this situation—and counseling. Then, because the case is so severe, I would talk to his counselors and get their opinion as to whether we should retain him or not. I would at least want to look at the possibility that the employee may change.

**DALE MASI:**

Selling drugs is a separate issue from taking drugs. How you found out about it doesn't matter. If your company has a policy that says drug dealing will not be permitted, then you should follow the policy.

If the policy doesn't specify that drug dealing is only prohibited on company premises, then that policy needn't be limited to company premises. And, unless you're part of the federal government, you have the right to write a policy that applies to employees' off hours.

**SHELLY GINENTHAL:**

I would assume the policy refers only to the workplace. Employers don't really govern what you do outside, so I don't think the company's policy could be enforced. I would have stayed out of this entirely and really stuck to the performance issues: Has the employee's arrest affected his attendance? If it has, he might be suspended and referred to an EAP, which could suggest a drug program. Although the company can offer assistance, it cannot demand that he receive treatment. Then I would continue to monitor his performance carefully.

**JIM KELLEY:**

Is Charles protected by a union contract or not? That will become the major point. In the absence of a union contract, most employers would terminate him, especially if they were serious about eradicating drugs in the workplace. There is particular concern about drug dealers: The theory is that employees who sell drugs are likely to sell to their coworkers, since that's an obvious, accessible market. And even though Charles was caught off company premises, the policy is enforceable; most state laws don't protect illegal conduct.

But if Charles has a union contract, the picture changes. Under most common contracts, it's questionable whether the company can enforce his termination, un- less it can prove some relation to job performance.

---

### THE REAL-LIFE OUTCOME

This is the only case in this article in which names and details have not been changed, because they are a matter of public record. In 1985, the Florida Power Corp. dismissed Charles Waters under the circumstances described. However, Waters *was* protected by a union contract, and his union, the International Brotherhood of Electrical Workers, filed a grievance. A labor arbitrator reviewed the case, found that the anti-drug policy was unclear in its application to off-premises activity and ordered Waters reinstated with back pay.

Florida Power fought the arbitration by filing to have it vacated in district court. The company won its filing, but the union appealed to the U.S. Court of Appeals, Eleventh Circuit, and that court reinstated the arbitrator's decision.

*Andrea is a brilliant, young computer designer who recently won an award for her work. However, she has been showing up to work with bloodshot eyes and slurred speech. Her company sends her to its EAP for testing, and her system is found to contain painkillers for which she has a prescription. She had started taking them to help with a back problem, which has long since improved, but she has now become dependent on the painkillers. She lies about her symptoms to get more drugs. EAP professionals send her to a rehabilitation clinic. After staying clean for four months, she again comes to work impaired. Should she be fired?*

*Norm Bush,* president and chief operating officer, ENSCO Inc. in Virginia.

### NORM BUSH:

I would consider the circumstances of Andrea's situation. She didn't get into this for kicks. She got involved because of a real problem, and *then* she got hooked. I would be more sympathetic to her than to someone who started taking drugs recreationally.

I would probably put her on probation and give her more time. I might invite her to work part time while getting treatment. In general, I would hang in there longer before I gave up on this situation. But she'd have to be working toward getting off the dependence. I hired her to do the work at a certain quality level, and she's not meeting that level.

### DALE MASI:

It depends on what the policy is. If the policy says that a drug user who has a relapse should be fired, then you should follow the policy. If she were the porter that cleaned up the plant, would you give her another chance? I don't think so. And all employees obviously have to be treated equally.

I don't think firing on the first relapse is a good policy. It's better to give employees a second chance and fire on the third incidence of drug use. But even if you have a bad policy, you can't start making exceptions. You shouldn't give mixed signals. It's not fair to the other employees.

### SHELLY GINENTHAL:

I would let her know in what areas her performance wasn't satisfactory and give her a referral back to the EAP. We would go through all the counseling again, and we would have many conversations about how important it is to stay off the drugs. Then I would warn her that this was her last chance.

It doesn't really matter whether the drug is legal or illegal. I'm not looking at the drug problem. I don't see a big difference between a person using drugs, or having a marital problem, or working a second job during the night and coming in too tired to function. What I care about is her performance, and she's not performing. She needs to get that fixed, and I'm willing to supply her with whatever she needs to do it.

### JIM KELLEY:

The drugs Andrea is using are not legal: They were fraudulently obtained, even if she does have a valid prescription. Abuse of prescription drugs is a major problem in the workplace, and many drug policies address this circumstance exactly. If you don't have a specific policy, essentially, you have to evaluate the relationship between Andrea's lapse and her job performance. You might want to accommodate her if she's still doing a good job.

You might also have legal problems if you fire her: Under many state disability statutes and the federal Rehabilitation Act (which applies to government contractors), she might qualify as disabled. If she were an alcoholic, most courts would say you have to give her another chance. They are less understanding about drugs, but they might still take that view with a drug user who was in a rehabilitation program.

---

### THE REAL-LIFE OUTCOME

The policy in Andrea's company is that an employee who tests positive for drugs within a year of rehabilitation is terminated, and so it was determined that she had to leave. However, because the drugs she was abusing were legally obtained, she was allowed to resign, rather than be fired.

---

*Nancy is a security guard in a manufacturing plant. For several months, she has been coming to work impaired by marijuana and depressants. Laura, Nancy's immediate supervisor, has discussed the problem with her several times, each time suggesting that Nancy seek counseling at the company's EAP. To let Nancy know that she cares, Laura has even gone to Nancy's home. Laura has the power to fire Nancy if she does not go to the EAP, but she lets the situation drag on. Laura is not doing her job effectively. Is it time for Laura's boss to step in?*

**Dale Masi,** D.S.W., professor at the University of Maryland School of Social Work and president of Masi Research Consultants Inc.

### DALE MASI:

It's very common for supervisors to avoid confronting drug users and holding them responsible for their behavior. Laura has got to remain uninvolved in Nancy's problem, while dealing with Nancy's performance. Going to Nancy's home is inappropriate; Laura is not a social worker.

As Laura's supervisor, I would tell Laura that she is responsible for Nancy's behavior. It's going to affect Laura's performance evaluation unless she handles the situation quickly. And that's the only way you'll get Laura to move.

### SHELLY GINENTHAL:

I would try to get Laura some training. But because this is a safety issue, I would probably go over Laura's head and deal with the employee first. If it weren't a safety issue, I would coach and counsel Laura, give her an opportunity to handle the situation, or show her how it's done by meeting with her and Nancy together. I would send Laura to the EAP, and I would certainly want her to learn how to use the EAP in supervising people in crisis.

### JIM KELLEY:

I would deal very severely with both supervisor and employee, especially given the nature of the job. At a minimum, I would give Laura a very serious counseling session. While she may believe she's being compassionate, she isn't helping Nancy—and she's harming the company.

As for the employee, this guard is worse than no security at all; I would get her off the job very quickly. Then I would give her a reasonable period of time to think about it—say, three days or a week—either without pay or as sick leave. During those few days, Nancy must decide whether she wants to go to the EAP. If not, she should be subject to disciplinary action, including discharge. Remember, an individual has to have an element of choice in going to an EAP—even if the option is losing her job.

### NORM BUSH:

Because Nancy is in a position where security is paramount, she would be terminated immediately. When we hire someone in security, that person has to understand better than anyone how important it is. Because we deal with the Defense Department, we cannot tolerate any deviations at all that might jeopardize our classified material. If that happens, and the government decides we're not secure, they can cancel our contract and put the entire company out of work.

As for Laura, I would counsel her and tell her I want Nancy removed. I'd explain that by trying to be understanding and sympathetic with Nancy, she'd failed to understand my concerns for the company. If she delayed further, I might have to put someone else in charge of security in the future.

---

### THE REAL-LIFE OUTCOME

After several months of inaction—during which she'd been patiently briefed by her company's EAP head—Laura still had not dealt effectively with Nancy's drug problem. One day, Laura's boss, fed up with the situation, simply appeared at the security department and ordered Nancy to accompany him to the EAP. According to the EAP head, this forced Nancy to deal honestly, both with her counselor and herself, about what she was doing. As a result, he has high hopes for Nancy's recovery.

*CASE 4*

*David is a former drug user who has spent time in jail. For the past three years he has been straight, and he now operates a forklift at a small construction company. Lately, however, he's begun having seizures, or "flashbacks," as a result of his earlier use of the drug PCP. He has been carefully evaluated by EAP professionals, and found to be clean of current drug use; indeed, they say flashbacks of this nature are quite common in ex-addicts. Mishandling of David's machine could be potentially dangerous to him and his coworkers. However, he has already had flashbacks while at the controls, and in each case the seizure caused him to release a handle, which simply stopped the machine. It is the only work he is qualified to do within this company. Should he continue on the job?*

**Shelly Ginenthal,** director of human resources, Macworld Communications, Inc., San Francisco.

**SHELLY GINENTHAL:**

That's a tough one. I'd go right to David himself and really enlist his help in solving this problem. Then I'd put the situation to his coworkers—I'd maintain confidentiality about his prison record—and try to have them come up with a solution, rather than try to impose one. For instance, a coworker could be assigned to keep an eye on him at all times, ready to react if something happened. I would probably ask them to try this on a trial basis, so the situation could really be monitored.

**NORM BUSH:**

What I'd be tempted to do is retrain him for a different job and get him out of a potentially dangerous situation—where he could cause harm to himself and his coworkers. Even if it involved a cut in pay, it might mean a more permanent future.

**Jim Kelley,** partner in the law firm Morgan Lewis & Bockius, Washington, D.C.

**JIM KELLEY:**

Terminate him. You have no choice: He is physically unable to do the only work you have for him. Just because he's been lucky a couple of times doesn't mean this is a risk you or your company should take. It's unfortunate because he's clearly made an effort to stay away from drugs.

This is the kind of thing you tell high school kids about when you're warning them about the dangers of drugs.

**DALE MASI:**

I would not let the EAP make the decision. It's a medical decision, and I would want a brain scan and a full medical examination. I'd want to see what a psychiatrist who specializes in flashbacks had to say. I'd do that before assuming the seizures are flashbacks. It's a mistake people make often, and many patients are misdiagnosed. If the seizures aren't flashbacks, it may be possible to treat them.

If the people who do the examination are willing to sign off on him, and give him a clean bill of health, I'd let him go back to the forklift. Otherwise he might have to be retrained for another job in the company. If not, my hunch is you're eventually going to have to let him go.

---

**THE REAL-LIFE OUTCOME**

Company executives took a good look at David's history with seizures, including the fact that all of his seizures had been non-violent, and carefully considered the workings of the forklift he was operating. They took into consideration that he was drug-free. Eventually, executives decided that he posed no threat and allowed David to continue working the forklift. There have been no accidents so far.

CASE 5

*Joe has been working at a large manufacturing company for about 20 years. Seven years ago, he had a serious alcohol problem. The company does not have a formal EAP, but Craig, his manager, gave Joe a referral to a rehabilitation program. With Craig's support, Joe stopped drinking. Recently, in the wake of a divorce, Joe has begun appearing at work under the influence again. This time, Craig has decided to fire him. The company's HR department wants to veto Craig's decision: Joe is only nine months away from retirement. Early retirement might be a solution, but Joe refuses that option, claiming the benefits are too low. How would you handle this?*

### NORM BUSH:

If the guy has been productive all these years, there is no way I would fire him with retirement only nine months away. I would try to get a bit more creative and figure out what to do, even if I had to keep him on the payroll at $1 a week until he retired. I would also make an evaluation as to whether he intended to continue working past retirement. And I would try to get the EAP to help him. If Craig insists that he still wants Joe out of the workplace, I would respect his decision, but tell him that we can't fire Joe.

### SHELLY GINENTHAL:

I wouldn't allow Joe to be fired. Instead, I would somehow negotiate a deal that would get him out of the office. I would counsel Joe on what help was available and explore other options. It seems Craig should be satisfied just having Joe out of the picture. After all, the problem isn't that he needs to fire Joe, it's that he needs someone who can do the job.

### JIM KELLEY:

I'd bring him in and say, "Look, Joe, you're late, you're often absent, and we can't deal with your unreliability. We would like to put you in a treatment program, or at least have you diagnosed." Whatever you do, Joe won't be left with nothing. Under federal law, you become vested in your retirement benefits after five years, although the benefits are much higher if he makes it to retirement.

But just because he's eight or nine months shy of retirement is no basis to say that we'll carry him so he can vest completely. If he looks you in the eye and says, "I don't have a problem," then you have to apply your disciplinary rules as if he were anyone else. As a manager, there's no common-sense reason to do otherwise.

### DALE MASI:

The chances are probably still very good for rehabilitation. Joe's been clean for years, and it was a crisis that caused him to drink again. What you need to do is get him back to the EAP—and he will go back there if he knows that his only other choice is going on early retirement. Even if rehabilitation takes up almost all of Joe's remaining work time, it will pay for itself in lower medical expenses, since medical benefits are usually part of a retirement package.

As for Craig, he's getting involved emotionally when he shouldn't be, and he needs help. He's taking it personally that his employee is drinking again, even though Joe's just been through a personal crisis.

---

### THE REAL-LIFE OUTCOME

Angry both at Joe and the HR department, Craig made it his personal mission to fire Joe before the nine months were up. Eventually, he succeeded.

---

# AIDS in the Workplace:

## Implications for Human Resource Managers

**Joseph G. Ormsby**
**Geralyn McClure Franklin**
**Robert K. Robinson**
**Alicia B. Gresham**

---

*Dr. Joseph G. Ormsby, is an Associate Professor of Management at Stephen F. Austin State University in Nacogdoches, Texas.*

*Dr. Geralyn McClure Franklin, is an Assistant Professor of Management at Stephen F. Austin State University in Nacogdoches, Texas.*

*Dr. Robert K. Robinson, is an Assistant Professor of Management at Southwest Missouri State University in Springfield, Missouri.*

*Dr. Alicia B. Gresham, is an Assistant Professor of Marketing at the University of South Alabama in Mobile, Alabama.*

Acquired Immune Deficiency Syndrome (AIDS) is recognized as a major health problem in the United States today. By 1990, it is estimated that over 300,000 individuals will have been diagnosed with the Human Immunodeficiency Virus (HIV). It is not surprising that a malady causing such national concern would become a major employee relations issue.

Organizations must be prepared to deal with this problem by establishing a corporate AIDS policy. Through this policy, conflicts arising over discrimination and the rights of the handicapped, the right to privacy, and employment and insurance issues can be handled without endangering the organization in costly litigation. Forming a corporate AIDS policy is a perplexing problem due to the constant barrage of medical and legal opinions concerning this catastrophic illness. Because the United States does not have any federal legislation that specifically addresses the employment rights of AIDS-afflicted individuals, legal parameters will continue to change. In the absence of legislation, courts will automatically presume that the civil rights of AIDS plaintiffs have been violated.

The purpose here is to provide information from recent court opinions, *Vincent L. Chalk v. U.S. District Court* and *School Board of Nassau County, Florida v. Arline,* and to explain how these opinions will affect organizations attempting to formulate a corporate AIDS policy. This article will present a simple but effective corporate AIDS policy and an outline of a program that could be used to educate your employees about AIDS.

### Personnel Implications from Recent Court Rulings

There are important implications for human resource managers in the *Chalk* and *Arline* decisions. Both apply *only* to employers subject to the provisions of the Vocational Rehabilitation Act of 1973. The Act applies specifically to employers who hold federal contracts of $2,500 or more, who are subcontractors to such an employer, or who participate in a federally-funded program. If an organization does not fall into one of these categories, it is subject only to state and local statutes. If no statutes exist, employers may follow the employment-at-will doctrine. Simply stated, an employer in a private organization may terminate an employee with or without specific cause unless there is a written employment agreement. This rule also assumes the employee may quit without reason and at any time.

If the employer is not exempt from the Vocational Rehabilitation Act, the AIDS-afflicted employee qualifies as a "handicapped individual" under Section 504 of the Act. Since AIDS affects the lymphatic system, the disease itself may not cause physical impairment; some employees testing positive for the HIV virus do not experience any physical deterioration. The question of whether a carrier of a contagious disease (such as AIDS) could be considered to have a

Reprinted from *SAM Advanced Management Journal*, Spring 1990, pp. 23–27. Copyright © 1990 by Society for the Advancement of Management.

"physical impairment" based upon contagion alone has not been answered. Both *Arline* and *Chalk* only cover employees who experience physical deterioration *and* contagiousness. For an employee to qualify as "handicapped," there must be definite signs of physical deterioration—a positive test for the AIDS virus by itself would not be enough. Thus, as in the case of *Chalk,* only certain AIDS-afflicted employees have been granted handicapped status.

Perhaps the elements of *Arline* and *Chalk* that most affect employers are the determination of health and safety risks, continuation of work, and reasonable accommodation. Employers must determine the danger an AIDS-afflicted employee imposes. They must know what the risk to coworkers and customers is, and how AIDS is transmitted. Since transmission is linked to sexual activity or the transfusion of infected blood, only those work environments which are conducive to such occurrences could justify terminations. Today, most organizations do not operate in a high AIDS transmission environment. Therefore, it would be difficult to prove that the AIDS-afflicted employee poses a serious transmission threat to coworkers and customers.

Three additional questions related to health and safety must be addressed. 1.) How long is the carrier infectious? Since there is no known cure for AIDS, the AIDS carrier is considered incurable and infectious for life. 2.) What is the potential harm to coworkers and customers? If infected, the harm is disastrous. Fortunately, this is offset by the low probability of infection in most work environments. 3.) What are the probabilities that the disease will be transmitted? Again, AIDS is not transmitted by casual contact. If job responsibilities do *not* increase the likelihood of coworkers and customers contracting the virus, an employer cannot substantiate termination.

If there is no risk in retaining the AIDS-afflicted employee, the employer must consider whether the employee was performing the job adequately before the discovery of the disease and, providing the employer made "reasonable accommodations," whether the employee could still adequately perform the job. If this is the case, the employee may not be terminated.

Importantly, courts have insisted that the employer make "reasonable accommodations" for these victims of AIDS. What constitutes reasonable accommodation has been difficult to determine. The guidelines developed for federal agencies can be considered a benchmark. For federal agencies reasonable accommodation may include, but is not limited to: 1) making facilities readily accessible to and usable by handicapped persons, and 2) job restructuring, part-time or modified work schedules, acquisition or modification of equipment or devices, appropriate adjustment or modification of examinations, the provision of readers and interpreters, and other similar actions.

However, if a federal agency feels that reasonable accommodation is imposing an undue financial or administrative hardship, it must provide the following verifiable information: 1) the overall size of the agency's program with respect to the number of employees, number and type of facilities, and size of budget; 2) the type of agency operation, including the composition and structure of the agency's work force; and 3) the nature and cost of the accommodation. If such guidelines are suitable for the federal government, they should be equally adequate for private sector employers.

Employers should remember that an AIDS-afflicted employee can be terminated once he or she can no longer perform the job. However, the employer must be prepared to substantiate that the employee's performance deteriorated below minimum standards, and that reasonable accommodation was made for the employee or would cause an undue financial burden on the employer. If the employer can show that these two requirements have been met, the AIDS-afflicted employee may be discharged as an "unqualified handicapped person." Termination under the "unqualified" label is the same provision set for all handicapped persons under the Vocational Rehabilitation Act (1973).

Employers must refrain from what may be called "constructive" reasonable accommodation. That is, removing the employee from his or her usual workplace for the purpose of isolating that employee. Quarantining an employee may be viewed as causing irreparable harm to the employee rather than as compliance with the Act. This would be especially likely in those instances where no reasonable accommodation is necessitated.

Employers are strongly encouraged to review their existing personnel policies to ensure that termination policies do not conflict with the guidance set forth in *Arline* and *Chalk*. Additionally, employers are warned to closely scrutinize their efforts in making reasonable accommodation for their employees. If an employer wishes to avoid allegations of irreparable injury, that employer should ensure that the organization has carefully documented that reasonable accommodation has been provided.

## Developing an Organizational AIDS Policy

When developing an AIDS policy, employers may want to review existing policies of other organizations. A number or corporate AIDS policies have been reprinted in various publications. The policy and procedures of Bank of America Corporation have received considerable praise from experts. This policy, along with other valuable information, can be found in *AIDS: the Workplace Issues,* a publication of the American Management Association.

The law firm of Schachter, Kristoff, Ross, Sprague and Curiale of San Francisco, California recommends the policy provided in Figure 1. It is imperative, however, that employers consult knowledgeable legal counsel in their respective states before finalizing such a personnel policy.

Organizations implementing an AIDS policy should check the coverage provided by the employee's insurance carrier. Currently, some insurance companies are treating AIDS as any other major disease and honoring existing contracts. Due to the tremendous costs involved in treating AIDS victims, this may change in the future.

## The Necessity of AIDS Education

To successfully function in an environment with AIDS-afflicted employees, organizations must understand that education of the workforce is vital. Potential benefits include: 1) an understanding of how AIDS is contracted and spread; 2) a forum for discussing employee questions and fears; and 3) information on AIDS treatment and sources of further information.

Education can also provide benefits for the employer. First, employers who currently are obligated to comply with the Vocational Rehabilitation Act would use such programs to prevent potential discrimination against AIDS-afflicted employees. This proactive measure would help keep the organization in compliance with the Act and would help avoid discrimination which could jeopardize federal contract(s) or grant(s). Additionally, the education program would insulate employers against possible litigation from AIDS-afflicted employees, or at the very least, provide evidence of the employer's concern about the disease. Similarly, employers subject only to state vocational rehabilitation laws may also benefit, since offering educa-

---

FIGURE 1
MODEL POLICY FOR AIDSDEVELOPED BY SCHACHTER, KRISTOFF, ROSS, SPRAGUE, AND CURIALE (SAN FRANCISCO)*

The unfortunate spread of AIDS in recent years has caused us to consider and adopt a policy regarding the employment of those who have, or may have, this disease. We have consulted medical experts and are satisfied that, according to the best medical evidence available to date, casual workplace contact with employees who have AIDS, or who have been exposed to the AIDS virus, will not result in the transmission of AIDS to others.

Therefore, effective immediately, our normal policy will be to employ employees or applicants who have AIDS, or are suspected of having AIDS, so long as such persons remain qualified to perform their jobs in accordance with our standards. Some exceptions or deviations to this policy may be necessary for certain positions, but our intent will be to maximize the employment opportunities of AIDS victims, while at the same time preserving the safety and morale of all our employees.

We will stay abreast of the latest medical knowledge regarding this disease. Should it ever appear that implementation of our policy may present a danger to our employees, we will make appropriate revisions to the policy.

If you have any questions about this policy, please contact _____ . If you wish to review medical information upon which the policy is based, we would be glad to make it available upon request.

*Used with permission

---

tional programs could protect against noncompliance litigation.

A second benefit for employers would be the economic and social benefits gained by adopting an AIDS education program. In a recent poll, one in four respondents openly stated that they would refuse to work next to someone with AIDS (Blendon and Donelan, 1988). It would be realistic to assume that these workers would feel adamantly enough about the issue to quit. The costs associated with such turnover could be substantially diminished through an education program which could reduce or eliminate these unfounded fears. This would be most beneficial for employers with skilled or professional workers, since the cost of replacing these employees is higher. Additionally, an education program would alleviate employee stress and anxiety by dispelling rumors and myths about the AIDS disease. Ultimately, the employer would benefit from the release of tension and the development of more peaceful relationships within the organization.

```
┌─────────────────────────────────────────┐
│              FIGURE 2                     │
│         AIDS SEMINAR OUTLINE              │
├─────────────────────────────────────────┤
│  I. Introduction (5–10 minutes)          │
│     A. Welcome                            │
│     B. Personnel policy (if applicable)   │
│     C. Introduce videotape                │
│ II. Videotape (15–30 minutes depending on │
│     video used)                           │
│ III. Discussion (30 minutes)              │
│     A. Highlight important facts from the │
│        videotape                          │
│     B. Respond to questions from the group│
│ IV. Closing Remarks/Brochure Distribution │
│     (5 minutes)                           │
│     A. Distribute AIDS information bro-    │
│        chures                             │
│     B. Distribute seminar evaluation forms│
│     C. Highlight company and community    │
│        resources                          │
│     D. Stress education and sharing infor-│
│        mation                             │
└─────────────────────────────────────────┘
```

## An AIDS Education Program

A variety of AIDS education programs are available from personnel clearinghouses, such as the Bureau of National Affairs. The guidelines that follow have been developed to keep the expense of the education program modest.

*Step 1: Research the disease.* Those responsible for the education program, typically human resource managers, should be prepared with the most up-to-date medical, legal, and social information about AIDS. This may require consulting local health officials and lawyers.

*Step 2: Appoint a task force.* This group should include representatives from the personnel, safety, and labor relations areas. In smaller organizations, a task force of employees who are interested in the program and willing to participate in such a project can be just as useful. Regardless of their specific backgrounds, each member should be responsible for gathering and distributing information and structuring the AIDS education program.

*Step 3: Train personnel who are to become AIDS resource specialists or enlist outside specialists to provide education programs.* Local health officials and officials of the American Red Cross are often available to train in-house specialists or provide education programs.

*Step 4: Introduce the topic.* Let employees know about the upcoming seminar through the com-

pany newsletter or a bulletin board, or send each employee a letter.

*Step 5: Educate supervisory employees.* Supervisory personnel are the heart of an AIDS education program as they are the link between the company and AIDS issues. Consequently, it is essential for supervisory personnel to be educated in medical and social issues AIDS concerns, including meeting the special needs of the AIDS employee and calming the fears of coworkers. In addition, supervisory personnel need to be familiar with the legal issues surrounding the employment of an AIDS-afflicted employee.

*Step 6: Educate all employees.* Employers will probably want to implement a program that is simple to follow and requires relatively little outside support. If the task force members or in-house specialists have been adequately trained, they can present the education program. Attendance of local medical and legal experts to answer employees' questions is also highly recommended. As a guide, an outline for an education program is provided in Figure 2. The use of a video tape is suggested in order to provide the basic facts about AIDS. For information, consult local health officials, the American Red Cross, or other references.

*Step 7: Distribute new information as it becomes available.* Due to the changing environment of medical information on AIDS, it is imperative for organizations to stay current on developments in this area. Distribute as much new information as possible since continual education is the best weapon for combating employees' fears.

## Conclusion

While many employers may feel that the development of a corporate AIDS policy and education program is difficult, it is certainly not impossible. Organizations must make every effort to act responsibly and in a timely fashion in order to deal with AIDS in the workplace. With active policy design, intelligent, reasonable application of those policies and firm-wide education programs, organizations will be well equipped to handle the AIDS dilemma.

**References**

Blendon, Robert J. and Karen Donelan. "Discrimination Against People with AIDS: The Public's Perspective." *The New England Journal of Medicine* 319 (October 13, 1988), 1022–1026.

# WHAT WOULD YOU DO?

# The Untouchables

*The South African company wanted help drafting an integrity code.*
*Was taking the assignment a step toward change in South Africa,*
*or an act of complicity with apartheid?*

*Doug Wallace*

*Doug Wallace does frequent consulting work on corporate ethics, and was formerly the vice president for social policy at Norwest Bank in Minneapolis.*

## THE CASE

It wasn't the first time the group had gone over this territory, Cynthia Stallings thought to herself. She suppressed a laugh as she realized: Those for and against the current proposal had arrayed themselves almost perfectly on opposite sides of the walnut conference table. As president of Stallings and Wesby, Cynthia would be the final arbiter: Should the consulting firm take on this new South African client?

The company in question was Nimma Financial Services, the fourth largest diversified financial services organization in South Africa. Nimma was an attractive prospect for Stallings and Wesby, a corporate consulting firm with a staff of twenty-five and revenues of several million, with a special focus on ethics. But the staff was divided on whether it was right to do business with a firm in South Africa.

Nimma's name had first come up eighteen months earlier. Jim Chopin, Stallings and Wesby's marketing director, had gotten a phone call from Chester Dorn, second in command at Nimma, who made a point of emphasizing Nimma's aggressive hiring and promotion of blacks. "I think you will find us in a leadership position of change," he explained.

In keeping with the policy of screening the values of potential clients, Jim checked out Nimma and presented his findings at a staff meeting: 30 percent of Nimma's employees and 3 percent of managers were black, and more than 60 percent of its home-loan portfolio was with black families. The industry association had given Nimma high marks. Several anti-apartheid groups were unhappy with Nimma's performance—but they were unhappy with all financial services companies in South Africa.

"Look," Jim had said, "Nimma wants to be better, that's why it's coming to us. Are we only going to work with companies that are already saved?" Half of the staff agreed, but the rest were vocal in their opposition—reminding Cynthia that they had come to work for her because of her focus on ethics. "Besides, how will other clients feel," one asked, "if we work with a white firm in South Africa?"

It was a difficult call, but Cynthia decided to turn down the work with Nimma for the time being.

Today, eighteen months later, the matter was back on the table. Chester Dorn—now president of Nimma Financial—had again asked for

Reprinted from *Business Ethics*, July/August 1991, pp. 24-26. *Business Ethics*, 1107 Hazeltine Blvd., Suite 530, Chaska, MN 55318. 612-448-8864.

145

*help. Earlier, Chester explained, he had sniffed some questionable behavior but suffered in silence. Now that he was in charge he had cleared the decks, and was looking for help drafting an integrity code to improve the corporate culture.*

*"A lot has happened in eighteen months," Jim told the staff. "Let's reconsider doing business with Nimma. President de Klerk has come out with strong proposals, and some British firms are dropping their embargo as a result. Can't we?" One colleague—who had been on the other side of the fence before—echoed his support. "Chester Dorn is a good guy," he said. "He's talking about having his company's mission reflect Third World values."*

*Others held firm in their opposition. "Until apartheid is totally abolished, there's no way we should be there at all," one said in anger. "I'm offended that you would even consider bringing this up again."*

*In a straw vote, Cynthia found the same split: fifty-fifty. As the staff filed out, her mood darkened. She no longer felt the least bit like laughing. Cynthia swiveled her chair and stared at the ceiling, wondering what she should do.*

## Harry Newman, Jr.

*Chairman, Newman Properties, Long Beach, California*

Cynthia's decision shouldn't be difficult to make. Stallings and Wesby has a specific mission of helping clients address ethical issues, and here is someone who is asking for ethical assistance. It's ridiculous to turn down this request. In a country with a tradition of repression, Chester Dorn has worked to get his company to take positive action. Dorn obviously wants to work on the problems in South Africa, and he wants help. I don't think there is any legitimate reason for refusing to help Dorn in his work at Nimma Financial Services.

I can't see any challenge for Stallings and Wesby if they work only for the "good guys." Apparently, that's what some of the staff wants the company to do. I would talk with those who are putting up so much resistance and get something straight. I'd let them know that the company is seeking work with clients who may not have the best track

record in the world, but who are seriously trying to do better. If some staff members can't buy that, then maybe they're working in the wrong firm.

## Steve Schueth

*Vice President, Socially Responsible Investing, Calvert Group, Bethesda, Maryland*

The future of a company like Stallings and Wesby is dependent on the credibility it develops with clients. For that reason, it must demonstrate care in how it handles this request. The extensive discussion that has already taken place is a plus in this regard.

But before making a decision, Cynthia needs more information. Some facts are missing. For example, what has been Nimma's position on the Sullivan Principles (the code of conduct for firms doing business in South Africa)? Also, are the interest rates charged black families the same as those charged whites? And is Nimma's goal to move blacks up in the organization? If so, the percentage of black managers (3 percent) is pathetic. Is there a risk here that the changes Nimma is making are only cosmetic? Is somebody trying to railroad us?

The bottom line is that no matter how good Nimma's intentions are, the company is still bound by the laws of South Africa. It exists within that system.

Cynthia needs to come down on the side of staff members who want to avoid all business with South African companies. But she should also keep the lines of communication open with Nimma. If I were her, I would consider taking on this specific project (writing a preliminary integrity statement) on a pro bono basis—for two reasons: First, the company doesn't want to profit from doing business in South Africa; and second, it can work on the assumption that Dorn and his company may be ahead of others when things really start to change in South Africa.

## Doug Wallace's Comments

We have here two sharply contrasting points of view on an important decision. Harry Newman focuses on the *mission* of the consulting firm and argues that to stay true to its purpose, it should accept the assignment. Steve Schueth's starting point is quite different. He begins by insisting that the context of the *system* makes it impossible, on the face of it, to accomplish Stallings and Wesby's mission. Who is right? I suggest that perhaps both are.

There are times when people are called to serve in the most abhorrent of situations: medics aiding soldiers in the midst of a misguided war, Jesus befriending Roman tax collectors who serve an oppressive ruler, the pacifist French community of Le Chambon acting in the middle of the Nazi Holocaust. Some would suggest that trying to act as an ethical agent of change within a resistive institution is simply a gesture of self-deception and unconscious complicity. And yet, at times that is exactly what certain people are called to do: to act for change without the safeguards of self-righteousness. To do so reflects a capacity for leadership with a tragic sense of life, an awareness of the absurdity of action in the face of overwhelming odds and moral ambiguity.

## WHAT ACTUALLY HAPPENED?

As is always true with "What Would You Do?" this case is a real one, though some facts have been changed to disguise the participants. The meeting portrayed here is a dramatized version of the actual dispute, which arose about a year ago, when South Africa was seeing hopeful signs of change—signs of change that continue still today.

After hearing both sides of the debate, Cynthia felt quite strongly that it was right to take on Nimma Financial as a client, and that doing so would give Stallings and Wesby a chance to be a progressive force in South Africa. But she was deeply concerned by the misgivings of her staff and didn't wish to take a step that would divide the company or damage staff morale. Despite her own discomfort, she reluctantly decided to decline the assignment with Nimma. Stallings and Wesby would stay out of business in South Africa until the government's policy of apartheid changed enough to demonstrate real progress.

# Emerging Ethical Issues in International Business

## David J. Fritzsche

Dr. Fritzsche is a professor at the University of Portland and has published numerous articles on business and marketing ethics and a book, *The Business Policy Game*.

*The process used to produce an industrial product which accounts for 20% of your firm's sales creates large quantities of Dio-Ethel-Atin-Tri-Hexophane (DEATH). This highly toxic compound has no commercial value, but its disposal represents a significant cost of production. A new competitor from Thailand has entered the market with a price just under your break-even level. The Thai firm is able to offer the product at that price due to the low cost of disposing of the DEATH compound.*

*Yesterday Tex-Tox called and offered to dispose of your DEATH compound for a quarter of your current cost. That would allow you to compete successfully with the Thai firm. Upon inquiry, you learn that Tex-Tox will ship the compound to an African country where it will be used for fill in a highway project. What will your decision be?*

This scenario places the decision maker in the realm of applied ethics. Applied ethics may be defined as the process of evaluating decisions with respect to the moral standards of the culture. In the international context, the question arises as to whose culture determines the standards. While there is often little difference in moral standards across cultures, the host country's standards would have to set the minimal acceptable levels where differences occur.

Moral standards have generally agreed upon distinguishing features.[1] Moral standards deal with issues that are considered to be of serious consequence to people. The validity of moral standards is based upon the acceptability of the reasons that support and justify them. Moral standards override self-interest. Finally, moral standards are based upon impartial rationale.

## When Ethical Issues Occur

As noted, ethical questions arise when issues involve moral standards. The three moral standards most often cited to evaluate moral issues are the principles of justice, rights, and utilitarianism.[2]

*Justice Principles.* The justice principles deal with issues of fairness when dealing with others. This includes *fair treatment* of individuals; persons who are similar to each other on relevant criteria should be treated as equals. People who differ on relevant criteria should receive treatment appropriate to the degree of difference.

*Fair administration of rules* is based upon the consistent application of rules to all parties involved. Rules should be administered in a fair and impartial manner. This applies to laws, policies of the firm, and actions of individual supervisors.

When an individual is injured or harmed, the individual is entitled to *fair compensation*. Compensation should be provided by the party responsible for the injury. To the extent possible, the compensation should return the injured party to his or her original state prior to the injury.

To be held accountable for an act, an individual must be in control of the act and thus justly receive *fair blame*. People cannot be held responsible for actions beyond their control.

Finally, individuals have a right to *due process*. When personal rights have been violated, the persons involved have a right to a fair and impartial hearing.

*Rights Principles.* There is a series of rights which our culture, as well as most others, believes an individual possesses simply by being human. Chief among these is the right to *life and safety*. A person's moral rights are violated if a decision is made that puts the individual

Reprinted from *SAM Advanced Management Journal*, Autumn 1990, pp. 42-46. Copyright © 1990 by Society for the Advancement of Management, Vinton, VA 24179.

unknowingly and unnecessarily in a harmful or life-threatening position.

An individual has the right not to be intentionally deceived in matters which the person considers important. Thus *truthfulness* in communication is a basic moral right.

A person has the right to *privacy* in personal life. This provides the individual the freedom to pursue his or her own interests outside the work environment. It also includes the right to control the dissemination of information about one's personal life.

Commonly accepted moral or religious norms provide guidance for people's behavior. An individual has a right to *freedom of conscience* and thus is morally correct in refusing to carry out orders which violate these accepted personal norms. Thus, management should not require an individual to act in a manner that would compromise personal norms.

*Freedom of speech* is a right we hold dear. This right guarantees the freedom to express opinions in a truthful and conscientious manner as long as they do not violate the rights of the individual or organization being criticized.

Finally we have the right to *private property*. Any individual has the right to hold private property in cultures which are not based upon collectivism. This right is especially strong to the extent that it provides the individual and associated family with shelter and other basic necessities of life. The right to private property is usually the first to be abridged when it conflicts with other rights.

The fact that an individual is entitled to specific rights imposes duties upon others. The right to truthfulness creates the obligation upon others to tell the truth. The right of free speech imposes an obligation not to interfere with honest criticism.

*Utilitarian Principles.* The essence of the utilitarian principles is to maximize the satisfaction of the organization's stakeholders. Notice the satisfaction is of stakeholders, not stockholders, although stockholders comprise one group of stakeholders. Thus, according to the utilitarian standard, the decision maker must evaluate any decision alternative in terms of the sum of the benefits provided to all of the organization's stakeholders. The alternative which yields the greatest overall benefit is deemed to be the most ethical.

As a corollary to maximizing stakeholder satisfaction, the utilitarian standard calls for the firm to attain its goals efficiently. Thus, for a given level of output, the required input plus the external costs borne by stakeholders should be minimized. The minimization of costs should enhance stakeholder satisfaction.

In addition, employees have an obligation to work toward achieving the goals of the organization. They must not deliberately hinder goal accomplishment either through actions designed to thwart the goals or by engaging in situations where personal interests would conflict with the goals.

### The Issues

In examining emerging ethical issues, few really new issues are likely to occur. What we can expect to see are familiar issues arising in new forms and new places. Therefore, it is useful to look at issues which raised serious ethical questions in the past. This can be done in summary form by examining Table 1.[3] The issues listed by order of frequency in the first column were obtained from two studies of *Harvard Business Review* readers who were asked to cite the unethical practice in their industry which they would most like to see eliminated. In the latter two columns, respondents were asked for the ethical issue which posed the most difficult ethical or moral dilemma for them.

It is interesting to note the similarity in the findings, particularly between the *Harvard Business Review* readers and the marketing managers. Some of the labels from the study of marketing managers group such issues as deception, collusion, and cheating under several headings, e.g., price and advertising.

### International Events Raising Ethical Issues

Ethical issues will emerge in the international arena due to significant changes in the environment. We will examine some of these changes and the potential issues they may cause.

*Europe 1992.*[4] In 1992, Europe will become an integrated economic market. To create this economic unity, Belgium, Britain, Denmark, France, Greece, Ireland, Italy, Luxembourg, the Netherlands, Portugal, Spain and . . . Germany will remove thousands of invisible trade barriers. Capital will be freed to flow anywhere in the 12 countries. Adjustments will be made to value-added and excise taxes to create more uniformity. European trade and professional workers will be able to practice their craft anywhere within the European Community (EC). The special "sweetheart" deals in government procurement will be gone, and the process will open up to anyone in the EC. Gone also will be the protected markets, price fixing, and the allocated market shares which have prevailed as a way of life.

According to EC officials, benefits from this unification include an increase in gross domestic product of between 4.3 and 6.4 percent (approximately $325 billion), a 6.1 percent decline in consumer prices, 1.8 million new jobs, an increase in government budget revenues of 2.2 percent of GDP [gross domestic product], and an improvement in the EC trade balance of 1 percent of GDP. These changes will be due to the strength gained by European firms operating in an enlarged home market (325 million people) and to their enhanced ability to compete in the world marketplace.

## Table 1
## Ethical Issues Faced by Business Executives

| Harvard Business Review Readers | Marketing Managers | Marketing Researchers |
|---|---|---|
| Gifts, gratuities, bribes; "call girls" | Bribery | Research Integrity |
| Price discrimination; unfair pricing | Fairness | Treating outside clients fairly |
| Dishonest advertising | Honesty | Research confidentiality |
| Misc. unfair competitive practice | Price | Marketing mix and social issues |
| Creating customers; unfair credit practices; overselling | Product | Personnel issues |
| Price collusion by competitors | Personnel | Treating respondents fairly |
| Dishonesty in making and keeping contracts | Confidentiality | Treating others in company fairly |
| Unfairness to employees; prejudice in hiring | Advertising | Interviewer dishonesty |
| Other | Manipulation of data | Gifts, bribes and entertainment |
| | Purchasing | Treating suppliers fairly |
| | Other issues | Legal issues |
| | | Misuse of funds |
| | | Other |

The evolving European marketplace and the increased competitiveness of European firms will change relationships, particularly in the areas of competitors and markets. This will bring pressure for foreign competitors to "buy" into the markets or be left on the sidelines. There is a real concern that the European Community will go protectionist. Numerous questionable deals are sure to arise.

Europe 1992 is also likely to provide opportunities (perceived as necessities in order to compete) to market questionable products, promote deceptively, and price dishonestly. If Japan or the United States responds with protectionist acts, either initiating or responding to the other blocs, the pressure to get into the EC will mount even more, creating even greater needs in the minds of some to act in a less acceptable manner.

*Regional Trading Blocs.*[5] A North American trading bloc was formed this past summer [1990] when Canada and the United States approved a free trade pact. The European Community will be a reality in 1992. The third bloc emerging is Japan and the "newly industrialized countries" (NICs). The NICs consist of Hong Kong, Singapore, South Korea, and Taiwan. Moving up in the wings ready to join these countries are China and Thailand. These three potential trading blocs create a new threat of divisions in the world.

If such divisions were to occur, there would be enormous pressure for firms in one bloc to penetrate another. Again, we have an example of significant changes in relationships. One could envision increases in payoffs, kickbacks, price discrimination, dishonest advertising, collusion, customer cheating and other unfair competitive practices. It should be noted that the formation of trading blocs in the 1930s was one factor in the political divisions which led to World War II.

*Air Pollution.* Neither chlorofluorocarbons (CFCs) associated with depleting the ozone layer nor $CO_2$ thought to foster the greenhouse effect respect national boundaries. Efforts to reduce CFCs, such as the agreement signed in Montreal by the European Community and 24 other nations which calls for halving the amount of CFCs produced by 1998, should help. $CO_2$ appears to be a problem due to the burning of fossil fuel and global deforestation.

Efforts to reduce these two gasses will likely result in more costly production and consumption processes, thus creating incentives for firms and even countries to cheat in the cleanup effort. Such actions would give an unfair advantage to the deviants at the expense of the complying firms. In addition, deception would likely occur when the products and services were sold. Consumers are not aware of the gaseous contents of products they consume unless told of the product's contents. A can labeled as containing an alternative propellant could, in reality, contain CFCs without being discovered.

*Biotechnology.*[6] The interest in biotechnology is growing in developed countries. Plant scientists in the Netherlands are ready to field-test potatoes which they have genetically engineered to contain a foreign gene to combat viral infection. Australian genetic researchers are planning to field-test protein enriched alfalfa which should boost wool production when fed to sheep. In the U.S., field tests are planned for corn containing a genetically altered bacterium designed to kill the European corn borer.

Animal scientists in Australia have given pigs an extra growth-hormone gene resulting in offspring that are 30 percent more efficient in converting feed to meat. Researchers in the U.S. have transferred a human gene to mice. The altered mice produce milk containing the TPA protein that dissolves blood clots. Work is going on in several countries to improve the genetic makeup of salmon.

Biotechnology raises a series of ethical questions.

The unknown environmental risks raise a set of important issues. Then there is the question of whether people have the moral right to patent animal life. Altering animal life is one step away from altering human life. The opportunities for lying, manipulation, and other dishonest practices are immense.

*Space.*[7] The launching of space vehicles, whether by countries or companies, produces a great deal of pollution. This may create a serious problem close to the earth in the near future. Both large and small objects can do serious damage to future craft. This quickly raises rights and justice issues concerning responsibility and compensation for damage done by space pollution.

In addition to pollution, there is the problem of fallout. In 1978 and again in 1983, Soviet satellites containing nuclear reactors fell back into the atmosphere. A third was expected to fall in October [1990], but the reactor was launched into a higher orbit prior to the reentry of the satellite. Earlier, two others had fallen back to earth during launch. Launching vehicles containing materials that could cause serious harm if control is lost again raises significant ethical issues of rights and justice.

*Exporting Waste.*[8] Waste disposal is becoming a major problem in developed countries, particularly the U.S. Site shortages and environmental regulations make waste disposal increasingly expensive. A solution tried by one city was to ship toxic incinerator ash to Guinea where children subsequently played on the ash "mountain." The waste removal contract was let by Philadelphia to a company which submitted the low bid based on foreign shipment.

Two Americans exported 1,500 gallons of cleaning fluid to Zimbabwe. Unfortunately for Zimbabwe, the cleaning fluid was actually toxic waste. Other toxic waste has arrived on the door step of developing countries labeled as "complex organic matter" or as "ordinary industrial wastes."

Zatec, a Netherlands firm, is building landfills in three African countries. It plans to ship chemical and industrial wastes to the landfills when they are completed. Disposing of toxic waste in developing countries is economically attractive, as costs paid to foreign governments and businesses for accepting the waste run as low as $3 to $50 per ton. In the U.S. and Europe the cost can be as much as $2,500 per ton.

The exportation of hazardous waste to undeveloped countries raises major ethical issues. In many cases, the receiving nations are very poor, have limited safe disposal capacities, and do not have the governmental infrastructure to deal with hazardous waste. Thus, the people of the country are exposed to serious hazards without knowing it. Their rights are violated, and there is little likelihood that they will receive compensation from the injuring party—or any party for that matter.

## Concerns

While the specific issue will vary with the location and the actors, numerous potential or early stage ethical issues have been identified. In most cases, the moral principles of justice and rights are violated. The actual issues encountered will take many forms, but what they all have in common is that they violate some dimension of one or more of the three moral principles.

The ethically-concerned firm can take several steps to encourage ethical behavior among its personnel. The empirical literature overwhelmingly supports the assertion that the CEO sets the ethical tenor of the organization. If the CEO communicates a strong concern for ethical behavior, the ensuing behavior is likely to be ethical. (It is not enough simply to be an advocate of ethical behavior if the advocacy is not communicated.) Corporate policy should also be developed which supports ethical acts. With strong CEO commitment supported by corporate policy, acting in an ethical manner becomes part of the organization's culture.

In addition, the organization should provide ethics training for its personnel at all levels. Training will sensitize employees to the ethical dimension of decision making as well as provide a framework in which to evaluate the ethics of decision alternatives. It also reinforces the belief that the organization is serious about the ethics of employee behavior.

Each manager should be alerted to look for potential ethical problems before they occur. The issues can then be given the proper consideration without operating in the mistake-prone crisis mode. In many cases, the "correct" decision alternative will not be obvious. More than one set of rights may be involved, and honoring one set of rights may conflict with the rights of others. For example, in the case of the DEATH compound mentioned at the beginning, the life and safety rights of the people in the African country will be abridged if the company agrees to the Tex-Tox offer. However, the property rights of stockholders will be violated if a major product must be dropped with no compensation.

The decision maker is in the position of playing judge in determining who wins and who loses. Some guidance is needed. In the area of rights, personal rights are generally considered to take precedence over property rights. The rights of the less powerful are generally given precedence over the rights of the more powerful when evaluating conflicting identical rights.

When conflict occurs between personal rights and utilitarian concerns, personal rights are considered to be dominant. However, property rights can be abridged in favor of utilitarian principles if the stakeholder gain is great enough, as in the exercise of eminent domain for highway construction.

Personal rights also override principles of justice. Again, property rights may take a back seat to justice principles if the result is to achieve a more fair distribution of benefits and burdens for society. Justice principles normally dominate utilitarian concerns. However, there are times when we are willing to trade off some equity if it results in greater benefit for all.

## NOTES

1. M. G. Velasquez, *Business Ethics: Concepts and Cases*, (Englewood Cliffs, NJ: Prentice-Hall, 1982): Chapter 1.

2. G. F. Cavanagh, *American Business Values*, 2nd ed. (Englewood Cliffs, NJ: Prentice-Hall, 1984): Chapter 5.

3. Taken from R. C. Baumhart, "How Ethical Are Businessmen?" *Harvard Business Review*, July–August 1961: 156–176; S. N. Brenner and E. A. Molander, "Is the Ethics of Business Changing?" *Harvard Business Review*, January–February 1977: 57–71; L. B. Chonko and S. D. Hunt, "Ethics and Marketing Management: An Empirical Examination," *Journal of Business Research*, Vol. 13: 339–359; and S. D. Hunt, L. B. Chonko and J. B. Wilcox, "Ethical Problems of Marketing Researchers," *Journal of Marketing Research*, August 1984: 309–324.

4. The following sources were drawn upon for this section: J. Yemma, "Setting sights boldly on unity," *The Christian Science Monitor*, June 27, 1988: 1 & 11; J. Yemma, "Businessmen: they grow them bigger in Europe," *The Christian Science Monitor*, June 28, 1988: 1 & 8: J. Yemma, "European states weigh the cost of . . . , "US and Japan size up new kid on the block," *The Christian Science Monitor*, June 30, 1988: 1 & 10.

5. D. R. Francis, "As big trade blocs rise, so does threat of new divisions in the world," *The Christian Science Monitor*, June 6, 1988: 16.

6. The following sources were drawn upon for this section: R. C. Cowen, "New wave crops headed for the farm," *The Christian Science Monitor*, June 1, 1988: 16–17; R. C. Cowen, " 'Value added' animals: what is on the horizon," *The Christian Science Monitor*, June 2, 1988: 16 & 17; R. C. Cowen, "Regulating biotech: how much is enough," *The Christian Science Monitor*, 16 & 17.

7. J. Oberg, "The nuclear waste that fell to earth," *The Christian Science Monitor*, June 29, 1988: 11.

8. The following sources were drawn upon for this section: K. Helmore, "Dumping on Africa: West exports its industrial wastes," *The Christian Science Monitor*, July 1, 1988; 1 & 8: Polly Diven, "Our Newest Hazardous Export," *The Christian Science Monitor*, October 27, 1988, p. 11.

# A Torrent of Dirty Dollars

*Money laundering is a runaway global industry
that serves customers ranging from cocaine cartels
to tax-dodging corporations*

**JONATHAN BEATY AND RICHARD HORNIK**

In Willemstad, the sunny Caribbean capital of the Netherlands Antilles, a banker ushers an American visitor through a hotel casino and into a dining room overlooking the harbor. During refreshments, the prospective customer says he expects a six-figure cash windfall soon and would like to bring the money "quietly" into the U.S. At first the banker responds cautiously. "This money isn't, ah, tainted, is it?" When the American assures him it is not, the officer of the Curaçao branch of the French-owned Credit Lyonnais Nederland smiles and orders another tonic water. In that case, says the banker, he can arrange a so-called Dutch sandwich.

Under this multilayered plan, the Paris bank would set up a corporation for the customer in Rotterdam, where he would deposit his cash in the bank's local branch. The American would control the newly created Dutch corporation through an Antilles trust company, but his identity as the owner would be protected by the island group's impenetrable secrecy laws. The Caribbean branch would then "lend" the American his own money held in Rotterdam.

If the American were questioned by the Internal Revenue Service or other authorities about the source of his wealth, he could point to his loan from a respected international bank. "Many of your largest corporations, many of your movie stars, do much the same thing here," says the banker. "We wouldn't want to handle criminal money, of course. But if it's just a matter of taxes, that is of no concern to us."

When U.S. drug agents tallied up the amount of cocaine they seized during fiscal 1989, their haul totaled 89 tons, or 44% more than last year's. The volume, which is believed to be only a small percentage of the tons flooding the country, is evidence of more than just a frighteningly effective drug-smuggling industry. The wholesale value of the coke, as much as $28 billion, is testimony to another kind of dark genius. This is the scandalous ability of the coke kingpins to launder billions of dollars in drug proceeds using many of the same financial services available to the FORTUNE 500. In a wash cycle that often takes less than 48 hours, the drug smugglers can turn coke-tinged $20 and $100 bills into such untraceable, squeaky-clean assets as money-market deposits, car dealerships and resort hotels.

The coke smugglers can accomplish this feat because they have plenty of help. They rely on a booming money-laundering industry that serves a clientele ranging from tax-avoiding corporations to the Iranscam schemers. The system depends on the collaboration, or often just the negligence, of bankers and other moneymen who can use electronic-funds networks and the secrecy laws of tax havens to shuffle assets with alacrity. The very institutions that could do the most to stop money laundering have the least incentive to do so. According to police and launderers, the basic fee for recycling money of dubious origin is 4%, while the rate for drug cash and other hot money is 7% to 10%.

Much is at stake as the powerful flow of narcodollars is recycled through the world's financial system. Drug lords and other lawbreakers are believed to be buying valuable chunks of the American economy, but clever Dutch sandwiches and other subterfuges make it almost impossible for U.S. authorities to track foreign investors. A case in point: blind corporations based in the Netherlands Antilles control more than one-third of all foreign-owned U.S. farmland, many of the newest office towers in downtown Los Angeles and a substantial number of independent movie companies producing films like Sylvester Stallone's *Rambo* pictures.

While businesses and individuals may conceal their assets for purposes that are completely legal, or dubious at worst, the systems set up for their convenience can be perversely efficient at helping drug barons launder as much as $100 billion a year in U.S. proceeds. "It is hard to understand why we failed for so long to institute adequate controls," says Massachusetts Democrat John Kerry, chairman of the Senate's Subcommittee on Terrorism, Narcotics and International Operations. The state of regulation is "so lackadaisical," says Kerry, "it's almost damnable."

President Bush, for his part, has declared money launderers a critical target in the war on drugs, allocating $15 million to launch a counteroffensive. While the sum is minuscule for the task, the declaration signals a change in philosophy for the Administration, which had resisted calls for tighter banking regulations. Only hours after Bush unveiled his anti-drug offensive last September, a federal task force began taking shape. The Financial Crimes Enforcement Network (FINCEN) hopes to zero in on money launderers with computer programs capable of spotting suspicious movements of electronic money.

In a high-tech game of cat and mouse, the Justice Department said last week that it had found and triggered the freezing of $60.1 million in bank accounts in five countries that contained the personal income of Jose Gonzalo Rodriguez Gacha, a leader of the Medellín cartel. Using financial records and computer disks captured by the Colombian government, U.S.

agents traced Rodriguez money to accounts in the U.S., Luxembourg, Switzerland, Austria and Britain.

Drug Enforcement Administration officials told TIME that one of Rodriguez's purported financial advisers, Panama-based Mauricio Vives, tried desperately to keep moving the money one step ahead of the agents. Vives called a British banker and told him to move several million dollars, fast, to an account in Luxembourg. If the bank were to delay, his Colombian client would kill him, Vives pleaded. The banker refused, and British authorities cooperating with the DEA froze the account. Not all countries were as helpful. U.S. agents said they tracked Rodriguez's money to the Cayman Islands, Spain and Montserrat, but local authorities said they could not cooperate, citing rigid bank-secrecy laws as an excuse.

What makes enforcement so difficult is a financial murkiness that has long frustrated tax collectors as they search for dirty money afloat in the world's oceans of legitimate payments. The multibillion-dollar flow of black money, the profits from criminal enterprise, moves through the world's financial institutions as part of a vastly larger quantity of gray money, as bankers call it. This dubious, laundered cash amounts to an estimated $1 trillion or more each year. Often legitimately earned, this money has an endless variety of sources: an Argentine businessman who dodges currency-control laws to get his savings out of the country; a multinational corporation that seeks to "minimize" its tax burden by dumping its profits in tax-free havens; a South African investor who wants to avoid economic sanctions; an East German Communist leader who stashed a personal nest egg in Swiss bank accounts; or even the CIA and KGB when they need to finance espionage or covert activities overseas.

The world's prosperity depends on a fluid and unfettered financial system, yet the lack of supervision is producing a large shadow economy. The IRS estimates that tax cheats skim as much as $50 billion a year from legitimate cash-generating businesses and launder the money to avoid detection. Banking experts calculate that the private citizens of debt-choked Latin American countries have smuggled more than $200 billion of their savings abroad in the past decade.

The money-laundering process, especially in the drug trade, begins with greenbacks. Much of the cash simply leaves the U.S. in luggage, since departing travelers are rarely searched. Larger shipments are flown out on private planes or packed in seagoing freight containers, which are almost never inspected. That explains, in part, why U.S. officials are unable to locate fully 80% of all the bills printed by the Treasury. Once overseas, the cash is easy to funnel into black markets, especially in unstable economies where the dollar is the favored underground currency.

But hauling cash out of the U.S. has its drawbacks. The interest revenue lost while cash is in transit pains a drug dealer as much as it would a corporate financial officer. And since narcotraffickers see America as a safe and profitable haven for their assets, they often launder and invest their cash in the U.S. The first and trickiest step is depositing the hot cash in a U.S. financial institution. Reason: the IRS requires all banks to file Currency Transaction Reports for deposits of $10,000 or more. During the early 1980s, launderers got around this scrutiny by employing couriers called Smurfs, named for the restless cartoon characters, who would fan out and make multiple deposits of slightly less than $10,000.

The Government now requires banks to keep an eye out for Smurfs, but launderers have developed new techniques. Since retail businesses that collect large amounts of cash are often exempt from the $10,000 rule, launderers have created front companies or collaborated with employees of such outlets as 7-Elevens and Computer-Land stores. To drug dealers, "an exempt rating is like gold," says a Wells Fargo Bank vice president. A restaurant that accepts no checks or credit cards can be an ideal laundering machine. Even a front business with no exemption is valuable because launderers can file the CTRs in the knowledge that they are unlikely to attract scrutiny, since the Government is swamped with 7 million such reports a year, up from fewer than 100,000 a decade ago. Other places where drug dealers can often dump their cash include the currency-exchange houses along the Southwest border and urban check-cashing and money-transmittal stores.

Once the money is in a financial institution, it can be moved with blinding speed. Communicating with the bank via fax machine or personal computer, a launderer can have wire transfers sent around the world without ever speaking to a banking officer. The goal of many launderers is to get their money into the maelstrom of global money movements, where the volume is so great that no regulators can really monitor it all. Such traffic has exploded because of the globalization of the world economy, which has multiplied the volume of international trade and currency trading. On an average working day, the Manhattan-based Clearing House for Interbank Payments System handles 145,500 transactions worth more than $700 billion, a 40% increase in just two years.

Much of the electronic money zips into a secret banking industry that got its start in Switzerland in the 1930s as worried Europeans began shifting their savings beyond the reach of Hitler's Third Reich. Later the country's infamous numbered accounts became a hugely profitable business. Chiasso, a quaint Swiss town of 8,700 inhabitants on the Italian border, has 18 banking offices. But during the past few years, Swiss secrecy has been weakened by

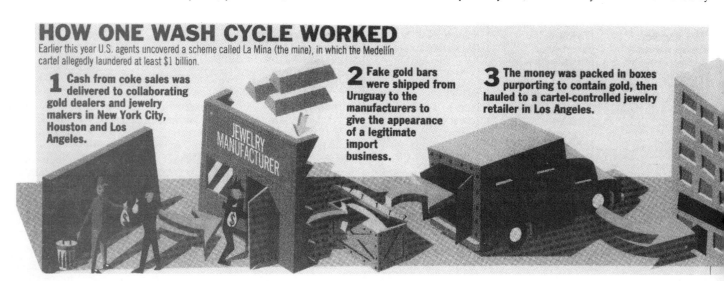

## HOW ONE WASH CYCLE WORKED

Earlier this year U.S. agents uncovered a scheme called La Mina (the mine), in which the Medellín cartel allegedly laundered at least $1 billion.

**1** Cash from coke sales was delivered to collaborating gold dealers and jewelry makers in New York City, Houston and Los Angeles.

**2** Fake gold bars were shipped from Uruguay to the manufacturers to give the appearance of a legitimate import business.

**3** The money was packed in boxes purporting to contain gold, then hauled to a cartel-controlled jewelry retailer in Los Angeles.

a series of cases involving money laundering. Switzerland is now preparing a new law that will make money laundering a crime punishable by prison terms. Explains Jean-Paul Chapuis, executive director of the Swiss Bankers Association: "Our hope is that the criminals will go to another country."

They apparently are, since many small countries have successfully attracted banking business by creating discreet, tax-free havens. In Luxembourg total bank deposits have grown from $40 billion in 1984 to more than $100 billion last year. In the wake of a drug-money scandal involving the Florida operations of Luxembourg-based Bank of Credit and Commerce International, the country has tried to burnish its public image by declaring money laundering a criminal offense, even while it has fortified its bank-secrecy rules.

The most inventive havens allow investors to set up shell corporations with invisible owners, which means that high rollers can secretly stash their money in real estate, corporate stock and other assets. The Netherlands Antilles, with cash flowing steadily from banking centers in Amsterdam and Rotterdam, is a favorite financial center for investors seeking a low profile. Many Hollywood filmmakers love the arrangement, since movie profits can be diverted to a nearly tax-free setting. Many actors, producers and directors set up so-called personal-service companies in the Antilles so they can collect their paychecks through such corporations and avoid U.S. taxes. "It has to be structured very carefully, since the rules are tortuously complicated, but it is legal," says a top entertainment lawyer. "However, the IRS may take a closer look after your story comes out."

Just as Hollywood paychecks pour into these havens to avoid taxes, mystery money flows out in search of well-paying investments. "The man I'm working with now," says a prominent screenwriter, "is an American representing vaguely described movie and cable interests in Europe who seem to have a waterfall of money from banks in Luxembourg and Amsterdam. He's all over town offering unlimited financing, but he won't show up himself at any of the meetings with the networks or studios."

Dozens of islands, from Britain's chilly Isle of Man to Vanuatu in the South Pacific, have boosted their economies by turning into havens for money. While narcotics traffickers launder their dollars through so-called brass-plate companies on these islands, the main business of the tax-free offshore havens is servicing some of the world's largest multinational corporations. "The idea is to put profits where there are the least taxes. Everybody does it," explains the president of a major U.S. corporation's foreign subsidiary.

One technique for minimizing taxes is a quasi-legal fabrication called reinvoicing, a paper shuffle that enables companies to re-book sales and profits into tax havens. For example, one FORTUNE 500 corporation imports raw materials through an offshore dummy company, which buys shipments at the lowest possible price and resells the material to the parent firm at a high mark-up. This dumps profits in the tax haven, while the U.S.-based company can boost its apparent costs to reduce taxes on the mainland. The profits can then be repatriated in the form of tax-free "loans" from offshore entities to the U.S. parent corporation.

While the IRS tolerates such schemes up to a point, the U.S. Government has tried to choke the river of drug money flowing through the same channels. Yet laundering hot spots tend to be moving targets. After the U.S. negotiated new treaties with Bermuda and Cayman authorities to allow limited access to banking records in narcotics cases, many of the launderers found new havens.

As the financial center of gravity in the world has shifted toward the Pacific Rim, new tax and secrecy havens have multiplied on such remote islands as Nauru in the western Pacific and Palau and Truk in Micronesia. Citizens of Vanuatu, a volcanic archipelago of some 80 islands formerly known as the New Hebrides, have found that international finance beats coconut and taro farming. In Port Vila, the capital, it is not unusual for a $100 million transaction between major international banks to take place on any given day.

Still, Hong Kong remains the pre-eminent laundering center in the Pacific. Almost everyone there does it, usually legitimately, at least according to the laws of Hong Kong, where even insider trading is no crime. By the puritan standards of the U.S., says one American banker, "the lack of public disclosure here is scandalous." The city is a mecca for arms dealers, drug traffickers and business pirates of every description. "Where else could I broker a deal that involves machine guns from China, gold from Taiwan and shipments traded in Panama City?" says a Brazilian arms merchant who maintains an apartment in Hong Kong.

In the U.S. a money-laundering center can be spotted by the huge surplus of cash that flows into the local branch of the Federal Reserve System. In 1985 the Miami branch posted a $6 billion excess. But after several years of intense federal probes of South Florida banks, Miami's cash glut fell last year to $4.5 billion. Much of the business went to Los Angeles, where the cash surplus ballooned from $166 million in 1985 to $3.8 billion last year. Despite such rocketing growth, the staffing of federal law-enforcement offices in L.A. still lags far behind the levels in Miami or New York City.

Both in the U.S. and abroad, financial businesses and even governments are often reluctant to impose regulations to keep out launderers. One reason is that a thriving financial industry brings jobs and income.

**4** The cash was deposited into banks as proceeds from the fictitious sale of the supposed gold and jewelry.

**5** Deposited money was transferred by wire to cartel-controlled bank accounts in Manhattan. From there, it was zapped through Panama into secret accounts overseas, primarily in Europe.

**6** The money finally arrived in Colombia, where some of it was used for operating expenses and to buy more coca. Some profits were sent back to the U.S., where they were spent on real estate and other investments.

South Florida's 100 international banks employ 3,500 workers and pump $800 million into the local economy. Even more appealing is the inflow of foreign capital. During the spend-and-borrow era of the 1980s, the gusher of flight capital into the U.S. from Latin America helped finance America's deficits. As in Hollywood, not many politicians were concerned about where the money was coming from. Alarmed by the tide, House Democrat John Bryant of Texas has long pushed for legislation to require disclosure of the identity of foreign investors. But for years, the Reagan Administration refused to go along, claiming that such openness might scare away capital.

Now that a consensus is building that the U.S. must pick out the black money from the gray, the tools at hand seem minimal for the task. Says Jaime Chavez, an international banking consultant: "The people who will probably be searching for it have a very limited knowledge of what money movement is all about. How is a third-rate employee of the Justice Department going to dissect the entire financial system to pinpoint the drug money correctly?" During the Reagan years, the budgets of agencies in charge of catching financial cheats failed to keep pace with the changing world of money manipulation. Even IRS agents are largely unprepared for the task of tracking transactions that can involve four or five banks, several shell companies and two or more currencies.

Few agents can be spared because IRS employees are working overtime to contain an explosion of smaller-time money-laundering cases involving car salesmen, ordinary investors, real estate agents and other entrepreneurs. In Florida undercover IRS agents operating a sting operation that they touted as a "full-service financial-investment corporation" have nabbed 50 would-be money launderers in the past year. "Some are lawyers and businessmen who are skimming cash from their businesses, and they've heard about what you can do through an offshore bank," says Tampa IRS supervisor Morris Dittman. "Others have cash that rolls out of the drug trade. When a druggie buys a big home and car for cash, you have a real estate agent and a salesman with sudden cash, and they begin wondering if they have to share it with the Government."

Such amateurs are running afoul of laws that professionals have already discovered. The statutes began tightening in 1986, when money laundering became a specific crime. Later it became illegal to evade the $10,000 currency-reporting requirements by making groups of smaller deposits. Banks have begun to exercise more internal supervision as well, prodded by a series of investigations in the mid-1980s in which such institutions as Bank of

## WHAT TO DO

**1.** Hold bankers responsible. Current requirements to report large cash deposits fail to deter professional launderers. Banks should have to investigate depositors as thoroughly as they do their borrowers.

**2.** Tighten controls on electronic banking. Computerized money transfers fall into a twilight zone of electronic pulses. The U.S. should require banks to keep standard customer information on all such wire shipments.

**3.** Insist on scrutiny abroad. The U.S. ought to call on foreign banks to cooperate in identifying the real owners of money. This should be considered the price of access to the global payments system that operates in the U.S.

**4.** Convene a bankers' summit. President Bush should bring together the heads of America's largest banks and financial companies to enlist their support in a unified effort to blockade drug loot.

**5.** Provide money, not just lip service. Bush's pledge to target launderers is not convincing without a larger budget behind it. Computers capable of helping trace the world's flow of money would be a national asset—and they would cost accordingly.

America and Bank of Boston were forced to pay hefty fines for their involvement in laundering schemes. Yet many major banks are still participants, witting or not, in ever more sophisticated laundering operations.

To close the gap, Bush's offensive against drug-cash handlers is being placed in the hands of a newly created task force that includes the CIA, the National Security Agency and the Pentagon, as well as a team of drug, tax and customs agents. FINCEN is already at work in a crowded Virginia office littered with discarded coffee cups, overflowing ashtrays, computer terminals and maps of the world. "We're going to be a financial think tank to help train cops who are deluged in financial data," says Gene Weinschenk, acting director of FINCEN's research-and-development division. "We're looking for money, not dope."

The biggest problem may be in deciding how to handle all the borderline illegality the task force will find. "How do you separate drug money from capital-flight money?" asks one of the mavens. "It will be more than drug money we come up with, and what happens when we stumble over a really major company and hold up its dirty linen? Maybe the banks will start turning in the narcotics people rather than lose their biggest customers."

To make a dent in the money-laundering

trade, authorities will need more support from the financial community. "They're now willing to tell us about people coming in with bags of cash," says a regulator, "but as far as anything else goes, you can forget it." Yet many bankers think the feds have become indiscriminate in their crackdown. "They are characterizing traditional, ordinary, international banking transactions as money laundering," gripes Gerald Houlihan, a Miami attorney who represents financial institutions in money-laundering and forfeiture cases. "They are not going after money launderers, but are attempting to terrorize banks in an effort to give the impression they are doing something about drugs."

U.S. bankers rightly point out that they must abide by relatively strict currency-reporting laws, while their counterparts in other countries play fast and loose. That discrepancy has prompted Washington to try to persuade the rest of the banking world to adopt the record-keeping system used by American institutions.

The biggest push could come from the provisions of the Kerry Amendment to the 1988 anti-drug abuse act. The law requires the Treasury Secretary to negotiate bilateral agreements on money-laundering detection and prevention with all U.S. trading partners. Countries that refuse to participate or that negotiate in bad faith could conceivably be excluded from the U.S. banking network and clearinghouses. Yet in hearings earlier this year, Assistant Treasury Secretary Salvatore Martoche indicated that the Bush Administration is reluctant to enforce the law zealously for fear of hampering the U.S. banking industry.

But there is more at risk than the dislocation of business as usual. Many experts believe the financial stability and national security of whole countries will be in jeopardy until the problem is solved. Says the head of the Italian treasury police, General Luigi Ramponi: "Now that they are too rich, the drug lords will start investing everywhere: in industry, in the stock market." In the U.S. some lawmakers have begun worrying about the impact of billions of drug dollars invested in U.S. institutions and wonder what influence the drug barons might eventually exert.

The money-laundering game is also creating a mess for investigators of other crimes, who are running into dead ends when they try to identify the players in fraud cases. Beverly Hills police are stymied by last August's Mob-style assassination of Hollywood entertainment executive Jose Menendez and his wife Kitty, who were shotgunned in the front room of their mansion. Menendez had been an executive and director of Carolco Pictures, an independent movie company that produced Sylvester Stallone's *Rambo* movies, and police have been unable to unravel his business affairs or identify all his partners. Carolco is controlled by a Netherlands holding company that is, in turn, owned by a tangle of offshore family trusts.

Financial experts are beginning to recognize that Washington will be unable to control drug money unless the U.S. compels offshore financial institutions to make their books "transparent" enough to show the true owners of the money. In the end, the Colombian drug cartels are about to force the world to re-examine the international financial system that has developed haphazardly over the 60 years since the Swiss first popularized secret banking. Countries may not yet be willing to make their banking transactions fully "transparent," but some light must be shed on everyone's books. Says Kerry: "It will take significant leverage and leadership. The President has to have the top bankers in and say, 'Unless you are part of the solution, you are part of the problem.'"

Yet there is still a deep-seated reluctance to take drastic measures. Briefing reporters after a Paris conclave on money laundering last September, a senior U.S. official declared that global efforts to trace drug money will have to be balanced against the freedom from unnecessary red tape. Too many controls, he declared, could "constipate" the financial exchanges. That is the kind of attitude that has brought the system to its current state, in which drug money freely mingles with the life force of the world economy, like a virus in the bloodstream. —*With reporting by Jay Branegan/ Hong Kong, S.C. Gwynne/Detroit and Jeanne McDowell/Los Angeles*

# Ethics and Social Responsibility in the Marketplace

- **Marketing Strategy and Ethics (Articles 38–40)**
- **Ethical Practices in the Marketplace (Articles 41–44)**

From a consumer viewpoint, the marketplace is the "proof of the pudding" or the place where the "rubber meets the road" for business ethics. In other words, what the company has promulgated about the virtues of its product or service has little meaning if the company's actual marketing practices and its treatment of the consumer contradict its claims.

At its core, marketing has a very noble and moral purpose: to satisfy human needs and wants and to help people through the exchange process. Marketing involves the coordination of the variables of product, price, place, and promotion to effectively and efficiently address the needs of consumers. Unfortunately, at times the unethical marketing practices of some firms have cast a shadow of suspicion over marketing in general. Since marketing is the aspect of business that is most visible to the public, it has perhaps taken a disproportionate share of the criticism directed toward the free enterprise system.

The generalization that all marketing practices are unethical is not supported by careful investigation of the marketplace. For example, one could contrast the marketing of Ford Pintos with Johnson & Johnson's handling of the Tylenol incident.

This section takes a careful look at the strategic process and practice of incorporating ethics into the marketplace. The first subsection, *Marketing Strategy and Ethics*, contains three articles describing how marketing strategy and ethics can be integrated in the marketplace. The first two articles provide a comprehensive and pragmatic conceptual base for combining social responsibility, ethics, and marketing strategy. The last article in this subsection, "Marketing With Integrity," examines the rights of consumers and the importance of marketing one's beliefs and values as much as one's products.

The next subsection is on *Ethical Practices in the Marketplace*. The first article explores some critical ethical issues encountered by professionals in their marketing and advertising practices. "The Magic of Herman Miller" exemplifies the significance of being a "value-led" organization. The last two articles focus on issues of sex, decency, and deception in advertising.

## Looking Ahead: Challenge Questions

Does an organization have a responsibility to reveal product defects to consumers?

Given the competitiveness of the business arena, is it possible for marketing personnel to behave ethically and both survive and prosper? What are some suggestions you would make that could be incorporated into the marketing strategy for firms that want to be both ethical and successful?

Which area of marketing strategy do you believe is most subject to public scrutiny in regard to ethics—product, pricing, place, or promotion? Why? What are some examples of unethical techniques or strategies involving each of these four variables?

In what ways does Herman Miller exemplify ethics and being "value-led" in their treatment of their workers, their customers, and their social concerns? What are some other organizations that you believe are very ethically minded? Why?

# Unit 4

# Social Responsibility, Ethics, and Marketing Strategy: Closing the Gap Between Concept and Application

The authors review the concepts of social responsibility and business ethics as well as some of the reasons why their adoption by marketing practitioners has been somewhat limited. An approach is developed to integrate these concepts into the strategic marketing planning process.

## Donald P. Robin & R. Eric Reidenbach

Donald P. Robin is Professor of Marketing, Mississippi State University. R. Eric Reidenbach is Director, Bureau of Business Research, University of Southern Mississippi. The authors thank four unidentified *JM* reviewers for their helpful insights.

THE quantity of discussion on social responsibility and ethics in marketing has increased in recent years. Most of the discussion has been descriptive, focusing on how or why marketers behave or fail to behave in a socially responsible or ethical manner. The discussion can be divided into general conceptual presentations (e.g., Baumhart 1961; Brenner and Molander 1977; Cavanaugh, Moberg, and Velazquez 1981; Clasen 1967; Gross and Verma 1977; Lavidge 1970; McMahon 1968; Newstrom and Rush 1975; Sturdivant and Cocanougher 1973); special-topic conceptual discussions including such areas as purchasing (e.g., Cummings 1979; Davis, Rudelius, and Buchholz 1979; Mayer 1970), field sales personnel (e.g., Dubinsky, Berkowitz, and Rudelius 1980), marketing research (e.g., Blankenship 1964; Tybout and Zaltman 1974), new product development (e.g., Varble 1972), and international marketing (e.g., Kaikati and Label 1980); model- or theory-based conceptual presentations (e.g., Ferrell and Gresham 1985; Hunt and Vitell 1986; Laczniak 1983); and survey-based empirical investigations (e.g., Chonko and Hunt 1985; Crawford 1970; Ferrell and Weaver 1978; Ferrell, Zey-Ferrell, and Krugman 1983; Hunt, Chonko, and Wilcox 1984; Krugman and Ferrell 1981; Laczniak, Lusch, and Strang 1981; Ricklefs 1983; Zey-Ferrell and Ferrell 1982; Zey-Ferrell, Weaver, and Ferrell 1979).

This line of research has led to a more complete and scientific understanding of social responsibility in marketing and marketing ethics. However, relatively few academic articles have suggested *how* marketing managers might use our current understanding of these subjects to build an actionable approach to social responsibility and ethics (e.g., Bartels 1967; Levy and Dubinsky 1983; Murphy and Laczniak 1981; Pruden 1971; Robin 1980). These efforts, though useful, all lack an integrated approach for making social responsibility and ethics part of the strategic marketing planning process. The purpose of this article is to offer one approach for accomplishing that end.

Because unanimity is lacking in perceptions of social responsibility and ethics, we first establish the meanings applied in our discussion. Then, because there is still some resistance to, and frustration with, implementing the concepts in any area of business, we establish the rationale for the use of social responsibility and ethics in business. We next provide a broad, general description of an approach for integrating social responsibility and ethics into the marketing planning process. We describe a role for each of the con-

Reprinted from *Journal of Marketing*, Vol. 51 (January 1987), pp. 44-58. Published by the American Marketing Association.

cepts and how those roles could be implemented in a capitalistic democracy. Finally, we offer more specific suggestions for implementing the approach and use several case histories to illustrate how the approach can prevent organizational/societal problems.

# Social Responsibility and Business Ethics: Differences and Similarities

The two concepts, corporate social responsibility and business ethics, have essentially different meanings. Corporate social responsibility is related to the social contract between business and the society in which it operates (e.g., Steiner 1972). Business ethics, in contrast, requires that the organization or individual behave in accordance with the carefully thought-out rules of moral philosophy. Though these two behavioral criteria often lead to the same conclusion, in many situations they do not. For example, actions that any given society defines as "responsible" in its social contract with business may be found by moral philosophers to be ethically neutral or even ethically unsound. Similarly, actions that would be dictated by moral philosophy could be seen as socially unacceptable. These inconsistencies are part of the problem faced by marketing managers when a decision must be made. Therefore the character of these two concepts must be explored in greater depth.

## Social Responsibility

An observation by Steiner (1972, p. 18) sets the basis for understanding the meaning of corporate social responsibility.

> At any one time in any society there is a set of generally accepted relationships, obligations and duties between the major institutions and the people. Philosophers and political theorists have called this set of common understandings "the social contract."

The social responsibility of business is a substantial part of this social contract. It is the set of "generally accepted relationships, obligations and duties" that relate to the corporate impact on the welfare of society. What becomes "generally accepted" is likely to be different for any two societies and is also likely to change within any society over time. In their book *Business and Society*, Davis and Frederick (1984, p. 41–2) note that in the United States

> . . . the trend since the 1960s has been toward more social involvement by business. . . . The public expects business to be part of the community and to act responsibly therein. This trend does not change the basic economic mission of business, because society still expects business to provide economic goods and services efficiently.

In addition to differences between societies and within a society over time, subcultures with diametrically opposed expectations are part of most major cultures. Almost any response to a call for "socially re-

sponsible" behavior by one group is likely to produce complaints by another group. The result seems to be a kind of paralysis fostered by the implicit suggestion that inaction is the safest response. However, inaction, or the failure to consider the social responsibility of certain outcomes, is often repugnant to much of society. A sense of frustration with "the system" is thus the fare of business managers at all levels in an organization.

Many individuals have observed and reported on the state of social responsibility in business. Glueck (1980), in his book on policy and strategic management, reviews several studies as examples of organizational objectives and comments (p. 37):

> Note that there was no mention of social responsibility in the list of major objectives in the studies above. Although much has been written about how firms ought to be more socially responsible, there is little evidence that social responsibility is a significant objective of most business, in spite of a good deal of pressure from some societal groups.

This lack of involvement in social responsibility at a strategic level seems to have occurred in spite of recognition of the need for it and the seeming willingness of executives to incorporate it. Even a decade ago, 81% of 248 corporate executives surveyed believed that wealth maximization and social involvement were not contradictory concepts (Edmonds and Hand 1976). In this last decade, business has responded to social needs in a variety of ways. Areas such as employee welfare, support for minorities, consumer satisfaction, community improvement, and environmental protection all have been targets for business support in varying degrees (Hill 1982). However, these efforts seem to lack a unified collective impact on public opinion. One suggested reason for this lack of impact is that the objectives of such efforts are often inexplicit and do not fit an overall plan (Hill 1982, p. 87).

The lack of a central theme and specific objectives is perhaps understandable because of the varied and changing societal expectations, but is intolerable if business in general, and marketing specifically, is to fulfill its role as an important and productive element of society.

## Ethics

Because it is an organized discipline, business ethics presents more coherent demands than does the concept of social responsibility; therefore, it provides a solid foundation from which to operate. Even so, the study of business ethics is not without problems of interpretation. Major ethical philosophies are sometimes in conflict with one another as to how a single issue may be resolved.

The two major traditions that dominate current thinking in moral philosophy are deontology and utilitarianism. In the recent marketing literature they have been used as the basis for a "General Theory of Marketing Ethics" (Hunt and Vitell 1986). One other tradition, virtue ethics, is used to help justify an approach we discuss subsequently.

Of the two dominant traditions, deontology is favored by many moral philosophers today. Further, deontological reasoning offers many people who are critical of marketing an approach for justifying their attacks. Utilitarianism, the other major tradition, has been attacked by moral philosophers because it seems to suggest certain untenable outcomes when applied to particular hypothetical situations. Utilitarian arguments are used historically to provide much of the ethical justification for the modern economic systems of capitalistic democracies.

*Deontology.* The reasoning found in deontological analyses suggests that there are *prima facie* ideals that can direct our thinking. Modern interpretations of these ideals suggest that they may be considered "universal" in character but not necessarily "absolute" (e.g., Ross 1930). The difference between absolute and universal is simply the recognition that situations sometimes arise in which one or more universal statements of "right" and "wrong" might be inappropriate. The absolutism of early deontological thinking would not admit to the nonabsolute character of rules, but more modern versions such as that put forth by Ross perceive these statements as *prima facie* universal in character and allow exceptions. In general, the concept is simply that these rules or duties are required, and a burden of proof lies with any exception to them.

Kant (trans. 1964) provided much of the reasoning that underlies modern deontology. His conclusions are based on two concepts. One is simply that the only possible basis for establishing a moral tradition is human reason or logic. The second concept is whether an action can be universalized. For example, one statement of his "categorical imperative" is that "one ought never to act unless one is willing to have the maxim on which one acts become a universal law." His reasoning is simply that good will, and only good will, can be universalized. Thus, a reasonable test for exceptions to universal rules is whether they can meet the criterion of universalized good will. For example, marketers could ask whether it is morally acceptable to market a product known to be potentially harmful to some individuals, such as A. H. Robins' Dalkon Shield, an intrauterine contraceptive device, or more recently G. D. Searle's Copper 7 IUD. The Kantian approach would force the marketer to ask whether he/she would be willing to live in a world where all producers were making a product known to be harmful to some people in its normal use. The *prima facie* response would likely be, "No." Thus, the burden of proof for treating the product as an exception is on the producer of the IUD.

Rawls provides a relatively modern statement of what is essentially deontological thinking. His work has had considerable impact on modern moral philosophy. His major work, *A Theory of Justice* (1971), has as its initial position the placing of all people behind a "veil of ignorance." Basically, people then are asked what kind of society they would want to live in, given that they know nothing about their own capabilities and potentialities. From this initial egalitarian position Rawls develops two principles of justice. One is that "each person is to have an equal right to the most extensive basic liberty compatible with similar liberty for others" (p. 60). The second principle has two parts and can be stated, "social and economic inequalities are to be arranged so that they are both (a) reasonably expected to be to everyone's advantage, and (b) attached to positions and offices open to all" (p. 60). The first principle and the latter part of the second principle are generally accepted by moral philosophers. The former part of the second principle has an undeniable egalitarian thrust which is perhaps not surprising given the initial "veil of ignorance" condition. Thus, the deontologist might define an activity as ethical if it involved true freedom of choice and action, were available to all, injured no one, and were a benefit to some. Obviously, price fixing, bribery, and marketing products that harm people are practices that are morally questionable to deontologists.

It is the egalitarian character of deontology, based on universalizing concepts, that provides the foundation for criticisms of the second major tradition in moral philosophy—utilitarianism.

*Utilitarianism.* The utilitarian ideal can be summarized by the phrase, "the greatest good for the greatest number." There are many variations of utilitarianism, as there are variations of deontology, and only a brief overview of the major ideas is presented here. The primary way of assessing "the greatest good for the greatest number" is by performing a social cost/benefit analysis and acting on it. All benefits and all costs of a particular act are considered to the degree possible and summarized as the net of all benefits *minus* all costs. If the net result is positive, the act is morally acceptable; if the net result is negative, the act is not.

Utilitarianism seems to have been accepted readily by business, in part because of its tradition in economics. Adam Smith (1776) and much of the ensuing economic philosophy of capitalism provide a rich traditional heritage for the utilitarian concepts. Capitalistic systems, by providing the greatest material good for the greatest number, are considered ethical from a perspective of economic philosophy. It should be noted that the utilitarian analyses of moral philosophers extend beyond "material good" to the much broader concept of "utility" from which the term is derived (e.g., Smart and Williams 1973).

Several technical criticisms of utilitarianism (e.g., the problems of quantifying goodness and requiring supererogatory acts; see Beauchamp 1982, p. 97–103; Smart and Williams 1973, especially p. 134–5) are of little interest in the context of this article. However, two criticisms are relevant to the discussion. One is the problem of "unjust" distribution of utility. Summarizing the costs and benefits as described above can conceal major negative occurrences to people in small social segments by allowing them to be offset by relatively minor increases in utility to larger segments of society. Though one version of utilitarianism (i.e., rule utilitarianism) would allow constraints so that negative outcomes could be eliminated, the criticism is still valid. For example, most of the arguments in support of the continued sale of infant formula by Nestlé to third world countries were utilitarian (e.g., Miller 1983). In this case, it was suggested that the greatest good to society was derived from the continued sale of the product. Other arguments, primarily deontological, seem to have prevailed because Nestlé agreed to severe marketing restrictions (e.g., World Health Organization's *International Code of Marketing of Breast-Milk Substitutes* 1981).

An additional problem for utilitarianism is concern for individual acts. If each act is judged solely on its own cost/benefit outcome, there is a lack of consistency and ability to generalize. Marketers may argue that fraudulent advertising is all right if no one is worse off, and a rule against such practices becomes less tenable. However, in spite of the weaknesses of utilitarianism, it is still a major tradition in moral philosophy and maintains substantial support.

A concluding point about the two major traditions is necessary. Deontology has the individual as its major concern and unit of analysis whereas utilitarianism is decidedly social in character and focuses on the welfare of society as a unit. This focus can, in a number of situations, put the two traditions at odds with each other, as in the Nestlé case. There is no totally accepted, absolute statement of what is ethical and what is not ethical—only important and carefully reasoned traditions.

## The Gap Between Concept and Practice

Several factors contribute to the gap between the conceptual and applied aspects of social responsibility and ethics. The strategic marketing process and marketing management literature is primarily, if not exclusively, aimed at identifying strategies and tactics for consummating the marketing exchange. Books, journal articles, and consulting efforts focus on identifying, creating, and servicing an exchange. Seldom are the moral or ethical dimensions of an exchange strategy integrated into the process. Though the marketing environment is a substantial part of this literature, it is analyzed primarily in terms of environmental effects on the marketing exchange rather than the effects of the exchange on the environment(s). Thus, the political, social, and legal environments of marketing usually are analyzed as they mandate, constrain, or eliminate certain marketing strategies. Zeithaml and Zeithaml (1984) substantiated this characteristic of the marketing literature and suggested that marketers think more proactively toward their environment.

We propose that just such a proactive approach toward moral decision making be adopted in marketing. Many critical decisions in marketing, as we are made increasingly aware, have multiple dimensions that are related jointly to marketing exchange and ethics (e.g., Ferrell and Gresham 1985). In other words, many marketing activities have ethical content, to a greater or lesser extent. Separate discussions of strategic and ethical decision making would be counterproductive. To the extent that ethics and social responsibility are considered in the strategic decision making literature, the material appears as a separate consideration, apart from the strategic plan. If a decision is made to adopt a particular strategic plan, the implication seems to be that deliberations on questions of moral appropriateness, if made at all, are a secondary consideration. To perform an *ex post facto* review of the decision for its moral appropriateness invites inefficient planning at best, or public exposure and moral rationalizing of alternatives at worst. Though authors of the strategic marketing literature probably do not intend that their social responsibility and ethics materials be interpreted in that way, the separate treatment, rather than full integration of the issue, promotes just such an *ex post facto* analysis.

Social responsibility and ethics often are treated as external to marketing's strategic planning process in corporate codes of ethics. Such codes have been found to be oriented more toward issues that influence profit than toward the concerns of society (Cressey and Moore (1983). Further, Chonko and Hunt (1985) found the recognized existence of such codes was not a significant factor in explaining individual perceptions of ethical problems. Only when top management internalized certain values was an effect noted.

Articles such as those by Friedman (1970), Gaski (1985), and Carr (1968) seem to garner at least some degree of tacit approval by marketers and bring into question the rationale for incorporating social responsibility and ethics into decision making. These articles state, either explicitly or implicitly, that business is amoral (i.e., neither moral nor immoral). However, the business ethics literature, though acknowledging such articles, strongly suggests that business must go beyond such thinking. The social realities in the United States and other developed capitalistic democracies seem to suggest that business and its leaders are to be held accountable for their behavior in a moral and ethical sense. For example, DeGeorge (1986, p. 4) states:

> The breakdown of the Myth of Amoral Business has been signaled in three fairly obvious ways: by the reporting of scandals and the concomitant public reaction to these reports; by the formation of popular groups, such as the environmentalists and the consumerists; and by the concern of business, as expressed in conferences, magazine and newspaper articles, the burgeoning of codes of ethical conduct, and so on.

One hundred years ago in the United States, the environment of business was predominantly *laissez faire* and business was given substantial freedom of action with a corresponding power "to act." Since then, concerns about predatory competition, concern for individuals as both employees and consumers, concerns about the environment, and a general disregard by business of common social values have produced a negative reaction by society and reduced some of this freedom and power. For example, the Iron Law of Responsibility (Davis and Blomstrom 1966, p. 174–5) suggests what business can expect if socially expected responsibilities are not satisfied. It states, "In the long run, those who do not use power in a way that society considers responsible will tend to lose it." In the case of corporate social responsibility, the lost power is likely to be the freedom to act and the freedom to choose.

Business is a human activity and, like most human activities, it has been and is likely to continue to be evaluated from a moral point of view. Moreover, business is a subset of a greater social activity and depends on the prevailing social morality in order to exist. For example, if stealing and lying were the social rule rather than the exception to it, business as we know it would be impossible. Both customers and employees would practice these behaviors to a much greater degree and the potential for consummating a marketing exchange would be greatly reduced. Arguments that do not hold business to the same social requirements as the rest of society are unrealistic. There is nothing extraordinary in the concept of business that excuses it from what society believes to be ethical and moral behavior.

Further, business cannot escape its moral role by appealing to its basic nonhuman nature, a frequently used rationalization. Though the corporation is essentially a legal entity, *people* are its legal agents and its owners, and both the organization and the individuals in it have been judged by society to be liable for the behavior of its agents. Society created the concept of the corporation and has the capacity, and apparently the will, to change it in any way it deems suitable. If moral considerations do not become a greater part of business practice, society, through its legislators, is likely to continue to impose corrective measures.

# An Approach for Closing the Gap Between Concept and Practice

Because the current situation in business and marketing seems questionable and inaction does not seem to be a feasible response, it is appropriate to search for a better approach. We suggest some of the major characteristics of such an approach, including a methodology for integrating the concepts of social responsibility and ethics into marketing strategy in a planned, logically consistent, easily understood manner.

## General Character of the Approach

The approach we suggest might be defined as the development or reformulation of a corporate culture. Just as anthropologists identify a culture by its values or beliefs, the key to the success of any corporate culture is the selection and implementation of an organizational profile identified by core values. When implemented and communicated to all involved parties, these values define the profile or "face" of the organization and become an integral part of the organizational mission. Because the mission or broadly defined objectives of an organization direct all marketing strategy, social responsibility and ethics can be successfully integrated if they become part of the marketing mission. The profile, relying heavily on these core values, should permeate the entire strategic planning process as well as the implementation of the final plan.

A major factor in developing successful socially responsible and ethical marketing programs is management's ability to integrate ethical core values throughout the organization's culture. Sathe (1986, p. 556) defines corporate culture as "the set of important assumptions (often unstated) that members of a community share in common." He goes on to make the point that "the content of a culture influences the direction of behavior" (p. 556). Two aspects of this enculturation process make it important: (1) what will occur in its absence and (2) the positive potential impact of integrating it into marketing's planning process.

In the absence of an overt, coherent, consistent, and integrated set of ethical core values, the organization will develop its own. The set of assumptions constituting the organization's value system come from the leadership of the organization and the experiences of its employees (Sathe 1986, p. 556). Two assumptions tend to thrive in most organizations' culture—profits and efficiency. Management preaches these twin values, and employees know they will be rewarded for practicing them. When profits and efficiency dominate the culture without the balancing effects of ethical core values, strategic marketing planning (and other behaviors) is directed principally, if not solely, by profits and efficiency. An example is Ford Motor Company's response to their defective fuel system problem in the Pinto. Ford's planners conducted a cost/

benefit analysis and concluded that it would be more profitable to settle out of court any claims resulting from the fuel system problem than to make the design change that would have eliminated the problem (Dowie 1977). An integrated set of ethical core values might have tempered their purely economic response with ethical considerations.

The myriad codes of ethics developed by organizations do not seem to fill the gap. Chonko and Hunt (1985) attest to the ineffectiveness of codes of ethics that have not been integrated into the corporate culture. These codes are often developed and put away. Their mere existence, without enforcement, is insufficient to effect ethical behavior.

A second aspect important to the enculturation process is the positive impact from the integration of socially responsible and ethical core values throughout the marketing activities of organizations. For ethical core values to have a positive effect on marketing planning, the integration of the values must follow the same pattern as marketing's strategic planning function. They must become part and parcel of the same planning procedure. To be most effective, these core values should become part of the marketing mission and part of the organization's culture. They should be tested against marketing's publics and monitored for their appropriateness as the organization and its environment change. Once achieved, these core values give ethical direction to the marketing activities of the organization. That direction tends to be more uniform and focused toward ends that are desired by top management.

The corporate culture approach, as supported by literature in the United States, has a strong basis in successful Japanese management practices. Deal and Kennedy (1982, p. 5) state:

> A major reason the Japanese have been so successful, we think, is their continuing ability to maintain a very strong and cohesive culture throughout the entire country. Not only do individual businesses have strong cultures, but the links among business, the banking industry, and the government are also cultural and also very powerful. Japan, Inc., is actually an expansion of the corporate culture idea on a national scale. Although this homogenization of values would not fit American culture on a national scale, we do think that it has been very effective for individual companies. In fact, a strong culture has almost always been the driving force behind continuing success in American business.

One example of the corporate culture approach in American business is seen in Cummins Engine (e.g., Sathe 1986). Historically the company has had close relations with an independent local union and a special concern for the community in which it is located. Further, the company has emphasized extraordinary service to its customers. Both of these activities represent core values of the company that were planned by top management, are communicated clearly to the

employees, and are presented as logically consistent with other goals and values of the organization.

This message is very similar to that fostered in the popular book, *In Search of Excellence* (Peters and Waterman 1982). It has considerable face validity as evidenced by its popularity in the business community. Other sources of related material are books and articles by Pascale (1984), Schein (1985), Tunstall (1983), and Wrapp (1984), which give more detail than can be presented here and are recommended for additional background information.

Before we discuss operationalization of the corporate culture approach, we must develop perspectives of business ethics and social responsibility that can be incorporated into a culture. The specific activities and the level of their performance are likely to differ among organizations, but general guidelines can be recommended for establishing them.

### A Business Ethics Perspective

The concept of the business organization has been created by society and its agents, and it must meet the expectations of that society or pay the price in consumerist and antibusiness legislation. If those expectations can be formulated in terms of ethical theory, they can be used in the development and testing of organizational values. Thus, it is appropriate to ask how two of the most popular ethical traditions, deontology and utilitarianism, are used in capitalistic democracies so that values in a marketing organization can be tested against them.

Many social systems seem to capture aspects of both deontology and utilitarianism in their laws and social policies. In the United States, cost/benefit analysis, a principal component of utilitarianism, is a tool of major importance in policy making at the national, state, and local levels. Further, the concept of capitalism has strong roots in utilitarianism. However, many individual rights are also protected at all levels of government. For example, the Declaration of Independence talks about "inalienable rights" and the U.S. Constitution has the "Bill of Rights." The United States, like many capitalistic democracies, can be viewed as adopting a blend of the two philosophies. Even so, the political, legal, and cultural environments of the United States and other capitalistic democracies have changed radically over the last century, with the business community being both a positive and negative agent in causing some of these changes. The blend of the two philosophies that is perceived as appropriate in a given society is subject to change. We believe such changes are evolutionary rather than revolutionary in most capitalistic democracies most of the time.

One problem is to determine how to treat this blend of philosophies. The language of deontology, a term derived from "duty," is fundamentally concerned with the individual and tends to dominate our thinking when the plight of individuals is deemed serious. Even when reasonably sound arguments about the "greatest good for the greatest number" can be made on one side of an issue, the deontological arguments on the other side tend to dominate if individuals' "rights" are seriously impaired. An excellent example is the case of Nestlé's sale of infant formula in third world countries. A recent book (Miller 1983) summarizes the utilitarian arguments made in the case, but the "final" resolution of the issue occurred when Nestlé agreed to follow the dictates of the World Health Organization (WHO) Code (1981). This code severely restricts even traditional marketing practices in an effort to protect individuals, and typical deontological arguments dominated the case made by its proponents. Thus, one theme that seems appropriate for marketers is:

> Marketing activities that have a foreseeable and potentially serious impact on individuals ought to be regulated by the values of deontological reasoning.

A positive example occurred when Procter & Gamble removed its Rely tampon product from the market. As reported by the *Wall Street Journal* (Rotbart and Prestbo 1980), P&G went through a short initial defensive reaction to protect the product. However, within a three-month period, as evidence connecting toxic shock with the tampon product increased, P&G agreed to do what it could to protect the public. Its actions included proposing a warning label, voluntarily halting production, removing the product from store shelves, offering to buy back all the unused product, pledging research for further study, and agreeing to finance and direct an educational program including a warning not to use Rely.

It is important to note two parallels between the Rely and Nestlé cases. First, in both situations, many of the problems can be attributed to a "natural" consumer misuse of the product. Rely was used for extended time periods beyond that deemed appropriate. Nestlé infant formula was overdiluted to save money and diluted with contaminated water in underdeveloped areas. In both cases, blame for the problems could have been directed partly toward the buyer, a tactic used by Firestone in defending the Firestone 500 product (Gatewood and Carroll 1981, p. 15). Second, utilitarian arguments could be developed in favor of retaining both products, and Nestlé supporters did generate such arguments. However, as seen with Nestlé, deontological arguments tend to prevail and it seems reasonable to suggest that P&G's actions with Rely were appropriate.

Alternatively, many and perhaps most marketing exchanges do not involve a "potentially serious impact on individuals." In those cases a second theme seems appropriate:

> For all marketing exchanges that do not have foreseeable serious consequences for individuals, the ar-

guments of utilitarianism seem appropriate within capitalistic democracies.

Thus, such issues as environmental concerns, import and export restrictions, competitive practices, and relations with supranational organizations such as the European Economic Community or OPEC all seem to be analyzed satisfactorily by means of utilitarian arguments. Though elements of society may argue differently (e.g., environmental groups), sound utilitarian arguments seem to satisfy or at least be understood by most of society. Marketing values addressing these issues can be developed and tested satisfactorily by means of the utilitarian model.

Moral philosophers also have analyzed the *level of performance* problem. The approach we suggest is borrowed from an older but still respected branch of moral philosophy called "virtue ethics." Aristotle proposed an ethics of prudence in his *Nichomachean Ethics* (see 1925 translation). Though a full description of this philosophical tradition is beyond the scope of our article, a brief presentation of how Aristotelian ethics can help solve the level of performance problem is warranted. The following abstracted statements describe how Aristotle perceived moral virtue (e.g., Beauchamp 1982, p. 161).

> Virtue is concerned with emotions and actions, where excess is wrong, as is deficiency, but the mean is praised and is right. . . . Virtue, then, is disposition involving choice. It consists in a mean, relative to us, defined by reason and as the reasonable man would define it. It is a mean between two vices—one of excess, the other of deficiency.

Thus, moderation or prudence is appropriate in the way we behave. The following examples of Aristotle's "mean" come from Fuller (1961, p. 209).

> . . . courage is the right or mean amount of the same activity as in deficiency constitutes cowardice, in excess, rashness. Temperance is a moderate love and pursuit of the physical pleasures; insensibility is too little interest in them, and self-indulgence or sensuality, too great a one; liberality is the golden mean between stinginess and prodigality; magnificence, between ostentatious and niggardly living; greatness of soul, between humility and vain glory; and so the list goes. Acts like theft, adultery, murder, and the like, and emotions like shamelessness, envy, and spite, Aristotle deals with by pointing out that they are in themselves already either excesses or defects, and therefore cannot exist in moderation.

We suggest that this same concept of moderation be applied to the system of values adopted by marketers. Neither excessiveness nor deficiency in performance would be acceptable. Rather, a "golden mean" of performance should be sought. For example, in the Rely tampon case, P&G might have been judged deficient by Aristotle had it adopted the approach of doing as little as possible. The company could have "held back," much like Ford Motor did with the Pinto or Firestone did with the 500 radial tire, and reacted only to the FDA and the Centers for Disease Control pressure, doing the minimum required in each case. However, P&G did *not* use that approach. It is important to recognize that under this recommendation extreme measures that could ruin the company are not required. Such extremes are outside the "golden mean" of performance. Thus, the level of P&G's performance in this case could be found acceptable.

## A Social Responsibility Perspective

In addressing demands to "be socially responsible," the marketing organization is faced with the variety of meanings discussed previously. However, an organized response is possible. We suggest that the organization build a parallel between its problems and the problems of an average family. This image of an average family using central values to solve family problems provides a benchmark for developing values within a marketing organization.

The parallels between the family and the marketing organization are *not* isomorphic. The sociology of the family identifies a number of family functions that are not relevant to the organization (e.g., procreation, sexual relationships, and a religious function). Nevertheless, by using the culturally established values of an average family as a *guide* in determining what its reaction to society ought to be, an organization can develop reasonable standards.

The lack of an absolute relationship between the concept of the average family and the social responsibilities of a marketing organization affords some flexibility in choosing the values to be adopted. We used United States cultural patterns as a basis for developing the set of potential parallels in Table 1. The average U.S. family is nuclear (i.e., husband, wife, and children) and Table 1 is constructed accordingly. The first relationship listed follows the Japanese model and suggests a nuclear family type of caring for the organization's employees, management, and stockholders. Many firms have not adopted this type of relationship with their employees, whereas others (e.g.,

Delta Airlines, Pepsico, and IBM) have moved direction. The slowly increasing use of organ ally sponsored daycare centers is an example o a caring relationship.

Customers are placed in a relationship parallel to that of close relatives. In a society where the nuclear family dominates, the caring for close relatives is great but not of the order of the caring for nuclear family members. However, such caring does go substantially beyond caring for neighbors and friends. Thus, customers should receive considerable concern and attention that goes beyond simply not harming them. Some organizations do seem to have adopted the value of treating customers like nuclear family members. For example, the Ronald McDonald Houses for families of sick children might be considered to represent more caring than is ordinarily required for customers or potential customers. Such deviations are subject to a variety of factors discussed in the next section.

The other parallels in Table 1 are not meant to be a complete list, but are examples of relationships that could be used. In all of these cases, the parallels drawn are very close or exact analogies and need no elaboration.

The most obvious question about the average-person approach arises from the nonhuman character of the organization. Because the organization is a creation of society and not a person, is it not reasonable to expect a *better* ethical performance than might be expected from a single average family? The problem with such an expectation is that the organization is a mythical creation, operating only through its agents who are human. Is it realistic to expect those people to have a higher level of moral performance as agents of the organization than in their personal lives? It seems more reasonable to expect a distribution of socially responsible performance for organizations that parallels the performance of the individual families of society. Hence, the mean or average family performance can be a reasonable guide in establishing

### TABLE 1
#### Parallels Between Basic Social Responsibility Values of the Family and the Organization

| Basic Family Values | Basic Organization Values |
|---|---|
| Caring for nuclear family members (i.e., husband, wife, children if any) | Caring for organization family (i.e., employees, management, stockholders) |
| Caring for close relatives (e.g., grandparents, aunts, uncles) | Caring for integral publics (e.g., customers, creditors) |
| Being a helpful and friendly neighbor | Being a helpful and friendly corporate neighbor |
| Obeying the law | Obeying the law |
| Being a "good" citizen in the community | Being a "good" citizen in the community, the nation, and the world |
| A portion of the family budget is allocated for philanthropic purposes | A portion of the organization budget is allocated for philanthropic purposes |
| Protecting and caring for the family's home and land | Protecting and caring for the physical environment on which the organization has an impact |

Ex: Atticus Finch in "To Kill A Mockingbird"

organizational values. Individual organizations may choose to strive for higher standards, and some undoubtedly might achieve lower ones, but the concept of the average person can provide at least a reasonably acceptable measuring device.

Another application of the concept is in establishing levels of performance for socially responsible activities. Even after marketers have created a system of values, the level of performance with respect to each value still can be questioned. For example, if a neighbor or employee were in trouble, how much help should the friend, neighbor, or organization be expected to give? Again, the concept of what the average family would do, combined with priorities in the system of values, can provide guidance. We are not *required* to threaten our own existence to help an employee or neighbor because the value of personal survival has a higher priority. Further, it is not something the average person would be expected to do. Thus, in questions pertaining to social responsibility, the selection of values and their level of performance can be analyzed by using the test of the average person. Carlyle, in *Past and Present* (IV.iv, p. 270), said, "In the long run every Government is the exact symbol of its people, with their wisdom and unwisdom." It is this sentiment, applied to the concept of corporate social responsibility, that we are suggesting.

## Integrating Social Responsibility and Ethics into the Strategic Marketing Planning Process

The preceding section provides a view of corporate culture that is instrumental in the integration of social responsibility and ethics into the strategic marketing planning process. The basis of this integration process is the idea of ethical core values acting as guidelines for the development of marketing plans.

Without the integration of concerns about ethics and social responsibility at the very beginning of the marketing planning process, as well as throughout the process, the organizational culture may not provide the checks and balances needed to develop ethical and socially responsible marketing programs. Corporate values of profit and efficiency tend to dominate most organizational cultures, particularly in the absence of the overt addition of counterbalancing ethical and socially responsible values. This situation arises because the organization reinforces its members at all levels on the basis of achieving profitability or efficiency objectives. Though profit and efficiency must remain central values within the culture, they must be balanced by other values that help define the limits of activities designed to achieve those objectives and by values describing other important ethical and socially responsible behaviors.

Figure 1 depicts the suggested parallel planning approach by which ethical and socially responsible core

values can be introduced into the organizational culture. It applies to the development of a new set of core values and marketing strategy. However, the development of one when the other already exists follows a similar pattern.

The organizational mission statement and ethical profile guide the development of marketing objectives. As these objectives are being developed, however, a feedback function also occurs, whereby the mission statement and the ethical profile are questioned, elaborated, and clarified. The next stage is an environmental analysis in which all affected publics are considered. Special attention is given to target markets prior to the development of the complete marketing strategy, but a dual emphasis is appropriate. The concern of the strategic planner in marketing is not just how a new marketing mix might induce the target customer to participate in the exchange, but also whether it might take advantage of weaknesses, ignorance, or simply lack of interest of the potential buyer. Similarly, other affected publics are analyzed from this dual perspective. The concern is not only how their actions will influence the effectiveness of a potential marketing strategy, but also how the marketing strategy is likely to influence them. Ethical and socially responsible questions are more likely to arise from the latter analysis than the former.

The parallel planning analysis in Figure 1 continues with the development of actionable ethical core values and the marketing mix. The feedback process between the two is perhaps most obvious at this level. For core values to be actionable and meaningful in daily marketing practices, their meaning must be explained in terms that apply to the marketing mix. Conversely, the marketing mix must satisfy the core values. Once the core values and the marketing mix have been established, enculturation and integration of core values are introduced with the implementation of the marketing strategy. The activity and change instigated by both activities must be monitored for both the effectiveness of the strategy in reaching the marketing objectives and the effectiveness of the core values in

### FIGURE 1
### Parallel Planning Systems for Integrating Ethical and Socially Responsible Plans into Strategic Marketing Planning

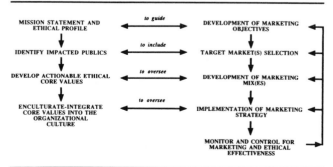

achieving ethically and socially responsible behavior. As with any plan, initial efforts may not be completely effective and changes may be needed at any level in the process.

## Mission Statement and Ethical Profile

Just as the organization's mission statement guides the marketing planning process, it also guides the development of the organization's desired ethical profile. The profile is a projection to external publics with whom the organization interacts, identifying how the organization chooses to interact with those publics. Its importance and function are similar to those of the mission statement in that it provides broad, general guidelines for identifying relevant ethical opportunities and developing more specific objectives.

There are numerous sources of ideas for aiding the marketing manager in developing an ethical and socially responsible profile. These sources parallel the ones that would be suggested for establishing any organizational mission. However, the application of these sources has a somewhat different connotation than that typically found in the marketing literature. Specific ideas for a socially responsible and ethical profile can come from threats, opportunities, organizational history and mission, current corporate image, personal preferences of management and owners, plus special marketing resources and competences. In fact, ethical profiles can be generated from any combination of these sources.

For example, threats to the organization can come from any of the publics affected by the basic marketing exchange, as well as any one of the uncontrollable environments. In this context, threats can be anything that might discredit the organization in the eyes of the general public or their representatives, or something that might be deemed unethical in the sense already described. Phillips 66 has reacted to a potential threat in the form of perceived environmental damage to areas in which it operates by promoting environmental concern. The company's positive record in this regard gives substance to this dimension of its profile.

Opportunities also provide a means of developing the profile of the organization. The social problems or needs of all elements of society are a beginning point for analysis. In addition, the problems of directly affected publics such as buyers, competitors, and marketing personnel should receive special attention in the search for opportunities. McDonald's concern for the needs of families of children who are chronically or terminally ill was the impetus for Ronald McDonald Houses, which were established near treatment centers to enable the family to stay together during the child's care. In this case, McDonald's is responding to an opportunity in a portion of its targeted market.

The organization's history, mission, and current image may provide some of the dimensions of the ethical profile. The financial industry typically relies on history and tradition as a source of its ethical profile to establish a sense of trust between an organization and investing publics. This profile has been tarnished somewhat by the actions of such financial firms as E. F. Hutton, cited for a check kiting operation, and The Bank of Boston, charged with the laundering of possible drug money. Personal preferences of top management or owners are a similar source of an ethical profile because these individuals provide its necessary support and enforcement (e.g., Chonko and Hunt 1985).

Finally, the special resources and competences that marketing organizations use to satisfy and facilitate the marketing exchange can be applied to project ethical and socially responsible profiles to the different publics. For example, Procter & Gamble loaned some of its special resource expertise to the Centers for Disease Control for investigation of toxic shock syndrome linked to the Rely tampon product (Rotbart and Prestbo 1980). A creative look at such competences and resources can be useful in suggesting dimensions of an ethical profile.

The profile acts as a standard with which marketing objectives can be compared to determine whether their *anticipated* impacts will be incongruent with the dimensions of the profile. The word "anticipated" is stressed because it is not always possible to predict all impacts of a marketing program. Specific profile dimensions might include such ideas as customer orientation, environmental concern and involvement, reliability, growth orientation, progressive/innovative behavior, and concern for quality. It is important to note that it is the total dimension rather than the individual dimensions that should be the focus of attention. All of the parts must fit together to produce a logical, internally consistent, and easily communicated ethical profile. The benefit of such coherency is similar to the benefit accruing from internally consistent individual behavior. Without a consistent profile and mission statement the organization projects a split personality to its external environment, as well as to its own stockholders, managers, and employees.

## Identifying Affected Publics

Identifying affected publics, the next step in the integration process, parallels the strategic marketing planning process step of identifying target market(s). The target market(s) identified will be one of the affected publics. However, other publics will be involved in this stage of the process, including the community in which the organization operates, competition, and society, plus internal publics such as managers, employees, and stockholders. Identifying affected publics enables the strategic planner to examine the *anticipated* consequences of marketing programs as they affect these other publics.

The identification of these potentially affected publics enables the strategic marketing planner to fine-tune the profile dimensions into specific core values that will be used in the enculturation stage. It is at this stage that the concern for marketing's impact on these identified publics is combined with the traditional marketing management concern for the impact of the environment on the effectiveness of the marketing mix and resultant profit expectations. This concern for the dual impacts (those of the environment on the organization and of the organization on the environment) represents a significant departure from typical planning processes in which the focus is generally one way. Moreover, this dual focus differentiates the concern for ethical and socially responsible planning from issue management, which is typically concerned with controlling the harmful effects of negative publicity (see Gatewood and Carroll 1981; Policano 1985; Sherrell et al. 1985).

To complete this step, each public identified must be analyzed carefully to determine the potential impact of a marketing action. Specifically, the broad ethical profile and its constituent dimensions are used as the basis for judgment in this analysis. If the marketing activity appears to be incongruent with the desired ethical profile, the activity must be reconsidered.

Such an analysis might have produced a different response from Nestlé in the marketing of infant formula to third world countries. In the Nestlé case, the affected public was one of the targeted markets, third world mothers. As originally conceived, marketing infant formula to third world countries was not only profitable but was initially defended as a beneficial and responsible action on the part of Nestlé. Subsequent experience with the product in third world countries revealed that individuals were not using the product correctly. The formula was being mixed with contaminated water, causing infants to develop diarrhea and dehydration that in some cases led to death. Nestlé's response was to continue marketing the product, claiming that it was not the company's fault that the product was being misused. With little concern for the wellbeing of third world customers being shown by Nestlé, several groups formed to make Nestlé respond in a more ethical and socially responsible manner (*Business Week* 1979). Finally, after boycotts and much pressure from international groups, Nestlé agreed to modify its marketing activities.

Nestlé's concern for profits outweighed concerns for the individual rights of the affected segments. An ethical profile and commitment to its use might not have prevented the initial problem, but would have provided guidelines for a more ethical and socially responsible response to the actual situation. The development and enculturation of ethical and socially responsible core values throughout Nestlé would have aided even more.

## Develop Actionable Ethical Core Values

The ethical profile is the ethical "face" of the organization that it presents to all its relevant external publics. Ethical core values are constructed directly from this profile and are the *internal* guidelines for maintaining and supporting the ethical profile. Each core value flows directly from discussions on ethics and social responsibility as well as concerns for affected publics. Deontological concern for the individual and utilitarian concern for the "greatest good" are combined in the construction of core values. Further, the family analogy shown in Table 1 is another ingredient in the design of an ethical value system. The content of each value is intended to direct the behavior of organizational members in both the level and nature of performance. These core values are combined with the economic and efficiency values of the organization.

Some of the profile dimensions identified before provide examples of how core values can be extracted and developed from the profile. One dimension is the idea of a strong customer orientation. The problem with such a profile dimension is that employees of the organization may not know how to implement it. An appropriate core value must be actionable and easily understood. Thus, an appropriate statement of a core value to support the profile dimension of customer orientation might be:

> Treat customers with respect, concern, and honesty, the way you yourself would want to be treated or the way you would want your family treated.

A profile dimension of quality orientation for products and services might be translated into:

> Make and market products you would feel comfortable and safe having your own family use.

Similarly, a societal core value toward being environmentally concerned and involved might become:

> Treat the environment as though it were your own property.

These core values, once developed, have a controlling function in the design of marketing programs, specifically overseeing the development of the marketing mix(es). In another sense, the development of these core values is analogous to the development of a marketing strategy. Though there may be several ways in which an organization can be customer-oriented, the approach identified through the development of the core values reflects the method or strategy selected by the organization. This selection of core values is governed by the idea that there is a limitation to the number of core values that can be assimilated effectively. Alternative core values should be developed to satisfy the affected public's needs, and each should be tested to determine the fit between the core values and the affected public's concerns. In addition, the selected core values should be examined in light of their internal consistency. If they are inconsistent, management must return to the alternatives to find values that are consistent with each other and the profile. The process is iterative until the core values and the profile achieve the desired results.

Core values become the day-to-day guidelines for developing marketing plans. They are a filter of sorts through which plans are passed to ensure their ethical content. They counterbalance profit and efficiency values which, in the absence of ethical core values, dominate the planning process. That several firms have let the values of profitability and efficiency dictate their marketing activities is evident in a number of well-known examples.

Ford Motor Company's reaction to the fuel system problem in the Pinto is a good example of marketing plans conceived in the absence of well-developed ethical core values. The Pinto was linked to more than 500 deaths and accidents resulting from collisions that ruptured the fuel system of the automobile and produced fires. Ford was aware of this problem even before the large number of accidents revealed it (Dowie 1977, p. 26–55). Ford management conducted a cost/benefit analysis of the situation and decided it was more cost effective to deal with the accidents than to institute a recall and repair the problem. Their decision shows a direct lack of concern for the ethics of the problem and the domination of the profit value.

Johnson & Johnson demonstrates the type of response that would be expected from an organization that has a well developed system of ethical core values. After the deaths of seven individuals who had consumed contaminated Tylenol capsules, Johnson & Johnson, within the week, had instituted a total product recall costing an estimated $50 million after taxes (Gardner 1982, p. 71). This action was taken even though the deaths were not the fault of the company but were attributable to the actions of some unknown individual outside the company. In addition, Johnson & Johnson spearheaded an industry move to develop more effective packaging to prevent tampering in the future. The company's behavior was reaffirmed when, after further tampering occurred, it quit producing capsules entirely. This action suggests that Johnson & Johnson considers the well being of the customer to be as important as profitability and is in direct contrast to the response made by Ford Motor Company.

### The Enculturation Process

Core values such as those suggested in the last section are also the principal tool for *implementing* the kind of ethical behavior desired. They are the major objectives of the enculturation of marketing personnel (see Pascale 1984 for insight into the enculturation process). This enculturation process instills the core values into each individual and integrates ethical and socially responsible concerns into the marketing planning process. Ideally, each member of the marketing organization would adopt those values when operating in his/her role of employee. Realistically, the process will not be perfect, but should reach most employees if carefully implemented.

Several companies that have experience with the enculturation of ethical values provide some guidelines for how this process can be accomplished. General Dynamics, in the wake of the recent controversy about overcharging the U.S. government on military contracts, has invested heavily in a program to increase the probability of future ethical behavior. General Dynamics uses seminars to communicate top management's concern for ethical behavior to its 100,000 employees (Moskowitz and Byrne 1985, p. 66). Backing up the seminars is a so-called "squeal clause" that not only protects whistle blowers who bring unethical behavior to the attention of the proper individuals, but also rewards them. Each division of General Dynamics has an "ethics program director" who is approachable when an employee feels it is inappropriate to go to his/her own immediate supervisor with a complaint. Over the ethics program director is a steering committee headed by two vice presidents whose responsibility it is to ensure implementation of the program.

E. F. Hutton chairman Robert Fomon suggests that effective enculturation involves education, training, and compliance. He goes so far as to say the program ". . . will have teeth and systems of enforcement" (Moskowitz and Byrne 1985, p. 66). Robert V. Krikorian, chairman of Rexnord, has videotaped a speech on ethics to be shown to all employees in which he tells them to "walk away from business when it means doing anything unethical or illegal" (Moskowitz and Byrne 1985, p. 66).

Educationally, projecting a total mission statement or profile is extremely difficult because it is couched in broad, general terms. Core values, in contrast, are more concrete and easier to understand, and hence are the primary vehicle for enculturation. With the selection of the core values, their communication, enculturation, and enforcement within the organization, top level management has begun a process conducive to ethical and socially responsible decision making at all levels of the organization. Further, much of the frustration that has accompanied traditional efforts in these areas because of a lack of well planned, logically consistent, and integrated efforts should be eliminated.

### Monitoring and Controlling Marketing Behavior

The enculturation process can take several years, and actually never ends as long as new members are added to the organization. There is a continual need to monitor marketing behavior to determine whether the en-culturation process is working. If the progress is too slow or if the core values are not producing antici-pated behavior, the reasons for these problems should be identified. Once understood, the(se) cause(s) may force a complete reevaluation of the process begin-ning with the first step in Figure 1. Alternatively, a slight change in the manner of enforcing the core val-ues or in the way they are stated may be all that is needed. Generalization is not possible, but a careful analysis of the reasons for the problem should be suggestive of its solution.

The successful enculturation of core values pro-vides an overseeing function on not only the imple-mentation of marketing programs but also the plan-ning of subsequent programs. It is at this point that the integration of ethical and social responsibility con-cerns into the marketing planning process is complete.

One other point is important. In addition to inter-nal enculturation or behavior problems, unexpected external reactions from affected publics can arise. For example, customers may misuse a product in ways no one would reasonably expect. When unanticipated and unintended ethical issues arise, moral excusing con-ditions might apply. DeGeorge (1986, p. 83) lists three categories of excusing conditions:

> . . . those conditions that preclude the possibility of the action; those conditions that preclude or diminish the required knowledge; and those conditions that preclude or diminish the required freedom.

Thus, in the Nestlé example, if it were unreasonable for Nestlé management to know the consequences of marketing infant formula in third world countries, they might be excused from moral responsibility. How-ever, once' they did know, they should be held re-sponsible. Clearly, this is not the case with Ford Mo-tor Company and its marketing of the Pinto. Ford management knowingly marketed a defective and dangerous product and should not receive the benefit of the excusing argument.

With the radically changing environment of mar-keting, the constant innovation of products and ser-vices, and the changing public ethos concerning the practice of marketing, the process of developing core values and their enculturation must be ongoing. Just as value systems evolve and change in a society, so, too, must the core values that guide an organization's marketing planning change. In both situations the value changes are reactions to shifts in the needs of society and its members.

## Conclusions

Thomas Donaldson, a philosophy professor at Loyola University in Chicago and coauthor of a popular busi-ness ethics book (Donaldson and Werhane 1983), is quoted in an article by Lewin (1983) as saying:

> . . . now almost everybody believes that corpora-tions should be concerned about something more than making money, that they have responsibilities not only to their shareholders but to their employees, to their customers, to the communities in which they work and to society at large.

Marketers who ignore their responsibilities to these other stakeholders face the prospect of a devalued cor-poration image and/or legal reprisals. However, to meet these responsibilities effectively, organizations must address both the direct and indirect concerns out-lined here in the development of marketing strategy. *Ex post facto* analysis of the issues will not afford a suitable opportunity for integration. What we ask for is more than a few stopgap rules or codes of ethics that basically tend to operate as constraints. Instead, we propose a positive, proactive approach to market-ing ethics and social responsibility based on careful analysis of the important potential impacts.

Is it possible for marketers to behave ethically in a competitive world and both survive and prosper? A central theme in books such as those of Dale Carnegie (1936) and more recently Peters and Waterman (1982) seems to suggest that such an approach will produce not just survival, but "excellence." Though both books have been criticized for their lack of scholarly ap-proach, they both seem to focus on a fundamental de-sire of individuals to be treated with respect and fair-ness and the fact that when people are so treated they react well. Thus, social responsibility and the major traditions of moral philosophy may not be at odds with sound marketing practice. We await the empirical evi-dence to confirm or refute this proposition. Mean-while, it is not unreasonable to expect the representa-tives of society to continue to create constraints and barriers for marketers whenever social values are vi-olated.

## REFERENCES

Aristotle (1925), *Nichomachean Ethics,* in *The Works of Ar-istotle,* William D. Ross, ed. and trans. Oxford: Clarendon Press, especially Books I–V, X.

Bartels, Robert (1967), "A Model for Ethics in Marketing," *Journal of Marketing,* 31 (January), 20–6.

Baumhart, Raymond, S. J. (1961), "How Ethical are Busi-nessmen?", *Harvard Business Review,* 39 (July–August), 6–31.

Beauchamp, Tom L. (1982), *Philosophical Ethics.* New York: McGraw-Hill Book Company.

Blankenship, A. B. (1964), "Some Aspects of Ethics in Mar-keting Research," *Journal of Marketing Research,* 1 (May), 26–31.

Brenner, Steven N. and Earl A. Molander (1977), "Is the Eth-ics of Business Changing?", *Harvard Business Review,* 55 (January–February), 57–71.

*Business Week* (1979), "A Boycott Over Infant Formula" (April 23), 137, 140.

Carlyle, Thomas (1855), *Past and Present.* New York: Harper & Brothers.

Carnegie, Dale (1936), *How to Win Friends and Influence People.* New York: Pocket Books, Inc.

Carr, Albert Z. (1968), "Is Business Bluffing Ethical?", *Harvard Business Review*, 46 (January–February), 145ff.

Cavanaugh, Gerald F., Dennis J. Moberg, and Manuel Velazquez (1981), "The Ethics of Organizational Politics," *Academy of Management Review*, 3, 363–74.

Chonko, Lawrence B. and Shelby D. Hunt (1985), "Ethics and Marketing Management: An Empirical Examination," *Journal of Business Research*, 13 (August), 339–59.

Clasen, Earl A. (1967), "Marketing Ethics and the Consumer," *Harvard Business Review*, 45 (January–February), 79–86.

Crawford, C. Merle (1970), "Attitudes of Marketing Executives Toward Ethics in Marketing Research," *Journal of Marketing*, 34 (April), 46–52.

Cressey, Donald R. and Charles A. Moore (1983), "Managerial Values and Corporate Codes of Ethics," *California Management Review* (Summer), 53–77.

Cummings, Gary F. (1979), "Are Purchasing Ethics Being Put to the Test?", *Iron Age*, 222 (September 24), 21–4.

Davis, Keith and Robert L. Blomstrom (1966), *Business and Its Environment*. New York: McGraw-Hill Book Company.

———— and William C. Frederick (1984), *Business and Society: Management, Public Policy, Ethics*, 5th ed. New York: McGraw-Hill Book Company.

Davis, Stanley M., William Rudelius, and Roger A. Buchholz (1979), "Ethical Problems of Purchasing Managers," *Harvard Business Review*, 57 (March–April), 8, 12, 14.

Deal, Terrence E. and Allan A. Kennedy (1982), *Corporate Cultures*. Reading, MA: Addison-Wesley Publishing Company.

DeGeorge, Richard R. (1986), *Business Ethics*, 2nd ed. New York: Macmillan Publishing Company.

Donaldson, Thomas and Patricia H. Werhane (1983), *Ethical Issues in Business*, 2nd ed. Englewood Cliffs, NJ: Prentice-Hall, Inc.

Dowie, Mark (1977), "How Ford Put Two Million Firetraps on Wheels," *Business and Society Review* (Fall), 46–55.

Dubinsky, Alan J., Eric N. Berkowitz, and William Rudelius (1980), "Ethical Problems of Field Sales Personnel, *MSU Business Topics*, 28 (Summer), 11–16.

Edmonds, Charles P., III and John H. Hand (1976), "What are the Real Long-Run Objectives of Business?", *Business Horizons*, 19 (December), 75–81.

Ferrell, O. C. and K. Mark Weaver (1978), "Ethical Beliefs of Marketing Managers," *Journal of Marketing*, 42 (July), 69–73.

————, Mary Zey-Ferrell, and Dean Krugman (1983), "A Comparison of Predictors of Ethical and Unethical Behavior Among Corporate and Agency Advertising Managers," *Journal of Macromarketing*, 3 (Spring), 19–27.

———— and Larry G. Gresham (1985), "A Contingency Framework for Understanding Ethical Decision-Making in Marketing," *Journal of Marketing*, 49 (Summer), 87–96.

Friedman, Milton (1970), "The Social Responsibility of Business Is to Increase Its Profits," *New York Times Magazine* (September 13), 33.

Fuller, B. A. G. (1961), *A History of Ancient and Medieval Philosophy*, 3rd ed., revised by Sterling M. McMurrin. New York: Holt, Rinehart and Winston.

Gardner, Judith B. (1982), "When a Brand Name Gets Hit by Bad News," *U.S. News & World Report* (November 8), 71.

Gaski, John F. (1985), "Dangerous Territory: The Societal Marketing Concept Revisited," *Business Horizons*, 28 (July–August), 42–7.

Gatewood, Elizabeth and Archie B. Carroll (1981), "The Anatomy of Corporate Social Response: The Rely, Firestone 500, and Pinto Cases," *Business Horizons*, 24 (September–October), 9–16.

Glueck, William F. (1980), *Business Policy and Strategic Management*, 3rd ed. New York: McGraw-Hill Book Company.

Gross, C. W. and H. L. Verma (1977), "Marketing and Social Responsibility," *Business Horizons*, 20 (October), 75–82.

Hill, Galdwin (1982), "The New Dimension," in *Participation III*. Los Angeles: Atlantic Richfield Co.

Hunt, Shelby D., Lawrence B. Chonko, and James B. Wilcox (1984), "Ethical Problems of Marketing Researchers," *Journal of Marketing Research*, 21 (August), 309–24.

———— and Scott Vitell (1986), "A General Theory of Marketing Ethics," *Journal of Macromarketing*, 6 (Spring), 5–16.

Kaikati, Jack and Wayne A. Label (1980), "American Bribery Legislation: An Obstacle to International Marketing," *Journal of Marketing*, 44 (Fall), 38–43.

Kant, Immanuel (1964), *Groundwork of the Metaphysics of Morals*, translation by H. J. Paton. New York: Harper and Row Publishers.

Krugman, Dean M. and O. C. Ferrell (1981), "The Organizational Ethics of Advertising: Corporate and Agency Views," *Journal of Advertising*, 10 (1), 21–30.

Laczniak, Gene R. (1983), "Framework for Analyzing Marketing Ethics," *Journal of Macromarketing*, 3 (Spring), 7–18.

————, Robert F. Lusch, and William A. Strang (1981), "Ethical Marketing: Perceptions of Economic Goods and Social Problems, *Journal of Macromarketing*, 1 (Spring), 49–57.

Lavidge, Robert J. (1970), "The Growing Responsibilities of Marketing," *Journal of Marketing*, 34 (January), 25–8.

Levy, Michael and Alan J. Dubinsky (1983), "Identifying and Addressing Retail Salespeople's Ethical Problems: A Method and Application," *Journal of Retailing*, 59 (Spring), 46–66.

Lewin, Tamar (1983), "Business Ethics' New Appeal," *The New York Times* (December 11), Section F, 4.

McMahon, Thomas V. (1968), "A Look at Marketing Ethics," *Atlantic Economic Review*, 17 (March).

Mayer, R. R. (1970), "Management's Responsibility for Purchasing Ethics," *Journal of Purchasing*, 4, 13–20.

Miller, Fred D., Jr., (1983), *Out of the Mouths of Babes: The Infant Formula Controversy*. Bowling Green, OH: Social Philosophy and Policy Center.

Moskowitz, Daniel B. and John A. Byrne (1985), "Where Business Goes to Stock Up on Ethics," *Business Week* (October 14), 63, 66.

Murphy, Patrick and Gene R. Laczniak (1981), "Marketing Ethics: A Review with Implications for Managers, Educators and Reseachers," in *Review of Marketing 1981*. Chicago: American Marketing Association, 251–66.

Newstrom, John W. and William A. Rush (1975), "The Ethics of Management and the Management of Ethics," *MSU Business Topics*, 23 (Winter), 29–37.

Pascale, Richard (1984), "Fitting New Employees into the Company Culture," *Fortune* (May 28), 28ff.

Peters, Thomas J. and Robert H. Waterman, Jr. (1982), *In Search of Excellence*. New York: Harper and Row Publishers.

Policano, Christopher (1985), "Case Study: A. H. Robbins and the Dalkon Shield," *Public Relations Journal*, 41 (3), 16–19, 21.

Pruden, Henry O. (1971), "Which Ethics for Marketers?" in *Marketing and Social Issues*, John R. Wish and Stephen H. Gamble, eds. New York: John Wiley & Sons, Inc., 98–104.

Rawls, John (1971), *A Theory of Justice*. Cambridge, MA: Harvard University Press.

Ricklefs, Roger (1983), "On Many Ethical Issues, Executives Apply Stiffer Standards than Public," *Wall Street Journal*

(November 1).

Robin, Donald P. (1980), "Value Issues in Marketing," in *Theoretical Developments in Marketing,"* C. W. Lamb and P. M. Dunne, eds. Chicago: American Marketing Association, 142–5.

Ross, William D. (1930), *The Right and the Good*. Oxford: Oxford University Press.

Rotbart, Dean and John A. Prestbo (1980), "Killing a Product," *Wall Street Journal* (November 3), 21.

Sathe, Vijay (1986), "How to Decipher and Change Organizational Culture," in *Managing Corporate Cultures*, R. H. Kilman and Associates, ed. San Franciso: Jossey-Bass, Inc.

Schein, Edgar H. (1985), *Organizational Culture and Leadership*. San Francisco: Jossey-Bass, Inc.

Sherrell, Daniel, R. Eric Reidenbach, Ellen Moore, Jay Wagle, and Thaddeus Spratlin (1985), "Exploring Consumer Response to Negative Publicity," *Public Relations Review*, 6 (1), 13–29.

Smart, J. J. C. and Bernard Williams (1973), *Utilitarianism: For & Against*. Cambridge: Cambridge University Press.

Smith, Adam (1776), *An Inquiry into the Nature and Causes of the Wealth of Nations*. New York: The Modern Library.

Steiner, George A. (1972), "Social Policies for Business," *California Management Review* (Winter), 17–24.

Sturdivant, Frederick D. and A. Benton Cocanougher (1973),

"What are Ethical Marketing Practices?", *Harvard Business Review*, 51 (November–December), 10–12, 176.

Tunstall, W. Brooke (1983), "Cultural Transition at AT&T," *Sloan Management Review* (Fall), 15–26.

Tybout, Alice M. and Gerald Zaltman (1974) "Ethics in Marketing Research: Their Practical Relevance," *Journal of Marketing Research*, 11 (November), 357–68.

Varble, D. L. (1972), "Social and Environmental Considerations in New Product Development," *Journal of Marketing*, 36 (October), 11–15.

World Health Organization (1981), *International Code of Marketing of Breast-Milk Substitutes*, Geneva, Switzerland.

Wrapp, H. Edward (1984), "Good Managers Don't Make Policy Decisions," *Harvard Business Review*, 61 (July–August), 8–21.

Zeithaml, Carl P. and Valarie A. Zeithaml (1984), "Environmental Management: Revising the Marketing Perspective," *Journal of Marketing*, 48 (Spring), 46–53.

Zey-Ferrell, Mary and O. C. Ferrell (1982), "Role-Set Configuration and Opportunities as Predictors of Unethical Behavior in Organizations," *Human Relations*, 7, 587–604.

———, K. Mark Weaver, and O. C. Ferrell (1979), "Predicting Unethical Behavior Among Marketing Practitioners," *Human Relations*, 7, 557–69.

# The Ethics of Virtue: A Moral Theory for Marketing

*The moral theory of virtue ethics holds much promise for guiding the behavior of marketers. Although the origins of this theory can be traced back to Aristotle, it has not received as much emphasis as the teleological and deontological theories within marketing. In the ethics of virtue, traits such as compassion, fairness, loyalty, and openness shape a person's and an organization's vision. Several marketing situations confronted by Johnson & Johnson are used to illustrate the theory of virtue.*

Oliver F. Williams and Patrick E. Murphy

Oliver F. Williams, C. S. C., is Associate Professor of Management at the University of Notre Dame. Patrick E. Murphy is Professor of Marketing at the same institution.

The field of marketing ethics is burgeoning. Although systematic study is just over 20 years old, recent emphasis on the subject has grown dramatically. Fueled by ethical transgressions by marketing managers, such as the widely reported events surrounding defense contractors and the infant formula industry's activities in developing countries, the examination of ethical behavior by marketers has received increasing attention from scholars (for reviews of this work, see Murphy and Laczniak 1981; Murphy and Pridgen 1990).

This article proposes that the ethics of virtue is a very relevant theory for improving the ethical conduct of marketers. Although this ethical theory has received only modest attention from marketing writers to date, it holds much promise for effectively examining and promoting ethical behavior. The point here is that much of the behavior cited as exemplary in the corporate world (for example, the Tylenol decisions by Johnson & Johnson or the Rely decision by Procter & Gamble), is not sufficiently explained as principled action alone. Rather, the top management of these firms became corporate heroes in the eyes of many because they exhibited uncommon virtue in maintaining allegiance to their principles. This was demonstrated, for example, in the courage to act to protect human welfare even

in the face of incomplete information and in the integrity and humility displayed in communicating with consumers about possible difficulties with a product. Before we discuss the theory of virtue in depth, we examine the ethical theories developed in moral philosophy that have been applied to marketing issues.

## ETHICAL THEORY APPLIED TO MARKETING

It is generally accepted that there are two classes of ethical theory, both of which yield principles for action: teleological and deontological. Useful definitions of each are proposed by Kimmel (1988):

> A teleological theory of ethics holds an action as morally right or obligatory if it or the rule under which it falls will produce the greatest possible balance of good over evil.

> The term deontology has evolved from the Greek *deon* (duty) and *logos* (science and reason), suggesting that certain acts are to be viewed as morally right or obligatory not because of their effects on human welfare, but rather because they keep a promise, show gratitude, demonstrate loyalty to an unconditional command, and the like (p. 44).

The most widely know teleological theory is utilitarianism, espoused by John Stuart Mill (Piest 1957). Two subcategories of utilitarianism—rule and act—are recognized. Ethical egoism falls within this theory. There are also two general approaches to deontology: duty-based theories, such as Kant's "categorical

From *Journal of Macromarketing*, Vol. 10, No. 1, Spring 1990, pp. 19-29. *Journal of Macromarketing*, published by the Business Research Division, College of Business, University of Colorado at Boulder.

175

imperative" (Wolff 1985) and Ross's (1930) prima facie duties, and the rights-based approach, whose best known proponent is John Rawls (1971).

Recognizing the crucial need to formulate principles that will guide the decision maker in establishing priorities among the various "goods" to be sought and "evils" to be avoided, marketing scholars have drawn on the deontological and utilitarian theories. Murphy and Laczniak (1981) summarize these theories and state that "ethics is fundamentally a matter of moral philosophy" (p. 252). Laczniak (1983) reviews three significant deontological frameworks proposed by Ross (1930), Garrett (1966), and Rawls (1971). He then applies their major principles to problems in marketing ethics. In their empirical examination of management behavior, Fritzsche and Becker (1984), drawing on the work of Cavanagh, Moberg, and Velasquez (1981), suggest that there are three prominent ethical theories—utilitarianism, rights, and justice (the latter two fall within the deontological theories).

Three major attempts to develop a theory of marketing ethics also utilize the teleology-deontology dichotomy as background for their work. Ferrell and Gresham (1985) discuss utilitarianism, the rights principle, and the justice principle as the components of the individual factors construct in their contingency framework for examining marketing ethics. Hunt and Vitell's (1986) article on the theory of marketing ethics contains an extensive discussion of moral philosophy, and they also employ these two ethical theories. They conclude, however, that "any positive theory of ethics must account for both the deontological and teleological aspects of the evaluation process" (p. 7). Most recently, Ferrell, Gresham, and Fraedrich (1989) reviewed these moral philosophies before proposing their "synthesis model" of ethical decision making.

The writings of Robin and his colleagues have built primarily on these two theories. Robin and Reidenbach (1988) develop their use of deontological and utilitarian theories onto the matrix of Miller's living system hierarchy. Robin and others (1989) evaluate corporate codes of conduct using deontological and utilitarian standards.

In a 1987 article in the *Journal of Marketing*, Robin and Reidenbach offer an insightful proposal for developing an ethical corporate culture in a business organization. Relying primarily on the widely used ethical theories of deontology and utilitarianism, this article presents a good example of the prevailing thinking in the field; for this reason their work, rather than one of the principles-based theories, will be cited in arguing the case for a new approach, which highlights a theory of virtue, to structuring an ethical corporate culture.

## THE MEANING OF SOCIAL RESPONSIBILITY AND ETHICS

Exactly what role do ethics play in determining a corporate culture?[1] Robin and Reidenbach (1987) are aware that the philosophers are not in complete agreement on this point. Therefore, they chart out their understanding of ethics and social responsibility and how these might be incorporated into a business culture. Following much of the "business and society" literature, they make a distinction between social responsibility and business ethics.

> Corporate social responsibility is related to the social contract between business and the society in which it operates. ... Business ethics, in contrast, requires that the organization or individual behave in accordance with the carefully thought-out rules of moral philosophy (p. 45).

The assumption is made that a business culture ought to reflect the dominant ethical values present in our capitalistic democracy. It is further assumed that "two of the most popular traditions," deontology and utilitarianism, are the best means of reflecting the ethics of democratic capitalism. Two principles are enunciated to guide corporate culture. First, marketing activities that have a foreseeable and potentially serious effect on individuals ought to be regulated by the values of deontological reasoning. Second, for all marketing exchanges that do not have foreseeable serious consequences for individuals, the arguments of utilitarianism seem appropriate.

Both deontology, with its concern for

---

[1] A common definition of corporate culture, and one to which we subscribe, is offered by Uttal (1983): the system of shared values (what is important) and beliefs (how things work) that interact with a company's people, organizational structures, and control systems to produce behavioral norms (how we do things around here).

individual "rights," and utilitarianism, with its social focus on "the greatest good for the greatest number," have a role to play in adjudicating ethical quandaries. In addition, the authors offer a third theory, virtue ethics, which, according to them, counsels that "neither excessiveness nor deficiency in performance would be acceptable." Rather, "a 'golden mean' of performance" should be sought (p. 51). Moderation, or "prudence," is highlighted.

Once an organization has a mission statement, an appreciation for the rules of deontology and utilitarianism, and a cognizance of the import of family values (which Robin and Reidenbach propose are similar to those held by organizations—Table 1 in their article), the firm's managers then formulate the core ethical values that will become the organization's hallmark. For example, if the mission statement emphasizes a strong customer orientation, the authors articulate the core value as follows: "Treat customers with respect, concern, and honesty, the way you yourself would want to be treated or the way you would want your family treated" (p. 55). Core values guide marketing plans and inform day-to-day practice.

## WHAT A THEORY OF VIRTUE MIGHT PROVIDE

When analyzing some of the difficult cases that have captured the widespread attention of the American public, such as the Tylenol or Rely product recall decisions, what becomes clear is that business experts, using one or the other theories of principles, were quite divided on the "right" response to the crises. Even at its best, moral reasoning does not yield unambiguous results. A case could have been made, and was made, for *not* withdrawing the Tylenol and Rely products. To be sure, the principles provided by the ethical theories offer some guidance to decision makers as they seek the right choices between the conflicting goods (here referring not to products but to alternative choices). But in the face of divided opinion and the fear of making a mistake, some individuals have the ability to see what to do, rise to the occasion, and muster the courage to act; these people often become our heroes. It may be that a theory of virtue best explains these human strengths and can assist in cultivating organizations that foster their development.

Most often today, discussions of virtue ethics in the literature are inadequate. The Aristotelian ethics of virtue, as retrieved in the work of the contemporary philosopher Alasdair MacIntyre, offers much promise. MacIntyre defines *virtue* as "an acquired human quality the possession and exercise of which tends to enable us to achieve those goods which are internal to practices and the lack of which effectively prevents us from achieving any such good" (MacIntyre 1981, 178). The point here is that character or virtue is *acquired*; these human capacities or qualities are cultivated by choices and by the environments within which we live and work. An equally important point in the definition is that acting virtuously truly is its own reward, that is, while acting virtuously may indeed yield good results (such as increased market share for Tylenol), virtuous decision makers act primarily to be true to themselves. What MacIntyre is getting at here is that there is a range of goods (goods *internal* to practices) which are valued not because of their utilitarian significance, in that they yield desired outcomes, but because they are a part of what it means to be a person. The young student who exercises great discipline and masters a musical instrument may indeed get an "A" in the course (a good external and secondary to the practice), but the significant reward is the ability to enjoy good music at a new and higher level (a good internal to the practice). The claim is that virtues make life interesting and worth living. Some of the virtues highlighted for the professions by one ethicist advocating a theory of virtue include perseverance, courage, integrity, compassion, candor, fidelity, prudence, public-spiritedness, justice, and humility (May 1984).

When an ethics of virtue informs a corporate culture, a shared theory of goods and a common consensus on the hierarchy of goods guides organizational life. The Johnson & Johnson credo expresses this lucidly when it states that the "first responsibility" is to customers and their welfare and the company's last responsibility is to stockholders and their need for profit (see Exhibit 1). The credo offers a vision of how Johnson & Johnson's efforts fit in with the good life that all seek for themselves and their loved ones living in a community. Rules and principles take on meaning, in that they are designed to promote and protect a humane way of life with all its values as they

# Our Credo

We believe our first responsibility is to the doctors, nurses and patients,
to mothers and fathers and all others who use our products and services.
In meeting their needs everything we do must be of high quality.
We must constantly strive to reduce our costs
in order to maintain reasonable prices.
Customers' orders must be serviced promptly and accurately.
Our suppliers and distributors must have an opportunity
to make a fair profit.

We are responsible to our employees,
the men and women who work with us throughout the world.
Everyone must be considered as an individual.
We must respect their dignity and recognize their merit.
They must have a sense of security in their jobs.
Compensation must be fair and adequate,
and working conditions clean, orderly and safe.
We must be mindful of ways to help our employees fulfill
their family responsibilities.
Employees must feel free to make suggestions and complaints.
There must be equal opportunity for employment, development
and advancement for those qualified.
We must provide competent management,
and their actions must be just and ethical.

We are responsible to the communities in which we live and work
and to the world community as well.
We must be good citizens — support good works and charities
and bear our fair share of taxes.
We must encourage civic improvements and better health and education.
We must maintain in good order
the property we are privileged to use,
protecting the environment and natural resources.

Our final responsibility is to our stockholders.
Business must make a sound profit.
We must experiment with new ideas.
Research must be carried on, innovative programs developed
and mistakes paid for.
New equipment must be purchased, new facilities provided
and new products launched.
Reserves must be created to provide for adverse times.
When we operate according to these principles,
the stockholders should realize a fair return.

*Johnson & Johnson*

are understood in the community of men and women living and working together. Concern for human welfare, as specified in the hierarchy of values elucidated in the credo, becomes the very glue that holds the firm and its purposes together.

The import of this discussion of virtue ethics may be further informed by returning to the Robin and Reidenbach article. Following a familiar pattern, the rationale offered as to why marketers ought to respond to society's demands is that, if they do not, further regulations likely will be enacted. Why, then, use the values of the family as a yardstick for business organizations? Is the only reason political (that is, to forestall the restrictive regulation that angry consumers might demand), or are there moral reasons (Frederick 1986; Epstein 1987)? Clearly there are, says the theory of virtue, for, on some level, the values or virtues that prevail in family life must permeate all of society if we are to avoid being overcome by greed and corruption.

The case of Nestle's sale of infant formula in developing countries is cited by Robin and Reidenbach (1987) as an illustration of how deontological arguments prevailed over utilitarian arguments; in the face of consumer pressure, the company finally "agreed to follow the dictates of the World Health Organization (WHO) Code" (p. 50). It is true that the final resolution was company adherence to the WHO Code, and it is probable that the force of moral arguments aroused the citizenry to consumer boycotts and other pressures which finally forced the company to comply. While compelling moral reasons may have marshalled the opposition to Nestle, however, these reasons are not captured clearly in the trade-off model of the two theories of principles (deontological and utilitarian) presented. A theory of virtue may provide deeper insight into the problem at Nestle and some direction for the future.

Nestle's failure was not that the firm did not *know* deontological reasoning and ethical core values; it probably can be safely assumed that management in the Swiss-based company was quite familiar with this scenario, if only because they had been hearing it from the activist opponents for almost six years before agreeing to conform to the WHO Code. Stressing the freedom of choice of consumers, Nestle management never seemed to give much weight to the fact the most Third World mothers did not have the capacity to make an informed choice about infant formula or to use the product safely. Even after it became clear that consumers were using the product incorrectly, Nestle still did not see the issue as its problem.

Unlike the credo-inspired corporate culture of fidelity of Johnson & Johnson, Nestle seemed to be operating with the outdated notion of *caveat emptor* (let the buyer beware). When the virtue of fidelity serves as the glue of a business organization, there is a promise by the business to its public that every effort will be made to look out for human welfare within the limits of its operation. The Johnson & Johnson Tylenol withdrawal was not so much a matter of telling the truth (principled action) as it was a matter of being true to this promise (virtuous action). Nestle management took its stand on freedom (principled action), but seemed to lack those qualities of character (such as prudence) which help orient one to the appropriate principle for the reality in question. The use of deontological reasoning makes it clear that Nestle had a blind spot, but this approach itself is not the remedy for the malady. An ethics of virtue helps make this apparent blindness understandable and points toward its cure.

## AN ETHICS OF VIRTUE

An ethics of virtue assumes that being human entails living in community and developing certain virtues or skills required for a humane life with others. By trial and error, human reason arrives at certain core virtues for community living—such character traits as honesty, truthfulness, compassion, loyalty, and justice. Various capacities have been highlighted during different eras; for example, the classical virtues discussed by Plato, Aristotle, and Cicero were prudence, justice, courage, and temperance. To be sure, the world view of Aristotle and his time is far from our own, but the theory of virtue still has much relevance.

In the ethics of virtue, or character, such traits or moral virtues as compassion, loyalty, and justice shape a person's vision. There is some truth to the saying that "only the good person knows the good"; only a person who has developed the moral virtues, who is compassionate, just, and so on, will perceive the right moral dilemmas and make correct judgments. Of course, these are not new ideas. Aristotle, particularly in the *Nicomachaen Ethics* (Irwin 1985) and the *Politics*, advanced an ethics that has much to say to our times:

> ...the same things do not seem sweet to a man in a fever and a healthy man—nor hot to a weak man and one in good condition. The same happens in other cases. But in all such matters that which appears to the good man is thought to be really so (Bk. X, Ch. 5, 1176a).

For Aristotle, virtues make a person good, and virtue entails affectivity; affectivity influences one's ability to "see" the moral dimensions of a situation:

> For to feel delight and pain rightly or wrongly has no small effect on our actions (Bk. II, Ch. 2, 1105a).

Affectivity, however, is learned behavior:

> Hence we ought to have been brought up in a particular way from our youth, as Plato says, so as both to delight in and to be pained by the things that we ought; for this is right education (Bk. II, Ch. 2, 1104b).

In a theory of virtue, the rightness or wrongness of an action, such as a TV advertisement, would be tied to how that ad likely would shape the viewers. Moral virtue is understood to be essential to making good assessments and judgments; that is, without having cultivated generosity, compassion, forgiveness, and so on, one will not "see" all that is there. With moral virtue, the intellect is affectively qualified in that it is attentive to certain features of experience which it otherwise might miss or undervalue.

A theory of virtue enables business organizations to develop consciously their own ethical corporate culture (see Williams and Houck 1978; Williams 1984). A business organization can so shape persons that they do not "see" the ethical dimensions of the professional world. When efficiency and productivity are the only values reinforced in the organization, people slowly are molded to do whatever will "get the job done", without adverting to broader considerations. Treating people functionally gradually may constrict their perspective so that their "world" is essentially functional. This can affect the features of their experience to which they attend and, consequently, how they describe situations. For example, a long-time employee who is not performing adequately in his or her present position may be seen as an "incompetent who must be fired" or as "a person in the wrong position who must be reassigned." To a large extent, it depends upon whether the cultural distortions of functionality and rationality dominate, or whether sensitivity to human dignity is shaping one's vision.

Most attempts to integrate the ethical dimension into the corporate culture concentrate on the two major theories of obligation without adverting to the integrative possibilities of the more comprehensive theory of virtue. What constitutes "good" and "ethical" marketing? In the commonly employed theories of obligation, the deontological and the utilitarian, this question is answered by referring to the standards of right and wrong, where rightness or wrongness is determined by rules and principles or by some assessment of the consequences of a practice. In theory of virtue, however, the central questions are "what sort of person am I shaping?" and "what sort of organization am I shaping?" by this proposed decision or policy. Thus the perspective of this ethical system is that all rules and principles are, at root, an attempt to preserve a human way of life; thus, our most fundamental task in ethics today is not primarily concerned with analyzing situations so that one can make the right decisions, but rather with reflecting on what constitutes the good life. The moral life is not so much a matter of thinking clearly as it is a way of "seeing" the world. The Johnson

& Johnson credo is a good example of an attempt to provide a humane world view for all constituencies.

The problem at Nestle was not that decision makers were not thinking clearly, but rather that managers were adverting to the wrong features of their experience. This is a problem explicitly addressed by the formation of an ethical corporate culture, for the culture does, indeed, shape one's vision. Underpinned by a theory of virtue, an ethical corporate culture, through an ingrained set of habits and perspectives, trains all those in its purview to see things in a certain way and hence is likely to predispose them toward ethical behavior.

In a theory of virtue, there is much attention to role models. The insight here is that being an ethical person is not simply an analytical and rational matter. It takes virtuous people to make right decisions, and virtue is learned by doing. Aristotle discussed the lives of obviously good Athenians in order to teach ethics. One learned the right thing to do by observing good people and by doing what they do.

> ...but the virtues we get by first exercising them, as also happens in the case of the arts as well. For the things we have to learn before we can do them, we learn by doing them, e.g. men become builders by building and lyre-players by playing the lyre; so too we become just by doing just acts, temperate by doing temperate acts, brave by doing brave acts (Bk. II, Ch. 1, 1103a).

The companies acclaimed for their ethical corporate culture most often can trace their heritage to one or several founders who were intent on managing an organization that respected human dignity and insisted on a humane way of life. Founders of such companies as Johnson & Johnson and Hewlett-Packard shaped their organizations so that they embodied the values and virtues that proved personally rewarding. The way of life in the company was not a result of a core values analysis or a code of conduct; rather, these vehicles were a later attempt to spell out exactly what was at the heart of the corporate culture already under way. For example, Bill Hewlett and Dave Packard did not formulate their company values in writing until after 20 years of operation. Only then, in order to ensure the the culture not be lost as the founders became more removed from the expanding work force, did top management draw up a statement of corporate values, initiate training seminars in the "HP Way," and install accountability procedures (Williams 1986).

For companies without a heritage of the Hewlett-Packard or Johnson & Johnson type, Robin and Reidenbach (1987) have provided some helpful practical steps to begin to develop an ethical corporate culture. They have not, however, delineated an ethical theory which can offer an account of what is happening in such a culture; the contention here is that the ethics of virtue is such a theory.

While principles are clearly essential to help guide the ethical choices of the decision maker, "principles without traits are impotent," in the words of a renowned philosopher (Frankena 1974, 65). Principles, whether they be of a deontological or utilitarian variety, need a context, a vision of what constitutes the good life. For example, the principle "be caring" would be understood one way by Ivan Boesky and quite another way by John Phelan, Jr., chairman of the board of the New York Stock Exchange and a leading exponent of ethical conduct on the "Street". The same principle would have different meanings for persons with divergent horizons of interpretation. The principle was designed to preserve a humane way of life in community, but it will only function in that fashion if its user has a vision of such a community in mind.

Actually, it is ingenuous to suggest the family as the horizon for interpreting moral principles for a business organization (Robin and Reidenbach 1987). The family unit is the one place where our humanity is evoked and virtuous relationships are almost always in place, at least as an ideal. The sense of what constitutes caring or honesty or most other virtues is easily grasped by looking to the family. A theory of virtue highlights the moral obligation to bring some of the virtues we all experience in the family into the workplace, as Hewlett-Packard has done. This is just another way of saying that a business organization ought to be a humane community. To be sure, one must be reasonable, and there is no iron-clad method for determining how much caring is required, but virtuous people can make prudent decisions.

## JOHNSON & JOHNSON: SOME FURTHER REFLECTIONS

As noted above, one company often singled out for its well-developed system of core values is Johnson & Johnson. While this assessment is accurate, it is more important to ask: From where do these values emanate, and how are they supported and sustained? The theory of virtue sheds light and offers an understanding of exemplary corporate cultures.

From its founding a century ago by three brothers, Johnson & Johnson has grown to a multinational firm with sales of more than $7 billion. The company operates 160 businesses in more than 50 countries. The hallmarks of the organization are that it is managed with a long-run view, decentralization is a key management philosophy, and the Johnson & Johnson credo (Exhibit 1) guides its business activities. Many of the phrases in the credo delineate what this company interprets as its hierarchy of "goods" and how the organization shapes the values of its stakeholders. The credo was first instituted in 1945 and has been revised twice since then. At the request of the then chairman, James Burke, the credo was "challenged" in the 1970s by Johnson & Johnson managers, and the consequence was basically an affirmation of it. The exercise resulted in a new 1979 credo with slight rewording of the previous one.

The company's reactions to the Tylenol poisonings of 1981 and 1984 are viewed by many observers as representing the type of responsible behavior all companies should exemplify. The firm's recall of the Tylenol capsules was a result of the culture in place at Johnson & Johnson for a long time and was more than just clear reasoning about the company values. One senior executive expressed the firm's perspective well when he said, "We never really thought we had much of a choice in the matter of the recall. Our code of conduct [credo] was such a way of life in the firm that our employees, including me, would have been scandalized had we taken another course. We never seriously considered avoiding the costly recall" (Nash 1988). The Johnson & Johnson decision was determined largely, then, by the firm's way of seeing the problem and its ingrained habits (not by reasoning about core ethical values). Virtues such as courage, compassion, and lucidity, long operative in the organization, came to the foreground in the quandary over the Tylenol crisis.[2]

---

[2] The most recent information indicates that the Tylenol brand was ranked the highest in terms of quality by a consumer study (Lipman 1989) and held the largest market share (27% versus 12% for second place) in the pain-remedy category (Deveny 1990).

A second illustration of Johnson & Johnson's virtuous corporate culture is found in the decision concerning operations in South Africa. After a careful moral analysis, the company decided to maintain its plants and investment there. Several constituencies in the United States have pressed strongly for disinvestment, but the firm disagrees on moral grounds and has not yielded to the pressure. Because of Johnson & Johnson's ethical corporate culture and long-standing commitment to humane values, their response has not been criticized, for the most part, even by those who justifiably hold a contrary position. Often it is in those cases where a theory of principle does not yield an answer compelling to all that a virtuous organization is readily apparent. Human strengths keep the argument about principles from taking a destructive tack; humility, intellectual caution, and good faith are virtues that preserve a humane community even while the dispute goes on.

A third example pertains to a successful advertising campaign that ran a decade ago for Johnson & Johnson Baby Oil (Baby, Baby! Turn on the Tan with Johnson's). At that time there was little concern about the sun's harmful effects on the skin. A medical acquaintance of a Johnson & Johnson executive later pointed out initial evidence that tanning might be harmful and that, since baby oil increases the rate of the burning and tanning process, the product could be indirectly harmful. After further investigation, Johnson & Johnson executives found this was the case and dropped the campaign. As the executive who made the decision stated, "It simply would be wrong to entice people to harm themselves" (Nash 1988, 98). To be sure, this was principled action, but action brought to the fore by the virtues of courage and integrity.

These examples convey how one company's behavior can be understood in the light of a theory of virtue. The pervasiveness of the Johnson & Johnson credo throughout the organization and the consistent ethical focus by managers show how moral reasoning is shaped by a virtuous environment and how that, in turn, influences managerial decision making.

## MARKETING AND THE THEORY OF VIRTUE

The theory of virtue has a bearing on the type of marketing mix decisions a company or manager makes. Implications for product, pricing, channel, and promotional decisions emanate from this theory. For product decisions, the theory of virtue would emphasize the product's effect on consumers' lives. Does the product pose potential harm to the consumer? For certain products, an especially vulnerable segment of the population may be harmed. What about targeting cigarette ads to young women or blacks, alcohol to young men, pornography to juveniles? In these cases, is there not a strong possibility of eroding the formation of virtue in a young life and of stunting public spiritedness and citizenship in the future? The theory of virtue thus highlights the need for marketers to consider how consumers are being affected by each product. We suggest that marketers should not sell products that retard character or virtue development.

The pricing area has received little attention from ethics scholars (Kehoe 1985). The theories of obligation as well as the theory of virtue would require marketers to place price in a perspective understandable to the potential market. For example, confusing airline fares and auto company financing plans may not meet the moral requirements of pricing products. Yet, complex fares may be viewed as more ethical (that is, virtuous) than a single monopoly price charged to consumers (as happened prior to deregulation), and multiple financing plans could be more ethical than a simple but very expensive one. Furthermore, the theory of virtue would emphasize the price-value trade-off about which consumers are concerned when entering into the exchange process for products. For example, clear delineation of list price, discounted price, and exceptions by retailers would embrace the spirit of the theory of virtue. It is interesting to note that these areas are being studied by the Better Business Bureau and a group of influential retailers (*Advertising Age* 1989).

The channel of distribution can present many ethical dilemmas for marketers because of the multiple intermediaries and the complex relationships among channel members that often exist. The theory of virtue would place priority on honesty and cooperation in dealings between channel members rather than on the coercion and conflict often cited. Furthermore, the move toward relational (that is, relationship-based) exchanges in the channel should be more conducive to virtuous behavior

(Gundlach and Murphy 1990). Larger organizations in the channel, which are growing in number, would not attempt unduly to coerce smaller ones if they were to follow this theory.

The theory of virtue also can be applied to the promotion element of the marketing mix. For personal selling, the emphasis would be on positive character traits, such as honesty, integrity, justice, and prudence. These are undervalued by companies that want aggressive, high pressure, short-term results oriented salespeople. Managers wishing to employ the theory of virtue might investigate how sales training and positive customer experiences can enhance sales results. The relationship that salespersons have with consumers also would be shaped by the theory of virtue. Consumers would be viewed as partners in the exchange process and not potential adversaries or pawns in the sales game. It appears that industrial salespeople often take a more "virtuous" stance because their relationship with customers is ongoing.

Advertising ethics also would take a different approach with an application of the theory of virtue. For example, a recent article on ethics in advertising examined how one should make a moral appraisal of advertising (Lee 1987). The literature is divided among those who believe that persuasive advertising is (1) moral as long as it promotes a useful or essential product, (2) never good, and (3) good as long as it does not affect individual autonomy. None of these positions adequately reflects the theory of virtue, which is concerned with how the person is being shaped, how the consumer's character may by formed by the advertisement.

The theory of virtue would demand that managers think about how advertising influences recipients. There is a growing concern by some professionals that through marketing, and especially advertising, people are being shaped and formed in inappropriate and perhaps harmful ways. For example, consider the views of psychiatrist Thomas Radecki, research director for the National Coalition on Television Violence, who argues that restrictions must be placed on the marketing of war toys on television. He cites substantial studies indicating that the massive promotion of war toys "encourages violent ways of interacting with the world." More hitting, selfishness, and cruelty to animals are evidenced in children exposed to such television, according to Radecki. While this is still a controversial finding, it highlights an increasing focus on the influences that shape young character or virtues.

Today, a whole new set of demands flow from a broader understanding of ethics, and these demands will pose a continuing quandary for marketers unless there is a genuine comprehension of the critics' positions. For example, advocates of less aggression, violence, and sex in advertising have an understanding of what constitutes "good" and "ethical" advertising that is well grounded in an ethics of virtue. It is in the marketer's interest to be familiar with this approach to ethics.

International marketing ethics are compounded by cultural, religious, social, and language differences, but the theory of virtue offers universal traits that can be applied across cultures. Exceptions obviously exist, but treating consumers with compassion, respect, and integrity would seem to transcend international boundaries. For example, Dow Corning conducts "ethical audits" at its plants and sales offices worldwide to make sure that the company's values statement is interpreted consistently everywhere. Likewise, many of the suspect practices of international marketers, such as product dumping and inadequate product usage information for infant formula, clearly violate the precepts of the theory of virtue.

## CONCLUSION

This article has summarized how ethical theory has influenced the marketing ethics literature. The major premise is that ethical analysis could be improved with a focus on the theory of virtue. Furthermore, the article has spelled out in detail what the theory of virtue is and how it can play a central role in the ethical development of marketers. It also shows how certain companies known for ethical behavior, in particular Johnson & Johnson, are much better understood in the light of a theory of virtue than from the perspectives of the other philosophical theories. The article also includes a discussion of how the theory of virtue could influence the marketing strategies used by companies.

Future research could build on the foundation developed here. An in-depth comparison of this theory with deontological and teleological theories could be used to evaluate specific marketing actions. Further study is also needed to determine how the theory of virtue might best complement other ethical theories (Beauchamp 1982, 163). Finally, this traditional ethical theory needs to be evaluated relative to other ethical approaches (Kohlberg 1969; Rest 1986) to see if they add specificity to this broad notion. The theory of virtue has much applicability to marketing ethics; even though more work needs to be done, the theory provides needed answers to the debate concerning a more ethical marketing system.

## REFERENCES

*Advertising Age* (1989). "Retail Code Worth the Price." 25 September.

Beauchamp, Tom L. (1982). *Philosophical Ethics: An Introduction to Moral Philosophy*. New York: McGraw-Hill.

Cavanagh, G. F., D. J. Moberg, and M. Velasquez (1981). "The Ethics of Organizational Politics." *Academy of Management Review*, 6 (July): 363-74.

Deveny, Kathleen (1990). "Painkiller Ads Strive to Give Foes Headaches." *Wall Street Journal*, 23 January: B1.

Epstein, Edwin (1987). "The Corporate Social Policy Process: Beyond Business Ethics, Corporate Social Responsibility, and Corporate Social Responsiveness." *California Management Review*, 29 (Spring): 99-114.

Ferrell, O. C. and L. Gresham (1985). "A Contingency Framework for Understanding Ethical Decision Making in Marketing." *Journal of Marketing*, 49 (Summer): 87-96.

Ferrell, O. C., L. G. Gresham, and J. Fraedrich (1989). "A Synthesis of Ethical Decision Models for Marketing." *Journal of Macromarketing*, 9 (Fall): 55-64.

Frankena, William K. (1974). *Ethics*, 2d ed. Englewood Cliffs, NJ: Prentice-Hall.

Frederick, William (1986). "Toward CSR2: Why Ethical Analysis Is Indispensable and Unavoidable in Corporate Affairs." *California Management Review*, 28 (Winter): 126-41, 152-53.

Fritzsche, D. and H. Becker (1984). "Linking Management Behavior to Ethical Philosophy—An Empirical Investigation." *Academy of Management Journal*, 27 (1): 166-75.

Garrett, Thomas (1966). *Business Ethics*. Englewood Cliffs, NJ: Prentice-Hall.

Gundlach, Gregory T. and Patrick E. Murphy (1990). "Ethical and Legal Foundations of Exchange." A paper presented to the Winter American Marketing Association Educators' Conference.

Hunt, S. D. and S. Vitell (1986). "A General Theory of Marketing Ethics." *Journal of Macromarketing*, 6 (Spring): 5-16.

Irwin, Terence, trans. (1985). *Nicomachean Ethics*, by Aristotle. Indianapolis: Hackett.

Kehoe, William J. (1985). "Ethics, Price Fixing, and the Management of Price Strategy." In *Marketing Ethics: Guidelines for Managers*, G. R. Laczniak and P. E. Murphy, eds. Lexington, MA: Lexington Books, pp. 71-83.

Kimmel, Allan J. (1988). *Ethics and Values in Applied Social Research*. Beverly Hills: Sage.

Kohlberg, L. (1969). "State and Sequence: The Cognitive Developmental Approach to Socialization." In *Handbook of Socialization Theory and Research*, D. A. Goslin, ed. Chicago: Rand McNally, pp. 347-480.

Laczniak, G. R. (1983). "Frameworks for Analyzing Marketing Ethics." *Journal of Macromarketing*, 5 (Spring): 7-17.

Lee, Kam Hon (1987). "The Informative and Persuasive Functions of Advertising: A Moral Appraisal—A Further Comment." *Journal of Business Ethics*, 6 (January): 55-57.

Lipman, Joanne (1989). "Top Brands Rank Low in Study of Quality." *Wall Street Journal*, 6 June: B5.

MacIntyre, Alasdair (1981). *After Virtue*. Notre Dame: University of Notre Dame Press.

May, William F. (1984). "The Virtues in a Professional Setting." *Soundings*, 67 (Fall): 245-66.

Murphy, Patrick E. and Gene R. Laczniak (1981). "Marketing Ethics: A Review with Implications for Managers, Educators, and Researchers." In *Review of Marketing*, B. Enis and K. Roering, eds. Chicago: American Marketing Association, pp. 251-66.

Murphy, Patrick E. and Dee Pridgen (1990). "Ethical and Legal Issues in Marketing." *Advances in Marketing and Public Policy*, forthcoming.

Nash, Laura L. (1988). "Johnson & Johnson's Credo." In *Corporate Ethics: A Prime Business Asset*, The Business Roundtable, ed., February: 77-104.

Piest, Oskar, ed. (1957). *John Stewart Mill, Utilitarianism*. New York: Macmillan.

Rawls, John (1971). *A Theory of Justice*. Cambridge: Harvard University Press.

Rest, James R. (1986). *Moral Development: Advances in Research and Theory*. New York: Praeger.

Robin Donald, Michael Giallourakis, Fred R. David, and Thomas E. Moritz (1989). *Business Horizons*. 32 (January-February): 66-73.

Robin, Donald P. and R. Eric Reidenbach (1987). "Social Responsibility, Ethics, and Marketing Strategy: Closing the Gap between Concept and Application." *Journal of Marketing*, 51 (January): 44-58.

——— (1988). "A Framework for Analyzing Ethical Issues in Marketing." *Business and Professional Ethics Journal*, 5 (2): 3-22.

Ross, William David (1930). *The Right and the Good*. Oxford: Clarendon Press.

Uttal, B. (1983). "The Corporate Culture Vultures." *Fortune*, 108 (October): 66-72.

Williams, Oliver F. (1984). "Who Cast the First Stone?" *Harvard Business Review*, 62 (5): 151-60.

——— (1986). "Can Business Ethics Be Theological? What Athens Can Learn from Jerusalem." *Journal of Business Ethics*, 5 (December): 473-84.

Williams, Oliver R. and John W. Houck (1978). *Full Value*. San Francisco: Harper and Row.

Wolff, Robert Paul, ed. (1985). *Foundations of the Metaphysics of Morals*, by Immanuel Kant. New York: Macmillan.

# Marketing

## WITH

# Integrity

*A marketplace of noise and hype
makes an effective backdrop for marketing
with integrity. When you believe in
the inherent worth of your products and customers,
and clearly demonstrate that belief,
customers will beat a path
to your door.*

TERRY MANDEL,
WITH MARJORIE KELLY

*Terry Mandel, a marketing consultant and speaker, conducts regular workshops in marketing with integrity, and works with a broad variety of clients on applying these principles in business. Her clients have included* Yoga Journal, *New Dimensions Foundation, The Earthwise Consumer, Hewlett-Packard, Providence Medical Center, and Tektronix.*

*Terry Mandel Communications, 864 26th Ave., San Francisco, CA 94121. Phone 415/668-7028.*

P eople are hungrier than ever for real human contact. But so much of what's done in business has to do with transactions rather than relationships. When people talk, for example, about getting employees to "buy in" to the company mission, they're using terms of commerce to talk about something that is fundamentally spiritual. This misuse of language trivializes people and their contributions, and it keeps work from being truly fulfilling.

Outside the organization, the same thing is happening. Everyday we're overwhelmed by massive amounts of information and advertising, most of it boring, much of it demeaning. We've been bombarded with lies so long, truth has become a novelty. And as Paul Hawken says in *Growing a Business*, "In a way, the junk ads are a boon to the honest, no-nonsense marketer. Honest copy and ads come across as refreshing change: we immediately recognize the authenticity and are disarmed."

Nothing builds trust more than au-thenticity. It's an interesting word, "authenticity"—it comes from the Greek for "author." So how might we become authorities about ourselves? We can start by asking, If I were my own customer, what would I want? How could I approach myself in a way that would be disarming? As we come to know ourselves, we realize perhaps others feel as we do: inspired or untouched or offended as we are by various ads and approaches.

## MOVING FROM TRANSACTIONS TO RELATIONSHIPS

T he key is to build relationships with customers, not simply as a better way to get them to buy products, but because you value them as fellow human beings. It means respecting their time and intelligence, communicating clearly who you are and what your product is, and trusting that the right people will be drawn to it.

The risk here, of course, is that customers—and this can be the internal customers, the employees—may realize what you're offering really isn't appropriate for them. It doesn't fulfill them as deeply as they had hoped. So they go elsewhere. But you see, if you truly want the best for your people, and you truly want the best for your vision, you'll be very happy to support them in going elsewhere. That only opens the door for the people who really do want to support you.

This requires a shift from control to trust. When you stop using external means to pull people and start trusting the momentum of your inner vision to attract them, you move into an entirely different way of doing business: from a transactional stance to a relational one.

You must believe that whatever you produce is of such inherent value that the question is not, How can we convince the most people to buy this? but rather, Where will we find the people who are waiting for it? The product is diminished if you don't care whether it goes to a "good home" somewhere. If you don't respect what you do, others won't either.

In advertising, the question is: Are you trying to push people by using fear and distortion, or are you attracting them with trust and clarity?

In selling, the question is: Can you imagine that being yourself is enough? That's the secret of great salespeople—that they show who they are. Wouldn't all of us rather talk to a real person on the phone, someone who will tell us the truth?

Traditional marketing relies on commotion—excitement, agitation—because it takes a huge amount of energy to move something that's stuck. Marketing with integrity can be much quieter, because it takes just a little, well-directed push to move something that's already inclined your way. The essence of marketing with integrity is pro-motion: encouraging natural, positive motion.

## BALANCING OUTER EXPRESSION WITH INNER TRUTH

Marketing has traditionally focused on cultivating a company's outer face, but the more critical task is to balance outer expression with inner work. Image and substance must form a cohesive whole. How valuable is a carefully crafted mission statement if employees snicker about it in the lunchroom? Or the slick advertising campaign, if it raises customers' expectations only to disappoint them?

Everything we do and say communicates what we value. We market our beliefs as much as our products or services. Tom Peters points out that the least-valued employee often has the greatest influence on the customer's experience. We must be certain that employees have an experience consistent with what our advertising promises customers.

One of my favorite illustrations of balancing mission and message is Patagonia, the enormously successful company that sells climbing and outdoor gear. They have a separate toll-free number people can call to talk about climbing—and until recently it was their only toll-free number; to place an order, you had to pay for the call. Their catalogue also features real people doing real things: climbing, kayaking, hiking. The business is clearly a vehicle for supporting a community of people who love mountaineering, and everything they say and do communicates that.

## GETTING OUT OF THE MIND-SET OF GETTING THINGS DONE

When clients come to me, most are focused on a specific result: a direct mail package, a public relations program, an advertising campaign. But marketing with integrity is not just about getting things done; it explores how what we do fits into the larger context of who we are and what we value. Sometimes this means you have to be more committed to your truth than to getting something done next Thursday. This is deep work that not everyone wants to do, and people must go at their own pace.

When we take the time to ask provocative questions, and resist the temptation to rush into action, we're rewarded with clarity, focus—and results. When I worked with *Yoga Journal* on a new direct mail package, I asked them, Do you want to go deeper into the yoga community or reach out to a non-yoga audience? They wrestled with the implications of this seemingly straightforward question for months; it had unwittingly touched on deep philosophical issues that needed airing.

The clarity that resulted didn't change their mission, but did move the spotlight. Previously, they had been mailing a package that used back pain as the motivator, and the message was inconsistent with the magazine's positive editorial approach. Even the look was inconsistent; it had the feel of AM radio hype. The teaser on the new package—"Just say the magic words and we'll leave you in peace"—was more an expression of their essence, because that's what the magazine promotes: peace and tranquility. It's proven successful in reaching the broader audience they decided to target—and it's bringing in more money, *faster,* than the old package.

## RELYING MORE ON INNER GUIDANCE

As a consultant, my initial focus has shifted from solving problems to asking questions, challenging the client to explore new territory. Implicit in marketing with integrity is decreasing reliance on outside experts and increasing reliance on inner guidance. Traditional marketing asks, "What do people want?" But when we also ask, "What is it I/we fundamentally and uniquely have to offer?" the only place to find the answer is inside. I can help frame and support the exploration, but I can't presume to know that inner terrain.

In my workshops, I devote a significant amount of time to this kind of inner work. In guided meditations, participants explore unconscious beliefs and assumptions—which tend to mirror the marketing practices they deplore—and reconnect with their deep sense of life purpose. These profound personal discoveries serve as deep roots, supporting the growth of a healthier organization that communicates its aliveness through every branch and flower.

Of course, doing deep inner work doesn't imply that every realization or insight is appropriately brought into the public eye. Marketing with integrity is practiced by truth-telling, not soul-bearing.

I hasten to add that, while I value process, I'm very results-oriented. The point isn't to replace our focus on tasks with a focus on process, but to recognize that getting things done well in the outer world is enhanced by attending to our inner world. Intuition is becoming an accepted tool in business decision-making not by replacing analysis, but by supplementing it.

## LETTING GO OF THE MYTH OF COMPETITION

The myth of competition is that there's somebody out there who will take away what I want if I don't grab it first. But as long as we subscribe to the metaphor of "them and us," we're stuck in a mind-set that diverts energy away from pursuing our uniqueness—which is our true competitive edge. We're also in danger of approaching customers as if they're "them," some anonymous group we must coerce into taking the action we want.

By switching instead to a metaphor of "we're all in this together," we restore competition to its original meaning of "striving together." Then competitors become mirrors for us of where we need to strengthen our product or service, and of how we can polish our uniqueness.

Marshall McLuhan was absolutely right when he said that the medium is the message. But giving voice to the inner spark, being willing to speak from the heart and spirit, is not easy. The issue that arises time and time again in my work is the fear of being different, the fear of having to change. Underneath that fear lies an issue of self-esteem. The real barrier to speaking our truths, without worrying what others think, seems to be the question: Do I have the right? What gives me the right to do that? This seems to be a nearly universal concern.

The challenge when we bump up against our self-limiting or contradictory beliefs is to recognize the opportunity for growth, rather than beating up on ourselves. Too often, we judge ourselves for the very ways we're different from others. None of us is special—in the sense of better than—but each of us is wonderfully unique. And cultivating our quirks really helps people tell us apart from everyone else, which is the whole aim of marketing, isn't it?

I recall the story of Rabbi Zusya, who on his deathbed said: "In the coming world, they will not ask me, 'Why were you not Moses?' They will ask me, 'Why were you not Zusya?'"

# Marketing By Professionals:
# Some Ethical Issues and Prescriptions

**Patrick E. Murphy, Ph.D. and Gene R. Laczniak, Ph.D.**

*Patrick E. Murphy, Ph.D., is a Professor of Marketing at The University of Notre Dame in Notre Dame, Indiana. Gene R. Laczniak, Ph.D., is a Professor of Business at Marquette University in Milwaukee, Wisconsin.*

## Introduction

Ethical issues facing the professions is a relatively longstanding concern. It is common practice to mention the "professional obligation" of certain practitioners to behave ethically. Examples of such professional duties are the obligations of medicine to provide health, of law to provide justice and of clergy to provide spiritual guidance. Another almost universal characteristic of the professions is the presence of a formal code of ethics and the existence of enforcement mechanisms for the code. We focus here, though, mostly on ethical questions revolving around the marketing and advertising techniques used by professionals such as accountants, dentists, lawyers and physicians.

The use of marketing and advertising techniques by professionals is an emotional and controversial topic. As Exhibit 1 recounts, the debate has raged for some time. From the Supreme Court decisions in 1976 (*Virginia State Board of Pharmacy v. Virginia Citizens Consumer Council*) and in 1977 (*Bates v. State Bar of Arizona*) that struck down prohibitions on such advertising, this issue has generated much debate in various professional communities. Feelings run deep on both sides, as exemplified by the following comment by former Chief Justice Warren Burger: "The public should never, never, never employ a lawyer or doctor who finds it necessary to advertise." His statement can be contrasted with one by a FTC official who said: "At bottom, the prejudice against advertising is that it creates pressure to compete." Related to the competition issue, is the feeling that advertising will place undue emphasis on price at the expense of the provider's quality of service. A final point of contention is that consumers seem generally much more favorably disposed to the use of advertising than many professionals.

In this article, we review the forces that have and will cause professionals to increase their marketing and advertising expenditures. We summarize the arguments for and against the use of these techniques. Then, we examine a few specific ethical issues relating to accountants, lawyers and the medical community. We conclude with **Ideas for Executive Action**, which should help advertising and marketing by professionals remain on a high ethical plane.

### Exhibit 1

### Legal Advertising: An Old Controversy

Over half a century ago, James F. Brennan, a California attorney, wrote a spirited argument against the prohibition, legal advertising and solicitation of clients by lawyers. Young, inexperienced, poor lawyers, he said, are forbidden to advertise or to solicit clients. But there is a sense in which this is *not* true of those attorneys who are wealthy and well established. The wealthy lawyer goes to his club and solicits the business of other wealthy persons on the golf course, at poolside, during dinner, at cocktail parties, and at other social functions. Because he has plenty of leisure, he may join philanthropic organizations and, through his activities there, may meet other persons who may be inclined, after talking to him, to retain his services.

Moreover, many lawyers work for large firms, engaged not exclusively in the practice of law but in other forms of activity closely related to law. Such firms and associations as banks, insurance companies, brokerage houses, utilities, unions, and large corporations of every kind may have one or more lawyers on their payrolls. Banks and insurance companies may advertise services related to setting up trusts and drawing up wills, all of which is the kind of work that is best done by lawyers and is likely to be done by the company's attorneys or in consultation with them. Thus, *these* attorneys benefit from the advertising done by the companies or associations with which they are affiliated; but the novice who is attempting to set up a solo practice is forbidden to advertise or to solicit.

Still others are fortunate enough to marry into the law business or to inherit one. They can afford to entertain the people who have lucrative law business to give.

All of this, Brennan said, was unfair to the impoverished young lawyer when he is denied the right to solicit business in the only way open to him. Even worse, he pointed out, was the fact that the bar associations were loaded with lawyers who worked for the big casualty insurers. It was curious, he said, that they were so eager to prevent others from soliciting business.

> Is it for the public interest or for their own interest? If the injured party has no independent legal advice as to his legal rights, these casualty insurance companies can settle with him on what they advise him his legal rights are.....If (plaintiffs') attorneys file more than three personal injury cases in one year, an investigation is made in the county clerk's office and elsewhere to ascertain how they got their cases. Why not investigate attorneys for bank and trust companies, title insurance companies and casualty insurance companies to ascertain how they get their cases?

Brennan noted that an attorney may know of legal rights that a party has but of which the party himself is ignorant. Yet, if the attorney informs the party of his legal rights and offers to assist him, he violates the rule and may be disbarred.

From *Business Insights*, Spring/Summer 1990, pp. 5-9. *Business Insights*, published by the Center for Business Development and Research, College of Business Administration, The University of Southern Mississippi.

A poor man should be able to have a lawyer as well as the rich man, and he is more in need of one. The attorney who handles personal injury cases is the poor man's lawyer.

## Forces Stimulating Marketing by Professionals

There are a number of developments in the last two decades that have moved professionals out of their traditional mode of operation. The ones we believe to be the most important are: emerging legal developments, growing competition and marketing's applicability to professional practice in areas such as new service development and franchising.

*Legal Developments.* Historically, most state and national professional organizations historically had prohibitions against advertising in their codes of conduct. The *Virginia Board of Pharmacy* case ruled "unconstitutional" a Virginia statute declaring that advertising of prescription drug prices by any pharmacist constituted unprofessional conduct. The *Bates v. State Bar of Arizona* case challenged the state bar association's ban on publicizing legal fees. The case was appealed to the Supreme Court, and it ruled in June 1977 that attorneys have First Amendment freedom of speech rights to advertise fees for routine services and that consumers have the right to receive such information. But the Court did not foresee major changes in the way that lawyers and other professionals practiced. They wrote: "We suspect that with advertising, most lawyers will behave as they always have. They will abide by their solemn oath to uphold the honor and integrity of the profession and the legal systems." The major professional associations followed the edict of the Court and relaxed advertising restrictions for dentists in 1977, and for the accounting, legal and medical professions in 1978. These decisions, then, set in motion the marketing and advertising of the professions.

Two subsequent Supreme Court cases reaffirmed the right of professionals to advertise. The first decision (the *Zauder* case in 1984) ruled that the use of illustrations or pictures in newspaper advertisements serves an important communicative function. The second case (*Shapero v. Kentucky Bar Association* in 1988) stipulated that states may not prohibit direct mail advertising aimed at specific target markets. The obvious conclusion that can be drawn is that marketing and advertising can now be legally used by professionals to promote their practice.

*Growing Competition.* The world of the 1990s is much more competitive for everyone, including professionals. There appears to be two reasons for this growing level of competition. First, law, architecture, dentistry and several other professions have become overcrowded with the number of new professionals entering the field. Professional schools continue to graduate large numbers of students every year. This means that the newer professionals, especially, must use marketing and advertising techniques to attract clients.

The mentality of most professionals toward promotion has also changed. They have moved from the traditional "country club" contact method of publicizing their service to a more sophisticated marketing perspective. This is not only due to the changing legal climate, but also because they see marketing as a viable mechanism to compete effectively in this changing environment. Competition probably will not diminish in the future, and most professionals (some reluctantly, however) have recognized that marketing and advertising will continue to play a major role in this competitive world.

A third competitive development is the growth in different types of professional providers. Medicine and dentistry were dominated by individual practitioners who did not view themselves as competing directly with their colleagues. Now, in medicine for example, these individual purveyors are competing with clinics, group practices, HMOs as well as hospitals. In the accounting field, the so-called Big Six (reduced from eight) is not only competing with one another, but also with smaller firms, consulting organizations and specialty companies which provide highly specialized services (e.g., auditing for health care organizations). The pressure then is on all types of professional service providers to market themselves more aggressively against the new competitive forms.

*Marketing's Applicability to Professional Practice.* Some professionals have found that marketing concepts such as branding, new service development, alternate delivery mechanisms and franchising can be applied to their situation. If the professional wants to meet the needs of the time conscious and mobile consumer of the 1990s, such new approaches must be explored. Just as Burger King has found consumers to be loyal to their "brand", Humana has found that its brand of medicine is preferred by some consumers. The use of brand or corporate names has made it much easier to franchise legal, dental, optical and medical clinics. Such retailing of the professions began even before the Bates decision, but has gained popularity in the 1980s. Dental World, Omnidentix Systems, Nu Vision Centers and Sterling Optical are some of the best known professional services franchises.

As mentioned, even the more traditional professional practices have expanded their product line and altered their distribution network. For instance, ambulatory surgery, alcoholic rehabilitation, psychological counseling, personal injury law and management consulting by public accounting firms are recent additions to the product portfolio of service providers. Furthermore, professionals have begun using immediate care medical centers, satellite offices and expanded hours to appeal to time conscious consumers. These developments often necessitated some type of advertising to inform consumers of the change in service distribution by the professional.

## 4. ETHICS IN THE MARKETPLACE: Ethical Practices

### The Status of Advertising by Professionals

Though 15 years have passed since the Virginia Board and Bates decisions, the use of marketing and advertising by professionals is still a controversial topic. We now review some of the strongest arguments on both sides of the issue.

*The Case for Advertising by Professionals.* Several arguments can be advanced. Probably the strongest is that consumers demand such information. Individuals are in need of information about legal, medical, optical and dental services. They are used to getting information about other products and services via the newspaper and television. At minimum, consumers want to know the location of the provider and the range of services offered. Word of mouth is still the most effective information source for all products; but dissatisfied consumers, newcomers to an area and the poor may not have access to this source. Consequently, advertising offers them an easily accessible vehicle for gaining information about professionals. From an ethical standpoint, it is argued that according to the principle of distributive justice, the poor, elderly and market illiterates are more likely to be served if advertising of these services is permitted.

A second argument, and the one that legal decisions are mostly based upon, is the First Amendment right of free speech. Professionals should be able to communicate with consumers in any nondeceptive manner that they choose. Critics view advertising as "undignified", but Justice Blackmun noted in the majority opinion of Bates: "The assertion that advertising will diminish the attorney's reputation in the community is open to question. Bankers and engineers advertise, and yet these professions are not regarded as undignified."

Third, proponents contend that the costs to consumers are lower when advertising is present. This is an extension of the competition argument which states that more information in the market place will have the effect of driving down prices. In the absence of advertising, the professionals could collude and keep prices artificially high. The Federal Trade Commission has used this argument extensively and has found in one study that in cities where lawyers intensely advertised, legal fees have declined by 5%—13%. When the FTC analysis is combined with the consumer information argument, supporters suggest that advertising contributes to the efficient functioning of the market place/economy.

A final reason to support increased marketing by professionals is that it allows a new entrant to gain access to the market more easily. In the absence of advertising, it may take years for a new lawyer or accountant, or a new type of practice to make enough contacts to attain a thriving business. A specific example is Hyatt Legal Services, a legal services chain with over 200 offices nationwide employing over 600 attorneys. Hyatt spent several million dollars on T.V. ads using CEO Joel Hyatt as spokesperson to build its client base. Although this firm is one of the most successful, there are undoubtedly many more professionals who received at least modest aid from advertising.

*The Case Against Advertising by Professionals.* The critics of marketing and advertising by professionals articulate a number of variations on a common theme. Namely, it is "unprofessional" for individuals who consider themselves to belong to a professional community to lower themselves to use common business practices. The logical extension of this argument is that advertising undermines the relationship of trust which exists between a professional person and a client. One CPA spokesperson perceives that the best way to build a practice is to get involved in one's community. The emphasis should be on "quality control, not marketing concepts". This critic foresees a long term detrimental impact of the marketing orientation of current CPAs: "By cheapening our profession with distasteful advertising and gimmicks, will we slip undistinguished into the maze of financial service providers who also are certified, i.e., planners, life underwriters, etc.?"

A similar sentiment was expressed by a lawyer who felt that advertising contributes to the negative image of that profession. A survey conducted by a Florida bar association found that professionals are very conscious of their image with the public, and some believe that the "dignity" of the profession is compromised with the use of mass market advertising. The view that marketing by professionals has an impact on all practitioners, not just those who advertise, is well articulated by a Florida lawyer: "Advertising is a broad brush, which stains all lawyers. We tend to be perceived as greedy, self-interested people who do not care about our clients and are only interested in making a buck."

Another view expressed by critics of marketing and advertising is that the focus has shifted away from the professional's major job of healing, advising and counseling toward an emphasis on issues of lesser importance—generating a profit. They ask, do consumers want to shop for the lowest price for a heart transplant as one would for a used car? Probably not. Certainly there are some unethical professionals who do use advertising unscrupulously. Furthermore, consumers are interested in more than price. Most want a competent, knowledgeable practitioner who can solve problems; price is secondary in importance. In the final analysis, however, the Supreme Court has affirmed the right of professionals to market and to advertise their services.

### Ethical Issues in Marketing by Accountants

Accountants were also reluctant to embrace marketing and advertising concepts. Times changed dramatically during the 1980s. Many accounting firms both developed advertising campaigns and employed staff people in a marketing capacity. Some of the largest ones, like Arthur Andersen, initiated consulting divisions which were engaged in extensive marketing efforts. Consequently, questions regarding the ethics of these practices became more prevalent.

The definitive position on advertising in the accounting field is contained in Section 502 (Advertising and Other Forms of Solicitation) of the AICPA Code of Professional Conduct. The emphasis in the code is on *informational,* as opposed to persuasive, advertising. Section 502 delineates what is prohibited by the code as well as what is considered ethical in advertising by accountants. For example, past experience is acceptable to mention in advertising as well as the CPA designation. However, the advertiser cannot use self-laudatory statements unless they are based on verifiable facts. Certain advertising of the largest CPA firms (Deloitte, Haskins & Sells, and Price Waterhouse) has been contested on ethical grounds. Accounting firms that are concerned about the ethical posture of their advertising need to develop guidelines that delineate what is expected. For example, Arthur Andersen has a detailed book outlining the firm's position on "Ethical Standards/Independence", which includes the complete AICPA code as an appendix.

## Ethical Questions Regarding Lawyer Advertising

Some law firms have openly embraced marketing. As one CEO of a prepaid legal service commented, "We don't have attorneys that sit in the office and practice. We market law. That's all we do." The law firms that have most extensively used advertising are those specializing in personal injury, medical malpractice, immigration law or divorce. Lawyers now spend over $50 million on advertising, a ten-fold increase since 1980. The percentage of lawyers who advertise has increased from three percent to 32 percent over those years.

The American Bar Association has developed both a Model Code of Professional Responsibility and Model Rules of Professional Conduct. The state bar associations follow one of these two documents to serve as the official standard of conduct for lawyers. Several of the clauses are quite similar to those governing accountants. Alleged violations are reviewed by a state bar committee which can recommend one of several sanctions (e.g., reprimand, suspension or disbarment).

There are many potential ethical issues stemming from attorney advertising and marketing. Exhibit 2 lists some pertinent questions that could be asked about potentially unethical legal advertising. The sundry ethical issues include fear generating T.V. ads dramatized with sirens, ambulances, wrecked vehicles, or individuals being placed on stretchers, and ads that vow to help you "collect cash". An in-depth examination of law practice marketing listed over 20 categories of ethical issues including use of customer testimonials, non-informational adver-

tising and cold call solicitations. The study concluded with the following admonition:

> Inevitably, the standards which will govern all of lawyer business-getting activity will be those of honesty and fairness. Misleading and false statements and overreaching conduct will characterize prohibited marketing behavior.....The responsibility for ensuring that law practice marketing plans comply with ethical prescriptions rests squarely with the lawyers.....Lawyers who accept any marketing advice without scrutinizing its ethical propriety risk are wasting money on strategies which must be abandoned for ethical reasons. More importantly, they risk censure from the bar.

## Exhibit 2

## Some Ethical Questions About Lawyer Advertising

The principal difficulty, though, lies in determining just what is, for instance, misleading, or unfair, or dignified. Consider the following:

- A personal injury ad says, "No recovery—no fee". Is this misleading or deceptive for failure to mention the client may be responsible for litigation costs?
- Is a "24-Hour Legal Hotline" dignified?
- "Real People, Not a Professional Corporation or Legal Clinic". Is this misleading to the public and unfair to other lawyers?
- An ad seeking drunk driving cases shows a liquor bottle, a wrecked car, and a drunk. Is this dignified?
- "Twenty Years of Successful Criminal Practice". Is this self-laudatory; does it contain information about past performance; and does it create an unjustified expectation?
- "Low Rates". Is this sufficient fee information, or deceptive?
- In an advertising circular, "Bring this coupon in for a Free Consultation. Is this dignified or deceptive?
- "The Worst Injury of All May Be Not Being Properly Represented." Is this misleading or unfair?
- "Full Compensation for Your Injuries". Does this create unjustified expectations?
- "Everyday our lawyers are in court representing innocent people charged with crimes they didn't commit." Is this potentially fraudulent or deceptive?
- A T.V. ad for personal injury cases shows an accident, flashing lights, and injured persons being loaded into ambulances. Is this dignified or deceptive? Does it appeal to anger, fear or greed?
- "We took the fear out of legal fees." Is this deceptive? Is it telling the public to be fearful of lawyers and legal fees?
- A lawyers' referral service sells all referrals from certain counties to lawyers for a monthly fee. The service advertises an "800" phone number in the yellow pages, with a nationwide answering service based in Tennessee. The service has been approved only by a local bar association in California. Does this meet the letter and spirit of Rule 7.3?

Source: "Lawyer Advertising—Marketing, Professionalism, the Future," *Res Gestae,* August 1988, 63.

## Ethical Issues Facing Medical and Dental Marketing

Of all the professions, medicine has resisted marketing and advertising most vehemently. Survey results indicate that physicians are more skeptical than other professionals toward the benefits of marketing. It may be that they perceive marketing to be primarily a selling activity and far removed from their view of the responsibilities contained in the Hypocratic Oath. Although the medical community was covered by the *Bates* decision, the American Medical Association was charged by the FTC with conspiring with state and local medical societies to suppress all forms of medical advertising. The Supreme Court handed down another decision in 1982. It affirmed the right of physicians to advertise in a truthful, nondeceptive manner.

The majority of medical advertising is undertaken by clinics, HMOs and hospitals. One of the earliest, and most controversial, hospital ads was undertaken by Sunrise Hospital of Las Vegas. There are a number of codes developed by various associations to help insure ethical advertising. The Advertising Guidelines of the Council of Medical Specialty Societies contains 13 points which stipulate that the use of incomplete information, heavy fear appeals and misleading messages are unacceptable. Many of these ethical guidelines should hold for the advertising of any product. One especially ethically charged medical area is cosmetic surgery. It is heavily advertised in some parts of the country, such as California. A number of ethical hazards of advertising cosmetic surgery has been noted by critics, including the possibility of creating oversimplified expectations. The worst case scenario is where ads manipulate individuals to demand services that are downright unhealthy (suction-assisted lipectomy, i.e., fat suction is an especially controversial procedure). Another issue pertains to promoting the professional qualifications of individuals performing cosmetic surgery. Some physicians advertise themselves as specialists without the proper training or certification—a morally, medically, and legally dubious practice. Defenders of cosmetic surgery have noted three reasons why advertising such surgery may be ethically justifiable: (1) Medicine should serve human wants, and one's appearance may improve an individual's quality of life; (2) Patients demanding this surgery are not sick and are more free to ''shop around'' and find the best deal; and (3) The surgical costs are voluntarily borne by the consumer.

### Ideas for Executive Action

The three interested parties—professional associations, practitioners and ad agencies—must all work together to insure that advertising by the professions is on the highest ethical plane. We propose a specific suggestion for each of them.

**(1) Professional associations must continue to place emphasis on advertising issues through updated codes and guidelines, enforcement and conference sessions devoted to the topic.**

Professional societies in law, accounting, medicine and dentistry have had to change their posture toward advertising. As one practitioner aptly noted: ''The question is thus not whether but how physicians shall be permitted to advertise their services.'' It is in this spirit that associations should look at their role to assist and guide, but **not discourage,** advertising by their professionals. For example, the Indiana State Bar Association Lawyer Advertising Committee has recommended that the association publish articles outlining changes in rules governing legal advertising and prepare a brochure to be disseminated to the public so that they can better be protected from false and misleading advertising. Professional organizations need to scrutinize the marketing programs of their members keeping ethical questions in the limelight and holding sessions that discuss such questions at association meetings. Furthermore, sanctions must be enforced so that violators know they will be prosecuted.

**(2) Professionals who employ ad agencies must hold them to high levels of integrity and continuously monitor the messages they develop.**

Professionals need to be careful in the type of agency they select to do their advertising. One recommendation would be to monitor other noncompeting professional ads and to find out what agency prepares the ads that have high integrity and credibility. Just because an agency contends that they are an ''expert'' in legal or medical advertising does not make them an acceptable choice. Professionals can further monitor the effect of the ad on their clientele by asking their impression of it and doing some informal research on their own.

**(3) Ad agencies and marketing consultants who wish to serve professionals should position themselves as being sensitive to the unique needs of the professional community.**

Many agencies and consultants see the growing professional advertising market as an extension of their regular business. This is possibly a mistake. Professionals are different in their orientation. Taking the high road in marketing and advertising is not just expected; it is a necessity. Therefore, marketers should develop campaigns and programs that are unquestioned in terms of integrity. Understanding the philosophical perspective of a professional is more than a semantic challenge.

### References

Abbott, Andrew, ''Professional Ethics,'' *American Journal of Sociology,* Vol. 88, 1983, 855-885.

Balzer, John E., ''Attorney Advertising: Who's Really Afraid of the Big Bad Lawyer,'' *New England Law Review,* March 1988, 727-760.

Braun, Irwin and Marilyn Braun, ''Following a Decade of Advertising: Professionals Still Face Restraints,'' *Marketing News,* August 14, 1987, 21.

''CMSS Develops Guidelines for Physician Advertising,'' *Annals of Emergency Medicine,* December 1981, 100.

Dugas, Christine, "Marketing: The Prescription for Professional Practices?" *Ad Forum,* February 1983, 42-44.

Folland, Sherman, R. Parameswaran and John Darling, "On the Nature of Physicians' Opposition to Advertising," *Journal of Advertising,* Vol. 18, 1989, 4-12.

Hite, Robert E. and Cynthia Fraser, "Meta-Analyses of Attitudes Toward Advertising by Professionals," *Journal of Marketing,* July 1988, 95-105.

"Is Dignity Important in Legal Advertising?" *ABA Journal,* August 1, 1987, A-1 and A-2.

"Lawyer Advertising—Marketing, Professionalism, the Future," *Res Gestae,* August 1988, 59-64.

Leiser, Burton M., "Professional Advertising: Price Fixing and Professional Dignity versus the Public's Right to a Free Market," *Journal of Business and Professional Ethics,* Spring/Summer 1984, 93-110.

Macklin, Ruth, "Commentary on Leiser," *Journal of Business and Professional Ethics,* Spring/Summer 1984, 114.

"Major CPA Firms Accused of Violations of Professional Conduct," *The Practical Accountant,* April 1986, 43-44.

Morreim, E. Haavi, "A Moral Examination of Medical Advertising," *Business & Society Review,* Winter 1988, 4-6.

Moss, Frederick C., "The Ethics of Law Practice Marketing," *Notre Dame Law Review,* Vol. 61, 1986, 601-696.

North, Sterling, "Lawyers in the Age of Advertising," *New England Business,* August 3, 1987, 22-25.

Stafford, David C., "Advertising in the Professions," *International Journal of Advertising,* 1988, 7, 189-220.

Stewart, Larry, "Advertising: The Need For a Strong ATLA Policy," *ATLA Advocate,* July 1989, 2 and 4.

"Suggestions for Lawyer Advertising—Avoiding Deceptive & Unprofessional Ads," *Res Gestae,* February 1989, 394-398.

Trapani, Christopher, "Advertising v. Solicitation: Shapero Ends the Controversy Over Targeted Direct-Mailings by Attorneys," *Florida Bar Journal,* February 1989, 31-33.

Walsh, William J., "CPAs and Advertising: Another Voice," *Journal of Accountancy,* November 1986, 178-180.

"What Forms of Advertising Are Permissible Under the Ethics Code?" *Journal of Accountancy,* November 1986, 98-99.

*This paper is abstracted from a chapter entitled, "The Ethics of Social, Professional and Political Marketing", which will appear in The Higher Road: A Path to Ethical Marketing Decisions, to be published by Allyn & Bacon.

# THE MAGIC OF
# HERMAN MILLER

It has soared to become one of the 500 largest U. S. firms and is always cited as one of the best managed. Being "value-led" keeps Herman Miller a winner.

JOANI NELSON-HORCHLER

While many U. S. executives rolled in the excesses of unrestrained greed in the 1980s, Max DePree, chairman of Herman Miller Inc. (HMI), was continually working at fulfilling a "covenant" with his employees in which leaders *owe* their workers "a rational environment [that] values trust and human dignity and provides the opportunity for personal development and self-fulfillment."

And, while other executives railed on about the bottom line, Mr. DePree was writing in his well-read *Leadership Is an Art* (Doubleday, 1989) about giving employees "space so that we can both give and receive such beautiful things as ideas, openness, dignity, joy, healing, and inclusion."

Being "value-led" is at the heart of Herman Miller's success. Two of the company's key values—participative management and sharing of company profits among all employees—have put the Zeeland, Mich., manufacturer of office and health-care-facility furniture consistently at or near the top of practically every "best" list in the U. S.: best-managed, most-admired, best environment for women, best quality and design—the list goes on and on. With 1950 sales of $2 million and 1976 sales of $50 million, HMI has grown to $865 million today.

Even during these recessionary times, HMI's sales are growing at about 5%, twice the rate of the business-furniture industry. The company has had to lay off employees only twice in the last 10 years.

What jumps out at a visitor to HMI is that seemingly everyone in the company—from the factory-floor worker to the very top—talks about values and has intimate knowledge of the successes and problems of the corporation.

"The person making panels has the right and responsibility to know the big picture," says Michele Hunt, HMI's vice president of corporate development, who served for six years as its first "vice president for people." That's why videotapes of monthly officers' and directors' meetings reviewing all the business' operations are shown to all employees at work-team meetings. Having all the information keeps all employees very business-literate about the company's strategic goals, performance-to-plan, and objectives for the month ahead.

Scott Fisher, a production coordinator, who started as a chair assembler seven years ago, cites as the biggest challenge facing HMI "keeping an edge over our competitors in the dwindling economy we're facing."

Open communication is another key value. Jill Woods, a pattern maker, describes HMI as "a very personal company in the way people deal with each other."

A crew leader who has worked at Herman Miller for six years, Kevin Knowles says, "What always surprises me is that everyone in the company . . . is free to talk with anyone in management about whatever they'd like to talk about. That's why there's a fairly high level of morale here."

The open, trusting environment so pervades HMI that supervisors themselves often cite their own employees' ability to "go over our heads" as one of the major reasons for the company's success. "Employees have several channels to go straight to the top with their complaints," says Diane Bunse, supervisor-fabric. "There's no fear of retribution if you call someone three levels above, and people don't hesitate to say, 'I need to have Dick [Ruch, president and CEO] call this customer,'" says Dawn Johnson, vice president-sales, North America.

"People are not afraid to tell me I'm full of it!" laughs James Bloem, vice president and chief financial officer.

Another corporate value that strikes a visitor to HMI is the delight everyone there seems to take in telling stories about the company's founder, D. J. DePree (who recently died at age 99) and other aspects of the company's tradition.

"I find myself taking the values I've learned from D. J. and others at work over to my family life, which has created a better family life," says Jack Spidell, director of HMI's Holland, Mich., production.

Reprinted with permission from *Industry Week*, February 18, 1991, pp. 11-12, 14, 17. Copyright © 1991, Penton Publishing, Inc., Cleveland, OH.

This pleases Max, D. J.'s son, because he believes that one of the signs of corporate trouble is when its workers "stop telling tribal stories or cannot understand them." Among other telltale signs of sickness, says HMI's chairman, are "a dark tension among key people; no longer having time for celebration and ritual; leaders who seek to control rather than liberate; and an orientation toward . . . dry rules . . . rather than a value orientation which takes into account . . . contribution, spirit, excellence, beauty, and joy."

Being value-led is "not a strategy—it's a belief that for people to identify with an organization they have to believe in its values," says Ms. Hunt. The constant challenges, she says, are to unleash people's potential around common values and provide the kind of environment where "work-team members have a right and responsibility to challenge managers, and managers have a responsibility to listen and be open to influence and not get rankled when employees 'go above their heads.'"

**To reflect** the value system, infrastructure has been put into place to enable employees to constantly challenge the status quo. During the company's most recent annual employee survey, some employees said that certain company policies were "not enabling." In response, a cross-functional team is revising those policies.

Employees have always been encouraged to challenge the status quo in furniture products and design. When the company's competitors pushed indirect ambient lighting several years ago, "we were laughed at by the industry because we did not believe it was of benefit to our customers and would not promote it," says Phil Mercorella, senior vice president-sales, marketing, and distribution. He feels lucky to work for a company that didn't fire him for his part in the controversial decision. Three years later, HMI's—and Mr. Mercorella's—instincts were proved right when the trendy product virtually disappeared from the marketplace.

"It sounds syrupy, but the major thing that's helped us is that we've

## COMPASSION FOR AN AIDS VICTIM

### "Roving leaders" at Herman Miller take charge.

He had read horror stories of other employers firing AIDS victims. So Peter Hill (a pseudonym), a Herman Miller (HMI) employee in the company's Roswell, Ga., plant, didn't tell his co-workers he had AIDS when he was first diagnosed as having the human immunodeficiency virus (HIV). He did tell his supervisor, Bobbie Moody, after swearing her to secrecy.

But all his "worst fears went right out the window," he says, when he finally told his co-workers in November 1990—through Ms. Moody and Dr. Cecil Williams, director of health and wellness—that he had full-blown AIDS. "The response from everyone has been overwhelmingly positive, beyond belief," he says. "Herman Miller has really been there for me and gotten me through these bad times."

To Dr. Williams and Ms. Moody, the compassionate treatment of Mr. Hill is simply part of HMI's commitment to value "the dignity of each individual" and to "expect quality relationships based on mutual trust and integrity." (Mr. Hill is one of five employees at HMI who have been known to have AIDS. All have been treated in the same respectful way.)

The process exemplifies what HMI Chairman Max DePree calls "roving leadership." It demands that the corporate hierarchy allow "subordinates" to break custom and be leaders. "Roving leadership is a key element in the day-to-day expression of a participative process," Mr. DePree writes.

Once Mr. Hill decided that his illness should become known to his co-workers, Ms. Moody, a senior inventory analyst, immediately became the roving leader in charge. First, she told the human-resources manager, who knows Mr. Hill, and

they both broke down and cried. The plant manager and the management work team were the next to be told. Then Ms. Moody and the other two managers dispersed throughout the plant to tell each individual work team, a process that was completed within two hours.

"**The key was** telling everyone in the plant quickly so that no one had the chance to gossip about it," Ms. Moody says. As a result, "no one has said anything negative. Everyone was shocked and unhappy because he's a very hard worker and so well-liked here."

After the work teams were told, Dr. Williams flew down the next work day from HMI's Zeeland, Mich., headquarters to present an informational video on AIDS to all plant employees and to answer their questions. One thing Mr. Hill really appreciates is that Dr. Williams "was very emphatic during this session that other employees should avoid shaking hands with me or touching me if they have a cold," Mr. Hill says. "Dr. Williams stressed that, in the workplace, they are potentially more of a harm to me than I am to them."

Mr. Hill has been placed on medical leave for six months, during which time he is paid 100% of his salary for 13 weeks and 70% for another 13 weeks. After that, he'll be eligible for long-term disability—a company insurance policy that pays 70% of his pretax salary.

But what's most important, says Ms. Moody, is that HMI's value system "allows us to act on our instincts and know the company will support us. Because the value of each individual is important to us, we were able to stop the manufacture of furniture for one day to take care of Peter."

always focused on what is morally right to do, not what's expedient," says Mr. Mercorella. An example is HMI's decision two years ago to help Friends of the Earth protect rain forests by eliminating from its standard product line tropical woods such as rosewood that cannot be obtained from sustainable-yield forest sources. HMI is also working to recycle more and make its packaging more environmentally acceptable.

> "
> *The person making panels has the right and responsibility to know the big picture.*
> "

Leaders owe their workers a "sense of equality," Mr. DePree strongly believes. Thus, in the mid-1980s, HMI became the first of now hundreds of U. S. companies that protect *all* their employees—not just senior executives—with "silver parachutes" against the threat of hostile takeovers. Too, HMI was one of the first U. S. firms—and is still among only a handful—that limit their top executives' pay to a certain multiple of their average worker's pay. (In HMI's case, the CEO can't make more than 20 times the average manufacturing worker.)

Such action is consistent with Mr. DePree's harsh criticism of managers who "are at the leading edge of consumption, affluence, and instant gratification." Mr. DePree decries the current "throwaway mentality that discards goods and ideas, that discards principles and law, that discards persons and families."

In fact, Mr. DePree has emphasized continually over the years his goal of reflecting "God's mix" of population within his company's culture. That includes not only re-

cruiting and grooming minorities and women but also the physically handicapped. President/CEO Richard Ruch recently promoted cultural diversity—including the need to sometimes give external candidates job preference—in a videotape produced for employees.

A major component of HMI's value system is the "Scanlon bonus" through which all employees for the last 40 years have shared the rewards of increased productivity and profitability. In 1988, an ad hoc group of employees changed the way the bonus was calculated after finding it tended to measure things from HMI's point of view rather than that of its customers and investors.

**Even during** current recessionary times, HMI employees continue to earn substantial bonuses. For example, the payout in December 1990 was 11.1% of the individual's quarterly gross salary, and for the previous quarter it was 14.5%. Employees get their bonuses in separate checks called "our earned share." Bonuses are capped at $39,000 for executives and anyone on another incentive plan.

The benefits of this participatory system are reflected in a low absenteeism rate of between 1% and 2%, well below the U. S. average of about 6%. Employee turnover of 7% is less than half of the 15%-to-20% average of other U. S. firms. Employee suggestions have led to an estimated cost savings of an annual average during the last five years of $11.6 million.

Many managements fail miserably at fairly and competently appraising employees of their job performances. But HMI excels at it, mainly because top management stresses that all supervisors must take the matter seriously and do it continually. "To surprise someone with an annual appraisal is the worst thing to do," says Ms. Bunse, the fabric supervisor. "I like our quarterly appraisals."

All employees also have the opportunity to regularly, and anonymously, evaluate their work-team leaders. For example, the executive team evaluates Vice President Ms. Hunt's performance as a work-team leader. Then, when she is reviewed

by her boss, Mr. Ruch, he is able to evaluate her from several different perspectives—how her work team sees her, how she sees herself, and how he sees her. And Ms. Hunt, at the same time, evaluates Mr. Ruch.

Also, when HMI interviews people for key management jobs, it uses cross-functional teams to evaluate them.

HMI isn't perfect, and everyone interviewed warned against any employee's ever thinking that it is. The company has experienced slumps, such as in the mid-'80s when it became—as one employee admits—"too inwardly focused." For example, it used to reward employees through the Scanlon plan for on-time shipments even when they did not result in on-time deliveries to

> "
> *My own biggest problem is the time it takes to get where I want to be in this company because of so much internal competition for promotions.*
> "

customers. As a result of the company's 1986 "renewal," the calculation was changed. And now, once a year, employee representatives take a critical look at the entire participative process. Based on feedback from an annual employee survey and other input, they identify processes that need to be changed and discuss current business conditions that may be keeping HMI from reaching its goals.

From the factory worker's perspective, "our biggest frustration is that we set such high goals for interpersonal communication that they sometimes seem unattainable," says Mr. Fisher, the production coordinator.

In fact, being one of the most liked and respected companies in the U. S. has created some hurdles for HMI. For example, even for factory-floor jobs, the company attracts and retains highly skilled and educated workers such as Bill Warner, a crew leader in panel-making who has made $55,000 worth of implemented cost-savings suggestions and who studies electronics during his off-work hours under HMI's tuition-reimbursement program.

"My own biggest problem is the time it takes to get where I want to be in this company because of so much internal competition for promotions and because the company often streamlines operations rather than hire new people," he says.

**Other problems** persist. The biggest for Ms. Bunse, the fabric supervisor, is "getting a commitment from our vendors around the world to have things here and defect-free when we need them." However, Ms. Bunse notes, the situation has improved now that purchasing is tracking completions together with her department.

The heftiest challenge HMI faces in the view of pattern-maker Ms. Woods is "to keep up with being a big company while still retaining [our] very personal nature." Martin Dugan, vice president-facility man-

agement, notes that the number of employees leaped from about 600 in 1972 to 5,400 worldwide currently. The way to maintain personal relationships, Mr. Dugan believes, is to keep the number of individuals on work teams at about 12.

As HMI grows and becomes more complex, "getting out ahead of global change" is the greatest challenge in Ms. Hunt's view. "We must empower ourselves to create change around a common vision and not wait for a crisis to hit us and then respond," she declares.

No, Herman Miller isn't perfect. And it never will be perfect, by the admission and blessing of Mr. De-Pree. "Corporations," he says in his prophetic way, "like the people who comprise them, are always in a state of becoming."

# Sex and Decency Issues in Advertising: General and International Dimensions

## Jean J. Boddewyn and Heidi Kunz

*Jean J. Boddewyn is a professor of marketing and international business at Baruch College, City University of New York. Heidi Kunz is an assistant vice president and financial controller with FISERV, Inc., New York.*

*De gustibus et coloribus non disputandum—* one should not argue about tastes and colors. This medieval proverb is often cited concerning the futility of discussing subjective issues. However, in the case of "sex and decency in advertising," it seems that the discussion will go on forever. This issue and its implications have been much studied and debated recently by academics, feminist groups, advertising bodies, and parliamentary committees.[1] The following sections highlight key problems, factors, and remedies derived from these studies and from an International Advertising Association (IAA) survey (Boddewyn 1989).

### KEY FACTORS

There is usually no simple explanation of why a particular product or advertisement is considered offensive, although some factors are more readily identifiable than others. Religion and other value systems are certainly crucial in defining and sanctioning sex and decency. Moslem countries tend to frown upon all kinds of salacious displays and even indirect sexual references. Similar Christian standards operate in such countries as Ireland, South Africa, Mexico, and the Philippines. Other cultures may be considered rather tolerant in sexual matters (for example, French commercials on public television readily show live semi-nude models) but may prohibit any show of pubic hair (Japan), the promotion of contraceptives (France), or the lewd use of women (Scandinavia and the Netherlands) in advertisements. Values change,

however. Thus, the spread of AIDS has re-opened the issue of advertising condoms and other contraceptives in a totally difference context, which transcends the older concerns about birth control and venereal-disease prevention.

The law usually parallels religious and moral standards. There are often statutes dealing with public indecency (in Switzerland, Thailand, and the United Kingdom), the moral protection of minors, the restriction of violent displays (including sado-masochistic ones), and discriminatory job advertisements (particularly in Australia, the Netherlands, Norway, the

> *Self-regulation and a watchful public appear to be the best defense against advertising that demeans women and men alike.*

United Kingdom, and the United States). Restrictions on the publication and circulation of "sexy" magazines of the *Playboy* variety, with their usually more risqué ads, also belong to this category (Argentina, Lebanon, South Africa, and Thailand). Reflecting concerns about "sexist" portrayals, a 1979 amendment to the 1972 Norwegian Marketing Control Law states: "An advertiser and anyone who creates advertising matter shall ensure that the advertisement does not conflict with the inherent parity between the sexes, and that it does not imply any derogatory judgment of either sex or portray a woman or a man in an offensive manner." Similar provisions have been enacted in India, Peru, and Portugal to protect women against indecent or derogatory representations.

Still, the matter of constitutional freedom of speech as applied to advertising has raised serious questions concerning control of sex and decency in advertising. Swedish courts, for example, have not sustained some initiatives of the Consumer Ombudsman in this matter; and the Swedish parliament stated in 1977 that no law prohibiting ads discriminating against women could be introduced without amending the Freedom of the Press Act. U.S. courts keep struggling with the definition of obscenity in the context of the First Amendment.

The activism of religious and feminist groups clearly affects the stiffening of standards. Several Moslem countries (such as Iran and Saudi Arabia) are strongly resisting the invasion of Western advertising themes and approaches. Besides, a vocal minority of women are increasingly objecting to the deprecation of their sex (in Canada, the Netherlands, Norway, Portugal, and Sweden). They oppose ads that belittle women, insult their intelligence, depict them in an offending manner, imply sex inequalities, or display violence against them. Some people, including men, oppose commercials about personal-hygiene products (in Canada and the United States).

Media control is crucial whenever a strong clearance system exists (in Mexico and Taiwan), particularly where television and radio networks are government controlled or when general censorship prevails (in Indonesia and Saudi Arabia). In general, TV and radio commercials are more restricted than print and

> "An ad in Playboy or a commercial shown at midnight will be received differently from those appearing in general-circulation magazines or in prime time."

direct-mail ads, which are more selective in their audience-reaching; private networks are often more tolerant than public ones in such countries as Italy. In any case, much depends on the execution of the advertisements as well as on their placement and timing. An ad in

*Playboy* or a commercial shown at midnight will be received differently from those appearing in general-circulation magazines or in prime time. Restraint, grace, and wit may also make a difference.

Besides, the greater number and variety of publications, commercial broadcasting stations, and direct-mail advertisements are eliminating much of the rationing that allowed the media—particularly television and radio—to refuse ads for various controversial products and services simply because there was not enough time and space to accommodate all advertisers. As Colin Shaw, Director of the U.K. Broadcasting Standards Council, remarked (1989): "People buy newspapers largely to confirm their prejudices. In the whole, most people look at television and are constantly having their prejudices affronted." International editions of newspapers and magazines as well as the recent growth of satellite broadcasting are diffusing new types of advertisements about different products to countries unaccustomed to them.

Advertising self-regulation has played some role in curbing excesses in the matter of sex and decency—particularly in Australia, Canada, Germany, the Philippines, and the United Kingdom. These efforts are aimed at preventing further government restrictions and improving advertising's image. Problems are often minimized by corporate policies and by tacit understandings among advertisers not to advertise certain products or use certain media, as well as by their fear of negative reactions on the part of audiences. This kind of self-discipline helps explain the paucity of male-hygiene advertisements in Japan and of contraceptive advertisements in Argentina. Situations change, however, as some advertisers, advertising agencies, and media brave tradition and begin to promote products and services previously left to more discreet treatment.

"Sex and decency" is not a monolithic issue, in any case. The following sections review the problems associated with defining, explaining, and curbing the use of indecent and sex-related advertisements.

### DECENCY

Many dictionary definitions of decency could be cited, but all suffer from the use of equally vague synonyms to catch a very elusive subject. In the 1998 IAA survey, decency was defined in terms of "conformity to recognized standards of propriety, good taste and modesty"—all imprecise terms, to be sure. Britain's Advertising Standards Authority, its self-regulatory body, has repeatedly tried to develop more precise criteria to be used by its complaint-handling body, such as:

1. Would it offend a majority of the people?

2. Is it so deeply offensive to a few that their feelings should override the views of the majority?

3. Does it include the irrelevant use of certain words and images?

4. Is gratuitous vulgarity used?

However, this laudable effort still suffers from the use of relatively vague criteria left to the appreciation of its complaint-handling bodies.

Decency criteria are also very heterogeneous. People who are very liberal about editorial and artistic expression—including the show of nudity and sex in films as well as the publication of erotic materials—may blanch when they see an ad for pantyhose, contraceptives, douches, sanitary napkins, and toilet paper. Moreover, criteria and their application are and will remain subjective, outside of specific interdictions such as various strictures in Moslem countries against showing female bodies in advertisements, the prohibition of branded contraceptive commercials in most countries, and media acceptance rules that exclude various products and services (feminine-hygiene products and funeral homes).

Besides, decency standards are in flux, sometimes in opposite directions. In the United Kingdom, the television standards applying to foundation garments have been relaxed without generating much opposition, while the introduction of feminine-hygiene commercials in 1986 prompted many complaints. The recent concern about AIDS has allowed generic commercials and posters about the use of male contraceptives and other forms of protection (including abstinence), but there is little movement toward the advertising of branded contraceptives on television because vocal religious and conservative groups oppose ads about products that explicitly acknowledge sexual activity.

### SEXUALITY

This issue concerns the use of sexual imagery and suggestiveness as the primary attention-getters in advertisements. Its range is broad—from the modeling of sexy lingerie, to men and women eyeing or touching each other, to hints or displays of homosexuality, to the combination of sex and violence in advertisements.

The use of sexuality in advertising rests on the assumption that "sex sells"—at least in some cases. Since few men or women will deny that they are interested in the other gender, the use of sexuality can be successful because perfume, lingerie, and designer jeans are often bought for the very purpose of attracting the opposite sex. Besides, eroticism is as legitimate in advertising as it is in art, to the extent that it is contextually apt. Still, besides the obvious moral concerns about promoting promiscuity, there are the more practical problems for advertisers

of distracting potential consumers from the real advantages of their product or service, and of offending some of their targets. Sexy ads can also degenerate into objectification and violence.

Cultural differences are very evident here. In Malaysia, when a man and a woman are shown alone in a room for more than three seconds, it implies they had intercourse. In this highly conservative Moslem country, any display of female bodies or any hint of sexuality is strictly forbidden. However, Scandinavians do not insist on modesty in ads, and French advertisers frequently show partially clad or nude women and use sexually suggestive language. In the U.S., one commonly sees men and women in intimate and suggestive poses, but advertisers refrain from any display of frontal nudity, except in some fashion print ads and men's magazines.

A major factor is that of appropriateness, as is revealed by the results of a recent British Survey (ASA 1990): "The strongest expressions of offence among the public in general relate to advertisements which exploited nudity, semi-nudity, or sex in a manner which could be said to be irrelevant to the product advertised. Although the survey shows a high degree of tolerance for nudity in advertisements when it is contextually apt, the public does react strongly to the inept use of sexuality, and to sexual innuendo either in illustration or text, and especially if the sole purpose is to draw attention to an advertisement."

### VIOLENCE TOWARD WOMEN

For some feminists, any portrayal of violence against women is the ultimate expression of male dominance and female submissiveness,

> "Besides the obvious moral concerns about promoting promiscuity, there are the more practical problems for advertisers of distracting potential consumers from the real advantages of their product or service, and of offending some of their targets."

which they totally reject. Still, some creative types in advertising agencies are constantly searching for new approaches to captivate jaded consumers, thereby pushing against current boundaries of acceptable sexual and semi-erotic advertising—until a backlash results. Thus, a South African manufacturer of industrial padding used an ad showing a semi-clad woman sprawled unconscious on a bed, with a knife resting at her side. The reaction in this very conservative Christian country was strong against this gratuitous implication of violence against women and against the irrelevance of using women in connection with this product. Similarly, Scandinavians are tolerant of nudity but object strongly to ads that negate the equality and dignity of the sexes.

The fact that some U.S. women's magazines are displaying more advertisements showing women in subservient and helpless positions is puzzling. This form of quasi-erotica is mostly found in men's and fashion magazines, but the introduction of sexual violence into the mainstream press and MTV videos suggests that some people, including women, find this type of display appealing and nonthreatening. Sexual violence may represent fantasy and not be considered as undermining seriously the position of women in society. Still, the growing awareness of battered wives and raped women may well turn sexual violence in advertising into a major issue.

## SEXISM/SEX-ROLE STEREOTYPING

Distinctions that diminish or demean one sex in comparison with the other—particularly through the use of sex-role stereotyping—are no longer a mere subset of the "poor taste" category of making fun of mothers-in-law, fussy wives, and fanatic homemakers. The debate

> *"It is obvious that the roles of women have multiplied and diversified in many countries. It is also acknowledged by more advertising practitioners that they have lagged in reflecting these new roles and aspirations."*

now centers on matters of "injustice and inequality," on "the myth of female inferiority," and on "the desired status of women." Is advertising a "mirror of society" that simply reflects the various roles of modern women—including those of wife, mother, and homemaker? Or is

its true but hidden purpose that of "keeping men in power"? These ideological issues match the broader contemporary concerns about racism and other forms of discrimination and disparagement, and they raise important questions about the impact of advertising on values and behaviors.

It is obvious that the roles of women have multiplied and diversified in many countries. It is also acknowledged by more advertising practitioners that they have lagged in reflecting these new roles and aspirations. The true challenges lie in: (1) eliminating blatant expressions of sexual discrimination that have no objective foundations, and (2) translating into good copy and images the fact that, at least in industrialized countries, both women and men play many roles in society, and thus they accept and even demand to be represented in multiple manners.

To the first task belongs the prohibition of employment ads that inappropriately specify gender for some occupations, the progressive elimination of sexist language in ads (sales*man*, house*wife*), and the increase of female voice-overs in commercials to dispel the notion that only men are experts and authority figures. The second task is really commonsensical in a marketing age that stresses market segmentation and the proper positioning of products and services. When more women work in better occupations and more husbands share in household and child-raising tasks—among other social-role developments—then advertising has no choice but to reflect these significant changes to be economically effective and socially accepted.

In this perspective, the counterarguments advanced by advertising practitioners lose much of their punch: that restrictions on sex-role stereotyping interfere with creativity; that the industry did not create the stereotypes but only uses them; that stereotyping is an appropriate shortcut technique to reach wide audiences, particularly in the context of very short commercials; and that negative stereotypes constitute only a small part in their overall use.

For critics of the advertising industry, instances of sexist advertising still abound, as revealed by this example given by Margaret Shields, New Zealand's Minister of Women's Affairs (1989):

> Car advertisements aimed at women give little factual information about what sort of performance we could expect from the vehicle. Instead, we find how sexually attractive we're going to look in it, how many shopping bags we can fit in the back, and how even those difficult parks, that we daren't have attempted in the past, are now accessible to us. Similar advertisements aimed at men frequently give detailed information about performance, econ-

omy and endurance. Women need this sort of product information as much as men do.

Yet this mandate is a complex one for advertising practitioners, because there are real differences between men and women, as revealed by the following Norwegian comment about what may or may not be acceptable:

Advertisements which exploit feelings of uncertainty in connection with menstruation are not necessarily open to challenge. However, an ad focusing on lack of mental balance during menstrual periods is open to assessment because the more or less well-founded claims concerning women's mental and physical problems connected with menstruation have been and still are one of the most effective means of inhibiting the activity of women in society by casting a derogatory judgment on them. (Melgard, no date)

Nevertheless, there are now dangers that new unrealistic prototypes are emerging (the "superwoman"), that women choosing to stay at home and raise children will be denigrated in turn, and that men will be portrayed unrealistically and even unfavorably. Regarding the latter, articles have begun to criticize the portrayal of men in U.S. and Canadian commercials (Freedman 1989, Goldberg 1989, Jung 1989). They point out that, while it is no longer acceptable to make fun of women, men are now the target of rough treatment and insults. Copywriters may be afraid to fool around with women's new roles, while the women get the best lines, as revealed by the following examples:

An airline commercial shows two reporters from competing newspapers. She's strong and smart. He's a nerd. He says to her: "I read your story this morning; you scooped me again." She replies to him: "I didn't know you could read."

A print ad for Stay-Put Shoulder Pads reads: "They're like a good man: a little bold, a little square, around when you need them, and they stay put. . . . They never lose their shape, which is more than you can say for most men."

Commercials showing women hitting men in the face, pouring cold water over them, pushing them into a lake, or patting their behinds are not uncommon in North America today. But they have elicited few reactions from viewers and the networks, who would be more likely to object if women were the victims of such treatments. It may be a case of overcompensating for the poor portrayal of women in the past, but such discriminatory treatment of men deserves equal criticism and correction.

Finally, one must acknowledge important national differences. Some cultures insist on keeping women in traditional roles. In Saudi Arabia and Malaysia, for example, women must be shown in a family setting—not carefree, not by themselves, and not appealing to the opposite sex in advertisements. Conversely, Canada, France, and Sweden are now stressing that sexism should be avoided in advertising directed to children to avoid associating certain toys and form of play with one sex or another, thereby nipping sexism in the bud.

## OBJECTIFICATION/REIFICATION OF WOMEN

Using women (mostly) as decorative or attention-getting objects, with little or no relevance to the product or service advertised, is also criticized. This objection emanates from both traditionalist and feminist women—the former objecting to the sex and nudity associated with such ads, and the latter more concerned about the limited roles assigned to women and about the way such ads deal with the relations among the sexes, particularly when women are presented in subservient positions. Clearly, the reification of women (that is, turning them into "things") overlaps with the issues of sexism (women are not presented as experts), decency, and sexuality (too much sex or the wrong kind).

Besides the fact that such ads reflect the traditional canons of male desires, the practical problem is whether they actually help sell anything in their crudest forms. Historically men have been perceived as the sole or main breadwinners and decision makers in families. Consequently, advertisements have reflected these values, even though much advertising was actually directed toward women. Because men are attracted to pretty and sexy women, and men were the primary purchasers of big-ticket items (cars, office equipment), the use of women as attention getters seemed appropriate and wholly acceptable.

The advent of the women's liberation movement in the 1960s changed this perception. Suddenly women were entering the work force in large numbers, some of them in mid-level and top managerial positions. Divorce was on the rise, and single parents became more common. At this point, attitudes toward the use of females as decorative objects took a major turn. Women, who for centuries had accepted their roles as wives, mothers, and inferiors to men, began demanding equal footing. They no longer believed they needed to direct all of their attention and efforts to looking young and attractive for men. A consequence of this change in attitudes has been the rejection of merely decorative roles for women.

However, advertisers have been slow in picking up on this change, and one still finds many instances of women being inappropriately used to sell products intended primarily for men, as is revealed by the following case from the Canadian Advertising Foundation (CAF):

A television message for a chewing gum directed at men drew many complaints from women. The 30-second message included shots of a variety of women while a 1960s rock song played. Only in the last two seconds was the product shown. The concept was to tie in "girl-watching" as a tradition with the use of gum as a tradition. The CAF consulted with the advertiser through several versions of the message, with the acknowledgment that no changes would bring the message in line with the guidelines. The final print did avoid overt examples of close body shots and scantily dressed women. However, it was still considered to be in contravention of the guidelines because the women's presence had no relevance to the advertised product.

Yet having attractive women in ads may help create a particular mood that the marketer is striving for. Thus, placing an expensively dressed and attractive woman in a men's clothing advertisement (or a man in a women's perfume ad) may imply quality. In this scenario, the woman or man bears no relevance to the product, but neither is she or he portrayed in an offensive manner. Therefore, the use of reification may not decrease when it shows women and men in a realistic lifestyle context, but the execution will be different from that of placing a bikini-clad woman on a forklift truck.

The use of reification in men's specialty magazines such as *Playboy* and *Penthouse* is better understood. These magazines are more or less dedicated to the exploitation and objectivication of women, so the use of women as decorative objects in their advertisements is in keeping with their character. Unless one is prepared to prohibit the sale of these magazines, as in South Africa and Thailand, such continued reification of women is to be expected in the pages of these special media.

## IAA SURVEY FINDINGS

A 1988 survey of 47 countries (Boddewyn 1989) revealed the following facts about the "sex and decency" issue, and about its control.[2]

1. Although much of the current literature suggests that decency, the use of sex stereotypes, violence against women, and objectification in advertising are "hot" issues

---

**Figure 1**
**Salience of Issues**

| | |
|---|---|
| Tasteless and indecent ads | 1.72 |
| Sexy ads | 1.72 |
| Using women as attention getters | 1.67 |
| Sexist ads | 1.57 |
| Violence against women | 1.42 |
| Predominance of male voice-overs in commercials | 1.24 |

*Note: These average scores for 47 countries were based on the following scale: 1 = minor issue; 2 = growing issue; 3 = major issue.*

---

in a host of countries, the survey results suggest they are of medium importance even though quite real and unlikely to disappear (see Figure 1).

2. The cultural, religious, and economic characteristics of the countries appeared to be the dominant factors explaining national patterns. Thus, Islamic countries were less tolerant of nudity, sexy advertisements, and the use of women as attention getters. Some Catholic countries (Ireland) and authoritarian regimes (the People's Republic of China) are also very conservative. More issues were labeled as "major" in less developed countries.

3. Even when done in good taste, ads for female over-the-counter contraceptives were the least acceptable ones around the world. Male contraceptives are also very restricted but some public-service advertising, without brand names being used, is beginning to be tolerated. (This is, by far, the major change since an earlier 1979 IAA survey on the same topic.) Other intimate-use products (douches, laxatives, sanitary napkins) are largely kept out of the broadcast and outdoor media.

4. As in 1979, very few objectionable advertisements have resulted in legal action or punishment. The majority of offenders were television and billboard advertisers, and the most frequent complaints were about indecency or the sexual exploitation of women. In most cases offenders were simply required to remove their ads.

5. Although two-thirds of the respondents indicated that self-regulatory guidelines in their respective countries were vague or lightly applied, only 14 countries expected increased regulatory and self-regulatory measures in the near future. Five countries anticipated some relaxation of the controls, particularly regarding the generic advertising of condoms in view of the AIDS epidemic.

6. Laundry detergent and household products were the categories generating the most complaints for sex-role stereotyping. Automobiles, auto supplies, and alcohol were the

prime sources regarding the use of women as attention getters. Film advertisements were the primary offenders as far as sexual violence against women was concerned.

7. Very few respondents were able to provide details concerning the number of complaints received annually in the areas of sex and decency. The absence of data may suggest that the issues are not major ones. However, given the number of self-regulatory guidelines aimed at addressing these issues, as well as the number of samples of sexist and sexy advertisements enclosed with the returned questionnaires, the likelihood of this scenario is slight.

8. Responses to a variety of hypothetical sexist situations (such as ads showing only women using a vacuum cleaner) revealed that self-regulatory guidelines are typically more common than laws. Broadcast media guidelines are also stricter than those of print in this respect (see Figure 2).

---

**Figure 2**
**Average Scores on Media Tolerance**

| | |
|---|---|
| Broadcast television | 2.9 |
| Radio | 2.6 |
| Posters/Billboards/Hoardings | 2.4 |
| Cable television | 2.4 |
| Newspapers | 2.0 |
| General magazines (e.g., *Time*) | 1.9 |
| Women's magazines (e.g., *Elle*) | 1.8 |
| Direct mail | 1.8 |
| Men's magazines (e.g., *Playboy*) | 1.4 |

*4 = Very Conservative; 1 = Very Tolerant*

---

9. Responses to a variety of hypothetically controversial commercials that could be seen on television were particularly negative concerning displays of homosexuality (mostly on the basis of self-regulatory guidelines) and of violence to women (the law is also strongly against it). Showing nudity, underclothing, and physical contact between men and women received their share of opposition from more conservative countries, including the United States.

Sex and decency in advertising is an important issue because it affects the acceptability of all advertising; even a few rotten ads can broadly discredit the industry. Besides, advertisers risk spoiling the intended impact of particular advertisements by offending consumers in the target market. Advertising, like other societal institutions, must operate within culturally defined and time-bound constraints. When norms vary and change, so must advertising, lest its effectiveness be impaired or its freedom be restricted.

More developed nations, particularly in Canada and northern Europe, already have some laws and self-regulatory guidelines as well as women's and other special-interest groups that actively publicize issues and educate both advertisers and the public. This policing by the public reduces the need for increased government intervention that is difficult to design and apply outside of outright cases of sex discrimination and obscenity. In addition, advertisers appear to be awakening to the reality that more women work outside the home than ever before and have become more important and more pervasive consumers. Still, the tug-of-war will continue between resurgent conservative and emerging modern values, with an outcome that cannot readily be predicted.

## NOTES

1. The useful comments of the following experts are gratefully acknowledged: Rena Bartos (New York), Niquette Delange (Conseil des Normes de la Publicité, Montreal), Maicen Ekman (National Swedish Board for Consumer Policies), Kjersti Graver (Nowegian Consumer Ombud Office), Suzanne Keller (Canadian Advertising Foundation), Patricia Mann (J. Walter Thompson, London), Prof. Dr. Christiane Schmerl (Bielefeld University, FRG), Alastair Tempest (European Advertising Tripartite, Brussels), Peter Thomson (London), Chiaki Shimads (JARO, Tokyo), Sally Washington (Ministry of Women's Affairs, Wellington, NZ), and Professor Robert G. Wyckham (Simon Fraser University, Canada).

2. In most cases, only one respondent provided answers for each country, although the respondents were people knowledgeable about the local situation: advertising practitioners, self-regulatory officials, legal experts, and government regulators.

## References

Advertising Association (UK). *The Portrayal of People in Advertisements: 1987 Peterhouse Seminar* (London: 1987).

Advertising Standards Authority (UK), *Annual Report 1986–87* (London: 1987).

Advertising Standards Authority (UK), *Herself Reappraised 1990* (London: 1990).

Rena Bartos, *Marketing to Women Around the World* (Boston: Harvard Business School Press, 1989).

Rena Bartos, *The Moving Target—What Every Marketer Should Know About Women* (New York: Free Press, 1982).

J. J. Boddewyn, *Advertising Self-Regulation: Sixteen Advanced Systems* (New York: International Advertising Association, October 1986).

J. J. Boddewyn, *Sexism and Decency in Advertising: Government Regulation and Industry Self-Regulation in 47 Countries* (New York: International Advertising Association, 1989).

Nadine Brozan, "Birth Control Ad: The Fight for

TV Time," *New York Times,* August 24, 1987, p. C12.

Jack Burton, "Malaysia Clamps Down on TV Advertising," *Advertising Age,* September 6, 1984, pp. 26–27.

Canadian Advertising Foundation, *Report to the Advertising Industry on Initiatives Re Sex-role Stereotyping for the Period April 1, 1987 to March 31, 1988* (Toronto: 31 May 1988).

Canadian Radio-television and Telecommunications Commission (CRTC), *Images of Women: Report of the Task Force on Sex-role Stereotyping in the Broadcast Media* (Hull, Quebec: Minister of Supply and Services, 1982).

Canadian Radio-television and Telecommunications Commission (CRTC), *Policy on Sex-role Stereotyping in the Broadcast Media* [Politique relative-aux stéréotypes sexuels dans les médias de la radiodiffusion] (Public Notice CRTC 1986–351: Ottawa, 22 December 1986).

A. E. Courtney and T. W. Whipple. *Sex Stereotyping in Advertising* (Lexington, Mass: Lexington Books, 1983).

European Advertising Tripartite, *The Portrayal of Women in the Media: An EAT Discussion Paper* (Brussels: August 1986).

European Parliament (EEC), *Report Drawn up on Behalf of the Committee on Women's Rights on the Depiction and Position of Women in the Media* [Marlene Lenz Report] (Strasbourg, France: 9 June 1987, Document A2-95/87).

J. H. Ferguson, P. J. Kreshel, and S. F. Tinkham, "In the Pages of *Ms.*: Sex Role Portrayals of Women in Advertising," *Journal of Advertising,* 19, 1 (1990): 40–51.

A. M. Freedman, "Never Have So Few Intimidated So Many," *Wall Street Journal,* March 20, 1989, p. B4.

M. C. Gilly, "Sex Roles in Advertising: A Comparison of Television Advertisements in Australia, Mexico, and the U.S.," *Journal of Marketing,* April 1988, pp. 75–85.

B. R. Goldberg, "TV Insults Men Too," *New York Times.* March 14, 1989, p. A29.

L. A. Heslop, J. Newman, and S. Gautier, "Reactions of Women to the Portrayal of Women in Magazine Ads," *Canadian Journal of Administrative Sciences,* June 1989, pp. 9–17.

M. B. Holbrook, "Mirror, Mirror on the Wall, What's Unfair in the Reflections on Advertising?" *Journal of Marketing,* July 1987, pp. 95–103.

Mary Jung, "Watchdog Group Lashes Out at Ads That Demean Men," *AMA Marketing News,* March 27, 1989, pp. 2ff.

F. W. Langrerh and C. L. Caywood, "An Assessment of the 'Sins' and 'Virtues' Portrayed in Advertising," *International Journal of Advertising,* 8 (1989): 391–403.

T. W. Leigh, A. J. Rethaus, and T. R. Whitney, "Role Portrayals of Women in Advertising," *Journal of Advertising Research,* October-November 1987, pp. 54–63.

Joshua Levine, "Fantasy, Not Flesh," *Forbes,* January 22, 1990, pp. 118–120.

Joanne Lipman, "Censored Scenes: Why You Rarely See Some Things in Television Ads," *Wall Street Journal,* August 17, 1987, p. 23.

M. Luqmani, U. Yavas, and Z. Quareshi, "Advertising in Saudi Arabia," *International Marketing Review,* 6, 1 (1989): 59–72.

Sissel Melgard, "Sexual Equality in Marketing" (Lysaker: Norwegian Consumer Ombud Office, no date).

National Swedish Board for Consumer Policies, *Könsdiskriminerande Reklam—Vad är Det?* ["Sexist Advertising—What Is That?"] (Vällingby, Sweden: Konsumentverket, 1987).

National Swedish Board for Consumer Policies, *Könsdiskriminerande Reklam—Nu Ska den Bort!* ["Sexist Advertising—Now It Must Go!"] (Vällingby, Sweden: Konsumentverket, 1989).

R. W. Pollay, "The Distorted Mirror: Reflections on the Unintended Consequences of Advertising," *Journal of Marketing,* April 1986, pp. 18–36.

L. N. Reid, C. T. Salmon, and L. C. Soley, "The Nature of Sexual Content in Television Advertsing: A Cross-Cultural Comparison of Award-Winning Commericals," in *1984 AMA Educators' Proceedings,* R. W. Belk et al., eds. (Chicago: American Marketing Association, Series No. 50, 1984), pp. 214–216.

H. J. Rotfeld and P. R. Parsons, "Self-Regulation and Magazine Advertising," *Journal of Advertising, 18,* 4 (1989): 33–40.

Randall Rothenberg, "Condom Makers Change Approach," *New York Times,* August 8, 1988, pp. D1.

Colin Shaw, "Sex and Violence, Plus Decent Research," *Marketing Review* (UK), February 1989, pp. 6–7.

Sherry B. Valan, "Broadcast Ad Standards for Personal Products," *Advertising Compliance Service,* December 21, 1987, pp. 5–7.

Laurel Wentz, "AIDS: Condom Advertising Charts Broader Course Overseas," *Advertising Age,* March 9, 1987, p. 62.

Aubrey Wilson and Christopher West, "The Marketing of 'Unmentionables,' " *Harvard Business Review,* January-February 1981, pp. 91–102.

World Federation of Advertisers, "The Portrayal of Women in Advertisements" (Brussels, April 1988).

R. G. Wyckham, "Self-Regulation of Sex Role Stereotyping in Advertising: The Canadian Experience," *Journal of Public Policy and Marketing,* 6 (1987): 76–92.

# Car Marketers Test Gray Area of Truth in Advertising

## Krystal Miller and Jacqueline Mitchell

*Staff Reporters of* The Wall Street Journal

DETROIT—Advertising executives are still shaking their heads in amazement at North American Volvo's blatant rigging of its "monster truck" commercial. The truth is, though, that some other auto ads aren't exactly what they seem.

In a **Volvo** ad from last year, a six-ton truck was lowered onto the roof of a Volvo car, which didn't sag at all under the truck's weight. But the car was propped up with jacks, which were hidden by shadows and thus invisible to viewers.

**Nissan Motor** touts its anti-lock brakes in a current spot that shows a side shot of a car screeching to a halt just in front of a standing man. But the man actually is closer to the camera than is the car.

**General Motors**' Oldsmobile division shows a car being dropped by parachute from the belly of an airborne cargo plane. The Olds 98 hits the ground and drives away. But it isn't the same car. The one dropped from the airplane, in fact, is just the empty shell of a car.

All three companies defend these ads, saying they don't make specific performance claims that are phony. And many ad specialists agree. But these experts add that commercials using trick photography can fall into an ethical gray area.

"There is nothing wrong with commercials that use skillful camera and film editing," says John Lichtenberger, managing editor of Advertising Compliance Service, a newsletter in Westport, Conn. "The problem arises, however, when those same techniques suggest product attributes that really don't exist."

Rajeev Batra, associate professor of marketing at the University of Michigan, says: "I don't find these commercials morally repugnant, or have any legal concerns about them." Nonetheless, he adds, "if you look at 100% literal truth, every day the consumer is getting deceived."

It isn't just auto ads that fall into gray areas; food and toy spots are among those that also use special effects to exaggerate their products. Many fast-food companies use coloring and special lighting to make their products look more appealing. "You couldn't find a hamburger that looks like that on TV in any restaurant," Mr. Lichtenberger says. "They spend days working on that hamburger."

Volvo's "monster truck" ad wasn't in a gray area. It depicted a pickup with oversized tires driving over the top of a row of cars, crushing the roofs of all except the Volvo. But the Volvo's roof was reinforced with lumber and steel that viewers couldn't see. And the other cars' roof-support pillars were severed or weakened.

Volvo has apologized for the ads, and the agency that made them—**WPP Group**'s Scali, McCabe, Sloves—resigned the account. But the company stoutly defends last year's ad showing a Volvo holding up a heavy-duty truck. It's a descendant of Volvo commercials from the early 1970s, which showed a Volvo holding up six other Volvos, also without sagging. In both the earlier and the latest ads, viewers saw the Volvos holding up lots of weight, but they didn't see the jacks placed between the cars' tires.

The reason: The ads were intended to show the strength of Volvo's roofs and bodies, which weren't reinforced, says a North American Volvo spokesman. They weren't meant to claim that Volvo's tires and suspensions can support such loads, he adds.

But some marketing specialists are skeptical of Volvo's justification. "That's an attempt to play mind games with the consumer," says Stephen A. Greyser, a professor of consumer marketing at Harvard Business School.

Mr. Greyser's objection is that some versions of the Volvo commercials didn't explicitly state that only the roof was being tested. One print version of the car-stacking ad did specifically discuss roof strength. But a print version of the truck ad didn't, saying: "What you see here is exactly what you think you see here." The TV ad that showed the truck being lowered onto the Volvo's roof simply stated: "How well does your car stand up to heavy traffic?" And the car-stacking TV ad said: "This Volvo is designed to be so strong it will also hold six Volvos."

Without the jacks, the Volvo spokesman says, the ads wouldn't have looked the same: "The tires would have exploded, and the springs would have compressed."

The Nissan commercial, in which a man appears to be standing directly in front of a moving car, wouldn't have looked the same without trick photography either. In fact, somebody might have been killed. During filming, the car ran "through" the plane of the man a couple of times, forcing re-shoots.

Still, John Rinek, Nissan's national advertising creative manager, says the ad is "an accurate braking demonstra-tion. The car was driving on wet pavement. It didn't skid when the brakes were applied."

**Honda Motor,** however, chose to put a "dramatization" label on a simi-lar commercial for the antilock brakes on its Acura luxury cars. In the com-mercial, an Acura car and a jet airplane appear headed straight toward each other on a runway, but stop just a couple of feet apart. In fact, the car and jet were filmed on parallel, adja-cent runways.

It's Honda's policy to use a drama-tization label "whenever we depict something in a commercial that could possibly be misconstrued," a spokes-man says.

The Oldsmobile air drop commercial isn't labeled a dramatization. That wasn't necessary, an Oldsmobile spokesman says, because the commer-cial doesn't discuss the car's performance. Instead, it touts the Olds-mobile customer satisfaction program, and the parachute is meant to represent the security that the program provides.

"Oldsmobile isn't making any claims that the car could drive away after a parachute drop," says Prof. Batra, and thus a disclaimer isn't nec-essary.

# Developing the Future Ethos and Social Responsibility of Business

Business ethics should not be viewed as a short-term "knee-jerk reaction" to recently revealed scandals and corruptions. Instead, it should be viewed as a thread woven through the fabric of the entire business culture—one that ought to be integral to its design. Businesses are built on the foundation of trust in our free enterprise system. When there are violations of this trust between competitors, between employer and employees, or between businesses and consumers, the system ceases to run smoothly.

From a pragmatic viewpoint, the alternative to self-regulated and voluntary ethical behavior and social responsibility on the part of business may be governmental and legislative intervention. From a moral viewpoint, ethical behavior should not exist because of economic pragmatism, governmental edict, or contemporary fashionability—it should exist because it is morally appropriate and right.

This last section is composed of five articles that provide some ideas, guidelines, and principles for developing the future ethos and social responsibility of business. Dr. Archie B. Carroll's article, "The Pyramid of Corporate Responsibility," begins this section by advocating that the total corporate responsibility of business entails simultaneously fulfilling the firm's economic, legal, ethical, and philanthropic responsibilities. He concludes his article by examining the important differences between immoral, amoral, and moral management. The next article points out the importance of establishing an ethical work environment and suggests steps and ingredients that a company can utilize in building a business ethics program. The last three articles elucidate why proper articulation of a corporation's environmental responsibilities and environmentalism will possibly be the most important area of focus for business in the 1990s.

## Looking Ahead: Challenge Questions

In what areas should organizations become more ethically sensitive and socially responsible in the next five years?

Do you agree with the author of "Environmentalism: The New Crusade" that environmentalism will be the most important issue for business in the 1990s? Why or why not?

Obtain codes of ethics or conduct from several different professional associations (doctors, lawyers, CPAs, etc.). What are the similarities and differences between them?

How useful do you feel codes of ethics are to organizations? Why?

Archie B. Carroll, in his article "The Pyramid of Corporate Responsibility," distinguishes between immoral, amoral, and moral management. From your perspective, which form of management is most prevalent in today's business landscape?

# Unit 5

# The Pyramid of Corporate Social Responsibility: Toward the Moral Management of Organizational Stakeholders

## Archie B. Carroll

*Archie B. Carroll is Robert W. Scherer Professor of Management and Corporate Public Affairs at the College of Business Administration, University of Georgia, Athens.*

F or the better part of 30 years now, corporate executives have struggled with the issue of the firm's responsibility to its society. Early on it was argued by some that the corporation's sole responsibility was to provide a maximum financial return to shareholders. It became quickly apparent to everyone, however, that this pursuit of financial gain had to take place within the laws of the land. Though social activist groups and others throughout the 1960s advocated a broader notion of corporate responsibility, it was not until the significant social legislation of the early 1970s that this message became indelibly clear as a result of the creation of the Environmental Protection Agency (EPA), the Equal Employment Opportunity Commission (EEOC), the Occupational Safety and Health Administration (OSHA), and the Consumer Product Safety Commission (CPSC).

These new governmental bodies established that national public policy now officially recognized the environment, employees, and consumers to be significant and legitimate stakeholders of business. From that time on, corporate executives have had to wrestle with how they balance their commitments to the corporation's owners with their obligations to an ever-broadening group of stakeholders who claim both legal and ethical rights.

This article will explore the nature of corporate social responsibility (CSR) with an eye toward understanding its component parts. The intention will be to characterize the firm's CSR in ways that might be useful to executives who wish to reconcile their obligations to their share-

> *Social responsibility can only become reality if more managers become moral instead of amoral or immoral.*

holders with those to other competing groups claiming legitimacy. This discussion will be framed by a pyramid of corporate social responsibility. Next, we plan to relate this concept to the idea of stakeholders. Finally, our goal will be to isolate the ethical or moral component of CSR and relate it to perspectives that reflect three major ethical approaches to management—immoral, amoral, and moral. The principal goal in this final section will be to flesh out what it means to manage stakeholders in an ethical or moral fashion.

## EVOLUTION OF CORPORATE SOCIAL RESPONSIBILITY

W hat does it mean for a corporation to be socially responsible? Academics and practitioners have been striving to establish an agreed-upon definition of this concept for 30 years. In 1960, Keith Davis suggested that social responsibility refers to businesses' "decisions and actions taken for reasons at least partially beyond the firm's direct economic or technical interest." At about the same time, Eells and Walton (1961) argued that CSR refers to the

**Figure 1**
**Economic and Legal Components of Corporate Social Responsibility**

| Economic Components (Responsibilities) | Legal Components (Responsibilities) |
|---|---|
| 1. It is important to perform in a manner consistent with maximizing earnings per share. | 1. It is important to perform in a manner consistent with expectations of government and law. |
| 2. It is important to be committed to being as profitable as possible. | 2. It is important to comply with various federal, state, and local regulations. |
| 3. It is important to maintain a strong competitive position. | 3. It is important to be a law-abiding corporate citizen. |
| 4. It is important to maintain a high level of operating efficiency. | 4. It is important that a successful firm be defined as one that fulfills its legal obligations. |
| 5. It is important that a successful firm be defined as one that is consistently profitable. | 5. It is important to provide goods and services that at least meet minimal legal requirements. |

"problems that arise when corporate enterprise casts its shadow on the social scene, and the ethical principles that ought to govern the relationship between the corporation and society."

In 1971 the Committee for Economic Development used a "three concentric circles" approach to depicting CSR. The inner circle included basic economic functions—growth, products, jobs. The intermediate circle suggested that the economic functions must be exercised with a sensitive awareness of changing social values and priorities. The outer circle outlined newly emerging and still amorphous responsibilities that business should assume to become more actively involved in improving the social environment.

The attention was shifted from social responsibility to social responsiveness by several other writers. Their basic argument was that the emphasis on responsibility focused exclusively on the notion of business obligation and motivation and that action or performance were being overlooked. The social responsiveness movement, therefore, emphasized corporate action, proaction, and implementation of a social role. This was indeed a necessary reorientation.

The question still remained, however, of reconciling the firm's economic orientation with its social orientation. A step in this direction was taken when a comprehensive definition of CSR was set forth. In this view, a four-part conceptualization of CSR included the idea that the corporation has not only economic and legal obliga-

tions, but ethical and discretionary (philanthropic) responsibilities as well (Carroll 1979). The point here was that CSR, to be accepted as legitimate, had to address the entire spectrum of obligations business has to society, including the most fundamental—economic. It is upon this four-part perspective that our pyramid is based.

In recent years, the term corporate social performance (CSP) has emerged as an inclusive and global concept to embrace corporate social responsibility, responsiveness, and the entire spectrum of socially beneficial activities of businesses. The focus on social performance emphasizes the concern for corporate action and accomplishment in the social sphere. With a performance perspective, it is clear that firms must formulate and implement social goals and programs as well as integrate ethical sensitivity into all decision making, policies, and actions. With a results focus, CSP suggests an all-encompassing orientation towards normal criteria by which we assess business performance to include quantity, quality, effectiveness, and efficiency. While we recognize the vitality of the performance concept, we have chosen to adhere to the CSR terminology for our present discussion. With just a slight change of focus, however, we could easily be discussing a CSP rather than a CSR pyramid. In any event, our long-term concern is what managers do with these ideas in terms of implementation.

**Figure 2**
**Ethical and Philanthropic Components of**
**Corporate Social Responsibility**

| Ethical Components (Responsibilities) | Philanthropic Components (Responsibilities) |
|---|---|
| 1. It is important to perform in a manner consistent with expectations of societal mores and ethical norms. | 1. It is important to perform in a manner consistent with the philanthropic and charitable expectations of society. |
| 2. It is important to recognize and respect new or evolving ethical/moral norms adopted by society. | 2. It is important to assist the fine and performing arts. |
| 3. It is important to prevent ethical norms from being compromised in order to achieve corporate goals. | 3. It is important that managers and employees participate in voluntary and charitable activities within their local communities. |
| 4. It is important that good corporate citizenship be defined as doing what is expected morally or ethically. | 4. It is important to provide assistance to private and public educational institutions. |
| 5. It is important to recognize that corporate integrity and ethical behavior go beyond mere compliance with laws and regulations. | 5. It is important to assist voluntarily those projects that enhance a community's "quality of life." |

## THE PYRAMID OF CORPORATE SOCIAL RESPONSIBILITY

For CSR to be accepted by a conscientious business person, it should be framed in such a way that the entire range of business responsibilities are embraced. It is suggested here that four kinds of social responsibilities constitute total CSR: economic, legal, ethical, and philanthropic. Furthermore, these four categories or components of CSR might be depicted as a pyramid. To be sure, all of these kinds of responsibilities have always existed to some extent, but it has only been in recent years that ethical and philanthropic functions have taken a significant place. Each of these four categories deserves closer consideration.

### Economic Responsibilities

Historically, business organizations were created as economic entities designed to provide goods and services to societal members. The profit motive was established as the primary incentive for entrepreneurship. Before it was anything else, the business organization was the basic economic unit in our society. As such, its principal role was to produce goods and services that consumers needed and wanted and to make an acceptable profit in the process. At some point the idea of the profit motive got transformed into a notion of maximum profits, and this has been an enduring value ever since. All other business responsibilities are predicated upon the economic responsibility of the firm, because without it the others become moot considerations. **Figure 1** summarizes some important statements characterizing economic responsibilities. Legal responsibilities are also depicted in Figure 1, and we will consider them next.

### Legal Responsibilities

Society has not only sanctioned business to operate according to the profit motive; at the same time business is expected to comply with the laws and regulations promulgated by federal, state, and local governments as the ground rules under which business must operate. As a partial fulfillment of the "social contract" between business and society, firms are expected to pursue their economic missions within the framework of the law. Legal responsibilities reflect a view of "codified ethics" in the sense that they embody basic notions of fair operations as established by our lawmakers. They are depicted as the next layer on the pyramid to portray their historical development, but they are appropriately seen as coexisting with economic responsibilities as fundamental precepts of the free enterprise system.

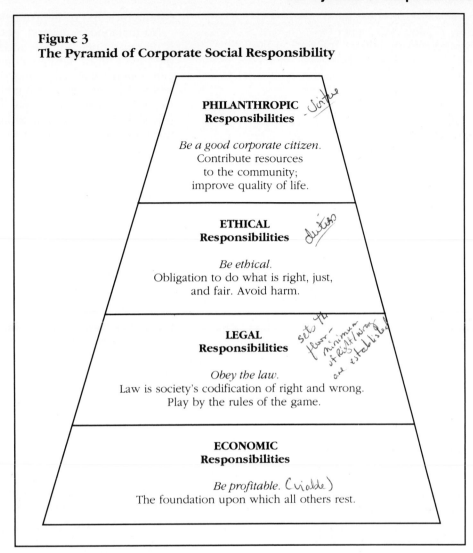

**Figure 3**
**The Pyramid of Corporate Social Responsibility**

**PHILANTHROPIC Responsibilities** — *Justice*

*Be a good corporate citizen.*
Contribute resources
to the community;
improve quality of life.

**ETHICAL Responsibilities** — *duties*

*Be ethical.*
Obligation to do what is right, just,
and fair. Avoid harm.

**LEGAL Responsibilities** — *set the floor - minimum of Right/Wrong and established*

*Obey the law.*
Law is society's codification of right and wrong.
Play by the rules of the game.

**ECONOMIC Responsibilities**

*Be profitable.* (viable)
The foundation upon which all others rest.

**Ethical Responsibilities**

Although economic and legal responsibilities embody ethical norms about fairness and justice, ethical responsibilities embrace those activities and practices that are expected or prohibited by societal members even though they are not codified by law. Ethical responsibilities embody those standards, norms, or expectations that reflect a concern for what consumers, employees, shareholders, and the community regard as fair, just, or in keeping with the respect or protection of stakeholders' moral rights.

In one sense, changing ethics or values precede the establishment of law because they become the driving force behind the very creation of laws or regulations. For example, the environmental, civil rights, and consumer movements reflected basic alterations in societal values and thus may be seen as ethical bellwethers foreshadowing and resulting in the later legislation. In another sense, ethical re-

sponsibilities may be seen as embracing newly emerging values and norms society expects business to meet, even though such values and norms may reflect a higher standard of performance than that currently required by law. Ethical responsibilities in this sense are often ill-defined or continually under public debate as to their legitimacy, and thus are frequently difficult for business to deal with.

Superimposed on these ethical expectations emanating from societal groups are the implied levels of ethical performance suggested by a consideration of the great ethical principles of moral philosophy. This would include such principles as justice, rights, and utilitarianism.

The business ethics movement of the past decade has firmly established an ethical responsibility as a legitimate CSR component. Though it is depicted as the next layer of the CSR pyramid, it must be constantly recognized that it is in dynamic interplay with the legal responsibility category. That is, it is constantly pushing the legal responsibility category to broaden or expand while at the same time placing ever higher expectations on businesspersons to operate at levels above that required by law. **Figure 2** depicts statements that help characterize ethical responsibilities. The figure also summarizes philanthropic responsibilities, discussed next.

## Philanthropic Responsibilities

Philanthropy encompasses those corporate actions that are in response to society's expectation that businesses be good corporate citizens. This includes actively engaging in acts or programs to promote human welfare or goodwill. Examples of philanthropy include business contributions of financial resources or executive time, such as contributions to the arts, education, or the community. A loaned-executive program that provides leadership for a community's United Way campaign is one illustration of philanthropy.

The distinguishing feature between philanthropic and ethical responsibilities is that the former are not expected in an ethical or moral sense. Communities desire firms to contribute their money, facilities, and employee time to humanitarian programs or purposes, but they do not regard the firms as unethical if they do not provide the desired level. Therefore, philanthropy is more discretionary or voluntary on the part of businesses even though there is always the societal expectation that businesses provide it.

One notable reason for making the distinction between philanthropic and ethical responsibilities is that some firms feel they are being socially responsible if they are just good citizens in the community. This distinction brings home the vital point that CSR includes philanthropic contributions but is not limited to them. In fact, it would be argued here that philanthropy is highly desired and prized but actually less important than the other three categories of social responsibility. In a sense, philanthropy is icing on the cake—or on the pyramid, using our metaphor.

The pyramid of corporate social responsibility is depicted in **Figure 3**. It portrays the four components of CSR, beginning with the basic building block notion that economic performance undergirds all else. At the same time, business is expected to obey the law because the law is society's codification of acceptable and unacceptable behavior. Next is business's responsibility to be ethical. At its most fundamental level, this is the obligation to do what is right, just, and fair, and to avoid or minimize harm to stakeholders (employees, consumers, the environment, and others). Finally, business is expected to be a good corporate citizen. This is captured in the philanthropic responsibility, wherein business is expected to contribute financial and human resources to the community and to improve the quality of life.

No metaphor is perfect, and the CSR pyramid is no exception. It is intended to portray that the total CSR of business comprises distinct components that, taken together, constitute the whole. Though the components have been treated as separate concepts for discussion purposes, they are not mutually exclusive and are not intended to juxtapose a firm's economic responsibilities with its other responsibilities. At the same time, a consideration of the separate components helps the manager see that the different types of obligations are in a constant but dynamic tension with one another. The most critical tensions, of course, would be between economic and legal, economic and ethical, and economic and philanthropic. The traditionalist might see this as a conflict between a firm's "concern for profits" versus its "concern for society," but it is suggested here that this is an oversimplification. A CSR or stakeholder perspective would recognize these tensions as organizational realities, but focus on the total pyramid as a unified whole and how the firm might engage in decisions, actions, and programs that simultaneously fulfill all its component parts.

In summary, the total corporate social responsibility of business entails the simultaneous fulfillment of the firm's economic, legal, ethical, and philanthropic responsibilities. Stated in more pragmatic and managerial terms, the CSR firm should strive to make a profit, obey the law, be ethical, and be a good corporate citizen.

Upon first glance, this array of responsibilities may seem broad. They seem to be in striking contrast to the classical economic argument that management has one responsibility: to maximize the profits of its owners or shareholders. Economist Milton Friedman, the most outspoken proponent of this view, has argued that social matters are not the concern of business people and that these problems should be resolved by the unfettered workings of the free market system. Friedman's argument loses some of its punch, however, when you consider his assertion in its totality. Friedman posited that management is "to make as much money as possible while conforming to the basic rules of society, both those embodied in the law and those embodied in ethical custom" (Friedman 1970). Most people focus on the first part of Friedman's quote but not the second part. It seems clear from this statement that profits, conformity to the law, and ethical custom embrace three components of the CSR pyramid—economic, legal, and ethical. That only leaves the philanthropic component for Friedman to reject. Although it may be appropriate for an economist to take this view, one would not encounter many business executives today who exclude philanthropic programs from their firms' range of activities. It seems the role of corporate

**Figure 4**
**Stakeholder/Responsibility Matrix**

*Types of CSR*

| *Stakeholders* | Economic | Legal | Ethical | Philanthropic |
|---|---|---|---|---|
| Owners | | | | |
| Customers | | | | |
| Employees | | | | |
| Community | | | | |
| Competitors | | | | |
| Suppliers | | | | |
| Social Activist Groups | | | | |
| Public at Large | | | | |
| Others | | | | |

citizenship is one that business has no significant problem embracing. Undoubtedly this perspective is rationalized under the rubric of enlightened self interest.

We next propose a conceptual framework to assist the manager in integrating the four CSR components with organizational stakeholders.

## CSR AND ORGANIZATIONAL STAKEHOLDERS

There is a natural fit between the idea of corporate social responsibility and an organization's stakeholders. The word "social" in CSR has always been vague and lacking in specific direction as to whom the corporation is responsible. The concept of stakeholder personalizes social or societal responsibilities by delineating the specific groups or persons business should consider in its CSR orientation. Thus, the stakeholder nomenclature puts "names and faces" on the societal members who are most urgent to business, and to whom it must be responsive.

By now most executives understand that the term "stakeholder" constitutes a play on the word stockholder and is intended to more appropriately describe those groups or persons who have a stake, a claim, or an interest in the operations and decisions of the firm. Sometimes the stake might represent a legal claim, such as that which might be held by an owner, an employee, or a customer who has an explicit or implicit contract. Other times it might be represented by a moral claim, such as when these groups assert a right to be treated fairly or with due process, or to have

their opinions taken into consideration in an important business decision.

Management's challenge is to decide which stakeholders merit and receive consideration in the decision-making process. In any given instance, there may be numerous stakeholder groups (shareholders, consumers, employees, suppliers, community, social activist groups) clamoring for management's attention. How do managers sort out the urgency or importance of the various stakeholder claims? Two vital criteria include the stakeholders' legitimacy and their power. From a CSR perspective their legitimacy may be most important. From a management efficiency perspective, their power might be of central influence. Legitimacy refers to the extent to which a group has a justifiable right to be making its claim. For example, a group of 300 employees about to be laid off by a plant-closing decision has a more legitimate claim on management's attention than the local chamber of commerce, which is worried about losing the firm as one of its dues-paying members. The stakeholder's power is another factor. Here we may witness significant differences. Thousands of small, individual investors, for example, wield very little power unless they can find a way to get organized. By contrast, institutional investors and large mutual fund groups have significant power over management because of the sheer magnitude of their investments and the fact that they are organized.

With these perspectives in mind, let us think of stakeholder management as a process by which managers reconcile their own objectives with the claims and expectations being made on them by various stakeholder groups. The challenge of stakeholder management is to ensure that the firm's primary stakeholders achieve their objectives while other stakeholders are also satisfied. Even though this "win-win" outcome is not always possible, it does represent a legitimate and desirable goal for management to pursue to protect its long-term interests.

The important functions of stakeholder management are to describe, understand, analyze, and finally, manage. Thus, five major questions might be posed to capture the essential ingredients we need for stakeholder management:

1. Who are our stakeholders?
2. What are their stakes?
3. What opportunities and challenges are presented by our stakeholders?
4. What corporate social responsibilities (economic, legal, ethical, and philanthropic) do we have to our stakeholders?
5. What strategies, actions, or decisions should we take to best deal with these responsibilities?

Whereas much could be discussed about each of these questions, let us direct our attention here to question four—what kinds of social responsibilities do we have to our stakeholders? Our objective here is to present a conceptual approach for examining these issues. This conceptual approach or framework is presented as the stakeholder/responsibility matrix in **Figure 4**.

This matrix is intended to be used as an analytical tool or template to organize a manager's thoughts and ideas about what the firm ought to be doing in an economic, legal, ethical, and philanthropic sense with respect to its identified stakeholder groups. By carefully and deliberately moving through the various cells of the matrix, the manager may develop a significant descriptive and analytical data base that can then be used for purposes of stakeholder management. The information resulting from this stakeholder/responsibility analysis should be useful when developing priorities and making both long-term and short-term decisions involving multiple stakeholder's interests.

**To be sure, thinking in stakeholder-responsibility terms increases the complexity of decision making and may be extremely time consuming and taxing, especially at first. Despite its complexity, however, this approach is one methodology management can use to integrate values—what it stands for—with the traditional economic mission of the organization. In the final analysis, such an integration could be of significant usefulness to management. This is because the stakeholder/responsibility perspective is most consistent with the pluralistic environment faced by business today. As such, it provides the opportunity for an in-depth corporate appraisal of financial**

as well as social and economic concerns. Thus, the stakeholder/responsibility perspective would be an invaluable foundation for responding to the fifth stakeholder management question about strategies, actions, or decisions that should be pursued to effectively respond to the environment business faces.

## MORAL MANAGEMENT AND STAKEHOLDERS

At this juncture we would like to expound upon the link between the firm's ethical responsibilities or perspectives and its major stakeholder groups. Here we are isolating the ethical component of our CSR pyramid and discussing it more thoroughly in the context of stakeholders. One way to do this would be to use major ethical principles such as those of justice, rights, and utilitarianism to identify and describe our ethical responsibilities. We will take another alternative, however, and discuss stakeholders within the context of three major ethical approaches—immoral management, amoral management, and moral management. These three ethical approaches were defined and discussed in an earlier *Business Horizons* article (Carroll 1987). We will briefly describe and review these three ethical types and then suggest how they might be oriented toward the major stakeholder groups. Our goal is to profile the likely orientation of the three ethical types with a special emphasis upon moral management, our preferred ethical approach.

### Three Moral Types

If we accept that the terms ethics and morality are essentially synonymous in the organizational context, we may speak of immoral, amoral, and moral management as descriptive categories of three different kinds of managers. Immoral management is characterized by those managers whose decisions, actions, and behavior suggest an active opposition to what is deemed right or ethical. Decisions by immoral managers are discordant with accepted ethical principles and, indeed, imply an active negation of what is moral. These managers care only about their or their organization's profitability and success. They see legal standards as barriers or impediments management must overcome to accomplish what it wants. Their strategy is to exploit opportunities for personal or corporate gain.

An example might be helpful. Many observers would argue that Charles Keating could be described as an immoral manager. According to the federal government, Keating recklessly and fraudulently ran California's Lincoln Savings into the ground, reaping $34 million for himself and his family. A major accounting firm said about Keating: "Seldom in our experience as accountants have we experienced a more egregious

**Figure 5**
**Three Moral Types and Orientation Toward**
**Stakeholder Groups: Owners and Employees**

| Type of Management | Orientation Toward Owner/Shareholder Stakeholders |
|---|---|
| Immoral Management | Shareholders are minimally treated and given short shrift. Focus is on maximizing positions of executive groups—maximizing executive compensation, perks, benefits. Golden parachutes are more important than returns to shareholders. Managers maximize their positions without shareholders being made aware. Concealment from shareholders is the operating procedure. Self-interest of management group is the order of the day. |
| Amoral Management | No special thought is given to shareholders; they are there and must be minimally accommodated. Profit focus of the business is their reward. No thought is given to ethical consequences of decisions for any stakeholder group, including owners. Communication is limited to that required by law. |
| Moral Management | Shareholders' interest (short- and long-term) is a central factor. The best way to be ethical to shareholders is to treat all stakeholder claimants in a fair and ethical manner. To protect shareholders, an ethics committee of the board is created. Code of ethics is established, promulgated, and made a living document to protect shareholders' and others' interests. |

| Type of Management | Orientation Toward Employee Stakeholders |
|---|---|
| Immoral Management | Employees are viewed as factors of production to be used, exploited, manipulated for gain of individual manager or company. No concern is shown for employees' needs/rights/expectations. Short-term focus. Coercive, controlling, alienating. |
| Amoral Management | Employees are treated as law requires. Attempts to motivate focus on increasing productivity rather than satisfying employees' growing maturity needs. Employees still seen as factors of production but remunerative approach used. Organization sees self-interest in treating employees with minimal respect. Organization structure, pay incentives, rewards all geared toward short- and medium-term productivity. |
| Moral Management | Employees are a human resource that must be treated with dignity and respect. Goal is to use a leadership style such as consultative/participative that will result in mutual confidence and trust. Commitment is a recurring theme. Employees' rights to due process, privacy, freedom of speech, and safety are maximally considered in all decisions. Management seeks out fair dealings with employees. |

example of the misapplication of generally accepted accounting principles" ("Good Timing, Charlie" 1989).

The second major type of management ethics is amoral management. Amoral managers are neither immoral nor moral but are not sensitive to the fact that their everyday business decisions may have deleterious effects on others. These managers lack ethical perception or awareness. That is, they go through their organizational lives not thinking that their actions have an ethical dimension. Or they may just be careless or inattentive to the implications of their actions on stakeholders. These managers may be well intentioned, but do not see that their business decisions and actions may be hurting those with whom they transact business or interact. Typically their orientation is towards the letter of the law as their ethical guide. We have been describing a sub-category of amorality known as unintentional amoral managers. There is also another group we may call intentional amoral managers. These managers simply think that ethical considerations are for our private lives, not for business. They believe that business activity resides outside the sphere to which moral judgments apply. Though most amoral managers today are unintentional, there may still exist a few who just do not see a role for ethics in business.

Examples of unintentional amorality abound.

**Figure 6**
**Three Moral Types and Orientation Toward**
**Stakeholder Groups: Customers and Local Community**

| Type of Management | Orientation Toward Customer Stakeholders |
| --- | --- |
| Immoral Management | Customers are viewed as opportunities to be exploited for personal or organizational gain. Ethical standards in dealings do not prevail; indeed, an active intent to cheat, deceive, and/or mislead is present. In all marketing decisions—advertising, pricing, packaging, distribution—customer is taken advantage of to the fullest extent. |
| Amoral Management | Management does not think through the ethical consequences of its decisions and actions. It simply makes decisions with profitability within the letter of the law as a guide. Management is not focused on what is fair from perspective of customer. Focus is on management's rights. No consideration is given to ethical implications of interactions with customers. |
| Moral Management | Customer is viewed as equal partner in transaction. Customer brings needs/expectations to the exchange transaction and is treated fairly. Managerial focus is on giving customer fair value, full information, fair guarantee, and satisfaction. Consumer rights are liberally interpreted and honored. |

| Type of Management | Orientation Toward Local Community Stakeholders |
| --- | --- |
| Immoral Management | Exploits community to fullest extent; pollutes the environment. Plant or business closings take fullest advantage of community. Actively disregards community needs. Takes fullest advantage of community resources without giving anything in return. Violates zoning and other ordinances whenever it can for its own advantage. |
| Amoral Management | Does not take community or its resources into account in management decision making. Community factors are assumed to be irrelevant to business decisions. Community, like employees, is a factor of production. Legal considerations are followed, but nothing more. Deals minimally with community, its people, community activity, local government. |
| Moral Management | Sees vital community as a goal to be actively pursued. Seeks to be a leading citizen and to motivate others to do likewise. Gets actively involved and helps institutions that need help—schools, recreational groups, philanthropic groups. Leadership position in environment, education, culture/arts, volunteerism, and general community affairs. Firm engages in strategic philanthropy. Management sees community goals and company goals as mutually interdependent. |

When police departments stipulated that applicants must be 5'10" and weigh 180 pounds to qualify for positions, they just did not think about the adverse impact their policy would have on women and some ethnic groups who, on average, do not attain that height and weight. The liquor, beer, and cigarette industries provide other examples. They did not anticipate that their products would create serious moral issues: alcoholism, drunk driving deaths, lung cancer, deteriorating health, and offensive secondary smoke. Finally, when McDonald's initially decided to use polystyrene containers for food packaging it just did not adequately consider the environmental impact that would be caused. McDonald's surely does not intentionally create a solid waste disposal prob-

lem, but one major consequence of its business is just that. Fortunately, the company has responded to complaints by replacing the polystyrene packaging with paper products.

Moral management is our third ethical approach, one that should provide a striking contrast. In moral management, ethical norms that adhere to a high standard of right behavior are employed. Moral managers not only conform to accepted and high levels of professional conduct, they also commonly exemplify leadership on ethical issues. Moral managers want to be profitable, but only within the confines of sound legal and ethical precepts, such as fairness, justice, and due process. Under this approach, the orientation is toward both the letter and the spirit of the law.

Law is seen as minimal ethical behavior and the preference and goal is to operate well above what the law mandates. Moral managers seek out and use sound ethical principles such as justice, rights, utilitarianism, and the Golden Rule to guide their decisions. When ethical dilemmas arise, moral managers assume a leadership position for their companies and industries.

There are numerous examples of moral management. When IBM took the lead and developed its Open Door policy to provide a mechanism through which employees might pursue their due process rights, this could be considered moral management. Similarly, when IBM initiated its Four Principles of Privacy to protect privacy rights of employees, this was moral management. When McCullough Corporation withdrew from the Chain Saw Manufacturers Association because the association fought mandatory safety standards for the industry, this was moral management. McCullough knew its product was potentially dangerous and had used chain brakes on its own saws for years, even though it was not required by law to do so. Another example of moral management was when Maguire Thomas Partners, a Los Angeles commercial developer, helped solve urban problems by saving and refurbishing historic sites, putting up structures that matched old ones, limiting building heights to less than the law allowed, and using only two-thirds of the allowable building density so that open spaces could be provided.

## Orientation Toward Stakeholders

Now that we have a basic understanding of the three ethical types or approaches, we will propose profiles of what the likely stakeholder orientation might be toward the major stakeholder groups using each of the three ethical approaches. Our goal is to accentuate the moral management approach by contrasting it with the other two types.

Basically, there are five major stakeholder groups that are recognized as priorities by most firms, across industry lines and in spite of size or location: owners (shareholders), employees, customers, local communities, and the society-at-large. Although the general ethical obligation to each of these groups is essentially identical (protect their rights, treat them with respect and fairness), specific behaviors and orientations arise because of the differing nature of the groups. In an attempt to flesh out the character and salient features of the three ethical types and their stakeholder orientations, **Figures 5** and **6** summarize the orientations these three types might assume with respect to four of the major stakeholder groups. Because of space constraints and the general nature of the society-at-large category, it has been omitted.

By carefully considering the described stakeholder orientations under each of the three ethical types, a richer appreciation of the moral management approach should be possible. Our goal here is to gain a fuller understanding of what it means to engage in moral management and what this implies for interacting with stakeholders. To be sure, there are other stakeholder groups to which moral management should be directed, but again, space precludes their discussion here. This might include thinking of managers and non-managers as distinct categories of employees and would also embrace such groups as suppliers, competitors, special interest groups, government, and the media.

Though the concept of corporate social responsibility may from time to time be supplanted by various other focuses such as social responsiveness, social performance, public policy, ethics, or stakeholder management, an underlying challenge for all is to define the kinds of responsibilities management and businesses have to the constituency groups with which they transact and interact most frequently. The pyramid of corporate social responsibility gives us a framework for understanding the evolving nature of the firm's economic, legal, ethical, and philanthropic performance. The implementation of these responsibilities may vary depending upon the firm's size, management's philosophy, corporate strategy, industry characteristics, the state of the economy, and other such mitigating conditions, but the four component parts provide management with a skeletal outline of the nature and kinds of their CSR. In frank, action-oriented terms, business is called upon to: be profitable, obey the law, be ethical, and be a good corporate citizen.

The stakeholder management perspective provides not only a language and way to personalize relationships with names and faces, but also some useful conceptual and analytical concepts for diagnosing, analyzing, and prioritizing an organization's relationships and strategies. Effective organizations will progress beyond stakeholder identification and question what opportunities and threats are posed by stakeholders; what economic, legal, ethical, and philanthropic responsibilities they have; and what strategies, actions or decisions should be pursued to most effectively address these responsibilities. The stakeholder/responsibility matrix provides a template management might use to organize its analysis and decision making.

Throughout the article we have been building toward the notion of an improved ethical organizational climate as manifested by moral management. Moral management was defined and described through a contrast with immoral and amoral management. Because the business landscape is replete with immoral and amoral managers, moral managers may sometimes be hard to find. Regardless, their characteristics have been identified and, most important, their perspective or orientation towards the major stakeholder groups has been profiled. These stakeholder orientation profiles give managers a conceptual but practical touchstone for sorting out the different categories or types of ethical (or not-so-ethical) behavior that may be found in business and other organizations.

It has often been said that leadership by example is the most effective way to improve business ethics. If that is true, moral management provides a model leadership perspective or orientation that managers may wish to emulate. One great fear is that managers may think they are providing ethical leadership just by rejecting immoral management. However, amoral management, particularly the unintentional variety, may unconsciously prevail if managers are not aware of what it is and of its dangers. At best, amorality represents ethical neutrality, and this notion is not tenable in the society of the 1990s. The standard must be set high, and moral management provides the best exemplar of what that lofty standard might embrace. Further, moral management, to be fully appreciated, needs to be seen within the context of organization-stakeholder relationships. It is toward this singular goal that our entire discussion has focused. If the "good society" is to become a realization, such a high expectation only naturally becomes the aspiration and preoccupation of management.

## References

R.W. Ackerman and R.A. Bauer, *Corporate Social Responsiveness* (Reston, Va.: Reston Publishing Co, 1976).

A.B. Carroll, "A Three-Dimensional Conceptual Model of Corporate Social Performance," *Academy of Management Review*, 4, 4 (1979): 497-505.

A.B. Carroll, "In Search of the Moral Manager," *Business Horizons*, March-April 1987, pp. 7-15.

Committee for Economic Development, *Social Responsibilities of Business Corporations* (New York: CED, 1971).

K. Davis, "Can Business Afford to Ignore its Social Responsibilities?" *California Management Review*, 2, 3 (1960): 70-76.

R. Eells and C. Walton, *Conceptual Foundations of Business* (Homewood, Ill.: Richard D. Irwin, 1961).

"Good Timing, Charlie," *Forbes*, November 27, 1989, pp. 140-144.

W.C. Frederick, "From $CSR_1$ to $CSR_2$: The Maturing of Business and Society Thought," University of Pittsburgh Working Paper No. 279, 1978.

M. Friedman, "The Social Responsibility of Business Is to Increase its Profits," *New York Times*, September 13, 1970, pp. 122-126.

S.P. Sethi, "Dimensions of Corporate Social Responsibility," *California Management Review*, 17, 3 (1975): 58-64.

# Creating Ethical Corporate Structures

Patrick E. Murphy
University of Notre Dame

*Patrick E. Murphy is Associate Professor of Marketing at the College of Business Administration, University of Notre Dame. Dr. Murphy holds the B.B.A. degree from the University of Notre Dame, the M.B.A. degree from Bradley University, and the Ph.D. degree from the University of Houston. He is currently editor of the* Journal of Public Policy and Marketing.

ETHICAL BUSINESS PRACTICES stem from ethical corporate cultures, the author writes. How does an organization go about developing that kind of culture? The most systematic approach is to build and nurture structures that emphasize the importance of ethical considerations. This paper outlines several companies' experiences with three types of ethics-enhancing structures: corporate credos, programs such as training workshops and ethics "audits," and codes tailored to the specific needs of a functional area. *Ed.*

WHAT IS AN ETHICAL COMPANY? This question is not easy to answer. For the most part, ethical problems occur because corporate managers and their subordinates are *too* devoted to the organization. In their loyalty to the company or zest to gain recognition, people sometimes ignore or overstep ethical boundaries. For example, some sales managers believe that the only way to meet ambitious sales goals is to have the sales reps "buy" business with lavish entertaining and gift giving. This overzealousness is the key source of ethical problems in most business firms.

Employees are looking for guidance in dealing with ethical problems. This guidance may come from the CEO, upper management, or immediate supervisors.[1] We know that ethical business practices stem from an ethical corporate culture. Key questions are, How can this culture be created and sustained? What structural approaches encourage ethical decision making? If the goal is to make the company ethical, managers must introduce structural components that will enhance ethical sensitivity.

In this paper, I examine three promising and workable approaches to infusing ethical principles into businesses:

• corporate credos that define and give direction to corporate values;

• ethics programs where companywide efforts focus on ethical issues; and

• ethical codes that provide specific guidance to employees in functional business areas.

Below I review the virtues and limitations of each and provide examples of companies that successfully employ these approaches.

## Corporate Credos

A corporate credo delineates a company's ethical responsibility to its stakeholders; it is probably the most general approach to managing corporate

| Table 1 | The Credo of Security Pacific Corporation |
| --- | --- |

**Commitment to Customer**

The first commitment is to provide our customers with quality products and services which are innovative and technologically responsive to their current requirements, at appropriate prices. To perform these tasks with integrity requires that we maintain confidentiality and protect customer privacy, promote customer satisfaction, and serve customer needs. We strive to serve qualified customers and industries which are socially responsible according to broadly accepted community and company standards.

**Commitment to Employee**

The second commitment is to establish an environment for our employees which promotes professional growth, encourages each person to achieve his or her highest potential, and promotes individual creativity and responsibility. Security Pacific acknowledges our responsibility to employees, including providing for open and honest communication, stated expectations, fair and timely assessment of performance and equitable compensation which rewards employee contributions to company objectives within a framework of equal opportunity and affirmative action.

**Commitment of Employee to Security Pacific**

The third commitment is that of the employee to Security Pacific. As employees, we strive to understand and adhere to the Corporation's policies and objectives, act in a professional manner, and give our best effort to improve Security Pacific. We recognize the trust and confidence placed in us by our customers and community and act with integrity and honesty in all situations to preserve that trust and confidence. We act responsibly to avoid conflicts of interest and other situations which are potentially harmful to the Corporation.

**Commitment of Employee to Employee**

The fourth commitment is that of employees to their fellow employees. We must be committed to promote a climate of mutual respect, integrity, and professional relationships, characterized by open and honest communication within and across all levels of the organization. Such a climate will promote attainment of the Corporation's goals and objectives, while leaving room for individual initiative within a competitive environment.

**Commitment to Communities**

The fifth commitment is that of Security Pacific to the communities which we serve. We must constantly strive to improve the quality of life through our support of community organizations and projects, through encouraging service to the community by employees, and by promoting participation in community services. By the appropriate use of our resources, we work to support or further advance the interests of the community, particularly in times of crisis or social need. The Corporation and its employees are committed to complying fully with each community's laws and regulations.

**Commitment to Stockholder**

The sixth commitment of Security Pacific is to its stockholders. We will strive to provide consistent growth and a superior rate of return on their investment, to maintain a position and reputation as a leading financial institution, to protect stockholder investments, and to provide full and timely information. Achievement of these goals for Security Pacific is dependent upon the successful development of the five previous sets of relationships.

---

ethics. The credo is a succinct statement of the values permeating the firm. The experiences of Security Pacific Corporation (a Los Angeles–based national bank that devised a credo in 1987) and of Johnson & Johnson illustrate the credo approach.

Security Pacific's central document is not an ethical code per se; rather, it is six missionlike commitments to customers, employees, communities, and stockholders. The credo's objective is "to seek a set of principles and beliefs which might provide guidance and direction to our work" (see Table 1).

More than 70 high-level managers participated in formulating a first draft of the commitments. During this process, senior managers shared and analyzed examples of ethical dilemmas they had faced in balancing corporate and constituent obligations. An outside consultant, hired to manage the process, helped to draft the language. Ultimately more than 250 employees, from all levels of the bank, participated in the credo formulation process via a series of discussion groups.

Once the commitments were in final form, management reached a consensus on how to communicate these guiding principles to the Security Pacific organization. Credo coordinators developed and disseminated a leader's guide to be used at staff meetings introducing the credo; it contained instructions on the meeting's format and on showing a videotape that explained the credo and the process by which it was developed. At the meetings, managers invited reactions by posing these questions: What are your initial feelings about what you have just read? Are there any specific commitments you would like to discuss? How will the credo affect your daily work? Employees were thus encouraged to react to the credo and to consider its long-run implications.

Security Pacific's credo was recently cited as a model effort, and it serves internally both as a standard for judging existing programs and as a justification for new activities.[2] For example, the "commitment to communities" formed the basis for a

| Table 2 | Johnson & Johnson Credo |
| --- | --- |

We believe our first responsibility is to the doctors, nurses, and patients, to mothers and all others who use our products and services. In meeting their needs everything we do must be of high quality. We must constantly strive to reduce our costs in order to maintain reasonable prices. Customers' orders must be serviced promptly and accurately. Our suppliers and distributors must have an opportunity to make a fair profit.

We are responsible to our employees, the men and women who work with us throughout the world. Everyone must be considered as an individual. We must respect their dignity and recognize their merit. They must have a sense of security in their jobs. Compensation must be fair and adequate and working conditions clean, orderly, and safe. Employees must feel free to make suggestions and complaints. There must be equal opportunity for employment, development, and advancement for those qualified. We must provide competent management, and their actions must be just and ethical.

We are responsible to the communities in which we live and work and to the world community as well. We must be good citizens—support good works and charities and bear our fair share of taxes. We must encourage civic improvements and better health and education. We must maintain in good order the property we are privileged to use, protecting the environment and natural resources.

Our final responsibility is to our stockholders. Business must make a sound profit. We must experiment with new ideas. Research must be carried on, innovative programs developed and mistakes paid for. New equipment must be purchased, new facilities provided, and new products launched. Reserves must be created to provide for adverse times. When we operate according to these principles, the stockholders should realize a fair return.

program specifically designed to serve low-income constituents in the area. However, this credo should not be considered the definitive approach to ethics management. First, the credo could be interpreted simply as an organizational mission statement, not as a document about ethics. Indeed, the examples supporting the credo and the videotape itself do stress what might just be called good business practice, without particular reference to ethical policies. And second, the credo has not been in place long enough for its impact to be fully assessed.

Any discussion of corporate credos would be incomplete without reference to Johnson & Johnson, whose credo is shown in Table 2. This document focuses on responsibilities to consumers, employees, communities, and stockholders. (The current J&J president, David Clare, explains that responsibility to the stockholder is listed last because "if we do the other jobs properly, the stockholder will always be served.") The first version of this credo, instituted in 1945, was revised in 1947. Between 1975 and 1978, chairman James Burke held a series of meetings with J&J's 1,200 top managers; they were encouraged to "challenge" the credo. What emerged from the meetings was that the document in fact functioned as it was intended to function; a slightly reworded but substantially unchanged credo was introduced in 1979.

Over the last two years, the company has begun to survey all employees about how well the company meets its responsibilities to the four principal constituencies. The survey asks employees from all fifty-three countries where J&J operates questions about every line in the credo. An office devoted to the credo survey tabulates the results, which are confidential. (Department and division managers receive only information pertaining to their units and composite numbers for the entire firm.) The interaction at meetings devoted to discussing these findings is reportedly very good.

Does J&J's credo work? Top management feels strongly that it does. The credo is often mentioned as an important contributing factor in the company's exemplary handling of the Tylenol crises several years ago. It would appear that the firm's commitment to the credo makes ethical business practice its highest priority. One might question whether the credo is adequate to deal with the multitude of ethical problems facing a multinational firm; possibly additional ethical guidelines could serve as reinforcement, especially in dealing with international business issues.

When should a company use a corporate credo to guide its ethical policies? They work best in firms with a cohesive corporate culture, where a spirit of frequent and unguarded communication exists. Generally, small, tightly knit companies find that a credo is sufficient. Among large firms, Johnson & Johnson is an exception. J&J managers consciously use the credo as an ethical guidepost; they find that the corporate culture reinforces the credo.

When is a credo insufficient? This approach does not offer enough guidance for most multinational companies facing complex ethical questions in different societies, for firms that have merged recently and are having trouble grafting disparate cultures, and for companies operating in industries with chronic ethical problems. A credo is like the Ten Commandments. Both set forth good general principles, but many people need the Bible, religious teachings, and guidelines provided by organized religion, as well. Similarly, many companies find that they need to offer more concrete guidance on ethical issues.

## Ethics Programs

Ethics programs provide more specific direction for dealing with potential ethical problems than general credos do. Two companies—Chemical Bank and Dow Corning—serve as examples. Although the thrust of the two programs is different, they both illustrate the usefulness of this approach.

Chemical Bank, the nation's fourth largest bank, has an extensive ethics education program. All new employees attend an orientation session at which they read and sign off on Chemical's code of ethics. (This has been in existence for thirty years and was last revised in May 1987.) The training program features a videotaped message from the chairman emphasizing the bank's values and ethical standards. A second and more unusual aspect of the program provides in-depth training in ethical decision making for vice presidents.[3]

The "Decision Making and Corporate Values" course is a two-day seminar that occurs away from the bank. Its purpose, according to a bank official, is "to encourage Chemical's employees to weigh the ethical or value dimensions of the decisions they make and to provide them with the analytic tools to do that." This program began in 1983; more than 250 vice presidents have completed the course thus far. Each meeting is limited to twenty to twenty-five senior vice presidents from a cross-section of departments; this size makes for a seminarlike atmosphere. The bank instituted the program in response to the pressures associated with deregulation, technology, and increasing competition.

The chairman always introduces the seminar by highlighting his personal commitment to the program. Most of the two days is spent discussing case studies. The fictitious cases were developed following interviews with various Chemical managers who described ethically charged situations. The cases are really short stories about loan approval, branch closings, foreign loans, insider trading, and other issues.[4] They do not have "solutions" as such; instead, they pose questions for discussion, such as, Do you believe the individual violated the bank's code? Or, What should X do?

Program evaluations have yielded positive results. Participants said they later encountered dilemmas similar to the cases, and that they had developed a thinking process in the seminar that helped them work through other problems. This program, while it is exemplary, only reaches a small percentage of Chemical's 30,000 employees. Ideally, such a program would be disseminated more widely and would become more than a one-time event.

Dow Corning has a longstanding—and very different—ethics program. Its general code has been revised four times since its inception in 1976 and includes a seven-point values statement. The company started using face-to-face "ethical audits" at its plants worldwide more than a decade ago. The number of participants in these four-to-six-hour audits ranges from five to forty. Auditors meet with the manager in charge the evening before to ascertain the most pressing issues. The actual questions come from relevant sections in the corporate code and are adjusted for the audit location. At sales offices, for example, the auditors concentrate on issues such as kickbacks, unusual requests from customers, and special pricing terms; at manufacturing plants, conservation and environmental issues receive more attention. An ethical audit might include the following questions.

• Are there any examples of business that Dow Corning has lost because of our refusal to provide "gifts" or other incentives to government officials at our customers' facilities?
• Do any of our employees have ownership or financial interest in any of our distributors?
• Have our sales representatives been able to undertake business conduct discussions with distributors in a way that actually strengthens our ties with them?
• Has Dow Corning been forced to terminate any distributors because of their business conduct practices?
• Do you believe that our distributors are in regular contact with their competitors? If so, why?
• Which specific Dow Corning policies conflict with local practices?

John Swanson, manager of Corporate Internal and Management Communications, heads this effort; he believes the audit approach makes it "virtually impossible for employees to consciously make an unethical decision." According to Swanson, twenty to twenty-three meetings occur every year. The Business Conduct Committee members, who act as session leaders, then prepare a report for the

*Developing a structure is not sufficient by itself. The structure will not be useful unless it is supported by institutionalized managerial processes.*

Audit Committee of the board. He stresses the fact that there are no shortcuts to implementing this program—it requires time and extensive interaction with the people involved. Recently the audit was expanded; it now examines internal as well as external activities. (One audit found that some salespeople believed manufacturing personnel needed to be more honest when developing production schedules.) One might ask whether the commitment to ethics is constant over time or peaks during the audit sessions; Dow Corning may want to conduct surprise audits, or develop other monitoring mechanisms or a more detailed code.

When should a company consider developing an ethics program? Such programs are often appropriate when firms have far-flung operations that need periodic guidance, as is the case at Dow Corning. This type of program can deal specifically with international ethical issues and with peculiarities at various plant locations. Second, an ethics program is useful when managers confront similar ethical problems on a regular basis, as Chemical Bank executives do. Third, these programs are useful in organizations that use outside consultants or advertising agencies. If an independent contractor does not subscribe to a corporate credo, the firm may want to use an ethical audit or checklist to heighten the outside agency's sensitivity to ethical issues.

When do ethics programs come up lacking? If they are too issue centered, ethics programs may miss other, equally important problems. (Dow's program, for example, depends on the questions raised by the audit.) In addition, the scope of the program may limit its impact to only certain parts of the organization (e.g., Chemical Bank). Managers who want to permanently inculcate ethical considerations may be concerned that such programs are not perceived by some employees as being long term or ongoing. If the credo can be compared with the Ten Commandments, then ethics programs can be likened to weekly church services. Both can be uplifting, but once the session (service) is over, individuals may believe they can go back to business as usual.

## Tailored Corporate Codes

Codes of conduct, or ethical codes, are another structural mechanism companies use to signal their commitment to ethical principles. Ninety percent of Fortune 500 firms, and almost half of all other firms, have ethical codes. According to a recent survey, this mechanism is perceived as the most effective way to encourage ethical business behavior.[5] Codes commonly address issues such as conflict of interest, competitors, privacy, gift giving and receiving, and political contributions. However, many observers continue to believe that codes are really public relations documents, or motherhood and apple pie statements; these critics claim that codes belittle employees and fail to address practical managerial issues.[6]

Simply developing a code is not enough. It must be tailored to the firm's functional areas (e.g., marketing, finance, personnel) or to the major line of business in which the firm operates. The rationale for tailored codes is simple. Functional areas or divisions have differing cultures and needs. A consumer products division, for example, has a relatively distant relationship with customers, because it relies heavily on advertising to sell its products. A division producing industrial products, on the other hand, has fewer customers and uses a personal, sales-oriented approach. A code needs to reflect these differences. Unfortunately, very few ethics codes do so.

Several companies have exemplary codes tailored to functional or major business areas. I describe two of these below—the St. Paul Companies (specializing in commercial and personal insurance and related products) and International Business Machines (IBM).

The St. Paul Companies revised their extensive corporate code, entitled "In Good Conscience," in 1986. All new employees get introduced to the code when they join the company, and management devotes biannual meetings to discussing the code's impact on day-to-day activities. In each of the five sections, the code offers specific guidance and examples for employees to follow. The statements below illustrate the kinds of issues, and the level of specificity, contained in the code.

• Insider Information. For example, if you know that the company is about to announce a rise in quarterly profits, or anything else that would affect the price of the company's stock, you cannot buy or sell the stock until the announcement has been made and published.

• Gifts and Entertainment. An inexpensive ball-point pen, or an appointment diary, is a common gift and generally acceptable. But liquor, lavish entertainment, clothing, or travel should not be accepted.

• Contact with Legislators. If you are contacted by legislators on matters relating to the St. Paul, you should refer them to your governmental affairs or law department.

The "Employee Related Issues" section of the code is the most detailed; it directly addresses the company's relationship to the individual, and vice versa. This section spells out what employees can expect in terms of compensation (it should be based on job performance and administered fairly), advancement (promotion is from within, where possible), assistance (this consists of training, job experience, or counseling) and communications (there should be regular feedback; concerns can be expressed without fear of recrimination). It also articulates the St. Paul Companies' expectation of employees regarding speaking up (when you know something that could be a problem), avoiding certain actions (where the public's confidence could be weakened), and charting your career course.

The company also delineates employee privacy issues. The code outlines how work-related information needed for hiring and promotion is collected. (Only information needed to make the particular decision is gathered; it is collected from the applicant/employee where possible. Polygraphs are not used.) The St. Paul informs employees about what types of information are maintained. Finally, information in an individual's file is open to the employee's review.

The code covers other important personnel issues in depth, as well. It touches on equal opportunity by mentioning discrimination laws, but the emphasis is on the company recognition of past discrimination and its commitments to "make an affirmative effort to address this situation in all of its programs and practices." Data acquired from the St. Paul supports this point. Between 1981 and 1986, hiring and promotion increased 60 percent for minorities in supervisory positions and 49 percent for women in management—even though overall employment rose only about 3 percent during this time. In addition, the code informs employees that the company will reimburse all documented business expenses. And it covers nepotism by stating that officers' and directors' relatives will not be hired; other employees' relatives can be employed, so long as they are placed in different departments.

Being an ethical company requires providing clear guidelines for employees. The St. Paul Companies' extensive discussion of personnel policies does just that. Employees may strongly disapprove of certain policies, but they are fully informed. The termination policy, for example, states that employment is voluntary and that individuals are free to resign at any time; the company, too, can terminate employees "at any time, with or without cause." Some people may consider that policy unfair or punitive, but at least the rules of the game are clear. One limitation of the code is that all sections are not uniformly strong. For example, the marketing section is only one paragraph long and contains few specifics.

The second illustration is of a code tailored to the company's major line of business. IBM's "Business Conduct Guidelines" were instituted in the 1960s and revised most recently in 1983. New employees receive a copy and certify annually that they abide by the code. It has four parts; the most extensive section is entitled "Conducting IBM's Business." Since IBM is, at its core, a marketing and sales organization, this section pertains primarily to these issues.

Six subsections detail the type of activities IBM expects of its sales representatives. First, "Some General Standards" include the following directives, with commentaries: do not make misrepresentations to anyone, do not take advantage of IBM's size, treat everyone fairly (do not extend preferential treatment), and do not practice reciprocal dealing. Second, "Fairness in the Field" pertains to disparagement (sell IBM products on their merits, not by disparaging competitors' products or services). In addition, it prohibits premature disclosure of product information and of selling if a competitor already has a signed order. Third, "Relations with Other Organizations" cautions employees about firms that have multiple relationships with IBM (deal with only one relationship at a time, and do not collaborate with these firms).

The fourth and fifth sections address "Acquiring and Using Information for or about Others." The code spells out the limits to acquiring information (industrial espionage is wrong) and to using information (adverse information should not be retained). Employees must determine the confidentiality of information gathered from others. The final section outlines IBM's policy on "Bribes, Gifts, and Entertainment." The company allows customary business amenities but prohibits giving presents that are intended to "unduly influence" or "obligate" the recipient, as well as receiving gifts worth more than a nominal amount.

One might contend that it is easy for a large, profitable company like IBM to have an exemplary code. On the other hand, one could also argue that a real reason for the company's continued success is that its sales representatives do subscribe to these principles. Is this a perfect code? No. The gifts area could use more specificity and, even though the company spends millions of dollars a year on advertising, that subject is not addressed in any section of the code. Further, IBM's legal department administers the code, which may mean that problems are resolved more by legal than ethical interpretation.

When should a company use a tailored code of ethics? If a company has one dominant functional unit (like IBM), or if there is diversity among functional areas, divisions, or subsidiaries, then a tailored code might be advisable. It allows the firm to promulgate specific and appropriate standards. Tailored codes are especially useful to complex organizations because they represent permanent guidelines for managers and employees to consult.

When should they be avoided? If a firm's leaders believe specific guidelines may be too restrictive for their employees, then a tailored code is an unsatisfactory choice. Codes are not necessary in most small firms or in ones where a culture includes firmly entrenched ethical policies. If a credo is similar to the Ten Commandments, and programs are similar to religious services, then tailored credos can be considered similar to the Bible or to other formal religious teachings. They provide the most guidance, but many people do not take the time to read or reflect on them.

## Conclusion

My research on ethics in management suggests several conclusions that the corporate manager may wish to keep in mind.

• **There Is No Single Ideal Approach to Corporate Ethics.** I would recommend that a small firm start with a credo, but that a larger firm consider a program or a tailored code. It is also possible to integrate these programs and produce a hybrid: in dealing with insider trading, for example, a firm could develop a training program, then follow it up with a strongly enforced tailored code.[7]

• **Top Management Must Be Committed.** Senior managers must champion the highest ethical postures for their companies, as James Burke of J&J does. This commitment was evident in all the companies described here; it came through loud and clear in the CEOs' letters, reports, and public statements.

• **Developing a Structure Is Not Sufficient by Itself.** The structure will not be useful unless it is supported by institutionalized managerial processes. The credo meetings at Security Pacific and the seminars at Chemical Bank are examples of processes that support structures.

• **Raising the Ethical Consciousness of an Organization Is Not Easy.** All the companies mentioned here have spent countless hours—and substantial amounts of money—developing, discussing, revising, and communicating the ethical principles of the firm. And in fact there are no guarantees that it will work. McDonnell Douglas has an extensive ethics program, but some of its executives were implicated in a recent defense contractor scandal.

In conclusion, let me add that managers in firms with active ethics structures—credos, programs, and tailored codes—are genuinely enthusiastic about them. They believe that ethics pay off. Their conviction should provide others with an encouraging example.

## References

*The author would like to thank Bernard Avishai, Gene Laczniak, Michael Mokwa, Lee Tavis, and Oliver Williams, C.S.C., for their helpful comments on an earlier version of this article.*

1
P.E. Murphy and M.G. Dunn, "Corporate Culture and Marketing Management Ethics" (Notre Dame, IN: University of Notre Dame, working paper, 1988).

2
R.E. Berenbeim, *Corporate Ethics* (New York: The Conference Board, research report no. 900, 1987), p. 15, pp. 20–22.

3
A more detailed discussion of Chemical's comprehensive program, and of Johnson & Johnson's, appears in *Corporate Ethics: A Prime Business Asset* (New York: Business Roundtable, February 1988).

4
One of the case studies appears in "Would You Blow Whistle on Wayward Colleague?" *American Banker*, 17 June 1988, p. 16.

5
Touche Ross, *Ethics in American Business* (New York: Touche Ross & Co., January 1988).

6
Berenbeim (1987), p. 17.

7
G.L. Tidwell, "Here's a Tip—Know the Rules of Insider Trading," *Sloan Management Review*, Summer 1987, pp. 93–99.

# Managing as if the Earth Mattered

## James E. Post

**James E. Post** is a professor of management and public policy in the School of Management, Boston University.

Alverino Gomez lives and works in Mexico City. He is the assistant plant manager for an American multinational corporation manufacturing industrial machines. The company's Mexico City facility is a major production center for its North American operations. The company has another Mexican facility near the U.S. border and other operations in the United States, Europe, and Asia. Mr. Gomez has a promising career in this company and hopes to continue his career development in Mexico, where his family is located. On this day, Mr. Gomez has received a telephone call from a government official from SEDUE, the Mexican environmental protection agency. The official ordered the plant to shut down because air quality had reached emergency levels. Mexico City is home to the world's largest urban population and lives with one of the world's greatest urban air pollution burdens. This is not the first emergency declared by environmental officials, but others have been widely ignored by industry. Business leaders often talk about the severe impact of a closing on production schedules and customer deliveries. Labor leaders are also unhappy with such emergencies because workers are sent home and receive no compensation for the hours not worked. Because the plant manager is away this day, Mr. Gomez must make the decision whether or not to close the plant.

Several thousand miles away, Peter Crumholz faces a different type of dilemma. He is an assistant product manager for a large consumer products firm and is responsible for maintaining the product's market share. The product is trademarked, dominates the consumer segment of the market, and has high buyer loyalty. Competition is based on price, image, and product quality. As his boss likes to say, "We have a mission and there is no room for error." A new study of the product's packaging has pointed out that customers are attracted to the presentation of the product but that the package contains substantial quantities of cardboard, polystyrene, and insulation made with ozone-depleting chlorofluorocarbons (CFCs). The study group recommends a major redesign to eliminate the CFC materials but believes it is unwise to reduce packaging size because of the marketing effects, despite the ability to reduce solid waste by 15 percent. Peter is to be the "point person" in developing a course of action for the company. He is scheduled to make a presentation, with recommendations, to the senior product manager and his counterparts in two days.[1]

Alverino Gomez and Peter Crumholz are both facing the increasingly common dilemma of reconciling routine business activity with emerging environmental concerns that force hard choices. For Mr. Gomez, there is the choice of closing the facility—thereby forcing economic injury on his work force and disrupting manufacturing processes and customers' plans—to meet an unevenly enforced emergency order that will not solve the air quality problems in any event. For Mr. Crumholz, there is the choice of endorsing packaging changes that are either too little to meet environmental needs or too much to guarantee the product will not be hurt in the marketplace.

Readers no doubt have ideas about clever ways to reconcile the conflicting dimensions of these issues. Considerable imagination can be—and actually was—brought to both of these cases. The dilemmas faced by these managers are not unique, and they raise unfamiliar problems of corporate responsibility. This article examines a variation on the central theme of this issue: What are a corporation's environmental responsibilities in a world where environmental problems are growing in number, severity, and complexity?

Business schools have largely ignored both this question and natural resource and environmental issues in their curricula (Post 1990). To the extent attention has been given to the dilemmas, it has been in the study of business-government and business-society relations. It is not sufficient that only such courses address these issues. The prevalence and seriousness of environmental problems and crises is becoming increasingly evident to managers everywhere. I believe environmental issues will be to business in the 1990s what quality issues were to business in the 1980s: a force of such power as to literally transform the way managers manage their businesses and think about the relationship of the firm to its internal and external stakeholders. This article develops the argument from two perspectives: (1) an analysis of why environmental problems are a basic new reality for managers and corporations in the 1990s; and (2) an assessment of what types of decisions managers and firms will be forced to make in reconciling environmental and economic considerations.

## ENVIRONMENTAL CHALLENGES[2]

The 1990s are being called the "decade of the environment." Public interest in preserving nature's ecological balance and a clean, healthy environment is high and growing. This means that business must strive to reconcile these goals with other, equally demanding goals.

In the desert near Tucson, Arizona, there exists what appears to be a giant greenhouse. When it is lighted at night, it shines against the dark, star-filled sky like an enormous beacon. Inside, eight human beings are living and working in a series of climatological zones called "biomes" that include a tropical rain forest, an ocean (complete with tides), a savannah, and a desert. Living in each zone are appropriate animals and plants, balanced in the best self-sustaining ways human beings can imagine. This environment will be sealed for two years, during which time the people, animals, plants, and other living organisms will try to survive. It is called "Biosphere 2," and it is a $30 million experiment to learn about ecological interdependencies. The scientists who developed Biosphere 2 say it will inform us about what must happen if humans are ever to build space colonies on distant planets. Also important are the lessons it may teach about our own relationship with Biosphere 1—the planet Earth (Allen 1991).

Thousands of miles away, crews of workers toil on the smoky desert and oily shores of the Persian Gulf. They are trying to cap the wells and clean the remains of one of the world's worst oil disasters, the intentional dumping of oil by Iraqi military officials during the 1990-91 war. Environmental experts helplessly watched the ecological carnage, aware it was taking place but unable to stop it. Many experts believe it will take years, even decades, for the desert and the Gulf to be ecologically restored. Some believe it will never happen.

People living near Prince William Sound, Alaska, the Rhine River that flows through Switzerland and Germany, and the Russian city of Kiev, a few miles north of Chernobyl, understand the importance of the biosphere and the terrible consequences of human damage to the environment. The Exxon Valdez oil spill, the explosion of a Sandoz AG factory in Basel, Switzerland, and the nuclear reactor fire at Chernobyl are tragic milestones in recent environmental history. Today the world is more aware than ever of the limited ability of earth to accept such ecological shocks. There is a new urgency to halting environmental damage, cleaning up the effects of past practices, and creating a new relationship between economic activity and environmental concerns.

Tragic events symbolize the major collision between industrial technology and nature's ecological systems. Agricultural chemicals, nuclear power, and the many other advances made possible by modern science and technology bring enormous benefits to humankind. But the human price and the pressures on the earth's ecological systems are sometimes unacceptably high. Finding a balance between industrial benefits and life-sustaining ecological systems is a major challenge facing business managers, government policy makers, and society in general. The work of the "biospherians" in Biosphere 2 is intended to advance our scientific understanding of humans and the environment. The work of business and government leaders, and society in general, is critical to meeting what has been called the challenge of "managing planet earth" (*Scientific American* 1989).

Ecology, the study of how living things interact with one another and their environment, is certain to become part of the modern managerial consciousness. In a general sense, business cannot be conducted today without an understanding and appreciation of the stakeholders and interdependencies that exist between the corporation and others. Specifically, managers in business, government, and nonprofit organizations are realizing the impact, power, and transforming potential of ecological issues.

The ecological challenge requires managers to formulate strategies, for the present and the future, that (1) make the most efficient use of scarce resources; (2) reduce wastes that pollute the environment; and (3) keep industrial production and other human activities within the limits set by nature's ecological systems. In the 1990s, this challenge is more formidable and more critical than at any time in human history. As global natural resources are depleted, the survival potential of the planet itself is at stake. Never before has Earth itself become a stakeholder of such significance to corporations and managerial decision making.

## The Global Commons

Throughout history, communities of people have created "commons." A commons is shared land on which, for example, a herder can graze his or her animals. The limited carrying capacity, or ability to sustain population on a given quantity of land that comprises the commons, is exceeded as each herder adds more animals to the land. If short-term decisions dominate each herder's thinking, the commons will be destroyed because each herder gets near-term advantage from grazing the maximum number of animals. In the long run, of course, the herder also loses because the commons is destroyed. The only solution in the near term is restraint, either voluntarily or through some form of coercion such as a law, that would limit the maximum number of animals. As the author of "Tragedy of the Commons" writes, "freedom in a commons brings ruin to all" (Hardin 1968).

The managerial dilemmas facing Mr. Gomez and Mr. Crumholz described at the beginning of this article are problems of the commons. We live on a global commons. As scientific evidence has demonstrated that we are testing—and surpassing in some instances—the earth's carrying capacity for pollution, our behavior is as threatening to the planet as that of the herders to the commons. Present dangers exist at two levels: (1) local environmental damage, such as toxic waste dumping, that leaves areas of the earth unable to support living organisms; and (2) global systems of climate, atmospheric protection, and food resources that are breaking down as the result of cumulative pollution. Depletion of the ozone layer (recently revealed to be occurring at a rate even faster than that previously understood), destruction of the rain forests, and desertification of land from topsoil loss are but a few of the ominous global environmental transformations now underway. These systems cannot be damaged or destroyed without affecting everyone. The deliberate destruction of wells and spilling of oil into the Persian Gulf damaged not just Iraq's enemies, but everyone in the region. Such events reinforce the message that preservation of the global commons is a new imperative for institutions, their managers, and all citizens.

## Sustainable Development

The World Commission on Environment and Development, including leaders from many industrialized and developing nations, has described the need for balance between economic and environmental considerations as sustainable development—"development that meets the needs of the present without compromising the ability of future generations to meet their own needs" (World Commission . . . 1987). There are two concepts within this idea that bear directly on business and society:

• First, the concept of "needs," in particular the essential needs of the world's population, rich and poor, to survive;

• Second, the concept of "limitation" imposed by the state of technology or social organization on the environment's ability to meet present and future needs.

Reconciling human needs, which are met through economic activity, with limitations imposed by ecological systems is the practical challenge that now confronts all managers. Protection of the global commons through responsible environmental management is a vital step toward sustainable development. But for companies and governments, and all their managers, the diagnosis is easier than the solution.

## MANAGING AS IF THE EARTH MATTERED

The twin ideas driving the environmental movement are preservation and conservation of natural resources on the one hand and control of pollution on the other. Conservationist thinking dates to the early 1900s in the U.S., when conservation leaders such as John Muir led campaigns to save natural resources, and political leaders such as President Theodore Roosevelt took actions to establish nature preserves. In the 1990s, this strain of thought is once again ascendant as biodiversity, preservation of wilderness, and animal habitat protection are sought by environmental advocates.

Concern about pollution has taken new forms in the 1990s. Scientific understanding of risks to human health and natural resources is more refined. The scientific measurement of exposures surpasses that of the past. Whereas "parts per million" was once the standard for quantifying toxins in air and water, it is now possible to state those exposures in parts per billion or parts per quadrillion. Whether such minute exposures are meaningful to humans is a question that provokes debate among scientists and policymakers. But as long as public fear of toxins is high, political pressure can be effectively exerted on business and government to reduce such perceived risks. Some have questioned the ethics of advocates—such as those who succeeded in banning Alar, a pesticide used on apples—as capitalizing on media hype and public fear. Whatever the merits of that criticism, it underscores the problem of creating reasoned dialogue about scientific information with a public that is highly emotional about toxic risks.

**Figure**
**Effects of Environmental Issues on Business Functions**

| Area | Example |
|---|---|
| Human Resources | Workplace risk exposures |
| Marketing | "Green" products |
| Finance | Liabilities; investment criteria; full environmental cost accounting |
| Operations/ Manufacturing | Waste reduction; energy use; process design |
| Product Development | Environmental life cycle; packaging |
| Research and Development | Use of animals; product specifications |
| Transportation | Vehicle mileage; alternative fuels; hazardous contents |

A complex set of scientific, social, and political values has also made environmentalism a powerful political philosophy today. "Green politics" describes a view of the world that uses environmental impact as a litmus test for all types of industrial, social, and technological decisions. In such European nations as Holland and Germany, green political parties have emerged, held office, and shaped the political debate. Hedrick Smith, author of *The New Russians* (1990), notes that if a green political party were permitted in the Soviet Union, it would almost surely be a significant political power given public concern in the aftermath of the Chernobyl disaster, the death of the Aral Sea, and innumerable toxic sites that have come to light since the fall of the Iron Curtain.

## Global Issues and Business Response

The preservation/conservation theme is especially powerful in our emerging understanding of global resource issues. Three global issues have profound consequences for business and society in the near and intermediate term: ozone depletion, global warming, and biodiversity. Each is a global commons-type issue; each presents itself to managers and firms with a degree of scientific uncertainty (Buchholz, Marcus, and Post 1992).

**Ozone depletion.** Since the 1970s, scientific concern for the depletion of stratospheric ozone has grown. The rapidly escalating estimates of skin cancers and agricultural damage caused by increasing amounts of ultraviolet rays from the

sun have prompted nearly unprecedented international action. The development of the Montreal Protocol as a political framework to reduce and eliminate chlorofluorocarbons (CFCs) that deplete stratospheric ozone has been signed by more than 100 nations. The industrial producers of CFCs—primarily located in the U.S., Europe, and Japan—have begun the phaseout of CFC production, and industrial users, including manufacturers of packaging, air conditioning, and computers, are moving to safer substitutes.

**Global warming.** The increasing temperature of the earth's atmosphere is subject to more uncertainty and debate than ozone depletion. Nevertheless, a broad scientific concern about global warming has moved business and government to consider the consequences if theories prove correct. Foremost among the effects is climate change, with direct effects on agriculture, food supplies, and human starvation. The release of carbon dioxide is a primary contributor to global warming, along with the release of other greenhouse gases used by industry. In the 1990s, efforts are underway to develop an international agreement like the Montreal Protocol to limit greenhouse gas emissions and slow the pace of warming. If not done, experts fear that polar ice caps will melt, raising sea levels and flooding coastal plains such as Bangladesh. The human and habitat costs of such climate change could be economically and socially devastating to many of the world's nations.

**Biodiversity.** Genetic diversity is essential for healthy species of plants, animals, and human beings. As in the Biosphere 2 example discussed above, habitats must be carefully balanced if they are to survive. As areas of rich natural resources, such as the tropical rain forests of Brazil, Malaysia, Costa Rica, and Mexico, are destroyed, many species of plant and animal life are endangered or eliminated. This has serious environmental balancing effects and high human costs as well. The pharmaceutical industry, for example, each year develops new medicines based on newly discovered plants from rain forest areas. As they are destroyed, so too is the stock of potential new medicines.

## Local Pollution and Business

Pollution is felt most immediately and acutely by local communities. Fouling of the air and water, for example, usually has its most direct effects on those citizens and communities living downriver or downwind of the source. As the example of Mexico City suggests, managers still face dilemmas when responding to these issues. In nations where governments have established environmental standards and engaged in vigorous and vigilant enforcement, progress in reducing pollution has been made. In nations where laws are weak or nonexistent and enforcement is lax, serious local air and water pollution problems plague communities. For those who make decisions, whether in business or government, the tradeoffs between cost and environmental standards remain difficult to make without visible public policy that encourages action favoring environmental protection.

Recent studies (Environmental Protection Agency 1990) indicate that United States' citizens and institutions spent more than $100 billion on pollution abatement in 1990. This is projected to double to $200 billion by 1995. In the U.S. and some European nations, approximately 2 percent of gross national product is now directed toward environmental protection. These data demonstrate that managers are making environmental investments every day. Government has moved to permit more incentive-oriented initiatives, such as "bubble concepts," pollution charges, and tradable emission rights. The EPA's policy decision to emphasize voluntary pollution prevention by industry is a landmark in U.S. environmental policy. Such approaches can only succeed, however, if companies make creative use of the flexibility to harmonize business decisions on plant location, product and process design, and operational standards with environmental goals. If voluntary action does not lead to improved environmental performance, more "command and control" regulation is likely to occur given the high societal importance placed on pollution control. The interplay of corporate policy and public policy thus directly shapes managerial behavior.

## THE GREENING OF MANAGEMENT

Environmental concerns touch all aspects of a business' operations. As illustrated in the **Figure**, modern environmental problems affect the management of a company's operations, marketing, human resources, and other activities. Even areas such as finance and accounting are directly affected. For example, federal rules now require a company to account for its toxic materials with an elaborate system of reports and an internal audit of environmental compliance. Financial officers recognize the increasing power of institutional investors, using environmental criteria such as the Valdez Principles (CERES 1989), to select companies for investment or damage those that fail to meet the criteria. The rise of environmental mutual funds and the attention of limited partnerships and venture capitalists to environmental businesses are also significant to the finance function. Some courts have ruled that the purchaser of property assumes full environmental liability, affecting the economics of some mergers and acquisitions and adding significantly to due diligence expectations.

Strategic and operational decisions are both affected. Management decisions about where to locate facilities, what product lines to develop, and environmental, health, and safety standards in all the company's facilities are major decisions. How a firm fuels its fleet of cars and trucks (gasoline, alternative fuels, electricity), designs energy efficiency into facilities, organizes employee transportation services, minimizes toxins in manufacturing, and communicates about all of these to communities and government officials affects its environmental profile.

Corporate environmentalism, a term that is sometimes used to describe responsible management responses to these issues, is neither a fad nor peripheral to the "real business" of decision making. Rather, it represents the commitment to environmental responsibility and a translation of that commitment into action. Research into the criteria that guide such efforts and the actions that distinguish an effective corporate environmental program is still relatively anecdotal. Yet a few studies have shown that corporate culture, reward and evaluation systems, and location and staffing of the environmental, health, and safety functions have some degree of influence on the effectiveness of environmental responses. Research programs now in progress should shed further light on these factors. They are important, for a commitment to environmental responsibility without a capability to translate rhetoric into action seems likely to lead to disappointing results.

More than 30 years ago, Edward Mason (1960) posed the central issues of managerial responsibility as two questions: To whom, and for what, is the modern corporation accountable? These questions still remain at the heart of today's discussion of what is expected of managers and the institutions they direct. Each attempt to extend corporate responsibility to meet the expectations of new stakeholders forces a reassessment of corporate accountability theory and practice. The emergence of environmental issues as the most prominent points on the modern political, economic, and social agenda in the U.S. and abroad poses a new type of challenge to theory and practice.

For some academics, environmental problems are unlike other social issues. The analysis of stakeholders that is so easily organized for most problems is radically different when earth itself is a stakeholder and the "stake" is nothing less than planetary survival. The stakeholder map one can draw for analyzing the water resources issue in Southern California is complicated, but it pales by comparison to that needed to assess global warming, climate change, or ozone depletion. In this context alone, environmental issues force thinking at levels of abstraction not normally used in managerial decision making.

It is not only to introduce value considerations that abstraction is required. It is vital to even define the nature of the problems we now face. What does global resource depletion mean in human terms? How can a manager like Alverino Gomez make a wise decision to shut down a plant that emits little but employs many? Is his company really accountable for Mexico City's air pollution problems? How can such a responsibility be met if it exists at all? Do conventional evaluation criteria suffice when global survival is at issue?

For managers and their companies, the problems are also complicated. Introducing good environmental management requires technical staff, commitment, and a receptive organizational culture. Meeting these needs in an era of global competitiveness exacerbates the challenge. Scarce resources become even less plentiful, and capital and human training needs are even greater. The greening of management is ultimately a matter of infusing environmental concerns, understanding, and commitment into each person's thought process. But it is also a matter of supporting those who wish to act through values that recognize the importance of environmental action, through systems that reward responsible behavior and deter unthinking action.

To manage as if the earth matters is not the same challenge as managing planet earth. But it requires no less a commitment to environmental preservation and no less an understanding of how international trade, competitiveness, and global resources are connected. Managers, like Alverino Gomez and Peter Crumholz, whose lives are not devoted to global and local environmental problems will still be affected by these issues. That is the nature of our world as this century closes. One hundred years ago, business was on the verge of defining a scientific way to manage enterprises. Today, we stand at the edge of another transformation, in which the planet imposes the boundaries within which efficiency and abundance are understood. It is a time of both promise and consequence. The promise is that we will find an environmentally sustainable path into the twenty-first century. The consequence of not doing so is, as Churchill said of defeat, unthinkable.

---

### Notes

1. Both incidents actually occurred. The first example was described to the author shortly after the events occurred. The names of both managers have been changed but other facts are presented as described by the participants.

2. This discussion is an adaptation of Frederick, Post, and Davis 1992, Chapter 19.

### References

John Allen, *Biosphere 2: The Human Experiment* (New York: Penguin Books, 1991).

R. Buchholz, A. Marcus, and J. Post, *Managing Environmental Issues: A Casebook* (Englewood Cliffs, N.J.: Prentice-Hall, 1992).

CERES (Coalition for Environmentally Responsible Economies), "The Valdez Principles," 1989.

Corporate Conservation Council, "Environmental Education: A Statement for Business Management," National Wildlife Federation/Corporate Conservation Council, 1991.

Environmental Protection Agency, *Environmental Investments: The Cost of a Clean Environment* (Washington, D.C.: U.S. Environmental Protection Agency, 1990).

William C. Frederick, James E. Post, and Keith Davis, *Business and Society: Corporate Strategy, Public Policy, and Ethics*, 7th ed. (New York: McGraw-Hill, 1992).

Garrett Hardin, "Tragedy of the Commons," *Science*, December 13, 1968, pp. 1243-1248.

W.M. Hoffman, R. Frederick, and E.S. Petry, Jr., eds., *The Corporation, Ethics, and the Environment* (Westport, Conn.: Quorum Books, 1990).

Edward Mason, ed., *The Corporation in Modern Society* (Cambridge, Mass.: Harvard University Press, 1960).

"Noah's Ark—The Sequel," *Time*, September 24, 1990, p. 72.

Robert Paehlke, *Environmentalism and the Future of Progressive Politics* (New Haven, Conn.: Yale University Press, 1989).

James E. Post, "The Greening of Management," *Issues in Science and Technology*, Summer 1990, pp. 68-72.

*Scientific American*, Special Issue: "Managing Planet Earth," September 1989.

Hedrick Smith, *The New Russians* (New York: Random House, 1990).

Peter Stillman, "The Tragedy of the Commons: A Re-Analysis," *Alternatives: Perspectives on Society and Environment*, Winter 1975, p. 12.

World Commission on Environment and Development, *Our Common Future* (New York: Oxford University Press, 1987).

# ENVIRONMENTALISM: THE NEW CRUSADE

It may be the biggest business issue of the 1990s. Here's how
some smart companies are tackling it.

*David Kirkpatrick*

**T**REND SPOTTERS and forward
thinkers agree that the Nineties will
be the Earth Decade and that environmentalism will be a movement
of massive worldwide force. How massive?
Listen to Gary Miller, a public policy expert
at Washington University in St. Louis: "In
the Nineties environmentalism will be the
cutting edge of social reform and absolutely
the most important issue for business." Futurist Edith Weiner of the Manhattan management consulting firm Weiner Edrich
Brown concurs: "Environmentalism will be
the next major political idea, just as conser-
vatism and liberalism have been in the past."

The smartest companies are not just facing this thunderous music, they're singing
along. Consider:
■ Du Pont is pulling out of a $750-million-
a-year business because it may—just may—
harm the earth's atmosphere.
■ McDonald's, which produces hundreds of
millions of pounds of paper and plastic
waste annually, has become a crusading proponent of recycling, and aims to become
one of America's leading educators about
environmental issues.
■ 3M is investing in myriad pollution controls for its manufacturing facilities beyond
what the law requires.
■ Procter & Gamble and other smart marketers are moving to cast their products in
an environmentally friendly light (see box).
■ Pacific Gas & Electric teams up with environmental groups—some of them outfits
it used to fight—to do joint projects, such as
a $10 million study of energy efficiency.
"The 1990s will be the decade of the envi-

REPORTER ASSOCIATE *Alicia Hills Moore*

ronment." That's not the chief druid of
Greenpeace talking, but rather the new
president of the Petroleum Marketers Association of America in a November speech.
Mere corporate ecobabble intended to pla-
cate the latest group of special-interest loon-
ies? Any company that thinks that way will
probably regret it. Exxon provides the obvious if inadvertent example of the bitter costs
of seeming unconcerned about the environment. Not long after the March accident in
Valdez, Alaska, 41% of Americans were angry enough to say they'd seriously consider
boycotting the company. Bill McInturff, senior researcher at the Wirthlin Group, a
polling firm with close Republican ties,
blames Exxon not for the accident but for its
response: "It was a disservice to American
industry the way the pullout last fall was handled. Exxon seemed satisfied with what they
had accomplished. It hardened the notion
that business is just interested in making a
buck and doesn't give a damn. It flabber-
gasts me that a company that size doesn't
get the drift." Even spending over $1 billion
on cleanup hasn't salvaged the oil giant's
reputation.

Such salvage won't get any easier. The
New York Times/CBS News poll regularly
asks the public if "protecting the environment is so important that requirements and
standards cannot be too high, and continuing environmental improvements must be
made regardless of cost." In September
1981, 45% agreed and 42% disagreed with
that plainly intemperate statement. Last
June, 79% agreed and only 18% disagreed.
For the first time, liberals and conservatives,
Democrats and Republicans, profess con-

cern for the environment in roughly equal
numbers.

Environmentalism is likely to continue as
an issue at the forefront for several reasons.
One is demographic. Says futurist Weiner:
"The combination of baby-boomers having
children and a significant part of the population moving into senior years means an
enormous percentage of the population is
taking the attitude of stewardship." The
Gallup Organization reports that 49% of
people over 50 feel strong identification
with environmentalism, compared with
39% of those between 30 and 49 and 31%
of those under 30. This reverses the pattern
that prevailed during the country's last up-
surge in environmentalism 20 years ago.

The new crusade will be different from
the old in other ways as well. Miller of
Washington University explains, "In the
Sixties, environmentalism was the tail end
of a period of social activism that was primarily based on civil rights and the
antiwar movement," while now it's a
movement of its own. The players are different. Far fewer activists of the 1990s will
be embittered, scruffy, antibusiness street
fighters.

**A**S AN EXAMPLE of the new
breed, consider Allen Hershkowitz,
who freely drops the names of his
CEO acquaintances. As a solid-
waste-disposal expert at the litigious Natural Resources Defense Council, Hershkowitz has won many legal battles with
business. Now high-ranking executives of
major companies regularly make the pil-
grimage to his office in the elegant, airy, and

## HOW ONE INVESTMENT FIRM RATES 25 COMPANIES ON THE ENVIRONMENT

| INDUSTRY | COMPANY | RATING 1=best, 5=worst | |
|---|---|---|---|
| CHEMICALS | H.B. Fuller | 1.5 | Environmental initiatives in HQ construction |
| | Monsanto | 4.0 | Pesticides, toxic dumps, offset by clean-air efforts |
| | W.R. Grace | 5.0 | Toxic dumps, several environmental lawsuits |
| COMPUTERS | Apple Computer | 1.5 | Recycles, lets environmental groups solicit on site |
| | IBM | 3.5 | High CFC emissions |
| ELECTRIC UTILITIES | Louisville Gas & Electric | 2.0 | Leader in installing smokestack scrubbers |
| | Southern | 5.0 | High SO₂ emissions contribute to acid rain |
| ENVIRONMENTAL SERVICES | Safety-Kleen | 2.5 | Leading recycler of solvents and motor oil |
| | Wellman | 2.5 | Leading recycler of plastic |
| | Browning-Ferris | 5.0 | Numerous landfill violations |
| | Waste Management | 5.0 | Numerous landfill violations |
| FOREST PRODUCTS | Jefferson Smurfit | 2.5 | Leading recycler of paper |
| | Louisiana-Pacific | 4.0 | Air and water pollution violations |
| NATURAL GAS | Consolidated Natural Gas | 2.5 | Promotes new, clean-burning technologies |
| | Panhandle Eastern | 4.0 | Substantial PCB pollution problems |
| OIL | Amoco | 2.0 | Strong waste-minimization program |
| | Exxon | 5.0 | Poor response to Valdez oil spill |
| PHOTO EQUIPMENT | Polaroid | 2.5 | Strong waste-minimization program |
| | Eastman Kodak | 4.0 | Substantial leaks in Rochester sites |
| STEEL | Nucor | 2.0 | State-of-the-art mills, uses recycled metals |
| | Bethlehem Steel | 4.0 | Old mills with numerous environmental problems |
| OTHER | Wal-Mart Stores | 2.0 | Promotes environmental products, recycling |
| | Borden | 4.0 | Toxic dumps, air and water complaints |
| | General Electric | 4.0 | Major PCB cleanup problems |
| | General Motors | 5.0 | Toxic dumps, air and water problems |

Franklin Research & Development of Boston, which calls itself a "socially responsible" investment firm and manages $200 million, bases these ratings on several factors. Each company starts with a score of 3, which then rises or falls based on corporate actions that harm or help the environment.

amply funded New York City headquarters of NRDC, coming to him lest he go after them. As he explains, "They come in here to see what they've got to cover their asses on." The cocky 34-year-old Ph.D., who serves as an adviser to banks and Shearson Lehman Hutton, among others, elaborates, "My primary motivation is environmental protection. And if it costs more, so be it. If Procter & Gamble can't live with that, somebody else will. But I'll tell you, Procter & Gamble is trying hard to live with it."

Still, for all his militancy, Hershkowitz is no fanatic or utopian. He understands that a perfect world can't be achieved and doesn't hesitate to talk of trade-offs: "Hey, civilization has its costs. We're trying to reduce them, but we can't eliminate them." Environmentalists of this stripe will increasingly show up even within companies. William Bishop, Procter & Gamble's top environmental scientist, was an organizer of Earth

Day in 1970 and is a member of the Sierra Club. One of his chief deputies belongs to Greenpeace.

Eager to work with business, many environmentalists are moving from confrontation to the best kind of collaboration. In September an ad hoc combination of institutional investors controlling $150 billion of assets (including representatives of public pension funds) and environmental groups promulgated the Valdez Principles, named for the year's most catalytic environmental accident. The principles ask companies to reduce waste, use resources prudently, market safe products, and take responsibility for past harm. They also call for an environmentalist on each corporate board and an annual public audit of a company's environmental progress.

The group asked corporations to subscribe to the principles, with the implicit suggestion that investments could eventual-

ly be contingent on compliance. Companies already engaged in friendly discussions included Du Pont, specialty-chemical maker H.B. Fuller, and Polaroid, among others.

Earth Day 1990, scheduled for April 22, the 20th anniversary of the first such event, is becoming a veritable biz-fest. "We're really interested in working with companies that have a good record," says Earth Day Chairman Denis Hayes, who predicts that 100 million people will take part one way or another. Apple Computer and Hewlett-Packard have donated equipment. Shaklee, the personal and household products company, paid $50,000 to be the first official corporate sponsor. Even the Chemical Manufacturers Association is getting in on the act, preparing a list of 101 ways its members can participate. The more than 1,000 Earth Day affiliate groups in 120 countries propose to shake up politicians worldwide and launch a decade of activism.

## 5. DEVELOPING FUTURE ETHOS AND SOCIAL RESPONSIBILITY

THE MESSAGE that leading environmentalists are sending, and progressive companies are receiving, is that eco-responsibility will be good for business. Says Gray Davis, California's state controller, who helped draft the Valdez Principles and who sits on the boards of two public pension funds with total assets of $90 billion: "Given the increasing regulation and public concern, there's no question that companies will eventually have to change their ways. The first kid on the block to embrace these principles will increase market share and profit substantially."

While that's hard to prove, few dispute that farsightedness today will pay off tomorrow. Environmental regulations will continue to be tightened. Says Lester Lave, a professor of engineering and public policy at the Carnegie-Mellon business school: "If you build a plant that just squeaks past now, you'll have to pay much more money down the line."

That is partly why Minnesota Mining & Manufacturing is going beyond the call of duty and government deadlines. For example, new federal regulations require replacement or improvement by 1998 of underground storage tanks for liquids and gases. The company decided to comply by 1992 instead, and to have all tanks worldwide in compliance by 1993. Cost: more than $80 million. "Regulations are about to overwhelm us," says Robert Bringer, 3M staff vice president for environmental engineering and pollution control. "The only way we see to deal with that is to reduce the number of materials we emit that trigger regulation."

Chastened in part by Exxon's example, some corporate bosses don't see red when faced with green activists—they see themselves. One of Edgar Woolard's first acts after becoming CEO of Du Pont in April (just after the Valdez spill) was to deliver a speech in London entitled—and calling for—"Corporate Environmentalism." Said the top man of the chemical giant in remarks subsequently reprinted by the company on recycled paper: "Avoiding environmental incidents remains the single greatest imperative facing industry today." He bemoaned industry's lack of credibility on the issue and called for spending more money than "mere compliance" with laws would require.

Woolard now meets at least once a month with leading environmentalists, and his company is taking what seem dramatic steps demonstrating its concern. In March 1988, Du Pont announced that, based on new evidence that chlorofluorocarbons (CFCs) might be seriously depleting the Earth's ozone layer, it would voluntarily suspend all production of CFCs—a $750-million-a-year business in which it leads the industry—by 2000, or sooner if possible. The company has already spent $170 million developing safe compounds to replace CFCs in cleaning, refrigeration, and other uses. It is prepared to spend as much as $1 billion on the best replacements discovered so far, but since even these compounds may slightly deplete the ozone layer, Du Pont wants guarantees that new plants will be allowed to function long enough to recoup the investment. Says Woolard: "In my opinion it has not been proven that CFCs are harmful to the ozone, but there is a fairly good probability, and we have to deal with that."

Evidence of increased environmental sensitivity is everywhere in Du Pont, perhaps partly because that's now one of the criteria in determining managers' compensation. The company voluntarily spends an estimated $50 million each year on environmental projects beyond what the law requires, like the $15 million it spent at a Texas plant to reduce the risk of dangerous gases being released. Du Pont's ultimate goal is zero pollution in all activities. While Woolard is certain this new priority will strengthen the company, he admits profits will suffer from the effort over the next few years.

Du Pont also sees business opportunity in environmental concern. Building on expertise gained in cleaning up its own plants, the company announced in early December the formation of a safety and environmental resources division to help industrial customers clean up toxic wastes. Management forecasts potential annual revenues of $1 billion from the new business by 2000. Defensive actions sometimes pay off too. Faced with protests over the ocean dumping of acid iron salts off the coast of New Jersey, Du Pont halted a practice its scientists were convinced was harmless. It then discovered the salts could be sold to water-treatment plants.

At 3M, CEO Allen Jacobson directs that pollution-control installations be judged by their environmental benefit, not only by return on investment. But 3M too has learned that environmental controls often lead to cost savings. The company specializes in coated products (such as videotapes and pressure-sensitive tapes) whose manufacture has long emitted significant pollutants. It has saved well over $1 billion since 1975 through a program called Pollution Prevention Pays. The program spotlights projects that reduce pollution as well as save money. Solvents that were once emitted to the atmosphere may be recycled and reused, or a volatile solvent may be replaced by a water-based one, eliminating the need for costly air pollution control equipment.

If, as many predict, alliances between environmentalists and corporations are the wave of the future, Pacific Gas & Electric has already learned to surf. But it took practice. In the mid-1970s economists and lawyers from the Environmental Defense Fund started fighting the company's plan to build several giant coal and nuclear power plants. The environmentalists proposed instead a combination of smaller-scale generating facilities like windmills or cogeneration plants on the sites of regional businesses, combined with aggressive conservation measures.

THE BIG PLANTS were never built. A persistent EDF campaign of pressure at utility commission meetings and sophisticated television advertising came just as the price of fossil fuels started climbing dramatically. PG&E's resistance gradually melted. The company took several steps to conserve energy, and much of the rest of the electric industry eventually followed PG&E's lead. Says EDF attorney David Roe: "We spoke to them in their own language. We used their type of computer models, their financial analysis sheets. We weren't saying, do what's good for the environment and it will cripple you. We were saying, it will save you economically."

While the company says it would have eventually taken most of the actions EDF proposed anyway, it acknowledges that the give-and-take was beneficial. Says PG&E attorney Kermit Kubitz: "I think both sides may have been closer together than either side realized at the beginning." Echoes Roe: "The basic point is, there's usually a lot more common ground than either side realizes."

Today PG&E has a policy of aggressively seeking discussions and joint projects with any willing environmental group, even those that have opposed the company in the past. Its board includes Melvin Lane, a well-known West Coast environmentalist. In November, PG&E announced a $10 million study, conducted in conjunction with the Natural Resources Defense Council, among others, to improve efficiency in the use of electricity. And that computer model EDF developed to demonstrate the relationships between conservation and electricity costs—PG&E now rents it from EDF for about $18,000 a year.

PG&E chief Richard Clarke believes that on the rocky coast of Northern California, where quality of life has long been a paramount public issue, he has seen America's environmental mood foreshadowed. A few guiding principles Clarke has learned:

■ "Make environmental considerations and concerns part of any decision you make, right from the beginning. Don't think of it as something extra you throw in the pot."

■ "Develop an internal cadre of environmentalists. They have minds of their own and will advocate things. They may not get everything they want, but there certainly are occasions where they prevail."

■ "Have a continuing dialogue with environmental groups."

■ "Put someone on your board to help you factor in environmental issues."

■ "Do these things because they are the right thing to do, not because somebody forces you to do them."

McDonald's might add another principle

# LEADING THE CRUSADE INTO CONSUMER MARKETING

There's money to be made catering to the public's mounting concern for the environment, as astute consumer marketers are beginning to learn. A July 1989 survey conducted for the Michael Peters Group, which provides consulting on products and design, found that 77% of Americans say a company's environmental reputation affects what they buy. Observes Howard Marder of the Hill & Knowlton public relations firm: "For the past 20 years the environmental movement in the U.S. has focused on cleaning up damage. Almost overnight the focus is changing to prevention. Marketers had nothing to sell before, but now they can say, 'Be part of the solution by buying our product.'" Among those now making just that pitch in the U.S.: Arco, Colgate-Palmolive, Lever Brothers, 3M, Procter & Gamble, and Sunoco.

Marketers with experience abroad have seen France and Britain quickly catch up to West Germany and Sweden in the responsiveness of their populations to environmental marketing, and experts have little doubt the U.S. will soon follow. In mid-November, Procter & Gamble began test-marketing its first domestic product with an explicit environmental claim: Downy Refill comes in a 21½-ounce milk-carton-type container and is intended to be mixed with water in a used plastic Downy bottle to make 64 ounces of fabric softener. Prominently printed on the carton: "Better for the Environment . . . Less packaging to throw away." With a package 75% smaller, Downy Refill costs 10% less than regular Downy. It's too early to gauge the product's success.

For Wal-Mart, environmentalism is "a cause and not a marketing scheme," claims William Fields, the chain's executive vice president for merchandise. The giant discounter in July asked its 7,000 suppliers to provide it with more recycled or recyclable products. About 100 are already in stores, with labels (printed on recycled paper) explaining their supposedly beneficial features. K mart and at least a dozen small to medium-size grocery chains have announced similar programs. Experts suggest Wal-Mart and the others proceed slowly. Overeager green-marketing campaigns in Britain and Canada have been attacked by environmentalists for unsubstantiated or inappropriate claims.

The London-based Body Shop, with 14 outlets in the U.S., puts environmental concerns at its core and in the process finds its way to the green in customers' pockets. The skin- and hair-care stores display literature on ozone depletion next to sunscreens and fill their windows with information on issues like global warming. Every employee is assigned to spend half a day each week on activist work. Customers get discounts if they bring their old bottles back to the store for recycling. In 1988 the chain collected over a million signatures in Britain on a petition asking Bra-zil's President to save the rain forests. In 13 years the Body Shop has opened 420 stores in 38 countries. Sales for the year ended February 1989 were over $90 million with pretax profits of about 20%.

Make sure your green-marketing claims amount to more than a fig leaf. British Petroleum got flak recently for promoting a new brand of unleaded gasoline in Britain with the claim that it caused "no pollution." It later apologized for what it called an inadvertent error. A plastic grocery bag used by some New York supermarkets says: "This 'Earth Sack' will begin degrading within 3 days of exposure to ultraviolet light . . . and will continue the process until it turns into a nontoxic environmentally safe dust." Scientists believe the statement can be misleading, and in landfills light can be in short supply anyway. Some environmentalists have targeted "degradable plastics" for protest.

In general, the more you tell your customers, the better off you'll be. Procter & Gamble environmental chief Geoff Place visited his brother's family in England recently and found them no longer using several P&G products because of environmental concerns. Later a family member told Place they'd started using Fairy Dishwashing Liquid again because P&G had improved it. In fact the company had simply added a statement on the label saying "Only biodegradable surface active agents are used in this product." That has been true since 1963.

to the list: Educate your customers incessantly. Faced with growing protests over the volume of waste it generates, especially the polystyrene foam packaging used for hot food, the restaurant giant has taken major steps to reduce waste at the source, to recycle what's left, and to explain what it is doing. Just by making its drinking straws 20% lighter, the chain eliminated one million pounds of waste per year. In October, McDonald's began collecting polystyrene waste in 100 New England outlets and recycling it; the company intends to include all 450 regional stores in the plan by March. Customers are asked to put polystyrene containers, such as those for Chicken McNuggets or Big Macs, in special bins. All napkins in U.S. stores are now made from recycled paper, as are carry-out drink trays and office paper at headquarters.

Shelby Yastrow, the company's general counsel and point man on environmental issues, says that since polystyrene is 100% recyclable, it is better for the environment than paper, which theoretically degrades but most commonly ends up in anaerobic landfills—virtually no oxygen gets through—which may instead preserve it for decades. Paper is also significantly bulkier than plastic in most uses, thus creating more waste. "Everything I look at tells me plastic is better," says Yastrow. "I have a little trouble convincing my children or my neighbors, but the scientific community isn't a problem."

To correct the misconceptions of those kids and neighbors and their peers nationwide, the company is embarking on a major educational campaign. McDonald's is describing its efforts and explaining recycling on the paper liners on customers' trays, in advertising, in brochures it hands out in stores, and in mailings to school teachers. That's a lot of describing and explaining: McDonald's serves 18 million customers in the U.S. each day, making its tray liners alone one of the largest of the nation's mass media.

EVEN IF IT IMPROVES public understanding of solid waste, McDonald's will continue to confront one of the nagging realities of the new environmentalism: Grass-roots local groups, many of them misinformed, wield increasing disruptive power. Says David Stephenson, a Boston public relations consultant who specializes in corporate environmental strategy: "The grass-roots groups are concerned about the value of their homes and the health of their children. That means they are relentless. In general, unlike the mainstream environmental groups, they are not interested in compromise or mediation." McDonald's successfully confronted antipolystyrene picketing at several of its Vermont stores with an aggressive local educational campaign. By the end, local activists were asking that the company convert its paper cold-drink cups to plastic.

ONE LESSON from the company's experience: Don't ever assume you've solved an environmental problem. As knowledge evolves, attitudes change, and so do solutions. McDonald's switched from paper to polystyrene packaging for Big Macs and other sandwiches in 1976 largely because the public was worried about cutting trees and the energy that paper production consumed. As recently as the early Seventies, CFCs, one of today's leading environmental villains, were believed to be a harmless and inert triumph of modern chemistry.

You have to keep looking ahead—way ahead. For gutsy environmental farsightedness, few companies can top Applied Energy Services. The private, Virginia-based power-plant management firm donated $2 million in 1988 for tree planting in Guatemala to compensate for a coal-fired plant it was building in Connecticut. The trees, which of course consume carbon dioxide, are intended to offset the plant's emissions of the gas, which may lead to global warming. Says CEO Roger Sant: "We pride ourselves on being part of the solution, not part of the problem. We weren't trying to do any more than salve our own guilt, I guess." The company expects to couple tree-planting programs with all seven new plants on its drawing boards. Several large outfits have contacted Sant to ask his help in refining similar plans.

One recent weekday afternoon, three men walked out of the Environmental Defense Fund's midtown Manhattan office on their way to have lunch together. On the left was EDF's senior economist. On the right was an environmental expert in the Soviet government. Between them was a businessman, a trader in the nascent enterprise of buying and selling pollution rights. Together that trio forms a picture of how the new environmentalism is shaping up: global, more cooperative than confrontational—and with business at the center.

# HERMAN MILLER: HOW GREEN IS MY FACTORY

## Protecting the environment pays off for the office-furniture maker

It was March, 1990, and Bill Foley was starting a ruckus. While taking a routine look at new woods to use, the research manager at office furniture maker Herman Miller Inc. realized that Miller's appetite for tropical hardwoods was helping destroy rain forests. He banned the use of two species—rosewood and Honduran mahogany—once Miller's existing supplies were exhausted. Unless top brass reversed his decision, Herman Miller's signature piece, the $2,277 Eames chair, would lose its traditional rosewood finish.

In the ensuing furor, everyone from executives to carpenters took sides. Some saw the move as ethical and far-sighted. Others thought it betrayed the original Eames design. Chief Executive Richard H. Ruch's first reaction was: "That's going to kill that [chair]." But Miller's executives approved a change to walnut and cherry. Now, they're waiting to see the effect on sales.

The rosewood tussle typifies the changes companies face as they try to do less damage to the environment. Herman Miller, based in Zeeland, Mich., uses recycled materials, recycles its own products, and nips toxic spills in the bud. Reducing packaging and building an $11 million waste-to-energy heating-and-cooling plant has cut the trash it hauls to landfills by 90% since 1982. "Herman Miller has been doing a superb job," says Stephen W. Allen, vice-president of the Michigan Audubon Society.

What's unique at Miller is the bottom-up nature of such initiatives. That's a product of the company's 40-year-old participatory-management tradition, plus strong corporate ethics that date from 1923, when D. J. De Pree, a devout Baptist, founded the company. Those factors make it easier to convert "personal beliefs . . . into action," says Foley. He and an in-house writer composed the new policy of using only wood from carefully managed forests.

Among the company's best idea people is Joe Azzarello. An engineer who oversees Miller's waste-to-energy plant, he found a taker last year for the 800,000 pounds of scrap fabric Herman Miller had been dumping annually in landfills. Now, the material is shipped to North Carolina, shredded, and made into insulation for car-roof linings and dash-boards—saving Miller $50,000 a year in dumping fees. When Azzarello found it wasn't practical to recycle the 800,000 Styrofoam cups Miller employees tossed out each year, he banished them and distributed 5,000 mugs. The mugs sport a Buckminster Fuller admonition: "On spaceship earth there are no passengers . . . only crew."

Azzarello's goal is to end trips to the dump by 1995. Already, the company is recycling leather, vinyl, foam, office paper, phone books, and lubricating oil. In 1982, Miller even began buying back, reconditioning, and reselling used Action Office furniture. The newest twist is cradle-to-grave design. Miller favors materials—such as recycled aluminum—that take little energy to fabricate, generate few pollutants, and come apart easily for recycling.

**BIG SAVINGS.** Far from pure altruism, "a lot of what we've done makes economic sense," says Ruch. Miller's energy plant, built in 1982, saves $750,000 a year in fuel and landfill costs. It will have paid for itself by the end of this year—a decade ahead of schedule. The company has also trimmed costs by cutting packaging. It has saved $250,000 a year in materials and shipping costs by eliminating 70% of the Styrofoam and cardboard packaging for the cloth-covered panels of its Ethospace office partitions. And it's getting suppliers to follow suit. One Grand Rapids maker of plastic shells for office chairs helped design returnable bins to enable reuse of cardboard and plastic shipping wrap. That saves Miller $300,000 a year, which is important in a recession: The company's net profit slipped 70%, to $14 million, on sales of $878 million in the fiscal year ended May 31.

Sometimes, Miller even spends a bit extra, if the environmental payoff is big enough. It just laid out $800,000 for two incinerators that burn 98% of the toxic solvents escaping from booths in which wood is stained and varnished. The furnaces go beyond what is required by last year's Clean Air Act. And they may become obsolete in as little as three years, if new water- and powder-based finishes are perfected. Miller's directors "put us through the wringer," says Ruch. But he won by arguing that buying the best is ethically correct—and that, if need be, he could recoup some of the investment by selling the furnaces to companies that still use toxic solvents.

Miller even maintains a spill-response team. Earlier this year, when 2,150 gallons of gasoline leaked from an underground tank at its main manufacturing plant, the team's quick action kept nearby wetlands clean. "I was impressed," says Thomas P. Berdinski, an environmental-quality analyst at the Michigan Natural Resources Dept.

**LOW PROFILE.** Oddly, Herman Miller hasn't joined the stampede of companies that advertise their efforts. Philip J. Mercorella, senior vice-president for sales, sees "green marketing" as a ploy that will eventually wear thin with cus-

**CUTTING COSTS BY CUTTING WASTE**

HERMAN MILLER'S ANNUAL SAVINGS FROM:

| | |
|---|---|
| WASTE-TO-ENERGY PLANT | $750,000 |
| REDUCED PACKAGING | $1.4 million |
| SELLING OR SWAPPING RECYCLABLE MATERIALS | $900,000 |

DATA: HERMAN MILLER

When 2,150 gallons of gas leaked from an underground tank, Miller's quick action kept nearby wetlands clean

tomers. And why advertise if you aren't perfect? Miller recycles only 15% of its corrugated cardboard; the rest goes to the energy plant, even though burning recyclable materials is considered an environmental no-no. Azzarello wants to modify the plant to burn safely the 1,820 tons of sawdust the company generates annually. When that's done, perhaps next year, all cardboard can be recycled.

Another Miller weakness, says Martin P. Dugan, vice-president for facility management, is that its plants outside Michigan tend to be less vigilant. For instance, at Helikon Furniture Co., a Connecticut subsidiary, solvents that were improperly stored had been seeping into the ground for years. It cost $200,000 to clean up the mess before Miller sold Helikon this year.

Still, Miller is setting an example. In the next century, says Mercorella, having a spotless environmental record will be "just part of doing business." And Miller's early start could be a big edge.

*By David Woodruff in Zeeland, Mich.*

# Credits/ Acknowledgments

Cover design by Charles Vitelli

**1. Ethics in Business**
Facing overview—United Nations photo by M. Tzovaras.

**2. Employees and the Workplace**
Facing overview—Saab-Scania.

**3. Business and Society**
Facing overview—U.S.D.A. Soil Conservation photo.

**4. Ethics in the Marketplace**
Facing overview—New York Stock Exchange photo by Edward Topple.

**5. Developing Future Ethos and Social Responsibility**
Facing overview—United Nations photo by John Isaac.

# ANNUAL EDITIONS ARTICLE REVIEW FORM

■ NAME: _____ DATE: _____

■ TITLE AND NUMBER OF ARTICLE: _____

■ BRIEFLY STATE THE MAIN IDEA OF THIS ARTICLE: _____

_____

_____

_____

_____

_____

■ LIST THREE IMPORTANT FACTS THAT THE AUTHOR USES TO SUPPORT THE MAIN IDEA:

_____

_____

_____

_____

_____

_____

■ WHAT INFORMATION OR IDEAS DISCUSSED IN THIS ARTICLE ARE ALSO DISCUSSED IN YOUR
TEXTBOOK OR OTHER READING YOU HAVE DONE? LIST THE TEXTBOOK CHAPTERS AND PAGE
NUMBERS:

_____

_____

_____

_____

_____

_____

■ LIST ANY EXAMPLES OF BIAS OR FAULTY REASONING THAT YOU FOUND IN THE ARTICLE:

_____

_____

_____

_____

■ LIST ANY NEW TERMS/CONCEPTS THAT WERE DISCUSSED IN THE ARTICLE AND WRITE A
SHORT DEFINITION:

_____

_____

_____

_____

*Your instructor may require you to use this Annual Editions Article Review Form in any number of ways:
for articles that are assigned, for extra credit, as a tool to assist in developing assigned papers, or simply
for your own reference. Even if it is not required, we encourage you to photocopy and use this page;
you'll find that reflecting on the articles will greatly enhance the information from your text.

# ANNUAL EDITIONS: BUSINESS ETHICS 92/93
## Article Rating Form

Here is an opportunity for you to have direct input into the next revision of this volume. We would like you to rate each of the 49 articles listed below, using the following scale:

1. **Excellent: should definitely be retained**
2. **Above average: should probably be retained**
3. **Below average: should probably be deleted**
4. **Poor: should definitely be deleted**

Your ratings will play a vital part in the next revision. So please mail this prepaid form to us just as soon as you complete it.
Thanks for your help!

| Rating | Article | Rating | Article |
|---|---|---|---|
| | 1. Business Ethics: A Manager's Primer | | 27. The Ethics Game |
| | 2. Developing an Ethical Climate for Excellence | | 28. Industry Ethics Edge Upward |
| | 3. Ethics in Practice | | 29. The Parable of the Sadhu |
| | 4. A CEO Looks at Ethics | | 30. Shades of Green: Eight of 10 Americans Are Environmentalists, At Least So They Say |
| | 5. Corporate Responsibility | | |
| | 6. Seven Reasons to Examine Workplace Ethics | | 31. New Trends in Relocation |
| | 7. Understanding Pressures That Cause Unethical Behavior in Business | | 32. A New Look at Women Executives |
| | | | 33. Combating Drugs in the Workplace |
| | 8. Ethics and Profits Don't Always Go Hand in Hand | | 34. AIDS in the Workplace: Implications for Human Resource Managers |
| | 9. Ethics and Common Sense | | 35. The Untouchables |
| | 10. A Farewell to Arms | | 36. Emerging Ethical Issues in International Business |
| | 11. The Corporate Ethics Test | | |
| | 12. An Employee's Right to Privacy? | | 37. A Torrent of Dirty Dollars |
| | 13. Balanced Protection Policies | | 38. Social Responsibility, Ethics, and Marketing Strategy: Closing the Gap Between Concept and Application |
| | 14. Why Corporations Can't Lock the Rascals Out | | |
| | 15. Silent Saboteurs | | 39. The Ethics of Virtue: A Moral Theory for Marketing |
| | 16. Stopping Sexual Harassment Before It Begins | | 40. Marketing With Integrity |
| | 17. Dealing With Sexual Harassment | | 41. Marketing By Professionals: Some Ethical Issues and Prescriptions |
| | 18. Companies Try a Variety of Approaches to Halt Sexual Harassment on the Job | | 42. The Magic of Herman Miller |
| | | | 43. Sex and Decency Issues in Advertising: General and International Dimensions |
| | 19. Many Minorities Feel Torn by Experience of Affirmative Action | | 44. Car Marketers Test Gray Area of Truth in Advertising |
| | 20. Older Workers Face Age-Old Problem | | 45. The Pyramid of Corporate Social Responsibility: Toward the Moral Management of Organizational Stakeholders |
| | 21. Hazing: Uncovering One of the Best-Kept Secrets of the Workplace | | |
| | 22. After the Downsizing | | |
| | 23. Ethical Values Underlying the Termination Process | | 46. Creating Ethical Corporate Structures |
| | | | 47. Managing As If the Earth Mattered |
| | 24. Changing Unethical Organizational Behavior | | 48. Environmentalism: The New Crusade |
| | 25. Implementing Business Ethics | | 49. Herman Miller: How Green Is My Factory |
| | 26. Take the Pap Out of Ethics | | |

*(Continued on next page)*

**ABOUT YOU**

Name_____ Date_____

Are you a teacher? ☐   Or student? ☐

Your School Name _____

Department _____

Address _____

City_____ State _____ Zip _____

School Telephone #_____

**YOUR COMMENTS ARE IMPORTANT TO US!**

Please fill in the following information:

For which course did you use this book? _____

Did you use a text with this Annual Edition?   ☐ yes   ☐ no

The title of the text? _____

What are your general reactions to the Annual Editions concept?

Have you read any particular articles recently that you think should be included in the next edition?

Are there any articles you feel should be replaced in the next edition? Why?

Are there other areas that you feel would utilize an Annual Edition?

May we contact you for editorial input?

May we quote you from above?